The Impact of EU Law on Health Care Systems

D1514432

P.I.E.-Peter Lang

Bruxelles · Bern · Berlin · Frankfurt/M · New York · Oxford · Wien

Martin McKEE, Elias MOSSIALOS
& Rita BAETEN (eds.)

The Impact of EU Law
on Health Care Systems

"Work & Society"
No.39

34.68091 I

This project was commissioned and funded by the Belgian Presidency of the European Union, with the support of the Belgian Ministry of Social Affairs, Public Health and Environment, the European Commission and the Belgian National Sickness and Disability Insurance Institute. The results were first presented at the conference on "European Integration and National Health Care Systems: A Challenge for Social Policy", organised by the Belgian Presidency of the European Union on 7th - 8th December 2001 in Ghent, Belgium.

© P.I.E.-Peter Lang s.a.
PRESSES INTERUNIVERSITAIRES EUROPÉENNES
Brussels, 2002
1 avenue Maurice, 1050 Brussels, Belgium
info@peterlang.com; www.peterlang.net
Printed in Belgium

ISSN 1376-0955
ISBN 90-5201-106-0
D/2002/5678/30

Die Deutsche Bibliothek – CIP-Einheitsaufnahme

The impact of EU Law on health care systems / Martin McKee, Elias Mossialos & Rita Baeten. – Bruxelles; Bern; Berlin; Frankfurt/M.; New York; Wien: PIE Lang, 2002
(Work & Society ; No.39)
ISBN 90-5201-106-0

*CIP available from the British Library, GB
and the Library of Congress, USA.*
ISBN   0-8204-4692-0

Table of Contents

List of Figures and Tables

Figures

Tables

Acknowledgments

We would firstly like to thank Mr. Frank Vandenbroucke, Minister for Social Affairs and Pensions, Federal Government, Belgium, for inviting us to edit this book and for his constructive comments on earlier drafts.

Our thanks also go to Mr. Jo De Cock, Director-General, National Sickness and Disability Insurance Institute (RIZIV-INAMI), Brussels, Belgium for co-organising with the Ministry of Social Affairs, the conference on "European Integration and National Health Care Systems: A Challenge for Social Policy", facilitating the meetings between the authors of this book and for commenting on several drafts.

Professor Jos Berghman, Professor of Social Policy, Catholic University of Leuven, Department of Sociology, Mr. Herwig Verschueren, Deputy Head of Unit "Free Movement of Workers and Co-ordination of Social Security Schemes", DG Employment and Social Affairs, European Commission, Mr. Eric Marlier, Task Force Europe of the Ministry of Social Affairs, Brussels, Belgium, Mr. Bart Vanhercke, Cabinet of the Minister for Social Affairs, Brussels, Mr. Paul Belcher, European Affairs Manager, European Health Management Association, Brussels and Mr. Michel Eggermont, Ministry of Social Affairs, Brussels, Belgium also offered thorough and detailed feedback on earlier drafts of this book and we extend to them our appreciation.

We would also like to extend our gratitude to Mr. Eric Teunkens at RIZIV-INAMI for organising all the meetings in Brussels and for his valued feedback on our work, Ms Caroline White of the European Observatory on Health Care Systems for diligently retrieving many often obscure references, Ms Valerie Cotulelli for her dedication to trace and complete missing details and for preparing the text and Mrs. Dorothy McKee for diligently proof reading the manuscript.

Last, but not least, we would like to thank the Observatoire social européen (OSE) for their overall co-ordination of this study.

It remains the case that the views expressed in this book are those of the authors alone and should not be taken as representing those of any of the organisations with which they are affiliated.

Martin McKEE, Elias MOSSIALOS and Rita BAETEN

CHAPTER 1

The Implications of European Law for Health Care

Martin MCKEE, Elias MOSSIALOS
and Rita BAETEN

In a Europe that is becoming ever more integrated, the place of health care in European law is increasingly unclear. From the earliest days of the European Community, health care has been seen as a national matter. While the structures vary in different countries, the financing and delivery of health care have been organised on a national basis. When health began to be included in European treaties it was clearly stated that, notwithstanding the importance of co-ordinating those aspects that had trans-frontier implications, the way in which health care was organised was a matter for national governments, a position that those governments subsequently have guarded jealously. Thus, the recent European Union Charter of Fundamental Rights established a right to medical care but "under the conditions established by national laws and practices".

Yet this position was always over-simplistic. Health care involves more than the distribution of funds or the building of hospitals. It involves people, whether as staff or patients, both of whom are increasingly mobile as borders fall within Europe. It involves goods, such as pharmaceuticals and technology, which have always been traded internationally. And it involves the provision of services, the nature of which is continually changing, whether due to technical advances, such as the growth of the Internet, or structural developments, as the border between public and private becomes blurred. Inevitably this creates tensions. How does one balance provisions to ensure international freedom of movement with national systems of regulation, whether of professionals or pharmaceuticals, in ways that take account of local circumstances but are not concealed protectionism? How does one enable those seeking care to take advantage of provision elsewhere while not undermining national solidarity?

The expanding scope of European law in areas that impinge on health care, coupled with a greater awareness by individuals and organisations within the European Union of the rights that this confers on them, has exacerbated the tensions and thrown into relief the challenge of ensuring that progress in developing an internal market enhances rather than undermines consumer safety and social protection. Resolving this challenge has become more important as the social dimension of what was first conceived as primarily an economic union has become more prominent.

European law is thus an increasingly important factor in the development and implementation of national and local health policy. Yet for many it remains shrouded in mystery. This is hardly surprising, as the European legislative process appears remote, with little coverage by either the popular or professional media. But the situation with regard to laws impacting on health care is especially problematic as, typically, consequences arise from policies designed primarily to address problems in other sectors, which then establish general principles whose applicability to health care only becomes apparent once interpreted by rulings of the European Court of Justice (ECJ). As the Court can only rule on the precise situation that has been presented to it, this means that the broader implications for health care are often unclear and highly contentious. Thus, initial rulings applying the Treaty freedoms to health services and products were held by many to be limited solely to health systems such as that of Luxembourg, from which they arose, that functioned on the basis of initial payment by the patient with subsequent reimbursement. It required a later judgement to clarify that health systems in which services were provided directly were also included.

In December 2001, during the Belgian Presidency of the European Union, Mr. Frank Vandenbroucke, the Belgian Minister for Social Affairs and Pensions, convened a conference in Ghent on the implications of European law for the social nature of health care. Two complementary books emerged from this process. This one provides an in-depth analysis of some of the most important issues facing health policy-makers in Europe, in which leading commentators provide their perspectives on the current situation and prospects for the future. Inevitably, while there is a high degree of consensus, there are areas where analysis (or interpretation) of the situation differ, reflecting the complex reality that presently exists. These chapters provide a detailed map of the often-labyrinthine body of European law, from a range of perspectives.

In a sister volume we have attempted to explore what these issues mean for the social nature of health care in Europe[1]. Despite differing in the detail of how they are organised, Europe's health care systems are united by the principle of solidarity. Yet, as the contributors to this book show, there are often tensions between free movement and social solidarity. How can these tensions be resolved? Is the present legal basis of the European Union sufficient to achieve this? We argue that it is not, and elsewhere we argue for the development of an explicit European health policy, based on a revision of the Treaties, and incorporating formal systems for co-ordination so that all can benefit from best practices wherever they arise. For now, however, it is essential that policy-makers be informed of the potential implications of European law for their work. This book seeks to provide this information.

The one health related area where the European Union has a clear competence to act that is enshrined in the treaties is public health. However, that competence is tightly constrained, with scope for action primarily limited to measures involving co-ordination of policies as well as a requirement to ensure that health is taken into account in other European Union policies. Yet, as Hervey notes in Chapter 2, an appearance of weakness in these provisions may lead observers to underestimate their impact. She shows how the European Union has often been able to go beyond what had been thought possible, developing programmes such as Europe against Cancer and Europe against AIDS, and argues that instruments of soft law (non-binding legal instruments) may be more significant forces for integration than might be thought. Thus they may provide a reference point for measures of hard law. They may promote convergence through expression of agreed recommendations, which may in turn prompt voluntary changes that bring national systems in line with an agreed "European norm". They may identify areas of "Community concern", where formal legal competence is lacking, thus paving the way for future developments in Community action, sometimes leading to enactment of binding legal measures. In this process, norms and policies promulgated at the European level interact with national norms and policies, contributing to the emergence of a multi-level European health policy.

Public health is not, however, an issue that has attracted widespread political interest in Member States. Instead, health and social affairs ministries have been more exercised by issues such as movement of patients across borders. In the past few years a series of rulings have challenged the previous consensus that non-urgent treatment abroad

---

[1] Mossialos, E. & McKee, M. with Palm, W., Karl, B. and Marhold, F. (2002), *EU Law and the Social Character of Health Care*, P.I.E.-Peter Lang, Brussels.

would, in most circumstances, require prior authorisation by the organisation responsible for paying for it. As Nickless shows in Chapter 3, this is no longer the case. He traces the evolving legal situation concerning free movement of patients, describing in detail successive rulings and showing how they have raised as many questions as they have answered. In reaching its decisions the Court has balanced many, often competing, objectives. These include supporting the right of free movement while protecting the finances and configuration of national health care systems and endorsing a Europe-wide approach while accepting the principle of subsidiarity. A particular challenge is definitional: precisely what are the boundaries of the health care system, as they differ widely between countries in terms of who is covered, for what, and by whom? But an even greater challenge is how to address issues of health care in the context of an internal market. Nickless reminds us why the principles of the market cannot be applied to health care, noting in particular the need for cross-subsidies if those in most need are to receive the care they require, as well as the high level of information asymmetry that exists.

In Chapter 4, Jorens explores this evolving situation further, focusing on the implications for patients seeking treatment abroad. Noting how patients are increasingly able to decide for themselves whether they wish to obtain health care abroad, he examines the extent to which the ECJ has permitted movement without prior authorisation. He notes how, while it was initially thought that this would not apply to hospital care, this is too simplistic an interpretation. Restrictions on the freedom of movement are only allowed if they are indispensable in providing a balanced hospital service accessible to all and must take account of the principle of proportionality, in other words, is the action being considered proportional to what it seeks to achieve? He questions what is considered as a hospital, given the increasing diversity of settings in which often complex care is provided.

While a long waiting list might be a justification for seeking care abroad, again the criterion of proportionality has to be taken into account and it remains unclear what is understood by the phrase "undue delay", which is incorporated in the relevant regulations.

While Member States are not obliged to reimburse the cost of treatment that is excluded from their national benefit package, a new consideration arising from a recent ruling is that the reimbursement criteria must be based on objective, non-discriminatory criteria. This means that the decisions on what is covered cannot only be judged at a national level, but must instead reflect an international perspective on effective care. Thus, the Court has introduced an international benchmark that is a first step towards a set of European standards, something that could emerge from the oncoming open process of co-ordination in the field of health care.

In Chapter 5, Hatzopoulos examines the consequences of EU law on state and public procurement for health services. He reminds us how the EU formally has limited competence to regulate health care services. The Treaty provisions provide a very weak legal basis for common action. However, the ECJ has progressively established how the Treaty provisions on the fundamental economic freedoms have a considerable impact on the organisation of health care services within Member States. He shows how the Court, in a series of controversial judgements, has established that health care services do qualify as "services" within the meaning of the Treaty. The Court went out of its way to decide that the free provision of such services, and indeed all the "free movement" provisions, should be assured under any circumstances, even where they are provided as part of, or financed by a social security scheme. The Court, however, acknowledged three series of exceptions to the above general rule. First, activities, which, by their nature and by the way they are set up constitute the core expression of the State's responsibility towards its citizens, expressed by the degree of solidarity they embody, may escape from the application of the Treaty rules. Second, overriding reasons of general interest, such as the maintenance of the financial balance of a national social security system, may justify restrictions to the Treaty freedoms. Third, restrictions may be permitted on grounds of public health.

The rules on both state aid and public procurement prohibit the discretionary and discriminatory allocation of public moneys to undertakings operating in a market environment, thus creating artificial market conditions. Hence, it is crucial to examine, for each one entity involved in the provision of health care services, whether and under what circumstances it may be viewed as an undertaking, or as an entity managing public moneys (*i.e.* public authority, contracting authority or other entity controlled by the State). In view of the specific nature of health care services and their linkage to the social security systems of Member States, he argues that it is impossible to draw sharp distinctions. Therefore, according to the criteria used by the Court, it would seem that a) treatment providers, b) hospitals and clinics and c) medical associations would, more often than not, qualify as undertakings. In contrast, central health authorities of Member States would qualify as state entities. The position is extremely finely balanced in relation to the activities of health insurance funds, which, depending on the way they are organised and governed and on the way they collect contributions and award benefits, may qualify either as undertakings or as state entities.

Consequently, there is a risk that money transferred within the framework of a social security scheme from one entity to another could be treated as a state aid when one of the entities involved qualifies as an undertaking and the other as a public authority. Thus, the ECJ has ruled that when the body managing social security contributions imposes reduced charges to some categories of undertakings this can constitute state aid, a view shared by the European Free Trade Association (EFTA) Court in a similar situation. By the same logic, the ECJ has ruled that for a social security fund to accept deferred payment of charges due from an undertaking also constitutes a state aid. These cases show the vigilance that the Commission applies to all forms of fund transfers between the entities involved in the provision of health care and emphasises the need for national systems to comply with EC rules.

He then considers rules on public procurement, noting how many of the entities involved in the provision of health care services are "contracting authorities" in relation to the Public Procurement Directives. Thus, the Court has ruled that a sickness fund in Austria remains subject to the rules on public procurement even when it wants to contract for a commercial activity that is offered within a competitive environment such as the reimbursement of the transport of patients.

It is thus apparent that national health systems must comply not only with general Treaty provisions, but also with specific rules such as those on state aid and public procurement. This, in turn, underlines the need for explicit definitions so that national authorities receive clear guidance as to what is permitted and what not under European law. This is unlikely to happen as long as the legal situation is evolving in a piecemeal fashion from a series of Court rulings, each addressing a specific situation but of uncertain generalisability.

In Chapter 6, Karl examines these issues further, with special reference to competition law. In particular she notes that, while many of the transactions within statutory systems may be exempt on social grounds, health authorities must be aware of the possibility of removing this protection through deregulation and privatisation. She notes how health care organisations can be considered as undertakings and that issues such as ownership or profit-seeking status do not affect this. What is important is whether they engage in economic activity. Moreover, each activity undertaken by an organisation must be judged on its merits; even where most of its activities are deemed to be non-economic, and thus exempt from competition law, it does not follow that everything it does is exempt.

She then examines those ways in which activities may qualify as being non-economic. They may be sovereign, in other words necessarily performed by the State when exercising official authority. However, the State must show that it is necessary for it to perform this activity, and must exercise caution when delegating its role to other bodies. It may be a social activity, but here it must demonstrate that it involves social protection and is based on the principle of solidarity. It may also be exempt because it involves no identifiable payment or because the activity simply involves the organisation concerned meeting its basic needs to continue to function. However, it is easy to see how poorly considered health care reforms, especially where they introduce market mechanisms and decentralisation, might render organisations unexpectedly subject to competition law.

One area where the legal situation is especially unclear is voluntary health insurance. Although only a minor component of health care financing in many countries, where it supplements national systems of social insurance, its importance is constantly growing. Policies to contain public health care costs have shifted part of the cost to households and, in some countries, supplementary health insurance is almost indispensable to achieve access to quality health care within reasonable time limits. Consequently, several countries have taken legal steps to ensure full coverage of vulnerable groups. At the same time, employers are taking an increasing interest in provision of collective health insurance benefits to their employees.

Unlike social insurance, voluntary health insurance has long been considered as primarily an economic activity, and so subject to the application of European law on the internal market. In Chapter 7, Palm shows that, although the European Union's regulatory framework, based on the third Non-Life Insurance Directive, recognises the specific nature and social importance of private health insurance that partially or completely substitutes for health cover provided by the social security system, it is unclear how far Member States can determine the method of operation of health insurers operating on their territory.

In the context of the integration of insurance markets, the non-profit mutual health funds, who have traditionally played a crucial role in securing health cover irrespective of financial and health status, face difficulties in preserving the principle of solidarity. Their specific legal status recognises their social mission and their broadly-based role, which includes involvement in activities related to health promotion, social cohesion, solidarity and reducing social inequalities in health, yet these are increasingly challenged as being market distortions and unfair competition. But the competition rules contained in the EC Treaty are intended to further all the Treaty objectives, including the goal of ensuring a high level of social and health protection. The challenge, as Palm notes, is how to achieve this.

Chapters 8 and 9 take us into the arena of trade in goods, specifically pharmaceuticals and medical devices. In Chapter 8, Hancher explores the evolution of the harmonisation of regulatory procedures for medicines for human use, as well as competition and free movement issues. The application of EU law to the pharmaceutical sector and, in particular, the rules on competition and free movement have been the subject of considerable commentary, analysis and controversy in recent years. This reflects the wide range of European legal problems, often raising novel issues, which have involved the pharmaceutical industry. She focuses on the interconnection between regulatory competition and free movement issues, as affected by evolving secondary legislation and Court rulings.

Important matters relating to the development and gradual harmonisation of the Community authorisation procedures, as well as advertising and marketing are now subject to increasingly complex bodies of secondary law. She also looks in some detail at recent case law, with respect to the application of the regulatory framework to generic products and parallel imports – the two main drivers for competition in the pharmaceuticals market.

She then examines further the legal and policy aspects of Community intervention in the controversial issue of industry pricing strategies as well as national regulatory controls with particular reference to the findings of the recent report by expert economists on the competitiveness of the European pharmaceutical industry. The report, entitled "Global Competitiveness in Pharmaceuticals: A European Perspective" commissioned by DG Enterprise, argued that the European industry has declined in competitiveness compared to the USA, albeit that there are large differences and trends across the Member States. It suggested that many national European markets are not sufficiently competitive, and that the nature and intensity of competition in final markets is too weak to nurture efficiency and innovation. Publication of this report, coinciding with the Commission's review of the current legal procedures for marketing or licensing products on the European market, raises many complex issues. Publication also coincides with important legal challenges to the Commission's powers to regulate the activities of pharmaceutical firms who seek to impose dual-pricing systems or other methods of sealing off competition from low-priced markets. She concludes that a reorientation in Community policy may well be timely: in the past the Commission has focussed on the supply side of the market, leaving the demand side essentially to the Member States. She proposes that the possibilities offered by information technology could be harnessed to change this approach in the future.

In Chapter 9, Altenstetter examines the regulation of medical devices in Europe, emphasising the similarities and differences of medical devices and prescription drugs; the timing of European Union medical device regulation; the nature of medical devices and drugs; and the distinct pathways to market authorisation as well as the boundary issues between the two sectors. She discusses the erosion of the boundaries between exclusive and shared responsibilities of the EU and Member States and argues that national medical device vigilance reporting systems and post-marketing surveillance are the weakest link in the European Union process. She asks whether the claim that patient safety is as important in the European regulatory regime as is free movement and competitiveness is really credible? If so, she argues, it will be necessary to make available additional resources. If patient access to effective, safe and high-quality medical devices is to be achieved then a series of other measures must be considered: how to achieve more coherence in the choice of European Union and domestic policy tools; how to produce information on compliance with European Union policy on vigilance and adverse incident reporting that is accurate, timely, reliable as well as comparable and available to the public; and how to make European Union decision-making in more committees more transparent and accountable?

Taken together, the contributors to this book demonstrate the complexity of European law as it relates to health policy, identifying many areas of ambiguity and contention. This situation is clearly far from satisfactory. But what is to be done?

One way forward is to take advantage of a new approach adopted at the Lisbon Council to address areas where there is considerable national diversity, but common goals. This is the "open method of co-ordination", a way of exchanging information on best practice and achieving greater convergence. It involves setting guidelines, combined with specific timetables for achieving the goals; establishing indicators of best practice; translating European guidelines into national and regional policies by setting specific targets and adopting measures that take account of national and regional differences; and periodic monitoring, evaluation and peer review organised as mutual learning processes. Thus, even without a legal basis to act in the area of health care, the open method of co-ordination can be seen as a compromise between integration and simple co-operation.

Ultimately, however, we believe that there is a strong argument for ensuring that health policy is considered explicitly during the next revision of the Treaty. There are too many areas in which internal market and social goals come into conflict. Including a clear statement concerning the social goals of health care in the Treaty, to which all

Member States should be able to agree given the coherence of their existing domestic policies, would enable the Court to draw on a counterbalance to existing provisions on the internal market.

Until then, however, we hope that the material in this book will contribute to a better understanding of this complex area, so helping to ensure that European law acts as a help rather than a hindrance to those trying to improve the quality and accessibility of health care for which they are responsible.

CHAPTER 2

The Legal Basis of European Community
Public Health Policy

Tamara K. HERVEY

Introduction

Outside the spotlight of high profile events in the health field, such as the litigation on the free movement of patients[1], the European Community has quietly developed its own small-scale public health policy, and begun to engage in integrative interactions with national health policy-makers. This chapter explores the legal basis and structures of the Community-level elements of this emerging policy, elaborating their development over time. The chapter proceeds from the view that legal and institutional structures are important[2], as they form a key element in policy-making processes within the European Community, and thus ultimately have an effect on policy content.

In the public health field, the mechanisms of integration used have not typically been "classic" harmonisation through the application of de-regulatory Community law, and reregulation by means of Community-level (minimum) regulatory standards[3]. The European Community does

---

[1] ECJ, case C-120/95, *Decker*, ECR [1998] I-1831; ECJ, case C-158/96, Kohll, ECR [1998] I-1931; ECJ, case C-368/98, *Vanbraekel*, ECR [2001] I-5363; ECJ, case C-157/99, *Geraets-Smits and Peerbooms*, ECR [2001] I-5473. For comments, see Chapters by Nickless and Jorens in this volume; van der Mei (1998 : 277); Cabral (1999: 387); Roscam Abbing (1999: 1); Baeyens (1999: 373); Sieveking (2000: 143); Mossialos and McKee (2001: 248). The British NHS has recently taken advantage of these rulings by sending patients to a hospital in Lille (*Times*, "European Beds for NHS Patients by the New Year", 31 August 2001 and "English Patients Take French Cure", 19 January 2002), and it appears that there are plans to use hospitals in other Member States, including Germany and Greece (*Times*, 31 August 2001; 19 January 2002 and 20 January 2002).

[2] A view not always made explicit by legal analyses. For exploration of this view, see for instance, Armstrong (1995) and Armstrong and Bulmer (1998).

[3] For exploration of these modes of integration see *e.g.* Weatherill (1995); Dehousse (1992: 383); Majone (1996); for a more legalistic view see Slot (1996: 378).

not have competence to develop a harmonised European-level public health policy (for a more detailed discussion, see Hervey, 2001a). Rather, in this field the Community institutions have sought to use persuasive methods of integration, such as financial support and measures of "soft law"[4]. Financial support may promote integration by encouraging certain types of activities over others, granting them finance in addition to that available at national or sub-national level. Indirect pressures for change at national level may arise as a result[5].

Measures of soft law (non-binding legal instruments) may be significant forces in the integration process for a number of reasons. They may provide an interpretative reference point for measures of hard law[6]. They may promote convergence through articulation of agreed statements of good practice and recommendations, against which national policies are measured[7], eventually prompting voluntary changes to bring national systems in line with the agreed "European norm". They may carve out areas of "Community concern", where formal legal competence is lacking, thus paving the way for future Community action, sometimes ultimately leading to the enactment of binding and directly effective Community-level measures (see Cram, 1997: 107-111)[8]. In all these mechanisms, norms and policy promulgated at the Community level interact with national norms and policies, thus creating an emerging multi-level[9] European health policy.

I. Historical Context

The original Treaty of Rome gave no explicit competence to the Community institutions in the field of health. However, European-level meetings of the ministers of Health of the Member States and the Commission have taken place since the late 1970s (Roscam Abbing, 1992: 24). The legal status of acts emanating from these meetings was

---

[4] For discussion of soft law, see, for instance, Wellens and Borchardt (1989: 267) and Kenner (1999: 33).

[5] For example, the Erasmus and Socrates programmes supporting migration of students within the EU played a role in prompting changes to national education policy, see Shaw (1999).

[6] See *e.g.* ECJ, case C-322/88, *Grimaldi*, ECR [1989] 4407; and more recently the opinion of the Advocate General in case C-173/99, *BECTU*, 8 February 2001.

[7] For example the "open method of co-ordination", in the context of employment policy, see Szyszczak (2001).

[8] For example in the areas of sex equality and racism/xenophobia see, respectively, Hoskyns (1996) and Geyer (2000: 164-171).

[9] For discussion of the EU as a "multi-level system of governance", see for instance, Hooghe and Marks (2001) and, in the context of social policy, Leibfried and Pierson (1995).

unclear. Article 2 EEC stated that one of the "objectives" of the Community was "raising of the standard of living". This was interpreted by some to imply that health protection was one of the aims of the Community. If this were so, Community action could lawfully be taken on the basis of Article 235 EEC (now Article 308 EC) (Verwers, 1992: 12; cited in van der Mei and Waddington, 1998: 132-3).

This broad interpretation of Articles 2 and 235 EEC underpinned some subsequent activity involving co-ordination of policies between the Member States in the field of health, prior to the inclusion of specific legal basis provisions on health in the Treaty. For instance, the Europe against Cancer programme (Council of the European Communities, 1988a)[10] was established in 1989, and the Europe against AIDS programme in 1991 (Council of the European Communities, 1991)[11]. As the enactment of these measures predated any formal legal competence on the part of the Community to take such action, the legal basis presented in Decision 88/351/EEC on Europe against Cancer is simply "the Treaty establishing the EC". The legality of this may have been dubious[12], but in practice, as the programme was not contentious, no party with *locus standi* sought to challenge the measure.

An explicit legal basis provision for health – Article 129 EC (now amended and renumbered Article 152 EC) – was introduced into the EC Treaty by the Treaty of Maastricht. Article 129 EC provided that "the Community shall contribute towards a high level of human health protection by encouraging co-operation between Member States, and, if necessary, lending support to their action". Action by the EU institutions was to be directed towards a number of specified areas, in particular major health scourges (including drug dependence); research into causes and transmission of these diseases; and provision of information and education on health.

---

[10] The programme encompassed anti-tobacco campaigns, improvements in nutrition, protection against carcinogenic agents, promotion of screening policies, provision of information to the public and professionals, and research.

[11] This programme encompassed training provision, information exchange on services, research and measures to promote the safety of blood. See further, Hervey (forthcoming) and McKee *et al.* (1996: 265).

[12] Article 5 EC (ex 3b) provides that the Community shall act within the limits of the powers conferred upon it by the Treaty. The EU institutions are obliged to state the legal basis on which they base legislative acts, see case 45/86, *Commission* v. *Council (Tariff Preferences)*, ECR [1987] 1483. Although Article 308 EC (ex 235) grants a residual power to the institutions to act where necessary to attain one of the objectives of the Treaty, where the Treaty has not provided the necessary powers, the Court has made it clear that this does not involve a limitless competence, see *Opinion 2/94*, ECR [1996] I-1759.

Article 129 EC also provided that health protection requirements are to form a constituent part of the Community's other policies. Various Community policies and activities may have an impact on the protection of human health. The "weak mainstreaming"[13] objective of Article 129 EC required that in policy areas not directly related to health, due regard should nevertheless be given to health issues (van der Mei and Waddington, 1998: 133). The presence of this objective in the Treaty arguably set health policy on the road to being established as a general Community policy. Such a conclusion is underpinned by the inclusion of the raising of "the quality of life" among the objectives of the Community (Article 2 EC) and a "contribution to the attainment of a high level of health protection" among the Community's activities (Article 3 (o)) (van der Mei and Waddington, 1998: 133; citing Verwers, 1992: 12 and European Commission, 1995).

The insertion of Article 129 EC into the Treaty of Rome established health as what is known as a "flanking policy" in the EU: an area in which activities of the EU institutions are limited to co-ordination, and harmonisation of national laws is explicitly excluded from Community competence. Member States are thereby placed under an obligation to liase with the Commission and to co-ordinate policies and programmes in the areas referred to above. Thus national health policy in these matters may not lawfully develop in a vacuum, but multi-level co-ordination is required. The Commission was formally granted a general power of initiative to propose measures that will promote co-operation between the Member States in those areas. Article 129 formed a legal basis on which Council and Parliament could adopt "incentive measures" according to the co-decision procedure[14], or recommendations, by qualified majority on a proposal from the Commission, in order to contribute to the achievement of the objectives set out in the provision. In fact, as we have seen, this grant of formal competence to take such action came after Community had acted, and put its earlier action on a firmer legal footing. Article 129 EC may be seen as representing a compromise between the governments of Member States who did not want any Community mandate in health and those who wanted to go further. Article 129 EC was seen by some as setting limits to the expansion of Community-level activities in the public health field, which had occurred in the past without any specific legal basis[15]. For others, it was a mere formalisation of what was already taking place

---

[13] Also known as "integration".

[14] For details of the co-decision procedure, in which Council and Parliament are "co-legislators", see Article 251 EC.

[15] It appears that the UK was instrumental in ensuring the rather weak final form of Article 129 EC, see O'Rourke (1999: 81-82).

(McKee *et al.*, 1996: 267). Ultimately, the proper construction of Article 152 (ex 129) EC is a matter for the ECJ, in the context of its jurisprudence on competence and legal basis (for further exploration, see Hervey, 2001).

The competence of the Community in the field of public health was expressed at greater length in 1993 in the Council Resolution on future action in the field of public health (Council of the European Union, 1993a). This resolution reiterates that "public health policy as such, except where the Treaties provide otherwise, is the responsibility of the Member States". The Resolution sets out four basic criteria for Community action. First, there must be a significant health problem, for which appropriate preventative actions are possible. Second, the proposed activity must supplement or promote other Community policies such as the operation of the internal market. Third, Community activities are to be consistent with those of other international organisations, such as the World Health Organisation, so stressing the desirability of European Community co-operation with other international organisations concerned with health. Fourth, the Resolution provides that the aim of the Community action must be such that it cannot be sufficiently achieved by Member States acting alone. This is a specific application of the general principle of "subsidiarity" in Community law (Article 5 EC). The principle of subsidiarity requires that proposed activities and functions of the EU institutions are demonstrably better performed at European, rather than national, level. In the health field, criteria to test proposed activities for compliance with subsidiarity might include a clear need for co-ordination of activity or for enabling Member States to learn from each other's experience in health care reform or innovation; functions which might be performed more cheaply for the EU as a whole (for instance, research into rare diseases which would be too expensive for one Member State acting alone); issues which cross national boundaries (for instance, epidemics, the environment or the consequences of free movement of persons); and action to support exchange of necessary information (for instance, standardisation of definitions) (see Abel-Smith *et al.*, 1995: 126).

The 1993 Council Resolution was fleshed out by a number of official Commission action programmes, including the first action programme for health promotion, information, education and training in the field of public health (European Commission, 1994a). This was agreed in 1995 after lengthy negotiations over budget size. As the budget is relatively modest, the setting of priorities for Community action is crucial. It was agreed by Council that action should not be spread thinly over a large area, rather that limited resources be directed at a few carefully chosen areas (McKee *et al.*, 1996: 269). The priority areas were drug dependence, cancer, AIDS and other communicable diseases, health data, information, accidents and injuries, pollution-related diseases, and rare diseases. The Commission's action programmes suggested a slight change of policy focus from that of the Council, towards health promotion and the broader determinants of good health. This refocus appeared to emanate from the Commission itself, and the agenda of those responsible in the Social Affairs Directorate-General, DG V (McKee *et al.*, 1996: 266). This is a change from the direction suggested by the wording of Article 129 EC, which appears to be more focussed on the prevention of major diseases.

The public health programmes proposed on AIDS, cancer, drug dependence and health promotion were implemented in 1996 (European Parliament and Council of the European Union, 1996a, b and c and 1997a); the fifth programme on health monitoring was implemented in 1997 (European Parliament and Council of the European Union, 1997b). The final three programmes – on injury prevention, rare diseases and pollution-related diseases were adopted in 1999 (European Parliament and Council of the European Union, 1999). These programmes support a number of projects covering, for instance, exchange of information and personnel, training, pilot projects, information campaigns, and networking of organisations and experts.

Originally there was no intention to amend Article 129 EC in the 1996 Inter-Governmental Council that culminated in the Treaty of Amsterdam (see Dommers, 1995: 46; cited in van der Mei and Waddington, 1998: 134). However, it seems that the BSE crisis – which made it clear that some threats to health merit a response at European level – galvanised the governments of the Member States into taking some action in that respect. The result was the new Article 152 EC, which provides as follows:

(1) A high level of human health protection shall be ensured in the definition and implementation of all Community policies and activities.

Community action, which shall complement national policies, shall be directed towards improving public health, preventing human illness and diseases, and obviating sources of danger to human health. Such action shall cover the fight against the major health scourges, by promoting research into their causes, their transmission and their prevention, as well as health information and education.

The Community shall complement the Member States' action in reducing drugs-related health damage, including information and prevention.

(2) The Community shall encourage cooperation between the Member States in the areas referred to in this Article and, if necessary, lend support to their action.

Member States shall, in liaison with the Commission, coordinate among themselves their policies and programmes in the areas referred to in paragraph 1. The Commission may, in close contact with the Member States, take any useful initiative to promote such coordination.

(3) The Community and the Member States shall foster cooperation with third countries and the competent international institutions in the sphere of public health.

(4) The Council, acting in accordance with [the co-decision procedure] ... shall contribute to the achievement of the objectives referred to in this Article through adopting:

   (a) measures setting high standards of quality and safety of organs and substances of human origin, blood and blood derivatives; these measures shall not prevent any Member State from maintaining or introducing more stringent protective measures;

   (b) by way of derogation from Article 37 [the Common Agricultural Policy], measures in the veterinary and phytosanitary fields which have as their direct objective the protection of public health;

   (c) incentive measures designed to protect and improve human health, excluding any harmonisation of the laws and regulations of the Member States.

   The Council, acting by qualified majority on a proposal from the Commission, may also adopt recommendations for the purposes set out in this Article.

(5) Community action in the field of public health shall fully respect the responsibilities of the Member States for the organisation and delivery of health services and medical care. In particular, measures referred to in paragraph 4(a) shall not affect national provisions on the donation or medical use of organs or blood.

A number of changes of emphasis from Article 129 EC should be noted.

The first sub-paragraph of Article 152 EC now contains the mainstreaming element, to the effect that health protection must be considered in the implementation of all other Community policies and activities[16]. This is consistent with the new provisions in Articles 2 and 3 EC. Public health interests must now be taken into account when pursuing potentially competing goals in other policy areas. The strengthening of the mainstreaming element in Article 152 EC is said to be in response to the arguments of the UK government in case C-180/96 UK *v.* Commission[17], concerning the emergency measures taken against

---

[16] Space precludes a detailed discussion of the mainstreaming obligation in this chapter. For further information, see Hervey (2001a).

[17] ECJ, case C-180/96, *UK* v. *Commission*, ECR [1996] I-3903.

BSE[18]. On a broad reading, Article 152 EC might require extra weight to be given to health goals, or indeed might render measures in other areas unlawful if a "high level of human health protection" cannot be guaranteed (van der Mei and Waddington, 1998: 134).

The Community's obligation has been strengthened from a requirement to "contribute" to ensuring a high level of protection of human health, to the duty to "ensure" a high level of health protection in all Community activities. Moreover, in line with the Commission's refocus, Community activities are no longer limited to *prevention* of disease, but have expanded to include *promotion* of good health (van der Mei and Waddington, 1998: 135). Article 152 (1) states that Community action "shall be directed towards improving public health, preventing human illness and diseases and obviating sources of danger to human health". The reference to the major health scourges, and health information and education remains. This new wording reflects a refocusing of EU policy towards health promotion and the broader determinants of good health, from the direction suggested by the wording of old Article 129 EC. As noted above, this refocus, if not change of policy direction, appears to have emanated from DG V of the European Commission (at that time competent for public health) (see McKee *et al.*, 1996: 266). However, its inclusion in the Treaty implies an acceptance by the governments of the Member States that this is an appropriate direction for Community health policy. Drug-related health damage has its own indent, again with an emphasis on prevention, rather than repression (Roscam Abbing, 1998: 172).

Article 152 (2) sets out the division of tasks and powers between the Member States and the EU institutions in the field of public health. The duty of co-operation on the part of the Member States remains unchanged. The provision makes it clear that, in accordance with the principle of subsidiarity, the main powers in the health field remain

---

[18] The UK argued that the measures (banning the export of bovines, meat from bovines and products obtained from bovines liable to enter the animal feed or human food chain, or materials destined for use in pharmaceuticals or cosmetics) were adopted on the basis of economic measures and the need to reassure consumers and protect the beef market. The UK sought an interim suspension of the ban with respect to various products for which the risk of BSE was not established or had been eliminated by national measures. Essentially, the UK argued that the ban was not justified for such products. The Court took the view that the potentially (at the relevant time, the link between BSE and CJD was not clear) serious harm to public health posed by BSE did justify the measures. Implicit in the Court's reasoning was the position that the protection of public health is a fundamental duty of the EU institutions, which cannot be disregarded in the pursuit of the common agricultural policy (paragraph 63). This implicit position was made more explicit by the "strong mainstreaming" of public health protection in all Community policies, effected at Amsterdam.

firmly with the Member States. This is underlined by Subparagraph 5. The Community is entitled to act only if "added European value" will result from the action. This point is taken up in the new public health programme, discussed below.

Article 152 (4) sets out the procedures by which the EU institutions may act in the health field, and delimits the types of measures that may be enacted. Two types of legislation are envisaged: the "measures" of (a) and (b) may include reregulatory harmonisation provisions; the "incentive measures" of (c) explicitly preclude such harmonisation. Article 129 EC gave legislative power to the Council to enact only such "incentive measures" in the field. Article 152 EC retains the power to adopt "incentive measures designed to protect and improve human health, excluding any harmonisation of the laws and regulations of the Member States" [Article 152 (4) (c)]. However, additional powers to adopt "measures" – by implication including harmonising regulations, directives or other acts – in two further areas are added to the pre-Amsterdam wording. These are "measures setting high standards of quality and safety of organs and substances of human origin, blood and blood derivatives" and "measures in the veterinary and phytosanitary fields which have as their direct objective the protection of public health" [Article 152 (4) (a) and (b)]. In one sense, these provisions, especially those in Article 152 (4) (b), are not an extension of Community competence, as they refer to areas of well-established EU policy. These latter provisions are an extension of (or rather a derogation from) the powers given to the EU institutions in (new) Article 37 EC to implement the Common Agricultural Policy. Their inclusion is apparently due to the BSE/CJD crisis. The provision removes veterinary and phytosanitary measures that are primarily concerned with human or public health from the scope of the Common Agricultural Policy (van der Mei and Waddington, 1998: 137). Significantly, a different legislative procedure (co-decision, rather than the basic procedure of Article 37 EC) is to be used[19].

The provisions in Article 152 (4) (a) are more obviously an extension of the power of the EU institutions. Their presence in the Treaty may be explained by various health scandals concerning blood and human organs, such as the distribution and transfusion of HIV-infected blood and blood products (van der Mei and Waddington, 1998: 137; see further Abraham and Lewis, 2000: 73-74 and Roscam Abbing, 1995: 295). It may also be relevant that an embryonic "market" in human

---

[19] Although the Council is to act by qualified majority under Article 37 EC, the role of the European Parliament is consultative only, rather than the co-decision role envisaged in Article 152 EC.

blood, organs and other substances is emerging in the EU. The use of the ordinary internal market provisions, including those on free movement of goods and consumer protection, to regulate this "market" is politically and ethically sensitive in many Member States, as these substances are neither conceptualised as "goods" nor the object of ordinary commerce or consumption. However, "consumers" of these "goods" do need to be protected within the EU's legal framework. Article 152 EC gives power to Council to enact the necessary protective regulations as public health measures, although the measures may well be modelled on existing internal market consumer protection regulation. Community requirements will set only a "minimum floor" of regulatory protection, and Member States are free to enact higher standards if they wish. Again, the subsidiarity principle is invoked with a specific exclusion in Subparagraph 5 for "national provisions on the donation or medical use of organs and blood". This refers to the differences in national legal systems concerning donor consent (see Roscam Abbing, 1998: 172).

Article 152 (5) is an explicit statement on the application of the principle of subsidiarity in the field of public health. Presumably, the main concern of the Member States is the preservation of national competence over the financing of national health systems.

What is perhaps most significant about new Article 152 EC is that it gathers together powers and activities of the EU institutions in the public health field in a much more coherent and logical manner than the pre-Amsterdam Treaty provisions. The EU can now truly be said to have its own (albeit modest) public health policy, which interacts with those at national level in the Member States. The details of that policy are a matter for elaboration among the institutions of the European Union.

II. Existing Community Public Health Action Programmes

Eight Community public health programmes were implemented in the mid and late 1990s. These were in the fields of health promotion, information, education and training; cancer; AIDS and communicable diseases; drug dependence; health monitoring; pollution-related diseases; rare diseases and injury prevention. To give a flavour of the kinds of activities financed under the programmes, elements of two – the cancer programme, and the AIDS dimension of the AIDS and communicable diseases programme – are discussed here. These examples have been chosen to illustrate the various types of actions funded under the programmes, and the legal and institutional contexts in which the interactions between national and EU-level health policies have developed by means of the programmes.

A. AIDS/HIV Programmes

EU interest in AIDS/HIV predates any specific formal legal Community competence to act in the field. The Council and Ministers of State for Health, meeting within Council, included on their agenda matters concerning AIDS/HIV from the mid-1980s (see *e.g.* Council of the European Communities, 1986, 1987 and 1988b)[20]. Thus, for instance, the conclusions of the December 1988 Council meeting (Council of the European Communities, 1989a) included an agreement to "improve and extend the current system for the rapid and periodic exchange of epidemiological data at Community level on cases of AIDS". This required co-ordination of criteria for assessment of effectiveness of preventive measures taken in the Member States. Links between AIDS/HIV and drug abuse[21], and matters concerning employment relationships[22] were also raised at this early stage, although no concrete action was proposed.

These early discussions led to the setting up of an *Ad Hoc* Working Party on AIDS for the exchange of information (Council of the European Communities, 1987). The Commission was requested by Council to draw up a proposal for a co-ordinated programme on combating AIDS/HIV (Council of the European Communities, 1989b). Both the Commission and the Working Party were to work closely with the World Health Organisation. The first EU-level programme specifically directed at AIDS/HIV followed this proposal (see Council of the European Communities, 1991). This action plan encompassed training provision, information exchange on services, research and measures to promote the safety of blood. This first action plan was followed by interim extensions by Council Resolution (Council of the European Union, 1993a) and Decision 1729/95/EC (European Parliament and Council of the European Union, 1995) up to the end of 1995.

A second "Europe against AIDS" programme was established by Decision 647/96/EC of the European Parliament and Council (European Parliament and Council of the European Union, 1996c). This measure adopted a programme of Community action on the prevention of AIDS and certain other communicable diseases within the framework for action in the field of public health. The programme was to run from

---

[20] Resolution of representatives of Governments of Member States meeting within the Council of 29 May 1986, OJ 1986 C 184/21.

[21] Elaborated in Council Conclusions of 16 May 1989 (Council of the European Communities, 1989b).

[22] Elaborated in Council Conclusions of 15 December 1988 (Council of the European Communities, 1989c).

1996-2000[23]. The legal basis for this measure is Article 129 EC. The objective of the programme is to "help contain the spread of AIDS and reduce mortality and morbidity due to communicable diseases" [Article 1 (2)]. The mechanisms by which this is to be achieved are "promoting co-operation between [national] prevention policies and programmes and supporting the activities of non-governmental organisations" [Article 1 (2)]. The explicit role for NGOs arose from pressure from the European Parliament[24]. The budget – a matter of contention between Council and the European Parliament in the adoption of the Decision (see Hilditch and Garman, 1998: 277)[25] – is € 49.6 million (Article 3).

The technical operation of the programme is set out in Article 5 of the Decision. The programme is to be administered by a committee comprising two representatives of each Member State, chaired by the Commission. The committee is responsible for establishing the annual work programme, including priorities for action, the criteria for selecting projects for financial support under the programme, the procedure for evaluating projects, and the arrangements for dissemination of results. The committee acts according to the "management committee" procedure, whereby the Commission submits proposals, and the committee votes according to the Council's qualified majority voting rules. If the committee does not support a Commission proposal then the matter goes to Council. The Council may then take a different decision, within a time limit specified by the Commission in its proposal, in accordance with the urgency of the measure. The significance of this mechanism of delegated legislation is that it preserves a position in which the influence of the governments of Member States, through the Council, is maintained, even where power to act has been delegated to the Commission[26].

Decision 647/96/EC, Annex, sets out four areas (or "chapters") for action under the programme (European Commission, 1997: 66-67). These are:

– surveillance and monitoring of communicable diseases;

---

[23] It was subsequently extended to 31 December 2002 (see European Parliament and Council of the European Union, 2001).

[24] See European Parliament's proposed amendments in European Commission (1994b).

[25] The authors describe how the "conciliation procedure" – a mechanism by which Council and the European Parliament resolve differences in amendments to proposed legislation – was used to good effect to resolve this and other differences of opinion, leading to quick adoption of the AIDS programme.

[26] For further discussion of "comitology" procedures, see, for instance, Bradley (1997: 230 and 1992: 691) and Boyron (1996: 293).

- combating transmission;
- information, education and training; and
- support for persons with HIV/AIDS and combating discrimination.

Actions under Chapter 1 will aim to improve understanding and dissemination of data and information on HIV and AIDS and other communicable diseases. Actions are also to improve the co-ordination of monitoring systems for those diseases, and of Community-wide responses, particularly in the event of an epidemic. Further EU-level support for control and surveillance of communicable diseases emanates from the setting up of a European network for surveillance, according to Decision 2119/98/EC (European Parliament and Council of the European Union, 1998a). Actions under Chapter 2 aim to prevent transmission of AIDS and other sexually transmitted diseases. There is a particular focus on environments and persons at risk, such as those involved in travel[27], prisons, sex-workers, and users of injectable drugs. Best practices are to be identified through the exchange of information and experience on different prevention methods and programmes in different Member States. Information, education and training, under Chapter 3, are mainly aimed at raising public awareness and information about HIV and AIDS. There is scope for focussing education on sexually transmitted diseases on children and young people. A contribution to training of health professionals is envisaged. Chapter 4 focuses on the position of seropositive persons and persons with AIDS. It aims to support exchange of experience and practice between networks of associations involved at national levels in the psychosocial care of such persons. Finally, Chapter 4 is concerned with combating discrimination against people with HIV/AIDS and the development of a code of good practice for HIV testing.

Overall, priority under the AIDS programme is given to flagship projects, effected by established, "tried and tested" organisations in the field. The projects must have a "Community dimension", involve co-operation between several Member States, and represent "real added value" in terms of achievement of the objectives of the programme (European Commission, 1997a: 67).

Article 7 of the Decision required an interim evaluation of the programme, which was carried out by the Commission in 1998 (European Commission, 1999a). The Commission report was based on a report

---

[27] The "flying condom" educational programme ran in summer 1994, aimed at young people on holiday to encourage the use of condoms (see European Commission, 1997a: 68-69).

from a team of external experts and the views of the representatives of the Member States on the relevant management committee. The interim report covers the years 1996 and 1997. Overall, budgetary support for Chapters 1-3 was broadly equal in amount, with Chapter 4 receiving around half the amount of the other chapters (Table 2.1).

Table 2.1: Budget Allocation for the Europe against AIDS and Other Communicable Diseases Programme

Area	1996		1997		Total	
	No. of projects	*M ECU*	*No. of projects*	*M ECU*	*No. of projects*	*M ECU*
A. Surveillance and Monitoring	6	3.246	9	3.316	15	6.562
B. Combating Transmission	15	2.190	17	2.351	32	4.541
C. Information, Education and Training	18	2.757	16	2.148	34	4.905
D. Support for persons with HIV/AIDS and combating discrimination	10	1.329	10	1.348	20	2.677

Source: European Commission (1999: 13).

The report highlights the issue of "consistency and complementarity" between the public health programmes, and other relevant Community policies, programmes and initiatives[28]. In order to promote such consistency, officials from the Public Health Directorate were invited to meetings of programme committees for specific relevant research programmes, and *vice versa*. Monitoring of the programmes was carried out by continuous review of the contractual obligations of the parties financed by the funds by the Commission.

In terms of the effectiveness of the programme, and the achievement of its aims, actual coverage by specific projects was reported to be "generally quite sufficient". In general, the AIDS projects delivered a range of appropriate and effective studies and interventions. Only one action (Action 10 on Member State vaccination policies and programmes) was not addressed by any project in 1996 or 1997. Positive results included improved co-ordination of surveillance systems, the production of a weekly electronic bulletin, and the creation and development of various European networks, for instance for HIV/STD pre-

---

[28] In particular, consistency is sought with the fourth (1994-1998) and fifth (1998-2002) framework programmes for research, technological development and demonstration.

vention among prostitutes, in prisons, and on European public policy on AIDS.

The projects utilised a mixture of innovative approaches and expansion of pre-existing effective projects. This confirms that the role of the EU is not limited to simply pilot projects or new ideas, but that the EU is willing to continue to finance worthwhile projects that have proved to be effective. In this respect, the EU is perhaps taking on some of the public health role of the Member States. The force for convergence between national public policies in the field, enhanced by Commission support of such programmes as the AIDS programme, was noted in terms of the "high intensity of inter-country exchanges, agreement on methods, achievement of a uniform and enhanced quality, and the production of common documents and statements".

There was some concern in the interim report that the populations targeted by the projects were not sufficiently focused on "high risk" groups, such as sexually active gay men, and intravenous drug users of all ages. Moreover, dissemination of results was felt to be limited to the traditional routes of scientific conferences and publications. The Commission would like to see the results of the projects it finances reaching wider audiences, although there are no concrete suggestions for who these audiences might be, or how they might be reached. Concern was also expressed that the issue of discrimination was not being adequately tackled. There is scope here for future improvement.

However, the most significant criticism of the interim report on the AIDS programme is in respect of the issue of EU-level "added value". This is seen to be the most crucial general objective, and one that was judged to be under-developed, especially in the initial projects. The experts report noted that

the project reports of the networks quite often fail to give a convincing picture of actual capacity to gather expertise and experience from all Member States and from all the relevant agencies in the Member States, as well as to disseminate information provided by those networks (European Commission, 1999a: 11).

In particular, the report draws a distinction between the *theoretical* position: "the project results in the majority of cases have significant practical relevance, and theoretically should better inform the HIV/STD policy framework and the design and delivery of programmes within the Member States"; and the *practical* position: "at present, there is only limited evidence that project results are actually being disseminated widely and influencing key policy-makers regarding future direction on HIV/STD issues within the Member States and in the European Union as a whole". The Commission is seeking to overcome this by stressing the "enhanced networking of applicants", although precisely what this means in practice remains rather undefined.

B. Cancer Programmes

As is the case with AIDS/HIV, the EU's involvement in tackling cancer predates the specific Treaty competence on public health. The European Council at Milan in June 1985 and Luxembourg in December 1985 called for a Community-level initiative to combat cancer. The Resolution of the Council and the Representatives of the Governments of the Member States, meeting within Council, of 7 July 1986 established the Europe against Cancer programme (Council of the European Communities, 1986). The original programme had three main elements: cancer prevention; information and public awareness; and training.

In December 1986, the European Council, at the London Summit, decided that 1989 should be designated "European Cancer Information Year". Accordingly, the Commission was charged, in collaboration with the Member States, with developing a "sustained and concerted information campaign" across the EU. This constituted the first action plan under the Europe against Cancer programme, established by Decision 88/351/EEC (Council of the European Communities, 1988a). The first action plan was effectively an information campaign, covering prevention, early detection and treatment of cancer. The budget for the campaign was € 10 million. The Commission was to co-ordinate information on the subject, for instance by contributing to production of televised information and health education programmes for the general public, co-ordinating exchange of experience with health education teaching materials, and involvement of health professionals.

On training, the Commission proceeded *inter alia* by calling on the Advisory Committees on Medical Training, Training in Nursing and Training of Dental Practitioners to review the ways in which the subject of cancer is taught to their respective professions, and to make recommendations for improvement. This review was carried out in 1987-1988. Each Committee then adopted a set of recommendations for training of medical professionals on cancer in the Member States. The recommendations included that each medical and dental school should include oncology in its undergraduate teaching programme; and that basic training of nurses should include the prevention, detection and diagnosis of cancer, and participation in public education about the benefits of prevention of and screening for cancer. All three Committees stressed the need for continuing education, based on current scientific knowledge. These recommendations are set out in the annex to Commission Recommendation 89/601/EEC (European Commission, 1989) concerning the training of health personnel in the matter of cancer. The Commission recommended that the conclusions of the Committees receive the widest possible circulation and discussion within the Member States.

The second phase of the Europe against Cancer programme (1990-1994) took forward the above initiatives. The Commission's action plan was adopted by Council and the Representatives of the Governments of the Member States meeting within Council in Decision 90/238/EEC (Council of the European Communities, 1990). This action plan established that Community-level action against cancer was to be an ongoing part of Community activity.

The three elements of the Cancer programme remained unchanged. However, while the first action plan had concentrated on information and public awareness, the second had a much stronger emphasis on prevention. For instance, the Commission was to stimulate projects of European interest concerning the prevention of nicotine addiction (especially amongst such target groups as young people, women, teachers and members of the health professions); pilot projects to teach methods of tackling nicotine addiction to members of the health professions and to teachers; and innovative information campaigns to prevent the use of tobacco among the general public and in the workplace. The Commission was also to stimulate medical research into matters such as diet and cancer; possible carcinogenic risks posed by certain chemicals, and screening programmes. Exchange of experience and networking was to be promoted, including the extension and monitoring of the European network of breast cancer screening programmes.

The health information and public awareness/education strands proceeded on the basis that the first action plan had been a success, and suggested a repeat of public European-wide information campaigns. However, an element of targeting of particularly vulnerable groups (at this stage undefined) was envisaged.

The training elements, especially the recommendations of the medical training Advisory Committees, were taken forward by Community-level support for measures to encourage exchange of experience between practitioners concerned with training in the Member States, encouraging the collection and exchange at Community level of teaching materials, and setting up of pilot European networks of medical, nursing and dentistry schools. Taking forward the Commission's recommendation, the Community was to finance national and regional meetings to promote the 1989 recommendations on the oncology element of medical training.

Significantly, the second phase of the Cancer programme also saw its institutionalisation within the Community legislature and administration. Decision 90/238/EEC, Article 1 (2) provided that the Commission is to be assisted in its implementation of the action plan by an advisory committee. The duties of the Committee were to assess projects to be co-financed from public funds, and to co-ordinate projects at national level partly funded by NGOs. Presumably "public funds" refers to both EU and national level sources of funding. The budget was set originally at € 50 million (Decision 90/238/EEC, Article 2), and this was adjusted to € 55 million in 1993 (Council of the European Union, 1993b).

The Commission submitted an evaluation of the Europe against Cancer programme from 1987-1992 on 23 March 1993. Both the European Parliament and the Council responded, essentially proposing that action taken under the Europe against Cancer programme be strengthened (European Parliament, 1993).

The Council invited the Commission to propose a further action plan, taking into account the revised objectives of the programme, based on the Commission's evaluation (Council of the European Union, 1993a). The Council's resolution took a different approach in establishing the areas of action, with a much stronger focus on prevention, as opposed to the other two areas. "Primary prevention" was to be given high priority in areas where the Community can continue to provide impetus for national action. Primary prevention was to take the form of information and health education. This is to be effected by dissemination of information on healthy lifestyles, both general and targeted at specific groups. "Secondary prevention" covers screening. Council noted that Community action in this field has allowed the knowledge and experience acquired in some of the Member States to be spread throughout the whole Community. Improvements could be made by Community-level interventions such as dissemination of best practice in the early diagnosis of and screening for cancer and by the continued study of effectiveness of and accuracy in screening. Finally, the Council Recommendation mentioned "other action", which was to include research, epidemiological studies, care and training.

The Council Recommendation envisaged a comprehensive approach to fighting cancer by using several complementary means: legal, financial, and co-operative. Council noted that "the legal means adopted by the Council must reinforce public health policy on cancer prevention in each Member State, particularly to promote healthy life-styles and to create an environment conducive to such efforts". It is not clear what Council meant by this statement. Such an environment might for instance include a European Union in which advertising of tobacco products is forbidden, a matter taken up by the Tobacco Advertising

Directive 98/43/EC (European Parliament and Council of the European Union, 1998b), subsequently held to be invalid by the ECJ[29].

The 1993 Council Resolution on future action in the field of public health (Council of the European Union, 1993c) included cancer among its priority areas for action. The third action plan to combat cancer was established in 1996 (European Parliament and Council of the European Union, 1996b). It was now possible to base the relevant Decision on the new Article 129 EC, introduced into the Treaty of Rome at Maastricht. In response to the Council and European Parliament's resolutions of 1993, the action plan contained revised – and more ambitious – objectives. However, the budgetary increase was relatively modest – from € 55 million to € 64 million (European Parliament and Council of the European Union, 1996b: Article 3) – and that to cover five years.

The general objective of the plan – reflecting the language of the (then) new Article 129 EC (now Article 152 EC) – was to contribute towards ensuring a high level of health protection. The action plan was to comprise actions aimed at preventing premature deaths due to cancer; reducing mortality and morbidity due to cancer; promoting quality of life; and promoting the general well being of the population, particularly by minimising the economic and social consequences of cancer. These actions are set out in detail in the annex, under the headings of data collection and research; information and health education; early detection and screening; training and quality control and guarantees. The plan envisaged significant progress towards a genuine European-level fight against cancer, with an emphasis on the practical details necessary to achieve such activity. Thus common objectives were to be established, comparable and compatible data on health were to be standardised and collected; the European network of cancer registers was to be developed; programmes for exchange of experience and of health professionals and for the dissemination of the most effective practices were to be supported; new information networks were to be created, European-scale studies were to be undertaken, with Europe-wide dissemination of results. The Decision gave authority for EU-level funding to be used to provide support for epidemiological studies focused on prevention, to implement pilot programmes and pilot projects, to compile reports (especially to monitor the measures taken on early detection and screening), to enable exchange of experience on quality control of the early detection of cancer and the prevention of its development (including experience of palliative care, methods for selecting priorities in cancer research, and experience of transferring results of

---

[29]   ECJ, case C-376/98, *Germany* v. *Parliament and Council (Tobacco Advertising)*, ECR [2000] I-8419. See further Hervey (2001b).

basic research into clinical trials) (European Parliament and Council of the European Union, 1996b: Article 1).

The Community's health programmes have thus developed from informal, *ad hoc* activities to on-going commitments with a firm legal basis in Community law. This is reflected in the formalisation of institutional arrangements, with the use of comitology structures promoting multi-level co-ordination between EU and national actors. The Commission's role is that of co-ordinator, and interactions are promoted between relevant national actors, including NGOs, especially those well established in the field. The content of projects supported by the plans is focused around information exchange and networking; education and training; disease prevention; health promotion; and research and data collection. In general, innovative pilot or flagship projects have been favoured, but there is increasing evidence of continued support for best practice. The budget has been a key area of difficulty, and this may explain the strong focus on groups specifically at risk, and the development of the notion of EU-level "added value". Questions remain over the extent to which actions taken under the programmes are really meeting the aim of promulgating at EU-level standards of best practice that actually penetrate into national and health policy[30].

III. The Proposed New Community Public Health Strategy

In April 1998, anticipating new provisions in the Treaty of Amsterdam, the Commission launched a debate on a new direction for Community public health policy (European Commission, 1998). The Commission took the view that the existing public health strategy was in need of fundamental revision for a number of reasons. First, experience of the existing strategy indicated some drawbacks. The approach of the 1993 programme was to propose eight separate programmes, rather than one overall strategy. The reason for this was to avoid serious delays in implementing the new provisions, arising from the differences between governments of Member States over the priorities to be addressed. However, the differentiated strategy caused a number of unforeseen problems. Each programme has its own "mixed" committee, with complex rules and structures, leading to a proliferation of bureaucracy. The differentiated strategy is inflexible, and cannot respond easily to developments not covered by the eight programmes, or to changes in priorities of the EU or its Member States. Each programme has a relatively small budget, and it is unclear whether the requisite "added value" at Community level can be delivered within these constraints. It

---

[30] This type of empirical enquiry is obviously beyond the scope of this paper, which concentrates on legal and institutional structures.

was difficult to ensure co-ordination between the programmes, and to avoid duplication or overlap of activities. Moreover, in practice, the focus of the programmes was on projects submitted to the Commission by organisations operating in the field. Thus the impetus for action came from those organisations, rather than from the EU institutions. The consequence of this procedure was that funds were spread among many projects, often with a relatively short time frame. Not all of these projects were necessarily relevant to all Member States. The Commission took the view that if fewer, larger-scale, sustainable actions had been supported a greater impact might have been achieved.

The second reason put forward by the Commission for a fundamental review was the emergence of new developments in health status and health systems within the EU, some of which could not have been foreseen in 1993. These include the emergence of new risks to health, chief among which is new variant Creutzfeldt-Jacob Disease (nv-CJD), but which also include avian flu and Ebola haemorrhagic fever. Levels of premature morality[31] remain high, particularly as a consequence of the so-called "lifestyle diseases"[32], such as cancer and cardio-vascular diseases. Wide variations and inequalities in health status remain across the EU as a whole, both between Member States, and within different population groups in each Member State. As a consequence of increasing life expectancies[33], more people are suffering from health problems related to old age, such as Alzheimer's and other degenerative disorders[34]. National health systems in the Member States are facing new pressures. Upward pressure on health care costs comes from demographic trends, technological advances, and increased public expectations. Member States have responded with cost-containment and efficiency measures. There is an increasing awareness of the importance of the health sector (as employer, and purchaser of goods and services) on the economy as a whole. Conversely, increases in unemployment may have drastic effects on national health services funded through income-related contributions.

Third, the process of EU enlargement to Central and Eastern Europe will present specific challenges in the public health field. It was felt that

---

[31] Defined for these purposes as death before the age of 65 years.

[32] So termed because behaviour patterns developed in childhood and adolescence, such as smoking, limited exercise and poor nutrition are major risk factors for these diseases in adulthood.

[33] Since 1970, life expectancy at birth for women in the EU has risen by 5.5 years and for men by almost 5 years. A girl born in 1995 can expect to live well over 80 years, a boy to nearly 74 years (European Commission, 1998: 1).

[34] It was estimated that by 2000, 8 million people in the EU would be affected by Alzheimer's (European Commission, 1998: 2).

the EU's health policy would have to be sufficiently flexible to deal with enlargement. The health status of the populations of Central and Eastern European States compares unfavourably with those of existing Member States. Any future EU health policy would have to find ways of tackling the problems and priorities of new Member States, and find ways of providing Community support to underpin the necessary restructuring of their health care systems.

The Commission proposed a Community public health policy comprising three strands:

- improving information for the development of public health;
- reacting rapidly to threats to health;
- tackling health determinants through health promotion and disease prevention.

The basic principles of the proposed new strategy were to make the best use of the limited resources available at EU level; to concentrate on a limited number of priorities; to emphasise the improvement of health; to be sufficiently flexible to respond to new developments; and to be credible and convincing from the point of view of citizens of the EU, reflecting their concerns. Without wishing to constrain the debate, the Commission suggested that one way forward would be to adopt a single "framework instrument" providing for subsequent adoption of separate instruments for each strand. This would have the benefit of creating a single budgetary heading, with an administrative structure to apportion funding between the strands.

The Council and the European Parliament (as well as the Economic and Social Committee, and the Committee of the Regions) responded positively to the Commission's 1998 proposals (Council of the European Union, 1998 and 1999a; European Parliament, 1999; ESC, 1998 and Committee of the Regions, 1998). These institutions also took the view that a single overall framework programme would be the best way forward. In order to ensure continuity, the existing programmes are to be continued until 31 December 2002 (European Commission, 2000a and European Parliament and Council of the European Union, 2001).

The proposal for a Decision adopting the new public health framework was originally put forward by the Commission in May 2000, and billed as a "very ambitious" "major new initiative" (European Commission (2000b: 5). The three priorities of the 1998 consultation – improving health information and knowledge; responding rapidly to health threats; and addressing health determinants – are to be maintained, and set out in Article 2 of the proposed Decision, which will implement the new framework. Each general objective is to be pursued by a number of sets of actions, as set out in Article 3 of the proposed

Decision, and elaborated in the Annex to the proposed Decision. The proposal envisages a broad range of different types of measures, such as support for preparation of EU-level legislation; support for health information in the Community Statistical Programme; support for preparation and dissemination of reports on specific health topics of interests to the EU and all Member States; development of networks of patients, health professionals and "other stakeholders" for the purposes of dissemination of information and consultation; support for the mobilisation of resources to tackle unforeseen health threats; support for building capacity to respond to health threats, including education and training; support for sharing of experience and exchange of information between the EU and the competent bodies within the Member States; provision of information, via the EU, to health professionals and the public; support for disease prevention and health promotion activities undertaken by NGOs; and support for innovative or pilot projects. Pursuant to the new competencies following Amsterdam in addition to the public health programme, the proposed new framework encompasses other potential legislative measures, including measures of harmonisation in the veterinary and phytosanitary fields, on standards of quality and safety of human organs, and on quality and safety of human blood and blood derivatives. The rationale for EU-level intervention, in the context of an area in which the main responsibilities for organisation and delivery of health care rest with the Member States, remains that of "added value".

The proposal envisages that the requirement to integrate public health in other EU activities and policies will be carried out by "joint strategies" and "joint actions" with related EU programmes and actions, such as those in consumer protection, social protection, health and safety at work, employment, internal market, information technology, research and technological development, telematic interchange of data between administrations (IDA), statistics, education, agriculture and environment[35]. The Commission is to ensure "consistency and complementarity" with other Community activities[36].

Various non-EU States may participate in the programme. These include the EEA countries, the "Europe Agreement" countries in Central and Eastern Europe, Cyprus, Malta and Turkey. Co-operation with international organisations competent in the sphere of public health shall

---

[35] See proposed Article 4 in European Commission (2000b) and Council of the European Union (2001).

[36] See proposed Article 6 in European Commission (2000b) and Council of the European Union (2001).

be fostered. The measure explicitly mentions the WHO, Council of Europe and OECD in this respect[37].

The Commission's proposal has, at the time of writing (February 2002) not yet been adopted. A number of issues have emerged as contentious or potentially contentious during the legislative process. Many of these issues concern the institutional arrangements for the new public health strategy, rather than matters of substance.

One at least potentially substantive issue, presumably arising at least in part from the litigation on free movement of patients, is the need to protect health and social systems from the stringencies of Community (economic) law. This was originally raised by the Economic and Social Committee (ESC, 2001)[38], and taken forward by the Commission in its amended proposal (European Commission, 2001). Recital 2 of the amended proposal read "health should be a priority beyond political or financial compromises". The Council's common position (Council of the European Union, 2001) removed this provision, but following the European Parliament's second reading report[39], the Commission has reinstated it in the current version of its proposal (European Commission, 2002). Council endorses the sentiment, but takes the view that this is not the appropriate context in which to promulgate it. The issue should be seen in the context of more general moves within the European Union to protect the "European social model" of social security (see, for instance, Council of the European Communities, 1992a and b and European Commission, 1997b and 1999b), *inter alia* through the "open method of co-ordination" introduced at Amsterdam (for further information, see Kenner, 1999: 33; Szyszczak, 2000 and 2001b).

The broad objectives of the programme have remained more or less unchanged throughout the legislative process. Matters of the scope of Community competence in public health are still the subjects of disagreement between institutional actors. For instance, the European Parliament sought to include among the Community's obligations that of developing a contribution to the definition of minimum quality standards applicable to health and patients' rights. The Commission originally took this proposal forward (European Commission, 2001: proposed recital 24), but in view of Council's position to the effect that "quality standards and guidelines and patients' rights are areas of Member State competence" (Council of the European Union, 2001: 39), has now taken the view that the development of generally accepted

---

[37] See proposed Articles 10 and 11 in European Commission (2000b) and Council of the European Union (2001).

[38] *Bulletin* 2000/11 1.4.55.

[39] Trakatellis Report A5/2001/420; *Bulletin* 2001/12 1.4.85, 26 November 2001.

standards of patients' rights would be beyond the scope of the programme (European Commission, 2002).

Thirdly, the European Parliament has sought to enhance the role of the EU in co-ordination and monitoring of public health data. The Commission's original proposal was that the EU was to develop and operate a health monitoring system, and to develop and use mechanisms for analysis, advice, reporting, information and consultation on health issues. Parliament, in its report of the first reading[40], proposed the setting up of a "Health Coordination and Monitoring Centre", as a separate EU-level agency. In addition to a data-monitoring role, the proposed Centre would co-ordinate EU measures and actions, and incorporate the work of existing and future Community networks in the field of public health at Community level. This proposal has found no support among other institutions and has not been taken forward in the current Commission proposal.

The Commission is to be responsible for adopting measures concerning the annual plan of work and for monitoring of the programme. According to the proposal, the Commission must identify performance indicators, monitor achievement of results and organise independent mid-term and ex-post evaluations. Evaluation reports must be publicly available. An attempt by the European Parliament to impose an obligation to provide it with annual reports was unsuccessful. The European Parliament had more success in modifying the original proposal in respect of the comitology procedures to be used to implement the programme. The original proposal was for use of the "advisory" procedure, but some elements are now to be subject to the "management" procedure (for details, see Council of the European Union, 1999b), "because of the particular sensitivity of the health sector and the scope of the programme under consideration"[41]. The significance of this is to enhance Member State control (and constrain Commission discretion) over the detailed implementation of actions taken under the programme.

The most contentious, and as yet unresolved, issue is that of the budget. The Commission remains committed to its original proposed budget for the overall programme of € 300 million (European Commission, 2002). However, the Council is suggesting a budget of € 280 million, and Parliament wants € 380 million to be allocated to the health programme[42]. Parliament takes the view that the new programme is

---

[40]   Trakatellis Report A5/2001/104; Bulletin 2001/4 1.4.64, 4 April 2001.

[41]   Trakatellis Report A5/2001/104 (page 50).

[42]   To put matters in context, the current (2001) budget for public health stands at € 44.6 million; whereas that for the European Regional Development Fund and other

much wider than the programmes currently in place, and that the higher amount is necessary to achieve its objectives. The Commission and Council dispute this, although the Commission adopted a revised financial statement in February 2002, with an increase in expenditure for technical and administrative assistance. Matters were complicated by the European Parliament's proposal, in its second reading, to the effect that a minimum of one quarter of the budget should be allocated to each objective. In the Commission's view, this removes flexibility necessary for the successful operation of the programme. The position at present is that Council has until April 2002 to consider the Parliament's proposal, and if rejected, the matter must be decided by conciliation between Council and Parliament. The allocation to "public health" in the 2001 budget was € 44.6 million, so Parliament's proposal, over five years, constitutes nearly a doubling of the budget, whereas Council's represents a modest increase. In addition to the obvious practical ramifications of an increased public health budget, the resolution of the budget represents an important symbolic struggle in terms of the increased competence of the EU in the field of public health.

Conclusion

This chapter has shown that Community public health policy has developed rapidly, from a situation of insecure legal and institutional basis, to one in which its place in the objectives and activities of the Community is legally and institutionally secure. While the competence to determine public health policies remains primarily at national level, in accordance with the principle of subsidiarity, the EU institutions now have a clear obligation to participate in the public health field. The incremental effects of the Community's public health programmes, as mechanisms of persuasive integration, are likely to continue to contribute to the determination of "European health policy" in the EU's multilevel system of governance. Whether the mobilisation of the programme in practice can deliver the much-sought-after "EU-level added value" remains to be seen.

Bibliography

ABEL-SMITH, B., FIGUERAS, J., HOLLAND, W., MCKEE, M. and MOSSIALOS, E. (1995) (eds.), *Choices in Health Policy: An Agenda for the European Union*, Dartmouth Publishing, Aldershot.

---

regional intervention stands at € 16,144.3 million and that for Agriculture at € 39,204 million.

ABRAHAM, J. and LEWIS, G. (2000), *Regulating Medicines in Europe: Competition, Expertise and Public Health*, Routledge, London.

ARMSTRONG, K. A. (1995), "Regulating the Free Movement of Goods: Institutions and Institutional Change", in SHAW, J. and MORE, G. (1995), *New Legal Dynamics of European Union*, Clarendon Press, Oxford, pp. 165-192.

ARMSTRONG, K. and BULMER, S. (1998), *Governance of the Single European Market*, Manchester University Press, Manchester.

BAEYENS, A. (1999), "Free Movement of Goods and Services in Health Care", *European Journal of Health Law*, Vol. 6, No. 4, pp. 373-383.

BOYRON, S. (1996), "Maastricht and the Codecision Procedure: A Success Story", *International and Comparative Law Quarterly*, Vol. 45, No. 2, April 1996, pp. 293-318.

BRADLEY, K. (1992), "Comitology and the Law: Through a Glass, Darkly", *Common Market Law Review*, Vol. 29, pp. 693-721.

BRADLEY, K. (1997), "The European Parliament and Comitology: On the Road to Nowhere", *European Law Journal*, Vol. 3, No. 3, pp. 230-254.

CABRAL, P. (1999), "Cross-border Medical Care in the EU – Bringing Down a First Wall", *European Law Review*, Vol. 24, No. 4, pp. 387-395.

COMMITTEE OF THE REGIONS (1998), Opinion of the Committee of the Regions of 19 November 1998 on the Communication from the Commission to the Council, the European Parliament, the Economic and Social Committee and the Committee of the Regions on the development of public health policy in the European Community (COM (98) 230 final).

COUNCIL OF THE EUROPEAN COMMUNITIES (1986), Resolution of the Council and the Representatives of the Governments of the Member States, meeting within the Council, of 7 July 1986, on a programme of action of the European Communities against cancer, OJ C 184, 23 July 1986, pp. 0019-0020.

COUNCIL OF THE EUROPEAN COMMUNITIES (1987), Conclusions of the Council and of the representatives of the Governments of the Member States, meeting within the Council of 15 May 1987 concerning AIDS, OJ C 178, 7 July 1987, pp. 0001-0001.

COUNCIL OF THE EUROPEAN COMMUNITIES (1988a), Decision 88/351/EEC of the Council and of representatives of the Governments of the Member States, meeting within the Council of 21 June 1988 adopting a 1988 to 1989 plan of action for an information and public awareness campaign in the context of the "Europe against Cancer" programme, OJ L 160, 28 June 1988, pp. 0052.

COUNCIL OF THE EUROPEAN COMMUNITIES (1988b), Conclusions of the Council and the representatives of the Governments of the Member States, meeting within the Council of 31 May 1988 concerning AIDS, OJ C 197, 27 July 1988, pp. 0008-0008.

COUNCIL OF THE EUROPEAN COMMUNITIES (1989a), Conclusions of the Council and the Ministers for Health of the Member States, meeting within the Council, on 15 December 1988 concerning AIDS, OJ C 28, 3 February 1989, pp. 0001-0001.

COUNCIL OF THE EUROPEAN COMMUNITIES (1989b), Conclusions of the Council and the Ministers for Health of the Member States meeting within the Council of 16 May

1989 regarding the prevention of AIDS in intravenous drug users, OJ C 185, 22 July 1989, pp. 0003-0005.

COUNCIL OF THE EUROPEAN COMMUNITIES (1989c), Conclusions of the Council and the Ministers for Health of the Member States, meeting within the Council, on 15 December 1988 concerning AIDS and the place of work, OJ C 028, 3 February 1989, pp. 0002-0003.

COUNCIL OF THE EUROPEAN COMMUNITIES (1990), Decision 90/238/EEC of the Council and the Representatives of the Governments of the Member States meeting within the Council, on 17 May 1990 adopting a 1990 to 1994 action plan in the context of the Europe against Cancer programme, OJ L 137, 30 May 1990, p. 0031.

COUNCIL OF THE EUROPEAN COMMUNITIES (1991), Decision 91/317/EEC of the Council and the Ministers for Health of the Member States, meeting within the Council of 4 June 1991 adopting a plan of action in the framework of the 1991 to 1993 "Europe against AIDS" programme, OJ L175, 4 July 1991, pp. 0026-0029.

COUNCIL OF THE EUROPEAN COMMUNITIES (1992a), Council Recommendation of 24 June 1992 on common criteria concerning sufficient resources and social assistance in social protection systems, OJ L 245, 26 August 1992, pp. 0046-0048.

COUNCIL OF THE EUROPEAN COMMUNITIES (1992b), Council Recommendation of 27 July 1992 on the convergence of social protection objectives and policies, OJ L 245, 26 August 1992, pp. 0049-0052.

COUNCIL OF THE EUROPEAN UNION (1993a), Council Resolution of 13 December 1993 concerning future guidelines for the Europe against Cancer programme following evaluation of it for the period 1987 to 1992, OJ C 15, 18 January 1994, pp. 0001-0004.

COUNCIL OF THE EUROPEAN UNION (1993b), Decision 93/362/EEC of the Council and the Ministers for Health, meeting within the Council of 27 May 1993 concerning the continuation in 1994 of the 1990 to 1994 action plan in the context of the Europe against Cancer programme, OJ L 150, 22 June 1993, p. 0043.

COUNCIL OF THE EUROPEAN UNION (1993c), Resolution of the Council and the Ministers for Health, meeting within the Council of 27 May 1993 on future action in the field of public health, OJ C 174, 25 June 1993, pp. 0001-0003.

COUNCIL OF THE EUROPEAN UNION (1998), Council Conclusions of 26 November 1998 on the future framework for Community action in the field of public health, OJ C 390, 15 December 1998, pp. 0001-0002.

COUNCIL OF THE EUROPEAN UNION (1999a), Council Resolution of 8 June 1999 on the future Community action in the field of public health, OJ C 200, 15 July 1999, pp. 0001-0002.

COUNCIL OF THE EUROPEAN UNION (1999b), Council Decision 99/468/EC of 28 June 1999 laying down the procedures for the exercise of implementing powers conferred on the Commission, OJ L 184, 17 July 1999, pp. 0023-0026.

COUNCIL OF THE EUROPEAN UNION (2001), Common Position 34/2001/EC of 31 July 2001 adopted by the Council, acting in accordance with the procedure referred to in Article 251 of the Treaty establishing the European Community, with a view to adopting a Decision of the European Parliament and of the Council adopting a programme of Community action in the field of public health (2001 to 2006), OJ C 307, 31 October 2001, pp. 0027-0040.

CRAM, L. (1997), *Policy-making in the EU: Conceptual Lenses and the Integration Process*, Routledge, London.

DEHOUSSE, R. (1992), "Integration v. Regulation? On the Dynamics of Regulation in the European Community", *Journal of Common Market Studies*, Vol. 30, No. 4, pp. 383-402.

DOMMERS, J. (1995), "Europese Integratie en volksgesondheid: handel noopt tot handelen", in ROSCAM ABBING, H.D.C. and VAN BERKENSTIJN, T.M.G. (eds.), *Gezondheidsbeleid in Europa*, Stafleu Van Loghum, Bohn.

ESC (1998), Opinion of the Economic and Social Committee of 9 September 1998 on the "Communication from the Commission to the Council, the European Parliament, the Economic and Social Committee and the Committee of the Regions on the development of public health policy in the European Community", OJ C 407, 28 December 1998, pp. 0021-0026.

ESC (2001), Opinion of the Economic and Social Committee on the "Proposal for a Decision of the European Parliament and of the Council adopting a programme of Community action in the field of public health (2001-2006)", OJ C 116, 20 April 2001, pp. 0075-0083.

EUROPEAN COMMISSION (1989), Commission Recommendation 89/601/EEC of 8 November 1989 concerning the training of health personnel in the matter of cancer, OJ L 346, 27 November 1989, pp. 0001-0007.

EUROPEAN COMMISSION (1994a), Communication from the Commission adopting a programme of Community action on health promotion, information, education, and training within the framework for action in the field of public health, COM (94) 202 final, OJ C 252, 9 September 1994.

EUROPEAN COMMISSION (1994b), Proposal for a European Parliament and Council Decision adopting a programme of Community action on the prevention of AIDS and certain other communicable diseases within the framework for action in the field of public health, COM (94) 413 final, OJ C 333, 29 November 1997, p. 0034.

EUROPEAN COMMISSION (1995), Report from the Commission to the Council, the European Parliament and the Economic and Social Committee on the Integration of Health Protection Requirements in Community Policies, COM (95) 196 final of 25 May 1995.

EUROPEAN COMMISSION (1997a), *Public Health in Europe*, Office for Official Publications of the European Communities, Luxembourg.

EUROPEAN COMMISSION (1997b), Communication from the Commission "Modernising and Improving Social Protection in the European Union", COM (97) 102 of 12 March 1997.

EUROPEAN COMMISSION (1998), Communication from the Commission to the Council, the European Parliament, the Economic and Social Committee and the Committee of the Regions on the development of public health policy in the European Community, COM (98) 230 final of 15 April 1998.

Tamara K. Hervey

EUROPEAN COMMISSION (1999a), Interim report from the Commission to the European Parliament, the Council, the Economic and Social Committee and the Committee of the Regions on the implementation of the programmes of Community action on the prevention of cancer, AIDS and certain other communicable diseases, and drug dependence within the framework for action in the field of public health (1996-2000), COM (99) 463 final of 14 October 1999 (http://europa.eu.int/eur-lex/en/com/rpt/1999/com1999_0463en01.pdf).

EUROPEAN COMMISSION (1999b), Communication from the Commission "A Concerted Strategy for Modernising Social Protection", COM (99) 347 of 14 July 1999.

EUROPEAN COMMISSION (2000a), Proposal for a Decision of the European Parliament and of the Council extending certain programmes of Community action in the field of public health adopted by Decisions 645/96/EC, 646/96/EC, 647/96/EC, 102/97/EC, 1400/97/EC and 1296/1999/EC and amending those Decisions, COM (2000) 448 final of 25 July 2000.

EUROPEAN COMMISSION (2000b), Communication from the European Commission on the European Community Health Strategy, Proposal of a Programme of Action of Community Action in the Field of Public Health (2001-2006), COM (2000) 285 of 16 May 2000.

EUROPEAN COMMISSION (2001), Amended proposal for a Decision of the European Parliament and of the Council adopting a programme of Community action in the field of public health (2001-2006) (presented by the Commission pursuant to Article 250(2) of the EC-Treaty), COM (2001) 302 final of 1 June 2001.

EUROPEAN COMMISSION (2002), Opinion of the Commission pursuant to Article 251 (2), third subparagraph, point (c) of the EC Treaty, on the European Parliament's amendments to the Council's Common Position regarding the proposal for a Decision of the European Parliament and of the Council adopting a programme of Community action in the field of public health amending the proposal of the Commission pursuant to Article 250 (2) of the EC Treaty, COM (2002) 29 final of 23 January 2002.

EUROPEAN PARLIAMENT (1993), Resolution on public health policy after Maastricht, OJ C 329, 6 December 1993, p. 0375.

EUROPEAN PARLIAMENT (1999), Resolution A4-0082/99 of 10 March 1999 on the Communication from the Commission to the Council, the European Parliament, the Economic and Social Committee and the Committee of the Regions on the development of public health policy in the European Community (COM (98) 230 final – C4-0393/98), p. 0035.

EUROPEAN PARLIAMENT and COUNCIL OF THE EUROPEAN UNION (1995), European Parliament and Council Decision 1729/95/EC of 19 June 1995 on the extensions of the "Europe against AIDS" programme, OJ L 168, 18 July 1995, pp. 0001-0006.

EUROPEAN PARLIAMENT and COUNCIL OF THE EUROPEAN UNION (1996a), Decision 645/96/EC of the European Parliament and of the Council of 29 March 1996 adopting a programme of Community action on health promotion, information, education and training within the framework for action in the field of public health (1996 to 2000), OJ L 95, 16 April 1996, pp. 0001-0008.

EUROPEAN PARLIAMENT and COUNCIL OF THE EUROPEAN UNION (1996b), Decision 646/96/EC of the European Parliament and of the Council of 29 March 1996 adopting an action plan to combat cancer within the framework for action in the field of public health (1996 to 2000), OJ L 95, 16 April 1996, pp. 0009-0015.

EUROPEAN PARLIAMENT and COUNCIL OF THE EUROPEAN UNION (1996c), Decision 647/96/EC of the European Parliament and of the Council of 29 March 1996 adopting a programme of Community action on the prevention of AIDS and certain other communicable diseases within the framework for action in the field of public health (1996 to 2000), OJ L 95, 16 April 1996, pp. 0016-0022.

EUROPEAN PARLIAMENT and COUNCIL OF THE EUROPEAN UNION (1997a), Decision 102/97/EC of the European Parliament and of the Council of 16 December 1996 adopting a programme of Community action on the prevention of drug dependence within the framework for action in the field of public health (1996-2000), OJ L 19, 22 January 1997, pp. 0025-0031.

EUROPEAN PARLIAMENT and COUNCIL OF THE EUROPEAN UNION (1997b), Decision 1400/97/EC of the European Parliament and of the Council of 30 June 1997 adopting a programme of Community action on health monitoring within the framework for action in the field of public health (1997 to 2001), OJ L 193, 22 July 1997, pp. 0001-0010.

EUROPEAN PARLIAMENT and COUNCIL OF THE EUROPEAN UNION (1998a), Decision 2119/98/EC of the European Parliament and of the Council of 24 September 1998 setting up a network for the epidemiological surveillance and control of communicable diseases in the Community, OJ L 268, 3 October 1998, pp. 0001-0007.

EUROPEAN PARLIAMENT and COUNCIL OF THE EUROPEAN UNION (1998b), Directive 98/43/EC of the European Parliament and of the Council of 6 July 1998 on the approximation of the laws, regulations and administrative provisions of the Member States relating to the advertising and sponsorship of tobacco products, OJ L 213, 30 July 1998, pp. 0009-0012.

EUROPEAN PARLIAMENT and COUNCIL OF THE EUROPEAN UNION (1999), Decision 372/99/EC of the European Parliament and of the Council of 8 February1999 adopting a programme of Community action on injury prevention in the framework for action in the field of public health (1999 to 2003), OJ L 46, 20 February 1999, pp. 0001-0005.

EUROPEAN PARLIAMENT and COUNCIL OF THE EUROPEAN UNION (2001), Decision 521/2001/EC of the European Parliament and of the Council of 26 February 2001 extending certain programmes of Community action in the field of public health adopted by Decisions 645/96/EC, 646/96/EC, 647/96/EC, 102/97/EC, 1400/97/EC and 1296/1999/EC and amending those Decisions, OJ L 79, 17 March 2001, pp. 0001-0007.

HILDITCH, L. and GARMAN, J. (1998), "Behind the Scenes: an Examination of the Importance of the Informal Processes at Work in Conciliation", *Journal of European Public Policy*, Vol. 5, No. 2, pp. 271-284.

GEYER, R. (2000), *Exploring European Social Policy*, Polity, Cambridge.

HERVEY, T. (2001a), "Community and National Competence in Health after Tobacco Advertising", *Common Market Law Review*, Vol. 38, No. 6, pp. 1421-1446..

HERVEY, T. (2001b), "Up in Smoke: Community (anti) Tobacco Law and Policy", *European Law Review*, Vol. 26, No. 2, pp. 101-125.

HERVEY, T. (forthcoming), "The European Union Dimension", in BRAZIER, M., MCHALE, J. and HARRINGTON, J. (eds.), *AIDS: Epidemics, Europe and Human Rights*, Oxford University Press, Oxford.

HOOGHE, L. and MARKS, G. (2001), *Multi-level Governance and European Integration*, Rowman & Littlefield, Lanham MD.

HOSKYNS, C. (1996), *Integrating Gender*, Verso, London.

KENNER, J. (1999), "The EU Employment Title and the 'Third Way': Making Soft Law Work?", *The International Journal of Comparative Labour Law and Industrial Relations*, Vol. 15, No. 1, pp. 33-60.

LEIBFRIED, S. and PIERSON, P. (1995), *European Social Policy: Between Fragmentation and Implementation*, Brookings, Washington.

MAJONE, G. (1996), "A European Regulatory State?", in RICHARDSON, J. (ed.), *European Union: Power and Policy-making*, Routledge, London, pp. 263-277.

MCKEE, M., MOSSIALOS, E. and BELCHER, P. (1996), "The Influence of European Law on National Health Policy", *Journal of European Social Policy*, Vol. 6, No. 4, pp. 263-286.

MOSSIALOS, E. and MCKEE, M. (2001), "Is a European Health Care Policy Emerging?", *British Medical Journal*, Vol. 323, No. 7307, 4 August 2001, p. 248.

O'ROURKE, R. (1999), *European Food Law*, Palladian, Bembridge.

ROSCAM ABBING, H. D. C. (1992), "European Community and the Right to Health Care", in HERMANS, H. E. G. M., CASPARIE, A. F. and PAELINCK, J. H. P. (eds.), *Health Care in Europe After 1992*, Dartmouth Publishing, Aldershot, pp. 20-32.

ROSCAM ABBING, H. D. C. (1995), "Human Tissue and Consumer Protection from a European Perspective", *European Journal of Health Law*, Vol. 2, No. 4, pp. 295-307.

ROSCAM ABBING, H. D. C. (1998), "Public Health in the Treaty of Amsterdam", *European Journal of Health Law*, Vol. 5, No. 2, pp. 171-175.

ROSCAM ABBING, H. D. C. (1999), "Editorial: Public Health Insurance and Freedom of Movement within the European Union", *European Journal of Health Law*, Vol. 6, No. 1, pp. 1-6.

SHAW, J. (1999), "From the Margins to the Centre: Education and Training Law and Policy" in CRAIG, P. and DE BÚRCA, G. (eds.), *The Evolution of EU Law*, Oxford University Press, Oxford.

SIEVEKING, K. (2000), "The Significance of Transborder Utilisation of Health Care Benefits for Migrants", *European Journal of Migration and Law*, Vol. 2, No. 2, pp. 143-155.

SLOT, P. J. (1996), "Harmonisation", *European Law Review*, Vol. 21, No. 5, pp. 378-387.

SZYSZCZAK, E. (2000), "The Evolving European Employment Strategy" in SHAW, J. (ed.), *Social Law and Policy in an Evolving EU*, Hart Publishing, Oxford, pp. 197-222.

SZYSZCZAK, E. (2001), "The New Paradigm for Social Policy: A Virtuous Circle", *Common Market Law Review*, Vol. 38, No. 5, pp. 1125-1170.

VAN DER MEI, A. P. (1998), "Cross-Border Access to Medical Care within the European Union – Some Reflections on the Judgments in *Decker* and *Kohll*", *Maastrich Journal of European and Comparative Law*, Vol. 5, No. 3, pp. 277-297.

VAN DER MEI, A. P. and WADDINGTON, L. (1998), "Public Health and the Treaty of Amsterdam", *European Journal of Health Law*, Vol. 5, No. 2, pp. 129-154.

VERWERS, (1992), "Towards a New EC Health Policy?" Uniting Public Health in Europe (European Public Health Association).

WEATHERILL, S. (1995), *Law and Integration in the European Union*, Clarendon, Oxford.

WELLENS, K. and BORCHARDT, R. (1989), "Soft Law in European Community Law", *European Law Review*, Vol. 14, No. 5, pp. 267-321.

CHAPTER 3

The Internal Market and
the Social Nature of Health Care

Jason NICKLESS

Introduction

In Raymond Kohll *v.* Union des Caisses de Maladie and Nicolas Decker *v.* Caisse de Maladie des Employés Privés, the ECJ used EU law on the free movement of goods and services to increase substantially a patient's options for receiving non-emergency health care in another Member State at the expense of his or her social health care system. However, these decisions left many unresolved questions, such as their impact on national health systems, their effect on the distribution of health care between rich and poor and the extent to which the EU can determine the range of care provided by a social health care system. It also raised the more fundamental issue of the extent to which economic rules should be applied to special areas like social health care.

The first section of this chapter introduces the Court judgements. The second section then advances a hypothesis concerning the limits of their application. This hypothesis is founded upon the principle of subsidiarity and balances national sovereignty with EU rules on fair trade without "persecuting" any particular model of social health care provision. It was previously proposed to the European Commission as part of a report produced by the Association Internationale de la Mutualité (AIM) (Palm *et al.*, 2000). The third section deals with two very recent decisions of the ECJ, Smits/Peerbooms and Vanbraekel. These decisions have clarified some of the uncertainty stemming from Kohll and Decker. This section also looks at whether these two new cases are consistent with existing models of patient mobility within Europe, and concludes with a flow diagram indicating when a patient may receive non-emergency social health care abroad. The final section of this chapter addresses the wider issues behind Kohll and Decker and what they mean for the balance between the economic and social domains of the European Union.

I. Kohll and Decker: The Facts and the Judgements

The Kohll[1] and Decker[2] decisions send a clear message to all those in the social health care sector that just because something is associated with social security it is not beyond the grasp of the internal market[3]. The cases concerned the provision of medical goods and services in another Member State at the expense of the patient's home social health care system. The EC Social Security Co-ordination Regulation 1408/71 clearly states that social health care can be provided in another Member State in several situations[4]. For example the home system will pay for emergency medical treatment needed during a visit to another EC State. Regulation 1408/71 EC also allows EU nationals to travel to another Member State for non-emergency medical care at the expense of their own health care system provided that their social health insurer or social health care administrator gives express authorisation beforehand. If this authorisation is provided, the patient's health care system then has to pay the foreign health care provider according to the rate and rules applied in the State where the treatment is received. When a patient uses this authorisation procedure this means that, in principle, they do not have to pay the foreign health care provider directly.

Mr. Kohll and Mr. Decker were Luxembourg nationals covered by the Luxembourg social health care system. Residents of Luxembourg receive health care coverage from social health insurers. The patients pay their health care provider directly and are then partially reimbursed by their insurer. Mr. Kohll wanted to purchase some new spectacles and Mr. Decker wanted orthodontic treatment for his daughter (a minor covered under his insurance scheme). Both the purchasing of spectacles and treatment by an orthodontist are provided for by the Luxembourg health insurance system and their costs are partially refunded by social health insurers.

However, Mr. Kohll and Mr. Decker did not want to purchase these goods and services in Luxembourg. Instead Mr. Kohll went to Belgium in order to get his glasses and Mr. Decker wished to take his daughter to an orthodontist in Germany. Neither Mr. Kohll nor Mr. Decker wanted to rely upon the authorisation procedure provided for in the EC Regulation. Instead, they wanted to go to the other Member State, purchase

---

[1] ECJ, case C-158/96, *Kohll*, ECR [1998] I-1931.

[2] ECJ, case C-120/95, *Decker*, ECR [1998] I-1831.

[3] For an excellent introduction to these cases see "Health Care without Frontiers within the European Union?", International Symposium, Luxembourg, 18 November 1998, available on request from Association Internationale de la Mutualité (Brussels).

[4] Article 22 Regulation 1408/71 (since amended) (Council of the European Union, 1996).

their medical goods and services, then return to Luxembourg and receive a refund from their social health insurer as if the treatment or products had been obtained in Luxembourg. They were prepared to pay the foreign health care provider directly and then be refunded according to the fees and rules that applied in their home State.

The Luxembourg social health insurers relied upon the national rules that implemented Regulation 1408/71 EC in order to refuse reimbursement. Mr. Kohll and Mr. Decker challenged these rules on the grounds that they violated the principles of free movement of goods and services contained "respectively" in Articles 28 and 49-50 of the EC Treaty.

The first point that the European Court of Justice (ECJ) addressed in its judgements was whether EU rules on the free movement of goods and services could be applied to social security systems. This is because the Luxembourg government and several intervening governments insisted that these were economic rules and so did not apply to the social security field.

The ECJ reviewed its case law in this area and concluded that Member States have a great deal of freedom in the organisation of their social security systems. In the absence of EU harmonising measures they are free to decide who can become affiliated to a social security scheme, what conditions must be fulfilled in order to receive benefits and how much these benefits will be. The Member States thus have a wide degree of discretion in organising social security but the Court concluded that this discretion cannot be used to breach EU law. As the Advocate General explained in his opinion:

> The Court's consistent view that "Community law does not detract from the powers of the Member States to organise their social security systems" by no means implies that the social security sector constitutes an island beyond the reach of Community law and that, as a consequence, all national rules relating to social security fall outside its scope.[5]

This means that just because something is closely associated with the social security system it is not necessarily exempt from EU law. Calling something a social security policy does not give Member States *carte blanche*. Member States have some discretion but that discretion is limited.

The rules concerning the free movement of goods and the free provision of services can be divided according to a two-stage test. The first stage determines whether there have been any restrictions on the free movement of goods and services across internal borders of the EU.

---

[5] Conclusions Advocate General Tesauro under cases C-120/95, *Decker*, ECR [1998] I-1831 and C-158/96, *Kholl*, ECR [1998] I-1931, paragraph 17.

If some restriction is identified then the second stage asks whether there is any reason that might justify this restriction.

According to European case law it is very easy to prove a restriction on the free movement of goods or services; the slightest hindrance to free movement, whether direct or indirect, actual or potential, is enough to breach Articles 28 or 49-50 EC Treaty[6]. Mr. Kohll and Mr. Decker explained that their social health care insurers would reimburse goods and services obtained in Luxembourg without demanding any formal authorisation, whereas if the same goods or treatment were to be provided outside Luxembourg prior authorisation was required. This extra requirement in the case of foreign goods and services was found to deter people from travelling to other States and this deterrent was sufficient to constitute a breach of Articles 28 and 49-50.

The Luxembourg government and the Luxembourg social health care insurers tried to justify the national rules in both Kohll and Decker by insisting, firstly, that prior authorisation was necessary to ensure the financial balance of the social security system and, secondly, that it was needed in order to maintain a functioning health care system open to all and thereby protect the public health.

As regards the first justification, the ECJ had ruled in previous cases that economic rules on the liberalisation of trade should not be applied where they jeopardise the delicate balance between contributions and benefits in a social security system[7]. However, in Kohll and Decker it explained that the individuals concerned only wanted to receive the same amount of money as they would had they purchased their goods and services in Luxembourg. The social health care insurers would not have to pay any more than they would have done had Mr. Kohll and Mr. Decker remained in Luxembourg. So the health care budget would remain undisturbed.

The second justification focused on the protection of human health, which is an express exception to the rules on the free movement of goods and services and is contained in Articles 30 and 46 of the Treaty respectively. It was argued that if prior authorisation were abandoned there would be no way to ensure the quality of the goods and services provided by orthodontists and opticians in other Member States. The ECJ dismissed this justification by referring to the mutual recognition of diplomas and the efforts made during the 1970s to harmonise training

---

[6]   ECJ, case C-8/74, *Dassonville*, ECR [1974] 497.
[7]   ECJ, case C-238/82, *Duphar*, ECR [1984] 523.

requirements for most health care professions[8]. It claimed that, on the basis of this mutual recognition and harmonisation, Member States could be assured of a minimum level of skill and qualifications from health care providers across Europe. The justification on the grounds of public health was thus dismissed. However, a closer inspection of the mutual recognition rules reveals that this was the wrong legal basis on which to base the assumption that there is a similar standard of health care right across Europe (Nickless, 2001).

It is important at this point to stress that the ECJ did not say that the justifications advanced by the parties could never be used to justify violations of Articles 28 and 49-50 of the EC Treaty. The Court merely made it clear that those justifications could not be used in the present cases because of their specific elements.

The ECJ held that the national rules did violate Articles 28 and 49-50 of the EC Treaty because they unjustifiably hindered the free provision of goods and services across the internal borders of the EU. However, the national rules were a very careful implementation of the authorisation procedure described in Article 22, Regulation 1408/71. It may have seemed logical that if the national rules were in violation of the Treaty then so was the Regulation. Nonetheless, the ECJ held that Regulation 1408/71 did not violate the Treaty. The ECJ explained that the EC Regulation only *suggested* one way of organising non-emergency social health care in another Member State; it was not an exhaustive list and did not prevent other mechanisms of trans-border treatment. The national rules, on the other hand, had been interpreted as an exhaustive list and thus violated EC law.

By applying the rules on the free movement of goods and services in this way and at the same time reaffirming the legitimacy of the procedure contained in Regulation 1408/71, the ECJ has created an alternative method of obtaining non-emergency social health care in another Member State. This means that a person may either:

- apply for authorisation and, then, travel to another State to receive medical goods and services, which are then paid for by the patient's own health care system (this means that patients do not theoretically need to take any money with them); or

---

[8] See for example Directive 93/16/EEC (Council of the European Union, 1993) which is a consolidation of all the mutual recognition legislation for doctors, specialised doctors and general practitioners.

- go straight to the foreigner provider and pay directly for the goods and services before returning home and being refunded as if the treatment or products had been purchased in his or her home State.

However, this creativity by the ECJ left many unanswered questions. The most obvious was, what if the social health care system does not operate a reimbursement mechanism? What if it is a national health service (NHS) type system or one where social health insurers contract with doctors directly and so patients do not have to pay all their costs up front? The decisions did not say whether or not they only applied to States with a reimbursement mechanism. Did this mean that some States were obliged to create a reimbursement mechanism, which would divert money from health care provision into health care administration? If a person was covered by a NHS system does this mean they are entitled to a 100% reimbursement, otherwise domestic treatment would be "free" and foreign treatment would be more expensive and thus "hindered"?

Issues were also raised about waiting lists; did these decisions mean that trans-European waiting lists would emerge? Did patients have to apply in advance to the foreign health care institution or could they just turn up and receive treatment? Were States allowed to give their own nationals priority or would this be unfair discrimination? What about the principle of equal access for rich and poor? Richer people will find it easier to cover travel costs and are more likely to have the liquid funds to pay foreign health care providers in advance.

How were these decisions going to effect health costs? It could be said that waiting lists in some systems are a means of controlling the flow of expenditure and the uncontrolled movement of patients abroad could compromise budgets.

There was also a degree of uncertainty about the precise scope of Kohll and Decker. In Kohll the ECJ referred to the fact that the service was provided outside any "hospital infrastructure". The Court did not explain precisely what it meant by this but it seemed to imply that it was somehow relevant to deciding whether or not treatment by an ortho-dontist in the context of social health care provision was really a service according to Article 49 EC Treaty. The Advocate General also referred to the concept of a "hospital infrastructure". He thought that services provided in the context of a "hospital infrastructure" were distinguished because the location and number of hospitals is determined by planning and the costs of one person's stay in a hospital cannot be separated from the costs of running the hospital as a whole. He concluded that if people were to receive treatment in hospitals abroad, the cost of maintaining an under-utilised hospital at home might well undermine the financial balance of the health care system. This could endanger the continued existence of hospital facilities for people who do not wish to travel. Kohll was not about hospital treatment and therefore the ECJ did not have to provide any further explanation of its position in relation to hospitals. The result was considerable uncertainty about whether or not social health care provided in a hospital infrastructure was really a "service" according to the EC Treaty.

The ECJ did not answer these unresolved questions because it did not have to. The ECJ is an adversarial court that argues only on the points that are raised by the parties and that are relevant to the specific case. These points were not raised during the proceedings and even if they were, it is arguable that they were not immediately relevant to the cases at hand. The ECJ is a judicial body that is not even indirectly democratically accountable. It has insufficient resources to conduct research on the full implications of its decisions.

Of course, the ECJ is only doing its job, ensuring an effective internal market and, where there is no guiding secondary legislation the only tool available to it is the EC Treaty itself.

The uncertainty created by the Kohll and Decker decisions led to a number of further references to the ECJ. Two of the most notable were those of Smits/Peerbooms and Vanbraekel. These two cases have now been decided by the ECJ and shall be discussed later in this chapter. However, before looking at these decisions I shall describe a hypothesis that was advanced to the EC Commission before Smits/Peerbooms or Vanbraekel were decided.

II. The Parameters of Kohll and Decker: A Hypothesis

The Kohll and Decker cases created legal and administrative uncertainty. The political responses of the Member States varied. Most simply argued that "my country is different", implying that the effects of these two judgements were confined to social health care systems that rely upon reimbursement. Those systems that operate a reimbursement mechanism were uncertain about the range of treatments covered by the decisions, for example did they include hospital services or simply outpatient care? It was clear that this uncertainty had to be resolved. This resolution had to take the form of a single model that respects EC law and national sovereignty without "persecuting" any particular system. This model had to be seen to apply to all countries regardless of whether they operate a reimbursement mechanism, a benefits-in-kind system or a national health service. Furthermore, it could not disturb the delicate financial balance of national social security systems or unduly impact upon national provisions aimed at limiting upward pressure on health care costs.

It is with these elements in mind that the following hypothesis was advanced to the EC Commission as a legal model by which to resolve the uncertainty that cloaked patient mobility for nearly two years.

The fundamental principle behind the Kohll and Decker decisions is that the patient should be able to go to another Member State and purchase goods and services there, that are then refunded *as if they had been delivered in the patient's home State*. This principle is clear from the Court's response to claims that unchecked patient immigration would disrupt the financial balance of the health care system[9]. The only way that the balance of the system can be protected is if the goods and services are refunded according to the boundaries of the social health care system in the patient's home State.

The boundaries of social health care are different in every Member State. These boundaries dictate which goods and services are covered by the social security system. When a patient steps outside these boundaries he or she ceases to be covered by the social system and becomes a "private patient" who must cover his or her own costs. The boundaries are determined by three basic elements:

- Personal scope: this refers to the range of people covered by the social health care system. The general principle is that of universal coverage, which demands that all citizens are entitled to health services. However, some States have chosen to exclude the richer members of their population as these groups can afford private insurance.

- Scope of treatment: every system lays down what treatment can or cannot be provided to its patients. A good example is the exclusion of cosmetic surgery in many countries or the creation of positive and/or negative lists of available pharmaceuticals.

- Scope of implementation (authorised providers): all health systems determine which health care professionals or institutions are entitled to give treatment that is financed by the social system. In some cases this may be State employees employed by the social health administration (as would be the case in a "pure" national health service). In other cases it might include all those with whom the health care system has a contract (typically seen in benefits-in-kind systems). It is also possible that a social system allows its patients to go to any health care professional in

---

[9] Paragraph 17 of Kohll and paragraph 21 of Decker.

its territory (which is the case in most reimbursement mechanisms). These three elements can be visualised in Figure 3.1.

Figure 3.1: The Scope of Social and Private Care

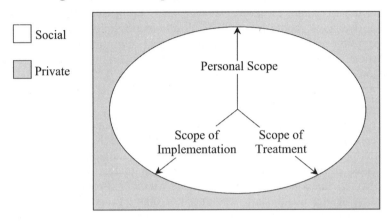

If a patient steps outside the lighter circle (because he or she is not
included in the personal scope, he or she asks for treatment that is not
covered by the system or he or she goes to a professional who is not
authorised by the social system) he or she steps outside the social
system and becomes a "private" patient.

Fears have been raised that the EC may be able to interfere with
these three essential elements and thus alter the boundaries of the
national social health care systems. These fears focus on both the EU
legislation and the ECJ.

Passing legislation at a EU level is a two-stage process. First the
legislator must find a legal basis in the EC Treaty that authorises law
making in the chosen field. Once a legal basis has been found the
proposed act must comply with the principle of subsidiarity. The EU
legislator has very few options by which to pass legislation in the social
security field. None of these options expressly empower it to determine
the scope of social health care packages[10]. However, the EU legislator
might be able to pass laws in this area according to a broad interpretation of the new Article 137(3) in the Social Chapter of the EC

---

[10]   For example Article 49 (ex 51) EC Treaty is confined to the co-ordination of social
security for migrant workers and may not be used to alter the substance of the
national systems. The new provisions on public health (Article 152 (5) EC Treaty)
expressly state that "Community action in the field of public health shall fully respect
the responsibilities of the Member States for the organisation and delivery of health
services and medical care".

Treaty. This article allows the adoption of Directives on "social security and social protection of workers", a competence that is shared with the Member States[11].

The principle of subsidiarity applies whenever the Member States and the EU share the power to legislate. The basis of this principle is that decisions should be made as closely as possible to the people who are going to be affected by them. Its legal definition can be found in Article 5 (ex 3b) EC Treaty. This article explains that the EC is only allowed to use its shared powers if it can be demonstrated that the objective cannot be achieved sufficiently by the Member States *and* the EC can do a *better* job.

There has been much political and academic debate about the precise meaning of subsidiarity in the EC Treaty (Toth, 1994; Steiner, 1994 and Emiliou, 1992) but there are some good arguments that favour the setting of national social health care parameters being left to the Member States and EU law. First, the Member States have been allocating scarce health care resources for many years. The financing of these resources usually comes from general taxation and/or social security contributions levied on a territorial basis. The EU has no power to influence directly the level or sources of social security financing or general taxation and does not make any substantial financial contribution to the provision of social health care services. Second, the health needs of the people of Europe vary among Member States (see Abel-Smith *et al.*, 1995). Furthermore, at the moment there is no European body charged with assessment of health needs and many States would argue that they are in the best position to respond to patterns of disease in their countries. The ethical framework also varies between States and it is important that sensitive issues such as abortion, blood transfusions and organ donations are dealt with at this level. Member States have been balancing health care budgets for a long time and it would be difficult for the EU to claim that it can do a better job, especially given the already strained resources of the European institutions.

Some guidelines for the application of the principle of subsidiarity were annexed to the EC Treaty in a Protocol following ratification of the Amsterdam Treaty. These guidelines set out examples of when EU action may be justified. One example refers to action at a Community level that would produce clear benefits by reason of its scale or effects

---

[11] The Social Chapter of the EC Treaty refers to a sharing of power between the EC and the Member States, this is clear from statements such as "[...] the Community shall support and compliment the activities of the Member States [...]" and "(t)he provisions adopted pursuant to this article shall not prevent any Member State from maintaining or introducing more stringent protective measures compatible with this Treaty" (Article 137(5) EC Treaty).

compared with action at the level of the Member States. This statement closely relates to the theory of economies of scale in which savings may be made when production takes place on a large scale. It also relates to the theory of specialisation that claims that efficiency is increased if people concentrate on the tasks they are good at and avoid unnecessary duplication. Economies of scale and specialisation may have a role to play in improving the delivery of social health care, and existing measures in border regions are testimony to this. It is therefore proposed that the subsidiarity principle does not exclude all Community action in the field of health care but merely, at the present time, the EC does not have the experience, resources or accountability to organise health care resources by setting the parameters of national social health packages.

But what is the role of the ECJ? In Kohll and Decker it made it absolutely clear that the principles of free trade can and will be applied to the social security sector. The question is then whether these principles could be used to undermine the boundaries of social health care in the Member States[12]. In the past the Court has tolerated restrictions of trade if these are necessary in order to maintain the financial balance of the social security system. Such restrictions will not be removed provided that they do not arbitrarily discriminate against goods and services from other Member States. For example in Duphar *v.* The Netherlands[13] that Court decided the exclusion of some pharmaceutical products from social security reimbursement could constitute a restriction of trade. However, this was justifiable "in order to promote the financial stability of health insurance schemes" provided that the criteria used to determine the range of drugs covered were fair and objective. In Kohll and Decker the Court accepted that this justification could be used but not in those specific cases.

Every State has its own criteria to determine who is covered by the social health care system, what interventions patients are entitled to, and which providers are authorised to provide them. If a social health care system was forced to accept a patient who is not normally covered, fund a treatment that is not usually available or pay a provider who would not otherwise be authorised then this will increase costs. These increases could then disrupt the balance of financing. Consequently it is unlikely that the promotion of free movement of goods and services could be used by the Court to alter the boundaries of social health care systems.

To understand this it is necessary to consider the elements of Kohll and Decker. The fundamental principle of these rulings is that the goods

---

[12] This issue was already raised in a case pending before the European Court of Justice, Peerbooms.

[13] ECJ, case C-238/82, *Duphar*, ECR [1984] 523.

and services received by the patient are treated as if they were delivered in the patient's State of residence. Thus, if patients step outside the social boundaries of their own system they will not be entitled to reimbursement. The system in Luxembourg states that the patient can receive treatment from any orthodontist registered in the territory of the Grand Duchy. In the "Euro-speak" of the internal market this is translated as any provider in the territory of the EU. However, had orthodontic treatment been excluded from the Luxembourg social health care package (*i.e.* from the scope of treatment) Mr. Kohll could have been refused a refund. If this were not the case then the Luxembourg health care system would be thrown off-balance. It therefore makes sense that, as patients step outside the boundaries of the system in their home State they cannot be refunded, the same applies in another State. So, in the context of a national health service, if a patient goes to a professional in another Member State who is not contracted with the national health service in that patient's home State then he or she has stepped out of the social and into the private sector. This means that no refund should be given. By this argument the Court and legislator must respect the sovereignty of the Member States to determine the parameters of their social health care packages.

This hypothesis favours those systems that limit their scope of implementation to certain contracted providers. However, it does not mean that Kohll and Decker have absolutely no impact upon them. The Court has made it clear that the balanced financing justification will only be accepted if the criteria used to control spending are fair, objective and free from arbitrary discrimination. This means that Kohll and Decker will have a two-fold impact upon systems that limit the range of authorised providers (mainly benefits-in-kind systems and national health systems).

Sometimes mechanisms exist whereby patients are pulled back from the private sector and into the social one. For example, in Spain if a patient is injured in front of a private hospital, and therefore closer to the private institution than the one contracted by the NHS, and his or her condition is life threatening, he or she will be taken to the private institution and the costs of treatment will be refunded in full by the national health service. The principle of non-discrimination dictates that if a Spanish resident sustains life-threatening injuries in another Member State then he or she will be entitled to a full refund even though the foreign hospital is not part of the Spanish social security system. Thus, any mechanism that allows the exceptional use of unauthorised providers or the special provision of otherwise excluded treatments should also apply to goods and services emanating from other Member States.

As the selection criteria have to be fair, objective and free from discrimination this means that it should be just as easy for a provider in State A to be contracted in State B as it is for providers in State B. In other words there should be no discrimination on the basis of nationality or territorial location. This means that direct discrimination will not be tolerated, for example by confining authorisation to those established in one country. However, indirect discrimination, where criteria appear at first glance to be neutral but in fact place a harsher burden on foreign goods and service, could be justified. For example, it may be lawful to place a restriction on contracting of non-emergency in-patient care where all institutions must guarantee that at least four hundred persons will be treated every year, otherwise they are not maintaining adequate experience.

This hypothesis respects national sovereignty and the principle of subsidiarity on the one hand whilst ensuring the EU principles of non-discrimination and free trade on the other. It applies to every system and therefore does not single out or "persecute" any particular countries, allowing a uniform application right across the EU.

III. Smits/Peerbooms and Vanbraekel: The ECJ Attempts to Define the Limits of Kohll and Decker

On the 12 July 2001 the ECJ delivered two decisions that resolved some of the outstanding issues raised by the Kohll and Decker cases. These two clarifying decisions were Geraets-Smits v. Stichting Ziekenfonds VGZ and Peerbooms v. Stichting CZ Groep Zorgverzekeringen[14] on the one hand and Abdon Vanbraekel and Others v. Alliance nationale des mutualitiés chrétiennes (ANMC)[15] on the other. This section will review the decisions and their impact in turn, beginning with Smits/Peerbooms. It shall then look at what these two decisions mean for patient mobility within the European Union.

A. Smits/Peerbooms

Mrs. Smits and Mr. Peerbooms were both insured under the benefits-in-kind system of social health care in the Netherlands. In the Netherlands social health care is provided by social health insurers who enter into contracts with care providers (such as doctors and hospitals). Insured persons are then entitled to treatment from health care providers who have a contract with the insured person's health insurer. When an insured person goes to a contracted doctor he or she receives treatment

---

[14] ECJ, case C-157/99, *Geraets-Smits and Peerbooms*, ECR [2001] I-05473.
[15] ECJ, case C-368/98, *Vanbraekel*, ECR [2001] I-05363.

and the health insurer then pays the doctor on their behalf. Insured persons in the Netherlands therefore do not have to pay health care providers directly for the full price of the treatment, although they may be asked to make a small contribution as a co-payment or "visit fee". The scope of implementation is thus confined to contracted providers.

The scope of treatment includes that provided by a general practitioner or a specialist "the [extent of which] shall be determined in accordance with what is normal in the professional circles concerned". If an insured person in the Netherlands wishes to obtain treatment from a doctor or institution that is not contracted with his or her health insurer (whether this institution is established in the Netherlands or not), he or she must obtain permission. Permission will only be granted for treatment abroad if the said treatment falls within the scope of treatment described above and is not available in time in the Netherlands.

Mrs. Smits suffered from Parkinson's disease and went to a specialised clinic in Germany to receive a multi-disciplinary, holistic programme of physiotherapy, medical treatment, ergotherapy and socio-psychological support. Mrs. Smits paid the German clinic directly and tried to obtain reimbursement from her Dutch health insurer according to the procedure created by Kohll. The reimbursement was refused because the treatment obtained was not considered as "normal treatment" and treatment for her individual symptoms was available in contracted clinics in the Netherlands.

Mr. Peerbooms was a 36 year-old man in a coma. He was transferred from a hospital in the Netherlands to receive neuro-stimulation in a clinic in Austria. Neuro-stimulation was practiced in the Netherlands at that time but it was only provided in two institutions, it was only available to people less than 25 years of age and it was still considered "experimental" by the social health care system. In Austria it was an accepted treatment covered by the social health care system. This treatment would not have been available to Mr. Peerbooms in the Netherlands. Fortunately Mr. Peerbooms did recover from his coma but when he tried to use the principles established in Kohll in order to recover the costs of his treatment in Austria, his Dutch health insurer turned him down.

Mrs. Smits and Mr. Peerbooms both initiated court action, claiming that they were entitled to a refund of the costs of their treatment under the EU rules on the free movement of services.

The ECJ had to decide if the Treaty provisions on the free movement of services applied to social health care provided in hospitals. It then had to decide if the requirement of prior authorisation for hospital treatment in another Member State violated these Treaty provisions and if so, whether the Dutch system of authorisation could be justified.

Do the Treaty provisions on the free movement of services apply to hospital treatment? The ECJ reaffirmed what it had said in Kohll about each Member State retaining a wide margin of discretion in the personal scope, conditions of entitlement and range of benefits. It also repeated that this discretion was subject to the rules contained within the EC Treaty, including the free movement of services.

The concept of "service" is defined in both the EC Treaty (Article 50) and EC case law[16] as an economic activity that is provided for remuneration. A number of governments insisted that in this context the patient does not pay for the treatment himself and that the person providing the service does not do so with the aim of making a profit.

The ECJ dismissed these arguments. It drew on previous case law that held that medical treatment was a service in the context of Article 50 EC Treaty and that it did not matter whether that treatment was provided in hospital or not[17]. The special nature of a service did not exclude them from the Treaty's scope, as was decided in Webb[18] which concerned the provision of labour mediation for unemployed persons. Furthermore, the hospitals attended by Mrs. Smits and Mr. Peerbooms in Germany and Austria were paid directly and so were remunerated. It was also noted that a service does not have to be paid for by the person who receives it in order for it to be classified as a service[19]. Finally it was also noted that contracted hospitals receive consideration for the treatment they provide which amounts to both remuneration and economic activity.

It was therefore decided that social health care treatment in a contracted hospital or foreign hospital was a service in the sense of the free movement of services in the EC Treaty.

Did the authorisation procedure in the Netherlands restrict trade between Member States? A person insured under the benefits-in-kind system in operation in the Netherlands can only obtain health care abroad under his or her social insurance if he or she obtains authorisation before hand. The ECJ concluded that prior authorisation

---

[16] See ECJ, case C-263/86, *Humbel and Edel*, ECR [1988] 5365 and ECJ, case C-159/90, *The Society for the Protection of Unborn Children Ireland Ltd.*, ECR [1991] I-4685.

[17] ECJ, joined cases C-286/82 and C-26/83, *Luisi and Carbone*, ECR [1984] 377 and ECJ, case C-159/90, *The Society for the Protection of Unborn Children Ireland Ltd.*, ECR [1991] I-4685.

[18] ECJ, case C-279/80, *Webb*, ECR [1981] 3305.

[19] ECJ, case C-352/85, *Bond van Adverteerders*, ECR [1988] 2085.

was not required for treatment in contracted hospitals in the Netherlands, which is the main way of obtaining social hospital treatment. Therefore the need to apply for authorisation for treatment abroad was an actual hindrance to the free movement of services across the internal borders of the European Union. The next issue was whether this hindrance could be justified.

The ECJ accepted that "seriously undermining a social security system's financial balance"[20] and "maintaining a balanced medical and hospital service to all"[21] both could justify the hindrance caused by a prior authorisation procedure provided that they were fair and that they were proportionate to their aims. The ECJ accepted that:

> it is well known that the number of hospitals, their geographical distribution, the mode of their operation and the equipment with which they are provided, and even the nature of the medical services which they are able to offer, are all matters for which planning must be possible (paragraph 76).

It went on to explain that this system of planning and contracting was necessary not just to provide hospital services but also to avoid wastage and control costs. The system was therefore justified both on the grounds of maintaining a balanced medical service for all and on the grounds of protecting the financial structure of a social security system. The ECJ stated:

> Looking at the system set up by the ZFW (the law on sickness funds), it is clear that, if insured persons were at liberty, regardless of the circumstances, to use the services of hospitals with which their sickness insurance fund had no contractual arrangements, whether they were situated in the Netherlands or in another Member State, all the planning which goes into a contractual system in an effort to rationalise, stable, balanced and accessible supply of hospital services would be jeopardised at a stroke (paragraph 81).

The ECJ then took a closer look at the authorisation procedure in order to ensure that it was fair and proportional. It did this by looking at the two tests used to decide whether authorisation should be given or not; firstly whether the treatment was regarded as normal in the professional circles concerned and secondly whether or not the treatment was available in sufficient time from a contracted provider in the Netherlands.

The "regarded as normal in the professional circles concerned" test is the rule that determines the scope of all social treatment, whether it is provided by a contracted hospital or not. The ECJ reaffirmed that Member States are free to set down the conditions of entitlement to

---

[20] See Kohll, paragraph 41.
[21] See Article 46 EC Treaty and Kohll, paragraph 56.

social security benefits and decide the amount of that benefit. It also confirmed that States may develop lists excluding certain products from social health care coverage[22] and went on to say:

> it follows that Community law cannot in principle have the effect of requiring a Member State to extend the list of medical services paid for by its social insurance system: the fact that a particular type of medical treatment is covered or is not covered by the sickness insurance scheme of other Member States is irrelevant in this regard (paragraph 87).

However, the ECJ also reminded us that this discretion had to be exercised in accordance with EU law and gave a clear indication of what this means for a prior authorisation procedure:

> Therefore in order for a prior authorisation scheme to be justified even though it derogates from such a fundamental freedom, it must, in any event, be based on objective, non-discriminatory criteria which are known in advance, in such a way as to circumscribe the exercise of the national authorities' discretion, so that it is not used arbitrarily (paragraph 90).

The "regarded as normal in the professional circles concerned" test could be interpreted in a number of ways; it could mean regarded as normal in the Netherlands or regarded as normal on an international level. The ECJ concluded that if the test was confined to professional opinion in the Netherlands this would effectively restrict treatment to that habitually provided in the Netherlands making it harder to obtain treatments readily accepted as normal in other Member States. If this were the case the system upon which prior authorisation is based would not be fair and objective. This objectivity can only be assured by interpreting "normal in professional circles" to include international professional circles. This is another example of translating national legislation into "Euro-speak". The same approach was used in Kohll where the Luxembourg system allowed its socially insured patients to visit any orthodontist in Luxembourg and the ECJ effectively interpreted this as any orthodontist in the EU.

The ECJ then went on to investigate the second aspect of the authorisation test, *i.e.* whether equally effective treatment could be obtained in time from a contracted hospital. It was accepted that using contracted providers whenever possible will ensure the continuation of a stable health care system and save costs, thereby protecting its delicate financial balance. However, it was made clear that the Dutch health insurers could not favour non-contracted hospitals in the Netherlands over non-contracted hospitals in other Member States. Essentially a non-contracted hospital is outside the boundaries of the social system and

---

[22]   Paragraph 86 and ECJ, case C-238/82, *Duphar*, ECR [1984] 523.

this is so whether that hospital is based in Maastricht, Brussels, London or Barcelona.

The case of Smits/Peerbooms affirmed that the economic rules for the creation of an internal market can and will be applied to social security systems. The ECJ further confirmed that hospital services provided as part of the social protection system still represent a service in the context of the EC Treaty.

The ECJ also confirmed that it would respect the boundaries developed by Member States when defining the scope of their social health care. The Member States thus remain free to determine which service providers provide what treatment to which patients. However, these boundaries have to be fair, objective, transparent and open to challenge. This means that the systems of contracting service providers should be open to doctors and institutions in other Member States and that express exclusion of providers from other Member States will only be tolerated on extremely limited grounds and that any rules that are apparently neutral but in fact make it harder for providers from other countries to join the social system will have to be justified. This justification could be based on the need to provide a sustainable health care service for all or the protection of the delicate financial balance of the health care system. This interpretation is very much in line with the hypothesis delivered above.

Finally a word must be said about the translation of national legislation into "Euro-speak". The ECJ accepted that Member States could draw up "limited lists" defining the boundaries of their systems (paragraphs 86 and 87). However, these limited lists will be interpreted wherever possible as referring not just to one State but the entire EU. Thus, enabling socially insured patients to attend any doctor in a country will be translated as any doctor in the EU. Offering to fully reimburse emergency treatment provided by non-contracted hospitals in Member State A provided that the patient's condition prevents him being taken in due time to a contracted hospital will also apply to non-contracted hospitals in Member State B. Therefore if a person is socially insured in Member State A and goes on holiday to Member State B where he or she is hit by a car, his or her condition will dictate that he or she could not be taken to a contracted hospital in Member State A and so is entitled to treatment in a non-contracted hospital in Member State B[23].

---

[23] It is true that emergency treatment is provided by the E111 procedure but under that procedure the patient is treated as if he were insured with the State of treatment, this means that he will be taken to a social hospital and will have to meet any co-payments that nationals of the State of treatment might be expected to make. In the scenario above the patient would be entitled to treatment in any hospital in Member State, even an expensive private one. Furthermore if his home state guarantees 100%

Legislatures and social administrators are thus going to have to take great care in how they phrase their legislation and policies in the future.

B. Vanbraekel

This case concerned Ms. Jeanne Descamps who suffered from bilateral gonarthrosis. Ms. Descamps was a Belgian national, living in Belgium and insured by a Belgian social health insurer. In 1990 she applied for authorisation from her health insurer to undergo orthopaedic surgery in France. The Belgian government had implemented Article 22(2) of Regulation 1408/71 that states that authorisation for treatment in another EC State must be given if the treatment is provided for under the legislation of the Member State of insurance and that treatment can not be provided in time in that State. Belgian law added that authorisation cannot be refused where better medical conditions are available abroad and a medical expert from a national university hospital declares that such treatment is essential.

Ms. Descamps application was refused because she had not obtained the opinion of doctor practicing in a national university hospital. Despite this refusal Ms. Descamps went to France and paid for the service herself. When she returned she appealed against the refusal and was successful. A Belgian court concluded that she should have been given authorisation. The problem then facing the court was whether she should be reimbursed according to the rules in France or according to the rules in Belgium. According to the procedure laid down in Articles 22 and 36 of Regulation 1408/71 when a patient is treated in another Member State that patient is treated as if he or she is part of the social security system of the State of treatment and all costs are reimbursed according to the rules in operation in the State of treatment. However, according to Kohll a patient is entitled to travel to another Member State for medical care and then be reimbursed by his or her social health care system as if the treatment had been provided in the State of insurance. According to the French system Ms. Descamps should have received FRF 38,608.99 (€ 5791.34) whereas according to the Belgian system she should have recovered FRF 49,935.44 (€ 7490.31). The Belgian national court wanted to know which amount had to be paid.

The ECJ explained that Regulation 1408/71 does not limit the circumstances in which authorisation for treatment in another Member State must be granted; this Regulation only suggests situations where such authorisation must be granted (paragraph 31). Thus, when the Belgian State grants authorisation or *should grant authorisation* under

---

reimbursement this may oblige it to pay any co-payments charged in Member State B as well (however, see case note on Vanbraekel below).

its own rules then this authorisation is effectively classified as authorisation under Regulation 1408/71.

The ECJ also confirmed that Regulation 1408/71 does not *prevent* reimbursement of medical costs incurred abroad if the State of insurance operates a reimbursement mechanism and the extent of reimbursement in that State happens to be higher than in the State of treatment. However, it goes on to say that Regulation 1408/71 does not oblige Member States to reimburse this higher amount. According to Articles 22 and 36 of the Regulation the costs of treatment are determined by the rules of the State of treatment, in this case France.

The ECJ followed its reasoning in Peerbooms and concluded that the EC Treaty rules on the free movement of services do apply to social hospital treatment (paragraphs 38-43). It then decided that if a Member State pays lower rates of reimbursement for treatment delivered abroad it discourages people from applying for authorisation and thereby receiving medical treatment abroad. This amounts to a hindrance to trade and a violation of the principle of the free movement of services.

Having found a hindrance to trade, the ECJ went on to determine whether that hindrance could be justified as it ensured a system of health care available to all or protected the delicate financial balance of the social security system. It decided that, as the patient would have received treatment in the State of insurance anyway, this would not interfere with the delicate balance of the financing of social health care. Furthermore as the patient in question is given authorisation to leave the State in order to receive treatment outside, *inter alia*, because treatment is not available in the home State, this does not jeopardise the sustainability of national health resources and, in fact, promotes the protection of human health.

The hindrance to trade could not be justified and the Belgian State is obliged by the economic rules on the free movement of trade to reimburse the higher amount.

The Vanbraekel case has important implications. When a patient travels abroad for medical treatment with the consent of his or her social health care system, Regulation 1408/71 should be used to calculate the amount of reimbursement according to the tariffs in operation in the State of treatment. However, Regulation 1408/71 does not prevent Member States from paying higher levels of reimbursement. In fact, if the State of insurance would have provided a higher level of reimbursement than that offered in the State of treatment then the economic rules on the free movement of services dictate that the higher amount should be paid. Nothing about this is mentioned in Regulation 1408/71 and therefore Vanbraekel joins Kohll and Decker as an example where the social system is extended beyond a Member State's legitimate expectations. No matter how carefully the social legislation in this area (Regulation 1408/71) was implemented there was no way to predict the effects of a ruling on free movement of goods and services. Allowing the ECJ to continue to describe the rigid and structured system established by Regulation 1408/71 as merely suggestive or non-exhaustive will only serve to perpetuate legal uncertainty.

Vanbraekel now leaves us with more unresolved questions. It is clearly set in the context of a reimbursement mechanism but how will it affect benefits-in-kind systems or national health systems? According to Regulation 1408/71 when a patient travels to another Member State for treatment he or she is treated as if he or she were part of the system in the State of treatment. This means that the patient should be subject to the same co-payments etc as are applied in the State of treatment. If the patient comes from an NHS system where treatment is free, or a benefits-in-kind system where the co-payments are lower, will the State of insurance have to make up the difference? This difference in costs represents a hindrance to free movement and, according to the reasoning in Vanbraekel, reimbursement of this higher cost will not affect the balanced financing of the social security system. The court did not explain what would happen in this situation because it did not have to, so now there is no way of knowing with any certainty how the situation will evolve in the future.

The combined impact of the Smits/Peerbooms and Vanbraekel Smits/Peerbooms has resolved some of the outstanding uncertainty that surrounded the Kohll and Decker decisions. It has confirmed the role that shall be played by economic rules in the social security sector and it has demonstrated a respect for the boundaries of social health care established in each Member State. It has shown that Kohll and Decker affects all types of social health care systems by declaring that the boundaries of these systems must be fair, objective, transparent and, wherever possible, translated into "Euro-speak". Vanbraekel on the other hand has created a degree of uncertainty and, just like Kohll and Decker, we must now wait for more cases to see where this legal path will go.

For now, however, Figure 3.2 portrays a flow chart that can be used to determine when and under what system patients are able to travel to another Member State in order to receive medical treatment covered by their social health care system.

**Figure 3.2: Entitlement to Non-emergency Social Health Care
in Another Member State**

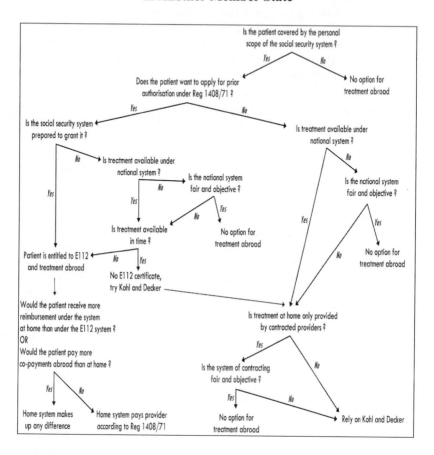

IV. The Internal Market and Social Health Care

Over the past three decades the ECJ has been particularly active in realising the EU dream of a genuine internal market. More recently there has been some debate about the extent to which the rules governing the internal market can be applied to the social security/health care field. Several academics have noted that the wide interpretations by the ECJ mean that the economic rules governing the internal market could be applied to providers, insurers and administrations that are responsible for statutory health care (see for example Pieters and Van den Bogaert, 1997). There are fears that the independence and sovereignty that

Member States have tried so hard to preserve in the social field shall be eaten away by the gradual penetration of internal market regulations. Health care funders and providers could be treated in the same way as hi-fi distributors and banana importers. There are strong arguments that the application of economic, market-oriented rules in these fields is not always appropriate and that the altruistic goals of social health care provision could be unnecessarily impeded.

This gradual infiltration of traditionally social fields by economic rules has been described as a process of "Euro-creep"[24] through which sovereign States see EU (economic) law creeping into areas they previously considered beyond the reach of EU "interference". Euro-creep is the product of the application of economic rules by the ECJ and is thus impervious to the limited legal bases and Member State's vetoes that apply to direct legislative action by the EU in the social field. The result is ironically that the restriction of legal bases for social action in the EC Treaty combined with the use of unanimous voting has blocked measures that are, arguably, necessary, whilst at the same time they have done nothing to stop the penetration of European law into sovereign national areas. The unanimous voting procedure has clearly failed to fulfil its role; it prevents binding law where it is necessary and fails to prevent EU interference where it maybe unnecessary and inappropriate.

The inappropriateness of applying internal market rules to the health care sector stems from the unique features of this sector. The internal market rules aim to create a fair and free market place where low prices and high quality are maintained by the threat of competition and the fear of bankruptcy. The producers in this ideal market are faced by consumers who know what they want and are (generally) capable of assessing (and comparing) the quality of the goods and services they receive. The primary objective of all the parties involved are selfish, consumers aim to maximise utility (low price with high quality) and producers aim to maximise profit (low costs and high prices). Failure means the prompt reallocation of resources and the production of a better good or service. The social health care "market" is not as simple as this. Going to the doctor is very different from getting a haircut or having your house painted. Many of the distinctive features of the health care market are related to the asymmetries of information that exist between a provider and his or her patient. The patient does not know what kind of treatment he or she may need and is completely reliant upon the advice of his or her doctor. Having received treatment there is often no way of assessing the real quality of that treatment. The result is that health care is a market where suppliers determine demand rather

---

[24] I first heard this term used by Berman's speech (1998).

than well-informed consumers. Our reliance upon health professionals transforms us from "consumers" into "patients". As Rudolf Klein (1996) explains:

> A patient is someone who is undergoing treatment or to whom things are being done. It is essentially a passive concept, implying the acceptance of direction from others. A consumer by contrast, is someone who uses a service or buys a commodity. It is essentially an active concept [...].

Furthermore, social health care patients rarely pay the full price of their health care directly. The final costs of health care are typically covered by taxation and/or social security contributions. Thus, there is no appreciation of the true costs of treatment and no incentive to reduce unnecessary consumption. Lack of appreciation of the costs of treatment, combined with the popular philosophy that large unmet demand is a prominent distinguishing feature of social health care. Medical goods and services are something to which many people, as economically active individuals, feel they have a right.

Indeed many national constitutions oblige the State to provide health care to everyone[25]. The principle of "universal coverage" can also be found in international law as a fundamental human right[26]. This means that even those in remote rural areas must be given access to facilities even if this is extremely expensive. Universal coverage also means that medical treatment should be available to those who have not contributed towards its financing and who are unable to pay their share.

The threat of failure is not the same for a hospital as it is for an advocate's office or hairdresser. The political implications of closing down health services are taken very seriously, as the closure of hospitals often generates protests and social disruption in the local community.

Therefore, the health market is a long way from the perfect market where egocentric consumers and producers ensure allocative and productive efficiency. Some States have tried to implement market principles into their social health care systems in an attempt to encourage administrative efficiency and cost savings. These elements of competition have been carefully introduced to limited areas, hence the term "quasi-market". Indeed, it is the absence of pure market forces that distinguishes private health care from social health care. Social health care should be available to everyone and is typically financed from taxes or social security contributions whereas private health care is provided

---

[25] See *inter alia* the Constitutions of Belgium (Article 23.3.1), Italy (Article 32), Finland (Article 15a), Greece (Article 21§3), Luxembourg (Article 11.4) and Portugal (Article 64).

[26] See *inter alia* International Covenant on Economic, Social and Cultural Rights (Article 12) and the Social Charter of the Council of Europe (Article 11).

on the open market and is available to all those who can afford it. It is thus arguable whether the economic rules designed to create the internal market should be fully applied in the social health care sector.

However, the social health care sectors in the EU employ and contract with millions of health professionals and every year they spend billions of euros on drugs and equipment. If Member States were allowed to discriminate against foreign providers, institutions or pharmaceuticals, it would reduce efficiency. It is not that the internal market has no role to play within the social health care sector but where it is introduced there must be no ambiguity. The right role for "Europe" in the health care sector could lead to improved treatment at lower costs. One of the most important differences between the social health care market and any other market is that saving money saves lives. What is needed is a balance and this balance cannot be achieved through Euro-creep. There is a great danger in sitting back and forcing the ECJ to fill in gaps. Governments, health care insurers, associations of professionals and other interested parties have to face facts; there is no resisting the relentless tide of Europe. It is better to let the internal market in through the front door than close one's eyes and let it creep through the back one.

Special internal market rules have been created for sectors such as transport[27], agriculture[28], sport[29] and military procurement[30]. These rules balance the interests of the internal market with the special features of those sectors; similar rules are needed for social health care. Social health care is an area that is too important, too specialised, too complicated and too diverse to leave entirely in the hands of an adversarial judicial body.

Bibliography

ABEL-SMITH, B., FIGUERAS, J., HOLLAND, W., MCKEE, M. and MOSSIALOS, E. (1995) (eds.), *Choices in Health Policy: An Agenda for the European Union*, Dartmouth Publishing, Aldershot.

BERMAN, P. (1998), "The Effects of Euro-creep on Health Care: 'Ostrich Policies or Anticipation'", Speech delivered at the Fifth Workshop on European Legislation and National Health Polities, organised by the Dutch Ministry of Health, Welfare and Sport, Oostende, 19 and 20 February 1998.

---

[27]   Title V EC Treaty.
[28]   Title II EC Treaty.
[29]   See Declaration on Sport of the Amsterdam Treaty.
[30]   See Treaty Article 296.

COUNCIL OF THE EUROPEAN COMMUNITIES (1993), Council Directive 93/16/EEC of 5 April 1993 to facilitate the free movement of doctors and the mutual recognition of their diplomas, certificates and other evidence of formal qualifications, OJ L 165, 7 July 1993, pp. 0001-0024.

COUNCIL OF THE EUROPEAN UNION (1996), Consolidated version: Council Regulation 118/97/EC of 2 December 1996 amending and updating Regulation 1408/71/EEC on the application of social security schemes to employed persons, to self-employed persons and to members of their families moving within the Community and Regulation 574/72/EEC laying down the procedure for implementing Regulation 1408/71/EEC, OJ L 28, 30 January 1997, pp. 0001-0229.

EMILIOU, N. (1992), "Subsidiarity: An Effective Barrier Against the 'Enterprises of Ambition'?", *European Law Review*, Vol. 17, pp. 383-408.

KLEIN, R. (1996), *Britain's National Health Service and the Consumer in Health Systems in Europe: Towards New Contracts Between Providers, Payers and Governments*, École nationale de la Santé publique/MIRE, Rennes.

NICKLESS, J. (2001), "A Guarantee of Similar Medical Standards Right Across Europe: Were the European Court of Justice Decisions in Kohll and Decker Right?", *Eurohealth*, Vol. 7, No. 1, Spring 2001, pp. 16-18.

PALM, W., NICKLESS, J., LEWALLE, H. and COHEUR, A. (2000), "Implications of Recent Jurisprudence on the Co-ordination of Health Care Protection Systems", Report produced for the European Commission Directorate-General for Employment and Social Affairs, May 2000 (www.aim-mutual.org).

PIETERS, D. and VAN DEN BOGAERT, S. (1997), *The Consequences of European Competition Law for National Health Policies*, Maklu Publishing, Antwerpen.

STEINER, J. (1994), "Subsidiarity under the Maastricht Treaty" in O'KEEFE, D. and TWOMEY, P. (eds.), *Legal Issues of the Maastricht Treaty*, John Wiley & Sons.

TOTH, A.G. (1994), "A Legal Analysis of Subsidiarity", in O'KEEFE, D. and TWOMEY, P. (eds.), *Legal Issues of the Maastricht Treaty*, John Wiley & Sons.

CHAPTER 4

The Right to Health Care
across Borders

Yves JORENS

I. Health Care Systems in Europe

Health costs have increased considerably in recent years, as measured by the rising percentage of Gross Domestic Product (GDP) spent on health services, which is now between 6.3% (Ireland) and 10.7% (Germany) of GDP among EU Member States. There are, however, enormous discrepancies within the EU in the various schemes of sickness and accident insurance (Stiemer, 1999: 227-253; van der Mei, 2001: 259-263 and Palm *et al.*, 2000: 16-18). Schemes differ in terms of:

- the basis of the right to benefits: insurance as an employed or self-employed person or as a previously employed or self-employed person on the one hand, or as a resident of the country on the other hand;
- the financing of care: financing from contributions or from taxes or a combination;
- the institution managing the funds: the provision of benefits by insurance institutions, or by health authorities, municipalities, counties or national government;
- the benefits involved: both the forms of medical care that make up the benefits and the degree to which persons entitled to benefits have to contribute to the costs themselves;
- the way in which the benefits are provided: in kind or reimbursement.

On the basis of these criteria, health care systems in Member States are generally divided into two categories: social insurance systems and national health systems.

The social insurance systems – found in the six original Member States are based on the Bismarckian model of insurance in which the law determines who is compulsorily insured. The categories of people who are insured have extended so all or virtually all of the population is now covered. The system is financed by the payment of premiums, mostly income-related and calculated on the basis of total expenditure. Administration is entrusted to local (semi) public bodies such as sickness funds.

In turn, social insurance systems can be divided into two groups. The first group is based on the principle of reimbursement, whereas the second group is based on the benefits-in-kind principle. Under the principle of reimbursement patients pay the medical provider and are, on the basis of a receipt, reimbursed by their sickness fund. Patients are entitled to choose their health care provider. This system is found in Belgium, France and Luxembourg. In systems based on benefits-in-kind, patients are entitled to obtain medical care from health practitioners who are paid directly by the health insurance institutions. In these cases an agreement is concluded between the sickness fund and a health care provider. As a general rule, patients do not have to pay a bill as long as they use a provider with whom the sickness fund has concluded a contract. This system exists in Austria, Germany and the Netherlands.

Unlike the social insurance systems, national health services are not based on an insurance model but on the Beveridge model, which offers a universal right to medical care. Health care is funded from tax revenues and is provided to the whole population according to the benefits-in-kind principle, with a uniformity of benefits, matching response to need. These systems were initially centralised although there is now increasing decentralisation. Patients, generally, do not pay directly, apart from a few flat-rate charges. This system exists in the United Kingdom, Ireland, Spain, Italy, Portugal, Greece, Denmark, Finland and Sweden.

Inevitably it is extremely difficult to distinguish between these three categories. Borderlines are rarely clear-cut; systems sometimes overlap, not least because all health care systems are confronted with the same challenges. Policies developed in one system are adopted by others, so leading to a certain amount of convergence.

The European Union and Health Care Policy

Although the Treaty of Amsterdam[1] has increased somewhat the competence of the Community in the area of health care it remains limited.

---

[1]   Article 129 of the Treaty of Maastricht introduced for the first time health protection as a separate policy domain that previously did not fall under the scope of the Community. The Community has to contribute towards ensuring a high level of human health protection. The adoption of this article demonstrated that the

Title XIII, Article 152 of the Treaty provides

[...] a high level of human health protection shall be ensured in the definition and implementation of all Community policies and activities. Community action, which shall complement national policies, shall be directed towards improving public health, preventing human illness and diseases, and obviating sources of danger to human health. Such action shall cover the fight against the major health scourges, by promoting research into their causes, their transmission and their prevention, as well as health information and education. The Community shall complement the Member States' action in reducing drugs-related health damage, including information and prevention.

Although the Treaty clearly shows that the European Community will ensure a high level of human health protection, it leaves the organisation of the system to the national legislature. This is clearly set out in Article 152 (5) of the Treaty.

Community Action in the field of public health shall fully respect the responsibilities of the Member States for the organisation and delivery of health services and medical care. In particular, measures referred to in paragraph 4(a) shall not affect national provisions on the donation or medical use of organs and blood.

Although the direct influence of European Community law on national health policy may be limited, it by no means implies that the social security sector is an island beyond the reach of Community law and that, as a consequence, all national rules relating to social security fall outside its scope[2]. Whilst Community law may not affect the competence of the Member States to organise their own social security systems, it means only that Community law does not regulate this matter directly and does not even take action when its application would compromise the very existence of the social security systems. Otherwise, Member States are bound to comply with Community law even when exercising the powers reserved to them in the field of social security[3].

Community is moving more closely from an economic to a social Community. Although the Treaty did not set out any provisions, the European Community had already been active in the field of health care through general programmes such as the Europe against Cancer Programme or the Europe against Aids Programme. The Treaty of Amsterdam replaced this Article 129 by Article 152 with specific provisions.

[2] Conclusions Advocate General Tesauro under cases C-120/95, *Decker*, ECR [1998] I-1831 and C-158/96, *Kohll*, ECR [1998] I-1931, paragraph 17.

[3] Conclusions Advocate General Tesauro under cases C-120/95, *Decker*, ECR [1998] I-1831 and C-158/96, *Kohll*, ECR [1998] I-1931, paragraph 22.

This applies in particular to the rules governing free movement, where fundamental freedoms have an effect on social security law unless there is a general interest justifying a limitation of such freedom, not least because the Court made it clear that medical products and medical treatment should be considered as goods and services within the meaning of European Community law. Moreover, it is not only health care providers that can invoke the principles of the free movement of services and freedom of establishment to set up business or provide services there. The freedom to provide services includes the freedom for the recipients of services to go to another Member State in order to receive a service there, without being obstructed by restrictions, even in relation to payments[4].

Although through its solidarity-based structure social security cannot be regarded as an enterprise within the meaning of EU law and the provisions of competition law (Articles 81 ff.) do not always apply, this does not apply to the domain of fundamental freedoms, in particular the framework in which social security services are provided. The provision of benefits in health care should therefore be regarded as an economic activity, which as such is subject to fundamental freedoms. In that sense social security institutions can be said to participate in the general economy[5].

II. The Territoriality Principle in National Health Care Systems

A common characteristic of all the social security schemes in the Member States is that the right to medical care is a territorial right. This means that people are only entitled to have the cost of medical care reimbursed in national territory. The cost of medical treatment provided abroad is reimbursed only in a limited number of cases, such as urgent medical treatment during a temporary stay abroad, or after receiving prior authorisation from the sickness fund. However, as the latter is at the discretion of the sickness fund, there is no genuine right to medical

---

[4]   ECJ, joined cases C-286/82 and C-26/83, *Luisi and Carbone*, ECR [1984] 377, paragraph 16.

[5]   Application of the principle of free movement provides considerable material for discussion but it is not related to the issue at hand so it will not be discussed here (application of European competition rules on medical providers and medical insurers; are medical care providers or care institutions companies within the meaning of Community law; to what extent do requirements in terms of diploma or occupation constitute an impediment to freedom of establishment and/or the provision of services for medical care providers? Price-fixing and parallel import of medicines? Pharmacy across the Internet etc.

care abroad. In most cases such permission is interpreted in a very narrow manner.

It is not surprising, therefore, that the ruling of the ECJ on such cross-border health care was eagerly anticipated. If the Court was to hold that national provisions forbidding the right to health care abroad or allowing it only under certain conditions countered the free movement of goods and services, then such provisions would be rendered invalid. Needless to say, this would have enormous implications for current cross-border health care regulations. For the Member States it could constitute a doomsday scenario, with medical tourism enabling patients to seek treatment anywhere in the European Union at the expense of their sickness fund. This might mean that a sickness fund would be obliged to repay the cost of medical treatment that is not in the national benefit package. It could also mean having to reimburse medical treatment that is much more expensive abroad than in one's own country and risk upsetting the financial balance of social security systems (see for example Cornelissen, 1997: 41; Jorens, 1997: 14).

There are other arguments against a growth in cross-border health care. It has been argued that there would be a risk of losing control over the quality of the health care. All Member States impose certain requirements in terms of qualifications of health professions or minimum standards for medical products. If patients were to seek treatment abroad that only met less strict standards than at home there would no longer be any way of guaranteeing quality.

Furthermore, granting patients an unconditional right to seek care anywhere they choose would also pose a threat to health planning. Member States calculate the number of facilities required to meet the needs of their population. There is a genuine risk, particularly in border areas, that certain hospitals might become overburdened as a result of free movement (see for example, Cornelissen, 1997: 41; Mavridis, 1996: 1092-1093; Zechel, 1995: 29 ff.). If too many insured were to go abroad, some units and hospitals might have to be closed down due to a lack of patients. A large proportion of a hospital's costs are fixed. Reduced size can be associated with lower quality in some areas[6]. In turn it could jeopardise the principle of effective care accessible to all.

On the other hand, the possibility of seeking treatment abroad also has positive consequences. Member States with waiting lists could see them reduced, provided the problem is not transferred to the recipient states. Some patients, particularly in border areas, would have easier

---

[6] Overburdening in a certain Member State may lead some states to wonder whether they should actually keep medical infrastructure at such high levels if it attracts citizens from other Member States (see Novak, 1998: 367-368).

access to health care, where that care is available just across the border but only at some distance in one's own country.

III. Cross-border Health Care in EC Co-ordination Law

A. Residing in Another State than the Competent State

The fundamental freedom of movement of people has meant that the EU has had to act to protect the rights to social security of cross-border workers, in EC Regulations 1408/71 and 574/72.

In principle, the co-ordination mechanism is quite simple. An insured person, and the members of his or her family[7], who stays within the territory of another Member State has the right to medical care[8] that is equivalent to what is legally available there, with the stipulation that they comply with all the conditions for the right to benefits in accordance with the legislation of the home Member State (Article 19 Regulation 1408/71/EEC). The institution in the insured person's place of residence provides this care.

---

[7] Members of family have this right insofar as they have no right to benefits based on the legislation of their country of residence. In cases of Member States where the right to benefits is based on residence, the cost of medical care of these members of the family is also at the charge of the institution which insures the employed or self-employed person, as long as the wife (husband) is not employed in the country of residence. This is a solution of equity: the State that obtains the contributions, has also to bear the costs of medical care. The definition of a member of the family can be found in Article 1(f) of the Regulation, although it makes for difficult reading. For the application of the definitions concerning sickness and maternity, it has always been assumed that the legislation in the country of residence determines who should be considered to be a member of the family. However, in ECJ (case C-451/93, *Delavant*, ECR [1995] I-1545) the Court of Justice ruled that "member of the family" can also be determined by the legislation of the competent Member State, when a person cannot be considered to be a member of the family according to the legislation of the country of residence.

[8] Benefits refer to benefits-in-kind, even when they take the form of an allowance for the costs of medical care, as is the case with restitution systems (ECJ, case C-61/65, *Vaassen-Göbbels*, ECR [1996] 257). Apparently, it has to involve the reimbursement of a well-defined treatment. In Molenaar (ECJ, case C-160/96, *Molenaar*, ECR [1998] I-843), the Court of Justice determined that German Pflegegeld was not a benefit in the sense of the Regulation, but an allowance. The argument for this stance was that Pflegegeld was not intended to reimburse the cost of a definite treatment. It involved a regular monthly payment for spending on the costs of nursing according to one's own discretion. Premium contributions for sickness insurance do not constitute benefits-in-kind within the meaning of the Regulation. Benefits-in-kind means benefits to be granted on the occurrence of an actual case of sickness or maternity. They do not include supplementary pension contributions which are intended as a contribution towards the financing of the beneficiary's sickness insurance (ECJ, case C-33/65, *Dekker*, ECR [1965] I-1135).

One must refer to legislation in the country of residence to ascertain whether care is a benefit-in-kind, which can be classified under the provisions for sickness and maternity care[9]. It is irrelevant whether the legislation of the home State considers it a benefit-in-kind. This could have important consequences for the home institution. However, it is in keeping with the system used by the Regulation by which the person concerned will receive benefits in accordance with the State where the benefits are provided as if he or she was insured there (Jorens, 1992: 86).

As well as the receipt of benefits, co-ordination has also been achieved on the payment of contributions. The general basis is that the insured person is liable to pay a contribution in accordance with the legislation of the Member State in which the institution is situated, that is accountable for the benefits according to the Regulation. In this case, no contribution can be imposed according to the legislation of, for example, the country of residence, even if the legislation of the Member State applies and the person concerned is insured and liable to pay contributions according to national legislation (Stiemer, 1999: 228).

B. Temporary Stay in Another State or Permission to Seek Treatment in Another State

The principles contained in national law, on whether or not someone is entitled to go abroad to seek treatment, are mirrored in EC Regulation 1408/71 on the social security of migrant workers. Article 22 of EC Regulation 1408/71 sets out two cases where persons who do not reside in another Member State are entitled to cross-border health care.

Unlike the other articles of the Regulation that only apply to employed or self-employed people, these provisions also apply to persons who are nationals of a Member State and are insured under the legislation of a Member State and to the members of their families residing with them.

The relevant factor is the place where the illness occurs, *i.e.* the Member State where a person resides temporarily or the Member State where he or she is insured. In the case of the former, such as during a temporary stay in another Member State, as on a holiday, for example, a person is entitled to medical care if they become ill and their condition

---

[9]   In point 1 of its Decision No. 175, the Administrative Commission determined that, with a view to the mutual reimbursement between institutions, benefits can be considered to be benefits for sickness and maternity insurance purposes, if they can be considered to be such based on the legislative regulation used by the institution that is providing them, insofar as the benefits can be obtained based on the provisions of the chapter on sickness and maternity.

requires immediate treatment[10]. This right is conferred by means of form E111 "provided the person's condition necessitates immediate benefits"[11]. This implies care that cannot be postponed until one has returned home without the insured person risking life or health (Stiemer, 1999: 231-232). Although it is not really clear who should rule on the condition necessitating immediate benefits, it seems reasonable to assume that the State providing the benefits should rule on their immediate necessity (Jorens, 1992: 96-97). In practice it seems that many Member States find the concepts "necessitates immediate care" and "urgent care" unclear. Although they should be interpreted under national law, there seems to be a need for a consistent interpretation. It is not always possible to discover how the border is drawn to define necessary health care (see also Jorens and Schulte, 2000: 44).

However, if the illness occurs in the insuring State, a person can receive treatment in another Member State after receiving prior authorisation from the sickness fund by means of a form E112. According to Article 22(2), 2nd paragraph, this authorisation may not be refused if the treatment in question is among the benefits provided for by the legislation of the Member State on whose territory the person resides but he or she cannot receive such treatment within the time

---

[10] The question arises whether this provision only applies if the necessity of medical care could not be foreseen before the person's departure or does it also apply to existing disorders which require medical treatment even during a temporary stay abroad? In this respect the Administrative Commission in its Decision No. 163 pointed out that regard must be had to preventing the improper use of the provisions of Article 22(1)(a) by persons who move temporarily to the territory of another Member State to obtain benefits-in-kind under this subparagraph without complying with the procedure laid down in Subparagraph (c) of the same Article, which makes the granting of such benefits subject to prior authorisation by the competent institution. On the other hand, an over-restrictive interpretation of Article 22(1)(a) would cause a significant obstacle to freedom of movement for persons whose condition necessitates continuous and regular medical treatment such that they will be likely to require immediate benefits in the event of a stay in the territory of another Member State. For this reason kidney dialysis or oxygen therapy provided in a Member State other than the competent Member State for a person entitled to invoke the provisions of Article 22(1)(a) of Regulation 1408/71/EEC or for a member of his or her family shall be regarded as being an immediate benefit within the meaning of the aforementioned provision if it is part of existing and ongoing dialysis or oxygen therapy, and in as far as the stay is for reasons other than medical reasons. The provisions of the previous paragraph shall apply without prejudice to the practical obligation on the person concerned to make a prior arrangement with a view to ensuring the effective availability of the treatment in question during a temporary stay in the Member State.

[11] Except for some employed or self-employed persons, such as posted workers, who according to Article 22b, benefit from these provisions for any condition requiring benefits.

normally necessary for obtaining treatment in that Member State, taking into account his or her current state of health and the probable course of the disease.

Thus, permission must be provided when the treatment cannot be given within the usual time period, for example due to long waiting lists. Barring such circumstances, it is, in principle, up to the Member States to grant permission for cross-border health care. They therefore have considerable discretionary powers in this regard[12]. It appears that this authorisation causes many problems due to diversity in practice between Member States. Some are very restrictive while others seem quite generous, or perhaps medical practitioners and patients are not well informed (see also Jorens and Schulte, 2000: 45).

In this respect it is important to look at the history of Article 22. Initially, Article 22(2) §2 provided that the authorisation could not be refused where the person concerned could not receive the treatment in question in the territory of the Member State in which he resides. In the Pierik case, the Court pointed out, firstly, that the words "who satisfies the conditions of the legislation of the competent State for entitlement to benefits" were exclusively intended to determine, who, in principle, is eligible for benefits. It did not mean that a patient who stays in another Member State could be denied the opportunity to receive benefits-in-kind provided by the legislation of that State to persons staying there if it was also granted in his State of residence[13].

Thus a worker insured in one State was entitled to the full range of benefits-in-kind provided for by the law of the place of residence. His treatment was not limited to benefits-in-kind provided for within his insuring Member State (Jorens, 1992: 98).

The duty laid down in Article 22(2) to grant authorisation covered both cases where the treatment provided in another Member State was either more effective than what the person concerned could receive in the Member State where he resides, or could not be provided in the home State[14].

This is also so the case in situations where the treatment in question is explicitly not included in the scheme of benefits-in-kind by the

---

[12] Since the costs relating to the treatment in question are chargeable to the competent institution which granted the authorisation, the institution of the Member State to which the person goes to receive the treatment is obliged to provide it upon presentation of such an authorisation even if, under the legislation which it administers, it does not have a duty but only a power to grant it (see Jorens, 1992: 100).

[13] ECJ, case C-117/77, *Pierik I*, ECR [1978] 825, r.c. 13.

[14] ECJ, case C-117/77, *Pierik I*, ECR [1978] 825, r.c. 22.

legislation administered by the relevant institution, for example on medical, or financial grounds or because the value of the treatment in question in the Member State in which the competent institution is established, in general not regarded as falling within the field of effective health care and furthermore is deliberately not provided by virtue of any other legislation of that Member State to which the regulation is applicable. When the competent institution acknowledges that the treatment in question constitutes a necessary and effective treatment of the disease from which the person concerned suffers, the conditions for the application of the second subparagraph of Article 22(2) of Regulation 1408/71 are fulfilled and the competent institution may not in that case refuse the authorisation referred to by that provision and required under Article 22(1)(c)[15].

The cost of benefits-in-kind provided on behalf of the competent institution by the institution of the place of stay or residence would be fully refunded. The decisive factor was that the worker in question received the treatment his or her condition required.

Thus, persons covered by Regulation 1408/71 were entitled to the best medical treatment they could get within the European Community. When the treatment in question would be more effective than that available in the home State, the home institution had to authorise treatment abroad (Jorens, 1992: 99).

To block the consequences of the court's judgement, the Council decided to change the wording of the Regulation to grant greater power of discretion to the Member States.

In this way one could argue that what might be considered as the first appearance of free movement of patients was blocked by the Council. The Member States made it patently clear that the decision whether a patient can go abroad for medical care at the expense of the sickness fund is made by them and not by the patients (van der Mei, 2001: 300). It is therefore clear that under EC Regulation 1408/71 there is no real right to free movement of patients. Consequently, one can argue that Article 22 has not really been affected by the Commission's proposal to simplify Regulation 1408/71 (European Commission, 1998). The proposed new Article 16 (temporary stay in another State) and Article 18 (permission to seek treatment in a State other than the competent State) leave intact the basic principles of Article 22. The only change is to extend the personal scope of application to everyone, not only EU nationals insured under the social security legislation of a Member State.

---

[15]   ECJ, case C-182/78, *Pierik II*, ECR [1979] 1977, r.c. 12-13.

IV. Cross-border Care under the Common Market Rules[16]

A. Health Care and the Common Market Principles: The Issue

The Kohll and Decker cases raise the fundamental issue of whether patients should have a say in deciding whether to seek cross-border health care. Do the provisions on free movement of goods and services set out in the EC Treaty preclude national rules under which reimbursement, in accordance with the scale applying in the State of insurance, is subject to authorisation by the insured person's social security institution?

These cases became the focus of considerable attention. Some called them "the Bosman case of sickness insurance" whereas others invoked "the denture menace" or "dentures under palm trees". Some welcomed the rulings because they introduced competition law to the health care sector, with an expectation of a reduction in costs; others believed they would inevitably lead to higher costs. One matter was striking: practitioners of social law were examining these cases with 'Argus' eyes. This was, perhaps surprising, as the Court had threatened to overturn a well-established principle in national legislation. Doomsday scenarios with medical tourism appeared threateningly on the horizon.

The Kohll, Decker and Bosman cases have the following in common: specialists in European law had been expecting these rulings for a long time because they were in line with earlier case law. Not only were experts not unduly shocked by these rulings, they dismissed them because they did not introduce anything fundamentally new. Indeed, one could ask why cross-border health care had escaped scrutiny by the ECJ until then. In this respect the cases are not revolutionary but a logical consequence of the dynamic development of European Community law and, in particular, the fundamental freedoms whereby national law, aided not least by the ECJ, is interpreted in an increasingly narrow manner.

---

[16]   Much has been written on the case law of the Court of Justice. In this respect we refer to the contributions/bibliography in the following seminars or books: *Grensoverschijdende gezondheidszorg in de Euregios: uitdaging of bedreiging/ Soins de Santé transfrontaliers dans les Eurégios: un Défi ou une Menace*, Europees Seminarie/ Séminaire Européen, Verslagboek/ Procès-Verbal, Alden Biesen, 1999; *Health Care without Frontiers within the European Union*, International Symposium, Ministry of Social Security of the Grand Duchy of Luxembourg, Association Internationale de la Mutualité, European Institute of Social Security, Luxembourg, 1999; Jorens and Schulte (2001) or the bibliography mentioned in Palm *et al.* (2000: 163-168).

B. Do Prior Authorisation Rules Hinder Free Movement?

In the Kohl and Decker cases the Court merely applied the well-known "Dassonville rule"[17]. Can national social security provisions be said to hinder, directly or indirectly, actually or potentially intra-community trade? This certainly appears to be the case. However, although national provisions, in principle, do not deter patients from seeking medical care abroad, they will be less inclined to do so in the knowledge that their costs will not be reimbursed by sickness funds[18].

Moreover, Advocate General Tesauro pointed out that this rule also has a negative effect on service providers established in another Member State. With the exception of a small number of rare cases where authorisation is granted, they will only offer non-reimbursable services[19]. This can also be said to constitute an obstacle to free movement (see Montagnie, forthcoming).

V. Justifications of Limitations to Free Movement

A. Grounds for Justification

Measures that limit free movement are not prohibited as such. The question is whether they are justified. Grounds for justifying a limitation may be the public interest, as set out in Articles 30 and 46) of the EC Treaty (for example health protection), or on the grounds of the "rule of reason" of the ECJ. According to the Court, a rule can only be justified where this is in the public interest or objectively justified by the need to ensure observance of professional rules of conduct[20]. In addition, such rules may not be discriminatory[21].

---

[17] ECJ, case C-8/74, *Dassonville*, ECR [1974] 837.

[18] In ECJ (case C-18/84, *Commission* v. *France*, ECR [1985] 1339) the Court had already ruled that by depriving newspaper publishers of certain tax advantages in respect of publications which they print in other Member States, the French Republic failed to fulfil its obligations under Article 30 of the EEC Treaty; the tax provision at issue may be regarded as an obstacle to intra-community trade. See also ECJ, case C-204/90, *Bachmann*, ECR [1992] 249.

[19] Conclusions Advocate General Tesauro under cases C-120/95, *Decker*, ECR [1998] I-1831 and C-158/96, *Kohll*, ECR [1998] I-1931, paragraph 43.

[20] See for example ECJ, case C-33/74, *van Binsbergen*, ECR [1974] 1299, paragraph 14; ECJ, joined cases C-110 and 111/78, *van Wesemael*, ECR [1979] 35, paragraph 29.

[21] In contrast to legal exception provided for by treaties, rule of reason exceptions can only be invoked for national measures which are not discriminatory and therefore apply without distinction to goods and services from national or Member States.

Although the Court recognised, in principle, that the three objectives cited in these cases, *i.e.* guaranteeing the financial equilibrium of the social security system, ensuring a balanced medical service accessible to everyone, and the protection of health may be grounds for justification, they were refuted in the actual rulings.

B. Protection of Health

The first potential justification is the protection of health. On the basis of prevailing national quality standards can doctors from country A be barred from treating patients in country B?

The desire to protect public health as grounds for justification does not raise any problems. It is explicitly referred to in Articles 30 and 46 of the EC Treaty. Recourse to these articles or to the rule of reason ceases to be justified, however, if Community directives provide for the complete harmonisation of national law[22].

The Court pointed out that the medical profession is the subject of mutual recognition between the Member States. Mutually agreed standards have been introduced and the conditions for taking up and pursuing a health professional have been the subject of several co-ordinating and harmonising directives. As a result, the quality of health care afforded by such health professionals is the same as that provided by those established on national territory.

According to the Court "these rules such as those applicable in the main proceedings cannot be justified on grounds of public health in order to protect the quality of medical services provided in other Member States."

At first sight this consideration would appear to be correct. If freedom of establishment precludes a Member State from imposing, in the interest of public health, stricter requirements on the formal training of doctors than those provided in these directives (who can therefore be granted permission to practice medicine in one country on the basis of a medical diploma obtained in another Member State), it seems logical to apply this reasoning to the provision of passive services, all the more so since the Court of Justice seems more inclined to allow limitations to freedom of establishment than obstacles to the free provision of services. Refusal to recognise the service provided by non-national health care providers cannot be justified on the grounds that they do not possess the requisite expertise. It is possible to ask whether requirements

---

[22] See ECJ, case C-5/77, *Tedeschi*, ECR [1977] 1555, paragraph 35 and ECJ, case C-k39/90, *Denkavit*, ECR [1991] 3069, paragraph 19.

imposed by national health care providers are based on a desire to protect the insured or to ward off competition.

In contrast, it could be argued that the Court actually starts from a hypothetical notion whereby, as the requirements for practising a health care profession are the subject of mutual recognition in Europe, this automatically implies that the quality of care provided in Europe is also uniform. The Court seems to hold that, fundamentally, quality standards are the same all over Europe so that there are no reasons for making medical treatment in another Member State subject to prior authorisation on the grounds of protecting health. Still, it cannot be denied that the EC guidelines to which the Court refers, tend to regard access to the profession rather than its actual practice[23].

It could, however, be argued that the treatment provided by foreign doctors does not meet the quality standards required in the national State. After all, the ECJ previously recognised that the existence of a Community regulation does not preclude a Member State from appealing to Article 36 to justify additional measures at national level if it is essential for public health[24].

All states impose certain requirements on those pursuing a health care profession regardless where he or she has obtained his or her diploma. It could be argued, therefore, that treatment given in another State by someone who does not meet such requirements cannot be reimbursed without prior authorisation. However, an important consideration is that, pursuant to the case law of the ECJ, restriction of the free movement of services cannot be justified on the basis of the common interest (because objectively it is not absolutely necessary) if this objective has already been achieved on the basis of comparative rules in the State where the service provider is established. Member States thus have to take quality control rules applicable in other States into account. A doctor established in another Member State may be exempted from license fees or registration with professional associations in the receiving State provided that he or she observes professional rules. If he or she were to practise activities under the national health insurance of the receiving State it is reasonable to assume that the standard provisions laid down by the legislation applicable to him or her, will apply.

Given the fact that the quality standards required for practising a medical profession are largely similar in the different States of the

---

[23] This is the case particularly in Decker where the Court refers to Directive 92/51 (Council of the European Communities, 1992).

[24] See ECJ, case C-72/83, *Campus Oil*, ECR [1984] 2727. See also Montagnie (forthcoming).

European Community, it is unlikely that a concern about quality could be used to justify the refusal to reimburse treatment provided in another State. Although quality standards exist for medical professionals, this is not the case for hospitals. To date there have been no harmonisation directives for hospitals.

C. Financial Balance of the Social Security System

Another potential ground for justification is the risk of upsetting the financial balance of the social security scheme. This could be the case if the cost of treatment provided in another State and reimbursed by sickness institutions were to be paid in accordance with the tariffs of the country where the medical services were supplied and, in view of the considerable differences that currently exist in terms of the cost of health care and the financing mechanisms of sickness funds. Although aims of a purely economic nature cannot justify a barrier to the fundamental principle of the free movement of goods, it is possible that the risk of seriously undermining the financial balance of the social security system[25] may constitute an overriding reason justifying a barrier of that kind[26]. In Duphar, the Court recognised that

> Community law does not detract from the powers of the Member States to organise their social security systems and to adopt, in particular, provisions intended to govern the consumption of pharmaceutical preparations in order to promote the financial stability of their health care insurance schemes [...] that it is not in principle incompatible with Community law for the Member State concerned, in a scheme which – like that in force in the Netherlands – is based on the principle of reimbursement in respect of all medicinal preparations which may be prescribed, with a view to achieving its aim of limiting costs, to prepare limitative lists excluding certain products from the reimbursement scheme.

---

[25] In this respect we want to refer to the new article 137 paragraph 4 of the Treaty of Nice. According to this Article, the provisions of the EC Treaty shall not affect the right of the Member States to define he fundamental principles of their social security systems and must not significantly affect the financial equilibrium thereof. It has to be seen if this Article would influence the Case Law of the Court of Justice. However, it could be said that these terms seem to be less strict than the wordings of the Court of Justice.

[26] See ECJ, case C-120/95, *Decker*, ECR [1998] 1831, paragraph 39; see also ECJ, case C-328/91, *Secretary of State for Social security* v. *Thomas*, ECR [1993] 1247, unequal treatment of men and women in matters of social security and financial balance of pension system and ECJ, case C-137/94, *Richardson*, ECR [1995] 3407 on exempting certain categories of persons from prescription charges and financial balance of pension systems. For a famous example on fiscal measures see ECJ, case C-204/90, *Bachmann*, ECR [1992] 249 on cohesion between fiscal system and the deduction of insurance premiums.

However, the Court later stated:

to be in conformity with the Treaty the choice of the medicinal preparations to be excluded must be free of any discrimination to the detriment of imported medicinal preparations. To that end the exclusionary lists must be drawn up in accordance with objective criteria, without reference to the origin of the products and must be verifiable by any importer.

Reimbursement according to foreign tariffs could be detrimental where costs are significantly higher in the State where care is received. In such cases prior authorisation is a sound instrument. In this case, however, such justification does not apply because the costs are reimbursed in accordance with the tariffs of the country where the concerned is insured and subsequently responsible for repayment, not pursuant to the tariffs of the country where the treatment was provided. It is irrelevant in which State the treatment was administered.

Hence, Article 22 of Regulation 1408/71 (that provides for reimbursement in accordance with the rates of the State where the benefits are administered provided prior authorisation is given) does not prevent the free movement of goods and services (see Article 22 of Regulation 1408/71/EEC). Some parties submitted that the applicability of Article 22 of Regulation 1408/71 should be questioned if national provisions are incompatible with free movement. The Court replied clearly that the fact that a national measure may be consistent with a provision of secondary legislation, in this case Article 22 of Regulation 1408/71, does not have the effect of removing that measure from the scope of the provisions of the Treaty.

Article 22 therefore does not prevent the reimbursement by Member States, at the tariffs in force in the home State, of costs incurred in another Member State without prior authorisation. This is logical because the Regulation may not restrict the rights of Community citizens granted on the basis of the Treaty[27]. This Article by no means requires that the cost of medical treatment has to be borne by the person concerned if permission was refused, or that they are not entitled to any form of compensation whatsoever.

It is not really clear why the Court refers to Article 22. After all, it may just as well have pointed out that national legal provisions were in breach of the general principles of free movement. The explanation may be that the Court intended to show that if something is allowed under EC law, it should be allowed under national law as well.

---

[27] Conclusions Advocate General Tesauro under cases C-120/95, *Decker*, ECR [1998] I-1831 and C-158/96, *Kohll*, ECR [1998] I-1931, paragraph 32.

Following these rulings, and the direct applicability of the principles of free movement of goods and services, Article 22 of Regulation 1408/71 has taken on a totally different role.

Indeed, in the wake of this case law a person who goes abroad to seek treatment or purchase a medical product now has two options, rather than simply pursuant to Article 22 of Regulation 1408/71:

- It may sometimes be more advantageous for the person concerned to request prior permission. An insured person who goes abroad to seek medical treatment after prior authorisation from the competent authority will be entitled to reimbursement of the cost pursuant to Article 22 of Regulation 1408/71, in accordance with the tariffs in the country where the treatment was given.

- Now he or she will be able to seek treatment abroad without prior authorisation. In such circumstances Article 22 does not prohibit the Member State concerned from reimbursing the treatment or product, in accordance with the scale of the state of insurance.

We shall come back to this point later.

D. Health Care for All

Granting everyone an unconditional right to health care anywhere in Europe could pose a threat to health planning. Member States calculate the number of facilities required to meet the needs of their population. There is a genuine risk, particularly in border areas, that certain hospitals might become overburdened as a result of free movement (see for example Cornelissen, 1997: 57; Mavridis, 1996: 1092-1093; Zechel, 1995: 29 ff.). If too many insured were to go abroad, some hospitals might have to close due to a lack of patients. Hospitals have high fixed-costs, regardless of the number of patients. Such reductions in volume could reduce quality.

That is why the Court states that the objective of maintaining a balanced hospital service, although intrinsically linked to the method of financing the social security system, may also fall within the derogations on grounds of public health under Article 56 (now Article 46) of the Treaty in so far as it contributes to the attainment of a high level of health protection. Article 56 (now Article 46) also permits Member States to restrict freedom to provide hospital services in so far as the maintenance of a treatment facility on national territory is essential for public health. This was not the case in the rulings in question as no one had shown that the service involved impaired provision of a balanced hospital service accessible to all.

VI. Reactions from Member States

A. Restricted Applicability only to Restitution Schemes?

Although the Kohll and Decker judgements were not revolutionary they provoked considerable reaction in political circles. This was perhaps due to the perceived threat that many patients would go abroad to seek treatment and the subsequent effect on social security systems. It is, however, most unlikely that hordes of people would go to foreign countries to consult foreign doctors (who may not even speak their language). In practice, few patients go abroad to obtain medical services, with three exceptions (Palm et al., 2000: 41):

- in border areas in cases where proximity to foreign medical services, cost, reputation, language, accessibility (waiting lists) administrative procedures, and familiarity encourage movement;

- for highly complex services where accessibility (waiting lists), the seriousness of the condition and the quality of the service-provider are decisive factors in the patients' choice;

- in cases were persons have at their disposal all the necessary information for making a rational choice.

At present frontier workers who are able to choose between treatment in either their country of employment or residence rarely use this option to seek treatment in the country of employment (De Buyser, 1997: 155). Cross-border health care takes only a marginal amount, between 0.3 and 0.5 of the total health budget (Palm et al., 2000: 37-40)[28].

Still, political reactions focused on other matters (see e.g. the following contributions Becker, forthcoming and Lugtenberg, forthcoming). Many Member States believed that Decker and Kohll applied only to health care systems such as those in Luxembourg and Belgium, i.e. where patients pay for health care costs and are reimbursed by their sickness fund. Consequently, the reasoning of the Court would not apply to benefits-in-kind systems (as in Germany and the Netherlands) or national health care systems (such as the United Kingdom). In such schemes the person concerned is not entitled to reimbursement of costs but to the care itself. An agreement exists between the care providers

---

[28] Luxembourg tops the list with 9%. This is due to the fact that this country only has limited medical infrastructure and authorisation to seek medical treatment abroad is much more frequently given. In addition, it would seem that practically all cross-border medical care is given within the six founding countries of the European Union, France being the most popular. In contrast, Italy is the greatest debtor in this respect.

and the insurance institutions and costs are paid directly by the insurance institutions. They fear that this regulation will be used to reform their national social security systems and that the Court will encourage the Member States, to replace benefits-in-kind systems by restitution schemes.

The question of whether or not these rulings apply only to restitution schemes is surprising. It would lead to a situation where a EU citizen, insured in a country with a restitution scheme, would be able to seek treatment abroad without permission whereas a EU citizen insured in a benefits-in-kind system would not have this possibility without prior authorisation from his or her insurance institution.

In addition, in some Member States with a benefits-in-kind system, certain categories of persons already have a right to reimbursement of benefits, which would lead to the strange conclusion that, within the same system, different rights to cross-border benefits would exist[29].

This problem was solved in the Geraets-Smits and Peerbooms cases. The question was whether systems, such as the Dutch one, where hospitals are paid by the fund with which the person concerned is insured, fall within the scope of freedom to provide services. Do these benefits apply in benefits-in-kind systems services? Several Member States and the Advocate General doubted this[30]. These services could not be seen as economical activities particularly when they are provided in kind and free of charge under the relevant sickness insurance scheme.

An economic activity requires remuneration, which is not the case in the Dutch system. Indeed general practitioners are not paid for individual treatments of patients. Doctors are paid on a capitation basis, regardless of whether or not patients make use of their services. The tariffs paid by the sickness funds to the hospital do not reflect real costs but have to be seen as means of fixing the annual hospital budget. Therefore we cannot speak of remuneration and Articles 49 and 50 (now Articles 40 and 41) are not applicable.

The Court clearly rejects these arguments. Medical activities fall within the scope of Article 60 (now Article 50) of the Treaty, there being no need to distinguish between care provided in a hospital environment and care provided outside it[31]. It is also established that the

---

[29]   For example in Germany for the voluntary insured.

[30]   See Advocate General Colomer under ECJ, case C-157/99, *Geraets-Smits and Peerbooms*, ECR [2001] I-5473, paragraphs 41-45.

[31]   See ECJ, joined cases C-286/82 and C-26/83, *Luisi and Carbone*, ECR [1984] 377, paragraph 16; ECJ, case C-159/90, *Society for the Protection of Unborn Children Ireland*, ECR [1991] 4685, paragraph 18, concerning advertising for clinics involved

nature of certain services does not exempt them from the fundamental principle of freedom of movement, so it is irrelevant that social security rules cannot exclude application of Articles 59 and 60 (now Articles 49 and 50) of the Treaty[32].

With regard to the argument that hospital services provided in the context of a sickness insurance scheme providing benefits-in-kind should not be classified as services within the meaning of Article 60 (now Article 50) of the Treaty, it should be noted that, far from falling under such a scheme, the medical treatment at issue in the main proceedings, which was provided in Member States other than those in which the persons concerned were insured, did lead to the establishment providing the treatment being paid directly by the patients. It must be accepted that a medical service provided in one Member State, paid for by the patient, should not fall outside the scope of the Treaty merely because reimbursement is applied for under another State's system that provides benefits-in-kind.

Furthermore, the fact that hospital treatment is financed directly by the sickness funds on the basis of established agreements is not sufficient to remove such treatment from the sphere of services within the meaning of Article 60 (now Article 50) of the Treaty. First, Article 60 (now Article 50) of the Treaty does not require that those on whom it is performed pay for the service[33]. Second, Article 60 (now Article 50) of the Treaty applies to services normally provided for remuneration and it has been held that, for these purposes, the essential characteristic of remuneration lies in the fact that it constitutes consideration for the service in question[34]. In the present cases, payments made by the sickness insurance funds under the contractual arrangements of the ZFW, albeit set at a flat rate, are a consideration for hospital services and unquestionably represent remuneration for the hospital that receives them and which is engaged in an activity of an economic character.

The Court clearly determines that, from the moment a patient has to pay for medical care abroad, which is normally the case, the rules on free movement of services and goods apply even if benefits are provided

---

in the deliberate termination of pregnancies; and ECJ, case C-158/96, *Kohll*, ECR [1998] 1931, paragraphs 29 and 51.

[32] ECJ, case C-279/80, *Webb*, ECR [1981] 3305, paragraph 10 and ECJ, case C-158/96, *Kohll*, ECR [1998] 1931, paragraph 20.

[33] ECJ, case C-352/85, *Bond van Adverteerders*, ECR [1998] 2085, paragraph 16 and ECJ, joined cases C-51/96 and C-191/97, *Deliège*, ECR [2000] I-2549, paragraph 56.

[34] ECJ, case C-263/86, *Humbel and Edel*, ECR [1998] 5365, 17.

for free in the home system[35], regardless of how that system operates[36]. In addition, services provided for in national health services have to be considered as services within the meaning of European Community law. Consequently, we may conclude that different means of organisation do not erode the application of fundamental freedoms. Otherwise Member States would be in a position to define unilaterally whether Community law is applicable or not. Yet, just because all health systems fall under the principles of free movement, it does not imply that there are no justifications for restricting free movement.

B. Intra-mural and Extra-mural Care

After the Kohll and Decker cases, it was questioned whether the reasoning of the Court of Justice only applied to extramural (or ambulatory) care or if hospital care was included. There is no doubt whatsoever that the arguments used by the Member States as justification for restricting free movement are more important with regard to intramural care. There is more scope for competition in extra-mural care. Hospitals have higher fixed costs and are heavily subsidised in many Member States. The consequence could be that foreigners, who have not contributed to this subsidy, now benefit from reduced hospital tariffs.

In the Kohll case the Court did not have to answer this question. Advocate General Tesauro did consider it an issue and believed that restrictions to free movement are allowed in the case of intramural care[37].

---

[35] The argument used in the Geraets-Smits and Peerbooms case that we could not speak about services, is all the more surprising as exactly these persons concerned had to pay for their benefits.

[36] In a certain way under the application of Regulation 1408/71 medical care provided under national health services was already considered as services which have to be paid for. The United Kingdom is indeed reimbursed for medical care provided on the basis of Article 22 of EC Regulation 1408/71 to a national of another Member State who needed immediate medical treatment.

[37] Also Advocate General Saggio in the Vanbraekel case (ECJ, case C-368/98, ECR [2001] I-5363) accepts restrictions to intramural care. The reasons, however, differ from these used by Advocate General Tesauro. According to Advocate General Saggio the rules on free movement do not apply to benefits which constitute, on the one hand, an integral part of public health systems in so far these are established and organised by the State and on the other hand are financed out of the public purse. Hospital care is therefore excluded from free movement. However, as already pointed out, the Court of Justice rejected this view in both the Vanbraekel case (r.o. 41) and in the Geraets-Smits and Peerbooms case (r.o. 53) by pointing out that medical activities fall within the scope of free movement, there being no need to distinguish between care provided in a hospital environment and care provided outside such an environment.

In his conclusions in the Decker and Kohll cases, Advocate General Tesauro accepted restrictions to benefits that must be provided to insured persons in hospitals. Unlike the benefits provided by individual practitioners, location and number of hospitals is determined by planning and cost of one person's stay cannot be separated from that of the hospital as a whole. Clearly, if a large number of insured persons chose to avail themselves of hospital facilities located in another Member State, their domestic hospitals would be under-utilised but would have the same fixed costs as if they were being used to full capacity. In other words, reimbursement by the home social security fund of benefits received in hospitals of other Member States, even on the basis of a flat-rate equivalent, would result in an additional financial burden for the system concerned. In the hospital sector, therefore, it remains essential to require prior authorisation, in order not to disrupt the financial balance of the system and to ensure the maintenance of a service that is accessible, both financially and logistically, to all (paragraphs 59-60).

Doubts could be raised, however, concerning such an unlimited restriction. Is it really true that overall health planning is endangered if one has the right to seek medical treatment in a foreign hospital? If not, is permission really necessary? If freedom to choose one's doctor and hospital were given, would there be an uncontrolled flow of patients from one Member State to another? Travelling across borders entails significant inconvenience, often including language difficulties and additional costs, if only for those persons accompanying the patient[38]. Moreover, in countries confronted with waiting lists, would not the fact that patients go abroad help these countries as it would decrease shortages? Is there still a danger that hospitals will close given the shift to outpatient care that has taken place in recent years? Does competition between private and semi-private hospitals not play a greater role?

In its judgement in Kohll the Court made clear that Member States may have to prove that restrictions are necessary to provide a balanced medical and hospital service open to all insured persons. However, concluding that every restriction is acceptable seems to be going too far (Jorens, 1999: 21 and van der Mei, 2001: 355). It is much more likely that the Court will judge on a case-by-case basis whether restrictions can be justified. The Court speaks about medical and hospital care, which can imply extramural care whereas the Advocate General only speaks about intramural care. As such the Court fails to differentiate the two (Jorens, 1999: 21). According to the Court, Member States will have to prove that the restrictions are "necessary" to provide a balanced medical

---

[38] See also Conclusions Advocate General Tesauro under cases C-120/95, *Decker*, ECR [1998] I-1831 and C-158/96, *Kohll*, ECR [1998] I-1931, paragraph 60, footnote 91.

and hospital service accessible to all and "indispensable" for the maintenance of an essential treatment facility or medical service on national territory. Strong arguments were therefore necessary to prove that this restriction is necessary and indispensable. The arguments used by Member States in the Geraets-Smits and Peerbooms case were judged by the Court to be sufficient. Explicitly referring to the observations submitted by governments, the Court argues that, in contrast to medical services provided by practitioners in their surgeries or at the patient's home, medical services provided in a hospital take place within an infrastructure with certain very distinct characteristics. The number of hospitals, their geographical distribution, the mode of their organisation, the equipment with which they are provided, and even the nature of the medical services that they offer, are all matters that it is possible to plan. Such planning meets a variety of concerns. First, it seeks to achieve sufficient access to a balanced range of high quality hospital treatment in the State concerned. Second, it helps to control costs and to reduce wastage of financial, technical and human resources. From both perspectives, a requirement that coverage of costs of hospital treatment provided in another Member State under a national social security system must be subject to prior authorisation appears to be both necessary and reasonable[39].

If insured persons were at liberty, regardless of the circumstances, to use services of hospitals with which their sickness fund had no contractual arrangements, whether they were situated in the competent State or in another Member State, all the planning which goes into the contractual system in an effort to guarantee a rational, stable, balanced and accessible supply of hospital services would be jeopardised at a stroke. The Court accepts that there are reasons that justify restrictions on free movement in case of hospitals. However, we may not conclude that every restriction is lawful. As the Court points out, national courts should ascertain that the conditions attached to each authorisation be justified with regard to the overriding considerations examined and must satisfy the requirement of proportionality.

It would be too easy to say that intramural care is entirely excluded. On a case-by-case basis one has to see whether the criterion of proportionality is fulfilled. The fact that a few patients would go abroad does not seem to be enough to allow an unlimited restriction of free movement.

In addition, it is also unclear if this reasoning applies only to hospital treatment as such, or if it is also applicable to every clinical facility

---

[39] ECJ, case C-157/99, *Geraets-Smits and Peerbooms*, ECR [2001] I-5473, paragraphs 76-80.

where medical care is provided. It is questionable if restrictions are also allowed concerning nursing homes or rehabilitation institutions, as arguments about the high financial cost are less applicable to these institutions. In addition the question of "What is hospital treatment?" could arise. Does it cover all treatment given in a hospital or is outpatient care excluded? One could perhaps argue that restrictions are only allowed with respect to medical care that normally cannot be provided for outside a hospital, however this may be defined.

C. Benefits not Covered by Insurance Packages

As medical benefits are reimbursed according to the tariffs in force in the competent State, one could expect that benefits not covered by the sickness insurance system in that State need not be reimbursed. On the other hand, one immediately understands that this limits to a great extent the principle of cross-border medical care. People would hardly see any reason to cross a border for obtaining medical care.

On the other hand, if medical benefits not covered could also be reimbursed, patients would have the possibility to seek the best treatment in the European Union.

The Court, following the opinion of its Advocate General, is quite clear in this respect. The Court refers to earlier case law where the Court decided that it is not incompatible with Community law for a Member State to establish, with a view to achieving its aim of limiting costs, limited lists excluding certain products from reimbursement under its social security scheme[40]. The same principle must apply to medical and hospital treatment when it is a matter of determining which treatments will be paid for by the social security system of the Member State concerned. It follows that Community law cannot in principle have the effect of requiring a Member State to extend the list of medical services paid for by its social insurance system: the fact that a particular type of medical treatment is covered or not covered by the sickness insurance schemes of other Member States is irrelevant in this regard[41]. Nonetheless, in exercising that power the Member State must not disregard Community law. Thus it follows from the Court's case law that the list of medicinal preparations excluded from reimbursement must be drawn up in accordance with Article 28 of the EC Treaty and that this will be so only where the list is drawn up in accordance with objective criteria, without reference to the origin of the products. Member States are thus

---

[40]   ECJ, case C-238/82, *Duphar*, ECR [1984] 523, paragraph 17.

[41]   ECJ, case C-157/99, *Geraets-Smits and Peerbooms*, ECR [2001] I-5473, paragraphs 86-87.

not obliged to reimburse benefits not provided for in their national legislation.

On the one hand, it is clear that this argument considerably limits the right of free movement of patients. On the other hand, the reasoning of the Court is also very terse. Is it a sufficient justification that the Member State decided not to include this benefit in their insurance package (see also van der Mei, 2001: 364-368)? In the Duphar case, which the Court refers to, the Court accepted that Member States could restrict the scope of care, not just because they have the power to do so, but also because this is necessary to ensure the financial stability of system (van der Mei, 2001: 365).

However, is it possible that treatment obtained abroad that is not covered by the home State, but which is cheaper than a similar intervention at home, be reimbursed? Specifically similar medical products are marketed under different names in different Member States. Consider the case that someone buys a medical product abroad and asks for reimbursement, which is not permitted as it is not on the list of the home State only because it is named differently. It seems strange that in these cases reimbursement would not be possible.

Thus, when Member States are structuring their insurance schemes they must respect European Community law, which implies that, when drawing up the list of reimbursable benefits, they must do so on the basis of objective criteria, without reference to the origin of products.

In this respect, prior authorisation cannot legitimise discretionary decisions taken by the national authorities, which are liable to negate the effectiveness of provisions of Community law, in particular, those relating to a fundamental freedom[42]. In order for a prior authorisation scheme to be justified, even though it derogates from such a fundamental freedom, it must, be based on objective, non-discriminatory criteria, known in advance, in such a way as to circumscribe the exercise of the national authorities' discretion, so that it is not used arbitrarily.

Such a prior authorisation scheme must likewise be based on a procedural system that is easily accessible and capable of ensuring that a request for authorisation will be dealt with objectively and impartially within a reasonable time. Refusals to grant authorisation must also be open to challenge in judicial or quasi-judicial proceedings.

---

[42] ECJ, joined cases C-358/93 and C-416/93, *Bordessa and Others*, ECR [1995] I-361, paragraph 25; ECJ, joined cases C-163/94, C-165/94 and C-250/94, *Sanz de Lera and Others*, ECR [1995] I-4821, paragraphs 23 to 28 and ECJ, case C-205/99, *Analir and Others*, ECR [2001] I-1271, paragraph 37.

The Dutch system of sickness insurance is not based on a pre-established list of treatments issued by the national authorities for which payment will be guaranteed. The Netherlands legislature has enacted a general rule under which the costs of medical treatment will be covered provided that the treatment is "normal in the professional circles concerned". It has therefore left it to the sickness insurance funds, acting where necessary under the supervision of the *Ziekenfondsraad* and the courts, to determine the types of treatment that actually satisfy that condition. In the present two cases, it is clear from the arguments submitted to the national court and from the observations submitted to the Court that the expression "normal in the professional circles concerned" is open to a number of interpretations, depending, in particular, on whether it is considered that regard should be had to what is considered normal only in Dutch medical circles, which seems to be the interpretation favoured by the national court or, on the other hand, to what is considered normal according to the standards generally accepted at international level. The point of view of the Netherlands Government that when a specific treatment constitutes professionally appropriate treatment having a valid scientific basis it is regarded as a qualifying benefit for the purposes of the ZFW, so that the application of the "normal" criterion must not have the consequence that only treatment normally available in the Netherlands can qualify for reimbursement, is considered by the Court as based on objective criteria. Only an interpretation on the basis of what is sufficiently tried and tested by international medical science can be regarded as satisfying the requirements of objective criteria. To allow only treatment habitually carried out on national territory and scientific views prevailing in national medical circles to determine what is or is not normal will' not offer those guarantees and will make it likely that Dutch providers of treatment will always be preferred in practice.

If, on the other hand, the requirement that treatment must be regarded as "normal" is extended to treatment that is internationally accepted, the authorisation sought under the ZFW can still be refused on the basis of the need to maintain a balanced supply of hospital care on national territory and to ensure the financial stability of the sickness insurance system, so that the restriction of the freedom to provide services by hospitals situated in other Member States, which might result, does not infringe Article 59 of the Treaty. Further, where, as in the present case, a Member State decides that medical treatment must be sufficiently evaluated before it will be covered under its social security system, the national authorities called on to decide, for authorisation purposes, whether hospital treatment provided in another Member State satisfies that criterion must take into consideration all the relevant information, including evidence from scientific literature, the opinions of specialists and whether the proposed treatment is covered by the sickness insurance system of the Member State in which the treatment is provided[43].

Although it is up to the Member States to decide themselves what services they want to reimburse, the new element in the case law is that the judgement about which benefits must be covered cannot be made only on national criteria. If a Member State recognises the reimbursement of a certain treatment for a particular disease, this State, when confronted with the question of whether or not other methods of treatment for that disease have to be reimbursed, has to take into account whether this other method is internationally tested and recognised. This is a first step towards European standards for health care and an invitation to use the method of open co-ordination. In addition, the criterion of being internationally recognised is a dynamic concept. This requires a constant exchange of information.

VII. Waiting Lists

It is clear that, in principle, the application of prior-authorisation rules to benefits for which waiting lists exist at home could infringe free movement and must be justified. It is up to the Member States to prove that restrictions are necessary in order to protect the financial stability of the system or the maintenance of a balanced service.

In Geraets-Smits and Peerbooms the Court argued that the condition concerning the necessity of the treatment can be justified under Article 59 (now Article 49) of the Treaty, provided that it is construed so that authorisation to receive treatment in another Member State may be refused only if the same or equally effective treatment can be obtained without undue delay from an establishment with which the sickness fund has contractual arrangements.

Furthermore, in order to determine whether there is undue delay, the national authorities must have regard to the specific circumstances in each case and to take due account not only of the patient's medical condition at the time when authorisation is sought but also of his or her past record. Such a condition can ensure the supply of hospitals on the national territory and the financial stability of the insurance system.

However, once it is clear that a contracted establishment cannot provide treatment, it is unacceptable for national hospitals without contracts to be given priority over hospitals in other Member States[44].

---

[43] ECJ, case C-157/99, *Geraets-Smits and Peerbooms*, ECR [2001] I-5473, 89-98.

[44] ECJ, case C-157/99, *Geraets-Smits and Peerbooms*, ECR [2001] I-5473, 103-107.

Restrictions are thus allowed to prevent financial problems or imbalances in the medical and hospital service. However, the proportionality clause has to be taken into account.

The Court uses a quantitative argument, referring to an "outflow of patients" and "logistical and financial wastage". It is clear that these criteria require further clarification. Until now, no massive outflow has taken place. Surely if patients go abroad to circumvent waiting lists, the lists will then fall so that accessibility to medical care will improve? This could be different if so many people were to go abroad that undercapacity turned into over-capacity. The Court argued, in the Kohll case, that it was concerned with the maintenance of an essential medical facility. Therefore it seems that only essential care could be made dependent on permission clauses. Restrictions could even be counterproductive and are sometimes no longer proportional in cases where care would no longer be available. In this respect there seems to be a limit under which protection makes no sense (Jorens, 1999: 21; du Pré, 1998: 370).

It is also unclear what should be understood as "undue delay". This has to be judged by the competent institution and the Court will only have a limited judicial input. According to the Court, the decision must take into account the patient's medical condition as well as his or her past history. Therefore decisions have to be taken on a case-by-case basis and no general rulings seem possible.

Yet the fundamental right to health care demands that this period be strictly interpreted and that the situation of the patient is central. "Without undue delay" involves not treating the patient in time, before his or her health deteriorates, but also avoiding pain and making symptoms bearable. In this respect it is very difficult to define what is to be considered as an acceptable waiting time. This will as a matter of fact not only differ from the national situation, but also from the disease concerned. Life-endangering disease will imply shorter waiting periods than, for example, a hip replacement.

VIII. Relation between EC Regulation 1408/71 and Common Market Principles

A. Two Methods of Cross-border Medical Care

As already pointed out, the Kohll and Decker cases created a second means of cross-border care. The Court made clear that Co-ordination Regulation 1408/71 does not provide an exhaustive list of the means by which someone may obtain goods and services in another Member State. According to both the spirit and intention of the Regulation, it can be interpreted as simply providing one method by which cross-border care could be provided. The cases only arose because national rules had been interpreted by national courts as precluding all other methods of obtaining health care goods and services.

The fact that there are now two methods of cross-border medical care raises the question of whether one prevails over the other (see *e.g.* Palm *et al.*, 2000: 137-140). The problem is that one can hardly establish a hierarchy between the two procedures. The Court confirmed that there is no conflict between the two procedures. As this article does not prevent partial reimbursement in cases where no prior authorisation is given, there is also no need to amend Article 22 and to state that in case of prior authorisation, reimbursement should be given in accordance with the tariffs of the Member State of insurance.

As Kohll and Decker is based directly on the EC Treaty, it will always apply whatever is provided for under the Regulation, unless the Treaty is changed to exclude health care from the provisions of free movement. Even if the Regulations would be changed, a patient could always rely on the principles of freedom of movement of goods and services and the Court could, in future, award greater rights under these principles. Modification of the Regulation can never lead to the disappearance of the procedure based on the Treaty. Thus it is very difficult to establish a hierarchical order of the two methods.

As there is no conflict between these two procedures, one cannot argue that the Regulation has priority on the basis of the *lex specialis*. We are therefore confronted with two different means of cross-border medical care that can exist next to each other and where each has its advantages and disadvantages (see *e.g.* Palm *et al.*, 2000: 137-138; Langer, 1999: 537-542).

As the Court pointed out under Article 22, no extra costs are incurred[45]. A person will be subject to the access conditions and form of payment applying in the country in which treatment is provided. When this treatment is given for free, this is also the case for someone who has the right to treatment under Regulation 1408/71. The patient is guaranteed reimbursement of the cost of care.

The procedure under Kohll and Decker is different if one considers the private services of the provider and does not take account of the

---

[45] By holding that a duty to full reimbursement only exists when prior authorisation is given, the Court could circumvent the problem of Article 36 according to which full reimbursement is provided for costs incurred by a State on behalf of another State. In cases where prior authorisation rules are not applied, partial reimbursement is permissible and precisely because partial reimbursement is possible there is also no need for making payment dependent on the prior authorisation.

system of social protection of the State of establishment of this service-provider. A patient is not bound by the obligations and conditions of this system. It is just as if the treatment had been performed in the country of the competent State. Consequently, there are no disadvantages, *e.g.* it is not necessary to contact a general practitioner first in order to obtain a referral to a specialist. This procedure may be more advantageous when the cover of the country of insurance is better or when the services of the foreign provider are not covered by the social protection of that country. In this respect this procedure can be used to obtain care which is not covered under Article 22 of EC Regulation 1408/71, such as non-urgent and non-authorised care, and care not covered by the social protection scheme in the State of stay as *e.g.* care provided by private providers or provisions not covered in that State. On the other hand, one cannot profit from the advantages conferred by the EC Regulation.

Under Kohll and Decker one always has to pay for treatment in advance. The difference between the level of reimbursement and actual price to be paid could even result in significant additional expenditure for the patient, which could preclude some people from advancing the costs. Could the right of choice therefore be limited economically? Would this lead to a two-track Europe where the right to health care will be different according to the financial situation of the person concerned?

One of the guarantees under Article 22 of the Regulation is that the person concerned has the same rights and will have to pay the same cost as someone who was insured in the country of treatment. There is no such guarantee under the Kohll and Decker procedure. Does this imply that medical providers who treat foreigners using the Kohll and Decker procedure can now charge what they want?

The answer is no. In Ferlini, the ECJ stated that Article 12 forbids private organisations from discriminating against nationals of other Member States. In Angonese[46] it extended this to private persons. Thus, providers are not allowed to charge foreigners fees that are higher than those applicable to members of their national social security scheme[47]. The criterion of affiliation to the national social security scheme, on which the differentiation of fees for medical and hospital care is based, constitutes indirect discrimination on the ground of nationality. Such differentiation could be justified only if it were based on objective considerations that were independent of the nationality of the persons concerned and proportionate to the objective legitimately pursued. A medical provider therefore has to apply the same tariffs to a person who is not affiliated to the national social security scheme as someone

---

[46]   ECJ, case C-281/98, *Angonese*, ECR [2000] I-4139, see further.

[47]   ECJ, case C-411/98, *Ferlini*, ECR [2000] I-8081.

affiliated to the scheme. However, it may be very difficult for the person concerned to prove that he or she is discriminated against.

Although both systems exist next to each other, one has to accept that this can cause administrative as well as judicial problems (see Eichenhofer, 1999: 117-122; Langer, 1999: 537-542). The Kohll and Decker procedure would be more difficult as one has to check the services provided abroad, identify them according to their own nomenclature and apply tariffs on the basis of the applicable legislation. It will be necessary to put services abroad into the same category as a service contained in the national list and then to apply an analogous charge, which will lead to administrative uncertainties.

People argue that this opens the way to abuse. If no permission is granted under Article 22 or if the urgent need is rejected, one can always fall back on the Kohll and Decker procedure. Some people wonder why one should still ask for an E112 form. On the other hand, however, abuse can never be avoided and that under Regulation 1408/71 the procedure of Article 22 was not always used for the purpose for which it was intended.

As the two methods have a different reimbursement tariff, the patient's choice of which procedure should be applied could be based on where he or she will receive the cheapest treatment, *i.e.* the best tariffs of reimbursement. If a person knows in advance which procedure is better, he could apply the Vanbraekel procedure directly.

This was made clear in the Vanbraekel case, where the relation between Article 22 of EC Regulation 1408/71 and the Treaty Provision of Article 59 (now Article 49) was examined.

The first question was whether, when a person who has requested authorisation on the basis of Article 22(1c) of Regulation 1408/71 has been refused by the competent institution and it is subsequently established that that refusal was unfounded, the reimbursement by the competent institution of the costs of the treatment should be made according to the relevant rules in force in the Member State in which the person concerned is insured or according to those laid down in the legislation of the Member State on whose territory the treatment was provided? According to Article 22 someone has a right to medical care according to the legislation of the Member State in which the treatment is given, while the competent institution remains responsible for subsequently reimbursing the institution of the place of stay, as provided for in Article 36 (now Article 30) of Regulation 1408/71. Both the practical effect and the spirit of those provisions require, moreover, that when the request of an insured person for authorisation on the basis of Article 22(1c) of Regulation 1408/71 has been refused by the competent institution and it is subsequently established, either by the competent institution itself or by a court decision, that refusal was unfounded, that person is entitled to be reimbursed directly by the competent institution by an amount equivalent to what would ordinarily have applied if authorisation had been properly granted in the first place. As, however, the amount reimbursable under the competent system is higher than the amount payable under the system where the benefits have been provided, the question arises whether the plaintiffs can also claim extra reimbursement to cover the difference between these two systems. As Article 22 of that Regulation is not intended to regulate any reimbursement at the tariffs in force in the Member State of registration, it does not have the effect of preventing or prescribing payment by that State of additional reimbursement covering the difference between the system of cover laid down by the legislation of that State and the system applied by the Member State of treatment, where the former is more advantageous than the latter and such reimbursement is provided for by the legislation of the Member State of registration[48].

There is no doubt that the fact that a person has a lower level of cover when he or she receives hospital treatment in another Member State than when he or she undergoes the same treatment in the Member State in which he or she is insured may deter, or even prevent, that person from applying to providers of medical services established in other Member States and constitutes, both for insured persons and for service providers, a barrier to freedom to provide services.

Is there any justification for this restriction? As the person concerned was in fact entitled to obtain the authorisation, it cannot be claimed that payment of additional reimbursement, would be liable to jeopardise the maintenance, in the Member State of registration, of a balanced hospital service open to all or the maintenance of treatment capacity or medical competence on national territory. Furthermore, since such additional reimbursement does not in theory impose any additional financial burden on the sickness insurance scheme of that State by comparison with the reimbursement to be made if hospital treatment had been provided in that latter State, it cannot be argued that making that sickness fund bear such additional reimbursement would be liable to have a significant effect on the financing of the social security system. Article 59 (now Article 49) of the EC Treaty is to be interpreted as meaning that, if the reimbursement of costs incurred on hospital services provided in a Member State of stay, calculated under the rules in force in that State, is less than the amount which application of the legislation in force in the Member State of registration would afford to a person receiving hospital

---

[48]   ECJ, case C-368/98, *Vanbraekel*, ECR [2001] I-5363, paragraphs 31-37.

treatment in that State, additional reimbursement covering that difference must be granted to the insured person by the competent institution[49]. Article 36 of Regulation 1408/71 cannot be interpreted as meaning that it follows from that provision that a covered person who has requested authorisation on the basis of Article 22(1c) of that Regulation and been refused by the competent institution is entitled to reimbursement of all the medical costs incurred in the Member State in which treatment was received once it is established that the rejection of his or her request for authorisation was unfounded.

In case the amount reimbursable under the competent State is higher than the amount payable under the system where the benefits have been provided, the person concerned can claim extra reimbursement. On the other hand, the person concerned is not allowed to enrich himself by asking for reimbursement according to the tariffs in the competent State of a product or treatment that is cheaper abroad. In our opinion, it seems that the competent institution is not obliged to apply its tariffs in an unlimited way. Reimbursement will be limited to the actual cost paid abroad. The wording of the Court of Justice justifies the conclusion that this reasoning of the differential amount applies to all health care systems and that it is not limited to restitution schemes.

The application of the Kohll and Decker procedure as a method of cross-border medical care has another advantage with regard to the Regulations.

With the principle of free movement of goods as well as the principle of free movement of services, the nationality of the recipient is irrelevant. In this respect, third country nationals who are insured in a Member State can in principle benefit from the Court's rulings. Until now, third country nationals have been excluded from the personal field of application of EC Regulation 1408/71. However, this will change in due course. Only very recently, on 3 June 2002, the Employment and Social Policy Council agreed to extend the personal field of application of the EC Regulation to third country nationals[50].

B. Modifications of EC Regulation 1408/71

Some proposals were made to change the Regulation radically. The most radical one was proposed by Professor Eichenhofer who combines the best options under the two systems: reimbursement according to the tariffs of the country where treatment was provided and the right to obtain abroad all the medical services one can obtain in the competent

---

[49] ECJ, case C-368/98, *Vanbraekel*, ECR [2001] I-5363, paragraphs 45-53.
[50] Not yet in force, August 2002.

State (Eichenhofer, 1999: 117-122). His idea is to change Article 22 of EC Regulation 1408/71 in such a way that everybody has the right to the medical care one is offered in the home State while in any other State, and be reimbursed according to the tariffs of the country where treatment has been given.

However, this solution disregards political reality. As the Court pointed out, Member States can determine how to structure their national social security system and financial concerns could limit the reimbursement of benefits obtained abroad. If States have to refund all that is provided abroad according to the tariffs of the State where treatment was given, they risk financial problems. This would be very problematic, particularly for the candidate States.

As the two methods exist next to each other and there is no possibility to order them in a hierarchical way, we believe that there is no need to change the EC Regulation[51]. As pointed out earlier, the case law is based on the principles of free movement. Consequently, criteria for cross-border medical care should be examined further and set out in, for example, a Communication and later a Directive. It is important to emphasise what was said earlier. Even when reference is made to the case law of the ECJ in newly adapted provisions of the EC Regulation 1408/71, it cannot be excluded that the Court will, in future, grant greater rights to the citizen. It should not be forgotten that the court made clear that EC Regulation 1408/71 is not the only means of cross-border care and that each system has its advantages. It is important to stress this.

However, as confusion can arise and people have to be informed about their rights, a declaratory modification could be made by pointing out, for example, that the Regulations will apply, notwithstanding rights obtained under the free movement of goods and services (see also Langer, 1999: 537-542). Clarification is needed. This is different from

---

[51] An exception has to be made with respect to Article 19 of Regulation 574/72 which foresees that in the case of frontier workers or members of their families, medicinal products, bandages, spectacles and small appliances may be issued, and laboratory analyses and tests carried out, only in the territory of the Member State in which they were prescribed, in accordance with the provisions of the legislation of that Member State, except where the legislation administered by the competent institution or an agreement concluded between the Member States concerned or the competent authorities of those Member States is more favourable. This article cannot be applied anymore after the case-law of the Court. Frontier workers can now choose on which side of the border they wish to obtain medical products. On the basis of Regulation 1408/71 (Article 20) alone, they had already that right. Article 19 of Regulation 574/72 limited this to a certain extent for medical products. It is clear after the Case Law of the Court that measures which should limit this right for frontier workers would be hardly acceptable.

modification. It could, for example, be pointed out that the authorisation by the competent institution has to be made on the basis of objective, non-discriminatory criteria known in advance. Abolishing the authorisation procedure altogether goes too far as it could still be advantageous for the person concerned to obtain prior permission.

Figure 4.1: Schematic Overview

Emergency care
Article 22, Regulation 1408/71

Non-emergency care

1. Prior authorisation given

   → Article 22, Regulation 1408/71

   → amount payable under competent state > amount payable under system where benefits have been provided: Payment of difference (Vanbraekel)

2. No Prior authorisation given or applied for. Benefits covered by insurance package ?

   YES
   ↳ existence of waiting lists ?

   ┌→ NO → Kohll/Decker
   └→ YES → Authorisation must be given: Article 22, Regulation 1408/71

   NO
   ↳ objective criteria/ medically normal (international standard) ?

   ┌→ YES → No treatment abroad
   └→ NO → Kohll/Decker

IX. Organisation of Health Care Systems after the Case-law of the Court of Justice

The choice of how to organise health services cannot undermine the application of the fundamental freedoms. Although it is up to the Member States to organise their own social security systems, both those that use a reimbursement system and those that provide benefits-in-kind or national health services will increasingly have to take into account ECJ case law and the effects of the fundamental freedoms. In the first place, systems will have to adapt to the principle of passive free movement of services and patients as guaranteed by EU law.

Sickness funds that do not offer reimbursement will have to understand that they must also finance medical services provided abroad and, when erroneously refused, the beneficiary has the right to be reimbursed. This by no means implies that countries with a benefits-in-kind or national health systems will have to turn their system into one based on reimbursement. But it also does not mean that if there is no reimbursement within the State, there should be no reimbursement outside its borders. This argument is wrong and the solution is a combined model with reimbursement for benefits provided abroad. This should not pose any problems for systems that already apply the reimbursement principle in some areas so only have to extend this system to benefits abroad (Jorens, 1999: 25).

The ECJ considers that the practical problems that could arise are no grounds for exemption from EU law. The argument that the providers of health services in the home country are subject to legal rules guaranteeing the quality of these services as well as their financial viability is, as pointed out by the Court, no reason to limit the reimbursement of benefits to providers in the competent State.

Although there is no need to change the national health system, pressure on systems cannot be ignored. The cases have shown that a patient is entitled to choose a doctor when he or she goes abroad, but that he will have not this right when he stays in his country. It is true that Community law is not applicable to purely internal matters, but national restrictions will come under increasing pressure. Previously we referred to similarities with the Bosman Case. Although European Community law would not affect restrictions on transfers in one country, as this is a purely internal matter, within country restrictions are no longer susceptible.

Member States have to adapt their system to take into account the passive right to free movement of services, but also to open their system to foreign medical providers. The Court made clear that, although Member States retain their competence in building their health system and may make the provision of types of care dependent on certain conditions, the criteria they use must be objective and non-discriminatory, without reference to the place of establishment of the service provider. This also has consequences for the scope of care included in the social protection scheme. European Community law requires that there may not be any discrimination, of a direct or indirect nature, against service providers on the basis of nationality or place of establishment, except where this is legitimately justified (Palm *et al.*, 2000: 121-130).

This implies that a Member State, when deciding with whom to sign contracts, may not discriminate against providers from other Member States and the criteria for evaluating applicants for contracts must be objective and must not discriminate (Palm *et al.*, 2000: 125-127).

Nationality or place of establishment does not preclude a foreign provider from signing a contract with the sickness institutions of another State.

This is most likely to arise in border regions, where different models have emerged involving agreements between sickness funds in one State and medical providers in another. Certainly, foreign medical providers will now be affected by quality standards in another State. In this respect EC law forbids application of quality standards other than those applicable to their own providers.

If more cross-border medical care emerges on the basis of the Community freedoms, it could lead to European standards on quality and prices[52], making these more transparent and aligning them[53]. The existing models in the border regions and the examples in Euregios play an important role in this respect. This would fit with the open co-ordination method of the European Union that aims to maintain and, where necessary, develop a high-quality health care system geared to the evolving needs of the population.

X. Private Health Care Insurance Contracts

The question could also arise as to whether the case law also has consequences for private health insurance contracts. Are restrictions in these contracts for reimbursement of medical care within the European Union still allowed?

Although these insurance contracts are private agreements between an insured person and an insurance company, the case law must also be applied.

It is now established that the fundamental freedoms have a horizontal effect and that private persons may not infringe the fundamental freedoms. Prohibition of discrimination must be regarded as applying to

---

[52] In Germany *e.g.*, contrary to some other Member States, the investment costs of hospitals are paid from taxes and are not reflected in the daily in-patient accommodation charge. Patients insured in another Member State who take up benefits in German hospitals will not – as they only pay the daily in-patient accommodation charge – have to participate in the investment costs of German hospitals. In cases where German insured people were to go a country where the investment costs are reflected in the daily in-patient accommodation charge, German sickness insurance funds which have to reimburse costs of medical treatment in hospitals abroad, would indirectly contribute to the investment costs in this country.

[53] For an overview of these cross-border activities and problems: see Pitchas (forthcoming) and Schirmer (forthcoming).

private persons[54]. Private measures that impede economic activities are forbidden. This also applies to forms of direct and indirect discrimination. However, individuals, just as States, can argue justification for restricting free movement[55]. Nevertheless, it is likely that private persons will find this difficult.

Conclusions

Health care has always been considered as within the national competence of Member States and has always been looked at from the supply side (Berghman, 1999: 69) where responsibility is taken for budgetary balance. A patient was never allowed to decide whether he or she could seek the best medical treatment abroad. Almost 25 years ago, the Court of Justice made clear, in the Pierik case, that under Regulation 1408/71 insured people would have the right to look for better treatment across borders. Member States did not accept this and changed the Regulation accordingly. Subsequently the Court has made clear that cross-border medical care is required by the fundamental freedoms. Patients now have the possibility to decide by themselves if they want to move abroad for health care. The purchase of health care across borders will increase, and in this respect these judgements can be considered as a milestone in the case law of the Court. However, they are definitively not the stone that will cause an avalanche to destroy the entire social security system. They have to be seen as a contribution to further European co-operation in the health care sector. Further alignment of regulations in the context of further development of a European Health Market is an enormous opportunity that will benefit not providers but also the insured people, in other words the citizens of Europe.

Bibliography

PALM, W., NICKLESS, J., LEWALLE, H. and COHEUR, A. (2000), "Implications of Recent Jurisprudence on the Co-ordination of Health Care Protection Systems", Report produced for the European Commission, Directorate-General for Employment and Social Affairs, Association Internationale de la Mutualité, Brussels, May 2000 (www.aim-mutual.org).

BECKER, U. (forthcoming), "De gevolgen van de arresten Decker en Kohll van het Europees Hof van Justitie voor de wettelijke ziektekostenverzekering in Duitsland" in JORENS, Y. and SCHULTE, B. (eds.), *Grensoverschrijdende gezondheidszorg in*

---

[54] ECJ, case C-281/98, *Angonese*, ECR [2000] I-4139, paragraph 36, see also ECJ, case C-36/74, *Walrave and Koch*, ECR [1974] I-1405 and ECJ, case C-415/93, *Bosman*, ECR [1995] 4921.

[55] ECJ, case C-415/93, *Bosman*, ECR [1995] 4921, paragraph 86.

Europa/ Grenzüberschreitende Gesundheitsversorgung in Europa, Die Keure, Nomos, forthcoming.

BERGHMAN, J. (1999), "Concluding Observations", International Symposium "Health Care without Frontiers within the European Union", Ministry of Social Security of the Grand Duchy of Luxembourg, Association Internationale de la Mutualité, European Institute of Social Security, Luxembourg.

CORNELISSEN, R. (1997), " 25ème anniversaire du Règlement (CEE) n° 1408/71, ses résultats et ses limites", Paper for the European Colloquium "25 Années du Règlement (CEE) n° 1408/71 sur la sécurité sociale des travailleurs migrants", Office National de la Sécurité sociale de Suède and Commission européenne, Stockholm, pp. 25-70.

COUNCIL OF THE EUROPEAN COMMUNITIES (1992), Council Directive 92/51/EEC of 18 June 1992 on a second general system for the recognition of professional education and training to supplement Directive 89/48/EEC, OJ L 209, 24 July 1992, pp. 0025-0045.

COUNCIL OF THE EUROPEAN UNION (1996), Council Regulation 118/97/EC of 2 December 1996 amending and updating Regulation 1408/71/EEC on the application of social security schemes to employed persons, to self-employed persons and to members of their families moving within the Community and Regulation 574/72/EEC laying down the procedure for implementing Regulation 1408/71/EEC, OJ L 28, 30 January 1997, pp. 0001-0229.

DE BUYSER, J. (1997), "Grensoverschrijdende gezondheidszorg" in JORENS, Y. (ed.), *Grensarbeid: sociaalrechtelijke en fiscaalrechtelijke aspecten*, Die Keure, Brugge, pp. 127-159.

DU PRÉ (1998), "Het EG-Verdrag door een ziekenfondsbrilletje", *Sociaal Maandblad Arbeid*, No. 9, pp. 364-376.

EICHENHOFER, E. (1999), "Der Europäische koordinierende Krankenversicherungs-recht nach den EuGH-Urteilen Kohll und Decker", *Vierteljahresschrift für Sozialrecht*, No. 2, pp. 101-122.

EUROPEAN COMMISSION (1998), Proposal for a Council Regulation (EC) on coordi-nation of social security systems, COM (1998) 779 final of 21 December 1998.

JORENS, Y. (1992), *Wegwijs in het Europese sociale zekerheidsrecht*, Die Keure, Brugge.

JORENS, Y. (1997), "Grensarbeid: algemene situering en probleemstelling", in JORENS, Y. (ed.), *Grensarbeid: sociaalrechtelijke en fiscaalrechtelijke aspecten*, Die Keure, Brugge, pp. 1-33.

JORENS, Y. (1999), "De betekenis van de arresten Decker en Kohll in een Sociaal Europa/L'importance des Arrêts Decker et Kohll dans une Europe Sociale", Grensoverschrijdende gezondheidszorg in de Euregios: uitdaging of bedreiging/ Soins de Santé transfrontaliers dans les Eurégios: un Défi ou une Menace, Europees Seminarie/Séminaire européen, Verslagboek/Procès-Verbal, Alden Biesen.

JORENS, Y. and SCHULTE, B. (2000), *European Report*, "European Observatory for the Social Security of Migrant Workers", DG Employment and Social Affairs, European Commission, Brussels.

Yves Jorens

JORENS, Y. and SCHULTE, B. (forthcoming), *Grensoverschrijdende gezondheidszorg in Europa/Grenzüberschreitende Gesundheitsversorgung in Europa*, Die Keure, Nomos, forthcoming.

LANGER, R. (1999), "Grenzüberschreitende Behandlungsleistungen- Reformbedraf für die Verordnung 1408/71", *Neue Zeitschrift für Sozialrecht*, No. 11, pp. 537-542.

LUGTENBERG, A. (forthcoming), "De arresten Decker en Kohll vanuit het Nederlandse standpunt", in JORENS, Y. and SCHULTE, B. (eds.), *Grensoverschrijdende gezondheidszorg in Europa/Grenzüberschreitende Gesundheitsversorgung in Europa*, Die Keure, Nomos, forthcoming.

MAVRIDIS, P. (1996), "Le citoyen européen peut-il se faire soigner dans l'État de son choix?", Droit Social, No. 12, décembre 1996, pp. 1086-1094.

MONTAGNIE, Y. (forthcoming), "De arresten Decker en Kohll in het licht van de rechtspraak van het Hof van Justitie van de EG", in JORENS, Y. and SCHULTE, B. (eds.), *Grensoverschrijdende gezondheidszorg in Europa/Grenzüberschreitende Gesundheitsversorgung in Europa*, Die Keure, Nomos, forthcoming.

NOVAK, M. (1998), "EG-Grundfreiheiten und Europäisches Sozialrecht", *Europäische Zeitschrift für Wirtschaftsrecht*, Vol. 9, No. 12, pp. 366-369.

PITCHAS, R. (forthcoming), "Grensoverschrijdende gezondheidszorg in Europa: De verbinding van zorgberoepen en de sociale verzekering in het Europese Gemeenschapsrecht ter veiligstelling van de kwaliteit", in JORENS, Y. and SCHULTE, B. (eds.), *Grensoverschrijdende gezondheidszorg in Europa/Grenzüberschreitende Gesundheitsversorgung in Europa*, Die Keure, Nomos, forthcoming.

SCHIRMER, H. (forthcoming), "Juridische mogelijkheden inzake de verstrekking van grensoverschrijdende medische diensten", in JORENS, Y. en SCHULTE, B. (eds.), *Grensoverschrijdende gezondheidszorg in Europa/Grenzüberschreitende Gesundheitsversorgung in Europa*, Die Keure, Nomos, forthcoming.

STIEMER, N. (1999), "Sickness Insurance viewpoint of the EU Member States", in JORENS, Y. and SCHULTE, B. (eds.), *Coordination of social security schemes in connection with the Accession of Central and Eastern European States*, "The Riga Conference", die Keure, Brugge, pp. 227-253.

VAN DER MEI, A. P. (2001), "Free Movement of Persons within the European Community, Cross-border Access to Public Benefits", Doctoral Thesis, Maastricht.

ZECHEL, S. (1995), *Die territorial begrenzte Leistungserbringung der Krankenkassen im Lichte des EG-Vertrages*, Erich Schmidt Verlag, Berlin.

CHAPTER 5

Do the Rules on Internal Market Affect National Health Care Systems?

Vassilis G. HATZOPOULOS

I. Do Health Care Services Form Part of the Internal Market?

In order to determine the extent to which EC law may affect health care services, it is important to ascertain the competences of the Community in this field. It is striking that, despite the existence within the Treaty of a specific provision stating that health care services fall within the exclusive competence of Member States, several instruments of secondary legislation interfere, indirectly but substantially, with this reserved domain. More importantly, there are fundamental Treaty rules that may be, and indeed, are, interpreted in a way as to affect national health care policies.

Starting from the Treaty, we find that the Title XIII entitled "Public Health" has been included in the Treaty only in its revision signed in Amsterdam in 1997. This new Title consists of a single Article (Article 152) and only provides for co-operation and some sort of co-ordination "supplementing" action by Member States[1]. Common action is to be pursued mainly in the field of relations with third countries and in the establishment of common standards. Community institutions may only intervene by using instruments of undetermined binding force, such as "measures" or "recommendations". Moreover, it is clearly stated in the concluding paragraph of this Treaty provision that "Community action in the field of public health should fully respect the responsibilities of the Member States for the organisation and delivery of health services and medical care". Hence, the Treaty only recognises limited competence by the Community in the field of health.

Within the Treaty there is one more provision acknowledging direct Community competence in the field of health, Article 137. This provi-

---

[1] Article 152 EC as it now stands is an unhappy "amelioration" of ex Article 129, introduced by the Maastricht Treaty.

sion, which is part of the Title XI, on social policy, is a quite limited "legal basis", since it only allows for action which supports or completes that by Member States, specifically as regards the "improvement of the working environment to protect workers". Community action in this field may, however, be pursued by means of binding measures, *i.e.* Directives issued by the Council.

These two Treaty provisions are very limited in scope, recognise the precedence of national over Community policy in the field of health care services and, to top it all, contain an express reservation of competence in favour of the States. There is no way in which they may account for any actual impact of EC law on national health care systems.

Instead, secondary legislation, dating back to the early 1960s, directly or indirectly touches on the way national health care systems are organised. These texts, mainly Directives and Regulations, have been adopted in pursuit of free movement of workers, free provision of services and freedom of establishment. Their legal basis is to be found in Title III of the Treaty (Articles 39 ff.), occasionally strengthened by Article 308 (ex 235). They have been provided for by the General Programmes[2] and may be classified into two broad categories: on the one hand, instruments that aim to ensure that workers moving within the Community continue to receive social and health care benefits and, on the other hand, that ensure mutual recognition of diplomas and other qualifications necessary for cross-border provision of health care services.

In the first category the main text is Regulation 1408/71[3]. This Regulation is an early and, hence, limited attempt by the Community Institutions to comply with their obligations under Article 42 (ex 51) of the Treaty. It falls sort of achieving any degree of harmonisation and limits its ambit to the co-ordination of basic national rules on the field of social and welfare benefits[4]. The Regulation follows the principle, confirmed repeatedly by the Court[5], that social security remains reserved to the competence of Member States. It therefore does not touch the core of national rules but only establishes some degree of co-ordination, so that fundamentally different systems may work together in order to secure minimal social and health care benefits.

---

[2] Programmes of the 18 December 1961, OJ (1962) L 62/32 and 62/36.

[3] Council Regulation 1408/71/EEC, best seen in the amended and updated Council Regulation 118/97/EC (Council of the European Union, 1996).

[4] On the qualification of this regulation as an instrument of co-ordination rather than as a means of harmonisation see the first recitals of the Regulation.

[5] Clearly in joined cases C-159/91 and C-160/91, *Poucet and Pistre*, ECR [1993] I-637 and constantly thereafter.

The provisions of the Regulation that are more specifically concerned with health care services are Articles 22 and 36. The basic mechanism established by these provisions is that any person wishing to receive health care services in another Member State has to obtain an authorisation by the competent fund in his or her home State, except for emergencies; once this authorisation is given the beneficiary is entitled to benefits-in-kind and/or reimbursement of the costs incurred[6].

In the second category of measures, aiming at the free movement of health professionals, the movement of six health professions has been harmonised extensively, while other professions fall under the catch-all umbrella of the "general systems" for the recognition of professional qualifications[7]. For the six main professions the method used is that of substantial harmonisation[8], based on pairs of Directives, whereby the first Directive harmonises the content, duration etc. of studies, while the second establishes the equivalence between diplomas or qualifications thus obtained. The harmonised professions are, in chronological order: physicians and, specifically general practitioners and specialists[9], nurses (Council of the European Communities, 1977a and b), dentists (Council of the European Communities, 1978a and b), veterinary surgeons (Council of the European Communities, 1978c and d), midwives (Council of the European Communities, 1980a and b) and pharmacists (Council of the European Communities, 1985a and b). Professionals who have obtained their qualifications in accordance with the harmonisation Directives may freely exercise their profession in any Member State, paying due respect to local professional rules.

---

[6]   For more extensive developments on the scope and application of these provisions, see *infra*, paragraphs 2 and 3.

[7]   Mainly Council Directive 89/48/EEC (Council of the European Communities, 1989), as completed by the Council Directive 92/51/EC (Council of the European Communities, 1992a).

[8]   Although described as "partial" or "minimal" within the texts of the Directives, subsequent experience showed that the degree of harmonisation achieved in these Directives is the highest ever achieved on the recognition of professional qualifications. It is significant to note that only the health professions have been regulated by pairs of Directives, while other profession-specific harmonisation (*i.e.* for Lawyers and Architects) has been restricted to single Directives. See for the various techniques and the different degrees of harmonisation, Hatzopoulos (1999: 327 ff.).

[9]   Initially regulated by Directives 75/362/EEC and 75/363/EEC (Council of the European Communities, 1975 a and b). These Directives have been modified by Directive 86/457/EEC (Council of the European Communities, 1986). The two directives and their modifications have been consolidated (and thus replaced) by Directive 93/16/EC (Council of the European Union, 1993a), which, in its turn, has been modified by Directive 97/50/EC (European Parliament and Council of the European Union, 1997) and Directive 98/63/EC (European Commission, 1998).

It is interesting to note that out of a total of eight professions whose exercise is harmonised, six concern health services; the other two concern lawyers and architects.

Professions not directly covered by these Directives fall, in principle, within the scope of the two "General Systems"[10]. The General Systems do not provide for any harmonisation of the conditions leading to the degrees or diplomas concerned. Instead, they establish a system of mutual recognition, whereby professionals may validate studies and professional experience acquired anywhere within the Community, in order to work in any other Member State.

In the rare cases where a profession is not covered by the specific Directives or by the General Systems, then the general principle of equivalence and mutual recognition, as implemented by the European Court of Justice (ECJ), offers the minimal guarantee that the qualifications and experience of the interested person will be given due consideration by the authorities of the host Member State[11].

It follows from the above that, notwithstanding the fact that the Community lacks the competence to intervene directly in the field of health care services, there are a number of specific measures that either co-ordinate or harmonise aspects of the administration of such services. However, the central question arising from this, and in the light of recent judgements by the ECJ, is the extent to which the general Treaty provisions on the Internal Market affect, by their direct effect, the provision of health care services. Thus, this chapter will examine thoroughly the rules on free movement of services and of freedom of establishment.

II. The Direct Application of the Treaty Provisions on Free Movement

Are health services "services" within the meaning of the Treaty? Ever since the judgement of the Court in the Luisi and Carbone case[12] health services are deemed to fall within the ambit of the "fundamental

---

[10] For more extensive developments on the scope and application of these provisions, see *infra*, paragraphs 2 and 3.

[11] See the leading case on this matter C-340/89, *Vlassopoulou*, ECR [1991] I-2357. On the creation and the application of the principle of equivalence and mutual recognition by the judge, see Hatzopoulos (1999: 114, Section I: "Instauration et application, par le juge, du principe d'équivalence et de reconnaissance mutuelle").

[12] Joined cases C-286/82 and C-26/83, *Luisi and Carbone*, ECR [1984] 377, paragraph 16.

freedoms". In this early case[13] the Court recognised, for the first time, not only that cross-border provision of health services is governed by Articles 49 ff. (then 59 ff.), but also that recipients of such services have the same rights as providers thereof. This was a breakthrough case and therefore it did not go into much detail. Subsequently, the Court in the Grogan case reiterated the finding that health services do fall within the ambit of Article 49 EC[14]. However, this case did not provide any further clarification on the issue, since the relevant Treaty provision was found inapplicable on the facts before the Court, due to the lack of an economic link between the students invoking Article 49 EC and the hospitals offering the contested health services.

Then came the Kohll case[15], sending shivers through all social security and health care funds[16]. In this case, the Court, following the view of Advocate General Tesauro, made it clear that Articles 49 ff. do apply to health services, even when they are provided in the context of a social security scheme. Or, as the Court put it: "the special nature of certain services does not remove them from the ambit of the funda-mental principle of freedom of movement" (paragraph 20 of the judge-ment)[17]. Moreover, the Court ruled that ensuing obligations might be comparable to the ones already stipulated by Regulation 1408/71[18].

Kohll was delivered the same day and based on the same opinion by Mr. Tesauro as the judgement in Decker[19]. In Decker the Court affirmed that national security and health care schemes should also respect Article 28 (ex 30) EC on free movement of goods. This case confirmed

---

[13] This is an "early" case in the field of services which, contrary to the case law of the Court in the field of goods, only developed considerably during the last decade, starting with the "tourist guide cases" C-154/89, C-180/89 and C-198/89, respec-tively *Commission* v. *France, Italy and Greece*, ECR [1991] I-659 ff., the "TV cases", C-260/89, *ERT*, ECR [1991] I-2925, C-288/89, *Gouda*, ECR [1991] I-4007 and C-353/89, *Commission v. The Netherlands, mediawet*, ECR I-4069 and, most importantly, Case C-76/90, *Säger*, ECR [1991] I-4221. For a comprehensive overview of this agitated field of the case law of the ECJ, *cf.* Hatzopoulos (2000).

[14] ECJ, case C-159/90, *Society for the Protection of Unborn Children Ireland*, ECR [1991] I-4685, paragraph 18.

[15] ECJ, case C-158/96, *Kohll*, ECR [1998] I-1931.

[16] For some comments of this case, see Mavridis (1988); Van Raepenbusch (1988) and Huglo (1988).

[17] This passage of the judgement has been repeatedly cited by the Court in its more recent judgements, see the developments further down in this paragraph.

[18] Council Regulation 1408/71/EEC, best seen in the amended and updated Council Regulation 118/97/EC (Council of the European Union, 1996). On the relationship between this Regulation and the Treaty rules, see below.

[19] ECJ, case C-120/95, *Decker*, ECR [1998] I-1831.

and extended the rule already established in the Duphar case[20]. Therefore, it would seem that Kohll is the logical transposition, to the field of services, of the Duphar/Decker case law, in accordance with the findings of the Court in Luisi and Carbone and Grogan[21].

This view is not, however, uncontroversial. In the meantime the Court, in two judgements, seemed to shift to the opposite direction. Hence, in the joined cases Poucet and Pistre[22] the Court, in the midst of great controversy, found that social security funds are not subject to the Treaty rules on competition. Four years later, in the Sodemare case[23], the Court ruled that the Italian measure that excluded profit-making health care providers from the national social security system was compatible with the rules on the internal market (mainly Articles 43 and 48, then 52 and 58 EC). This measure clearly restricted freedom of establishment but, in view "of the powers [the State] retains to organise its social security system" (paragraph 32 of the judgement) the Court upheld it merely because it did not discriminate on the basis of the place of establishment of the health care operators (paragraph 33 of the judgement).

Thus, it seemed that the core of social security schemes would enjoy a derogation to the application of the Treaty rules[24]. This view was further strengthened by three judgements of the same date rendered by the plenary Court in cases Albany, Brentjens and Drijvende[25]. In all these cases the Court held in identical terms that "agreements concluded in the context of collective negotiations between management and labour in pursuit of such objectives must, by virtue of their *nature* and *purpose*, be regarded as falling outside the scope of Article 85(1) [now 81(1)] of the Treaty"[26]. These three judgements were given some months after the judgement of the Court in Kohll and Decker, so it became unclear whether the effect of latter rulings had been changed. Moreover, the judgement in Kohll concerned medical treatment offered

---

20 ECJ, case C-238/82, *Duphar*, ECR [1984] 523.
21 All cases cited above.
22 ECJ, joined cases C-159/91 and C-160/91, *Poucet and Pistre*, ECR [1993] I-637.
23 ECJ, case C-70/95, *Sodemare*, ECR [1997] I-3395. In the meantime some uncertainty had been created by the judgement of the Court in the FFSA, case C-244/94, ECR [1995] I-4013.
24 The judgement of the Court in FFSA made it clear that the very notion of social security schemes would be strictly interpreted.
25 ECJ, case C-67/96, *Albany*, ECR [1999] I-5751, joined cases C-115/97 to C-117/97, *Brentjens*, ECR [1999] I-6025 and case C-219/97, *Drijvende*, ECR [1999] I-6121, respectively. On these three cases, see Idot (1999).
26 ECJ, case C-67/96, *Albany*, ECR [1999] I-5751, paragraph 60, emphasis added.

by a dentist acting alone, while it remained unclear whether it extended to treatment offered in a hospital infrastructure[27].

It is against this background that the plenary Court with its twin "summer" judgements in cases Vanbraekel[28] and Geraets[29], confirmed and extended the ambit of the Kohll judgement.

Do health services provided in the context of a social security scheme constitute "economic activities" in the sense of Articles 49-50? The Vanbraekel case concerned a Belgian lady seeking reimbursement from her social security fund for treatment received in a French hospital. According to Article 22(1) and (2) of Regulation 1408/71, any person who has obtained prior authorisation by their institution to receive treatment in another Member State is entitled to do so "as though he were insured with [the competent institution of this State]". This means that, if treatment is not provided for free and the patient has to pay medical expenses, he or she may recover them in accordance with the tariffs applicable in the State of the treatment.

However, in the case under discussion, benefits provided for by the French (host) legislation were lower than those offered by the Belgian fund for treatment obtained in Belgium. The question thus arose as to whether Regulation 1408/71 entitled beneficiaries to recover the higher benefits stipulated by the legislation in their home State or if any refund was limited to the level stipulated for by the host State legislation.

In the Geraets case the very requirement of prior authorisation, as implemented by the Dutch legislation, was challenged under the Treaty rules on services. Under the Dutch social security scheme, patients are treated for free by care providers, mostly Dutch, who have reached an agreement with the social security fund. Authorisation to be treated by a care provider with whom no agreement has been reached is only given by the fund if two conditions are met: the treatment for which authorisation is required should be considered as "*normal* in the professional circles concerned" and it should be *necessary* – both in terms of time and of quality – for the particular patient. In the light of the Kohll and Decker case law the question arose as to whether such a requirement of prior authorisation was compatible with the Treaty rules on services.

In both cases, some of the ten intervening Governments argued that the Treaty rules on services did not apply precisely because health care services provided in the context of a social security scheme do not fall

---

27 Paragraph 11 of Advocate General's Saggio opinion of 18 May 2000, in ECJ, case C-368/98, *Vanbraekel*, ECR [2001] I-5363

28 ECJ, case C-368/98, *Vanbraekel*, ECR [2001] I-5363.

29 ECJ, case C-157/99, *Geraets-Smits and Peerbooms*, ECR [2001] I-5473.

within the ambit of Article 49 EC, because they are not remunerated. Advocate General Saggio in his opinion in Vanbraekel (paragraphs 17-23 of the opinion) and Advocate General Colomer in his opinion in Geraets (paragraphs 35-45 of the opinion) adopted the same point of view.

The Advocates General first drew a distinction between, on the one hand, social security systems where patients are treated for free by care providers contracted by the social security fund (as was the case in the Netherlands) and, on the other hand, systems where the patient goes to the practitioner of his or her choice and is then entitled to refund (as was the case in Luxembourg). Therefore, the cases under discussion were distinguished *prima facie* from the judgements in Decker and Kohll.

Thereafter, both Mr. Saggio and Mr. Colomer focused on health care benefits offered and examined whether the element of remuneration, conditioning the applicability of Articles 49 ff. EC, is present. They both concluded in the negative. Mr. Colomer, recalling the judgement of the Court in Bond van Adverteeders[30], reasoned on the basis of a tri-partite relationship, whereby services offered by care providers to patients were paid for by a third party, the social security fund. Then he examined to what extent money transfers from the fund to care providers did indeed constitute consideration for the services provided. He found that the amount paid by the fund for each treatment offered by care providers was calculated by reference to a number of factors not directly related to the treatment itself and according to an abstract mathematical formula. He also found that some money transfers were made, even in the absence of treatment effectively offered, in order to secure the financial needs of practitioners and hospitals. Therefore, relying on the judgement in Humbel[31], where the Court had held that the national education system stands outside the scope of Article 50 (then 60) EC and that the eventual payment of registration fees does not constitute remuneration, the Advocate General concluded that health care services offered for free to patients do not qualify as "services" under the relevant Treaty rules. Mr. Colomer did not draw any distinction between services offered in hospitals and those offered by private practitioners. Mr. Saggio, on the other hand, followed a parallel reasoning, but focused on health care services offered within a hospital infrastructure. He concluded that such services fall outside the scope of Articles 49 ff. because "first, [they] form an integral part of the national health system,

---

[30] ECJ, case C-352/85, *Bond van Adverteeders*, ECR [1988] 2085, paragraph 16.

[31] ECJ, case C-263/86, *Humbel and Edel*, ECR [1988] 5365.

since they are set up and run by the State and second, they are financed through public funds"[32].

The Court, in contrast, in two very comprehensive sentences, phrased identically in both judgements, dismissed all the above arguments. Recalling the Luisi and Carbone, Grogan and Kohll case law, the Court affirmed that "it is settled case-law that medical activities fall within the scope of Article 60 of the Treaty, *there being no need to distinguish in that regard between care provided in a hospital environment and care provided outside such an environment*"[33]. Thus dismissing the distinction drawn by Advocate General Saggio, the Court goes on to clarify that the logic which prevailed in the Albany, Brentjens and Drijvende cases concerning the (non) application of competition rules to social security schemes is not to be transposed to the application of the fundamental freedoms. In this respect the Court reiterates the statement already made in Kohll[34], that "the fact that the national rules at issue in the main proceedings are social security rules cannot exclude application of Articles 59 and 60 (now 49 and 50) of the Treaty"[35].

The Court, then, went on to explain why it was not impressed by the arguments of the intervening Governments and of the two Advocates General. The Court's reasoning goes in two complementary directions. First, the Court rebuts the distinction on which both Advocates General distinguished these cases from the Kohll case. For the Court, differentiation of systems based on "free" treatment and systems establishing a refund procedure is irrelevant: patients who received services abroad, by care providers with whom the fund had no prior agreement, were only entitled to refunds. Thus, the Court focuses on the atypical situation where the social security scheme is involved with new care providers, and not those already participating in the scheme[36]. This "atypical" situation is the one that most non-national care providers are likely to come across and, of course, the one pertaining to the factual background of the Geraets case.

Second, the Court refers to the financing of the scheme and declares that "the fact that hospital medical treatment is financed directly by the sickness insurance funds on the basis of agreements and preset scales of fees is not in any event such as to remove such treatment from the

---

[32]   Opinion of the Advocate General Saggio, paragraph 21, as translated from the French by the present author.

[33]   Vanbraekel, paragraph 41; Geraets, paragraph 52, emphasis added.

[34]   Kohll, paragraph 21.

[35]   Vanbraekel, paragraph 42; Geraets, paragraph 53.

[36]   Geraets, paragraph 55.

sphere of services within the meaning of Article 60 of the Treaty"[37]. In this respect the Court refers to the rule in Bond van Adverteeders, that remuneration for services may be given by a third party. It then recalls the criteria established in Humbel as to the characteristics of remuneration, but, with no further explanation, the Court reaches the exact opposite conclusion from the one reached by both the Advocates General. Indeed, the Court affirms that

> in the present cases payments made by the sickness insurance funds [...] albeit set at a flat rate, are indeed the consideration for the hospital services and unquestionably represent remuneration for the hospital which receives them and which is engaged in an activity of an economic character.[38]

This is more an affirmation than an actual finding, since it is not supported by any sort of evidence or reasoning. The very wording of the judgement is revealing: the Court states that "albeit" (*i.e.* contrary to) what may seem logical, the exact contrary is "indeed" "unquestionably" true. The use of strong words instead of convincing arguments is an "unquestionable" sign of weakness of the judgement. It shows, however, the determination of the full Court, or at least the majority therein, to bring social security schemes within the realm of the Treaty rules.

However, the lack of actual reasoning makes it difficult to appreciate the exact content of the rule set by the Court. At any rate, the fact that the Court restricts its "unquestionable" finding to "the present cases" without any further explanation is extremely unfortunate, since it gives no clue as to how future cases will be decided.

The only safe conclusion that one may draw is that the notion of "remuneration", in the sense of Article 50 (ex 60) EC, has been stretched to cover payments that bear only an indirect relationship to the service provided[39]. The further conclusion that may be drawn is that, in most cases, health care services will be considered as services in the meaning of the Treaty. This, in turn, allows for a distinction to be drawn between, on the one hand, the Treaty rules on the fundamental freedoms which, as a matter of principle, apply to national social security schemes and, on the other hand, Article 81 EC on competition which, in view of

---

[37] Geraets, paragraph 56.

[38] Geraets, paragraph 57.

[39] From this perspective the judgements under discussion may be seen as a partial revision of the judgement in Humbel. It would seem that in the present case the Court distances itself from the purely economic relation between the service and the consideration and privileges an intent-based relation: money transferred by the social security funds is aimed to cover healthcare expenses.

the *object* and the *nature* of some agreements relating to the organisation of a social security scheme, does not apply[40].

The recognition that health services do constitute an economic
activity in the sense of Articles 49 ff. EC also has implications for the
application of the other Treaty provisions on fundamental freedoms,
especially the rules on establishment. It will be recalled that the rules on
services are of a "subsidiary" nature and only apply where no other
internal market rule applies. Further, it has been repeatedly stated by the
Court that trans-border service activities that entail some permanence,
duration, repetition or periodicity are to be treated under the Treaty rules
on establishment[41]. Therefore in Sodemare, the Court found that a
Luxembourg company that maintained elderly care homes in Italy
should be dealt with under the rules on establishment, since the company was "involved on a stable and continuous basis in the economic
life of Italy"[42].

Moreover, it should be recalled that, in the two recent cases, the
Court declined to distinguish between, on the one hand, health care
services offered within a hospital environment and, on the other hand,
treatment by independent practitioners. Both are covered by the Treaty
rules on the fundamental freedoms. Older cases on the right of establishment of health practitioners (general practitioners, dentists etc.) can thus
be seen in a new light.

On the other hand, cases like Duphar and Decker, demonstrate how
the extensive reading of Articles 49 ff. so as to cover health care services may also affect the scope of application of Articles 28 (ex 30) ff.
EC on the free movement of goods.

A recurrent issue in the recent cases is the relationship between the
rules set out in Regulation 1408/71 and the Treaty rules on establishment and services.

Cases Kohll and Decker concerned the scope for persons who had
not obtained the prior authorisation provided for in Regulation 1408/71
to receive refund of health expenses incurred in another Member State.
The Court, without invalidating the relevant Regulation, interpreted it in
such a way as to eliminate its alleged restrictive effects. The Court
stated that the existence of the Regulation does not preclude the application of the Treaty rules and went on to construe the two in a

---

[40]   ECJ, case C-67/96, *Albany*, ECR [1999] I-5751, joined cases C-115/97 to C-117/97,
      Brentjens, ECR [1999] I-6025 and case C-219/97, *Drijvende*, ECR [1999] I-6121,
      respectively. On these three cases, see Idot (1999).
[41]   See for a clear statement of the principle ECJ, case C-55/94, *Gebhard*, ECR [1995]
      I-4165.
[42]   ECJ, case C-70/95, *Sodemare* v. *Regione Lombardia*, ECR [1997] I-3395.

complementary way. Hence, the Court found that the authorisation procedure provided for in the Regulation allows the patient "to receive sickness benefits-in-kind, on the account of the competent institution but in accordance with the provisions of the legislation of the State in which the services are provided [...] without that person incurring additional expenditure"[43]. On the other hand, relying on the Treaty rules alone, one may claim "reimbursement for costs incurred in connection with treatment provided in another member State" but only at the tariffs in force in the State in which he is insured[44].

Consequently, the Court treats Regulation 1408/71 as a specific application of the general Treaty rules on free movement and not as the only occasion in which social security funds may be called upon to reimburse expenses incurred in other Member States. Hence, the very importance of Regulation 1408/71 on the reimbursement of health expenditures is greatly undermined.

In the Vanbraekel case the scope of Regulation 1408/71, in respect of refund of medical services received in another Member State, was further reduced, to the benefit of the Treaty rules. In this case the authorisation stipulated by the Regulation had been given to a Belgian patient for treatment in France. The patient was thus entitled to receive a refund based on the tariffs applicable in France, which happened to be lower than the ones applicable in Belgium. The question arose as to whether, under such circumstances, Regulation 1408/71 constitutes a hindrance to the basic Treaty freedoms, since it made health care services offered in France less attractive than those offered in Belgium. The Court further degraded, or even annihilated the importance of the relevant provisions of the Regulation since it deprived them of any clear content. The Court did not find the solution in the interpretation of the Regulation provisions, but opted for a cumulative application of both sets of rules. It found that the effect of the Regulation is limited to guarantee reimbursement according to the tariffs of the State where the treatment was administered. The Court, however, went out of its way to state that the Regulation provision

> does not in any way prevent reimbursement by Member States at the tariffs in force in the competent State, of costs incurred in connection with treatment provided in another Member State [... where] the tariffs applied under that legislation are more beneficial than those applied by the Member State in which the treatment was provided.[45]

---

[43] Kohll, paragraph 26; Decker paragraph 28.
[44] Kohll, paragraph 27; Decker paragraph 29.
[45] Vanbraekel, paragraph 36.

The existence of such an obligation has to be checked against the Treaty provisions on free movement.

In this respect the Court, referring to the judgements in Luisi and Carbone, Bachmann[46] and Kohll found that

the fact that a person has a lower level of cover when he receives hospital treatment in another Member State than when he undergoes the same treatment in the Member State in which he is insured may deter, or even prevent, that person from applying to providers of medical services established in other Member States and constitutes, both for insured persons and for service providers, a barrier to freedom to provide services. [... Hence,] additional reimbursement covering that difference must be granted to the insured person by the competent institution.[47]

However, the very requirement of prior authorisation has been up-held, albeit strictly circumscribed, by the Court in the Geraets case. In this case the said requirement was indirectly, through its implementation in Dutch law, challenged by reference to the Treaty rules. The Court, in a very similar way to the judgement in Vanbraekel, found that the national rule, and hence the Regulation, may "deter, or even prevent, insured persons from applying to providers of medical services established in another Member State and constitute, both for insured persons and service providers, a barrier to freedom to provide services"[48]. It went on to state, however, that such a restriction may be justified by "overriding considerations"[49] relating to the control of costs and to the maintenance of high quality hospital treatments within a Member State, and upheld the measure. Hence, the very requirement of a prior autho-risation stipulated by the Regulation is qualified *prima facie* as a restriction to the fundamental Treaty freedoms. Such a restriction may only be upheld, according to the Court, by virtue of some mandatory requirement, provided it satisfies the four-tier test clearly expressed by the Court in the Gebhard case[50].

From all the above it is clear that the Court treats Regulation 1408/71 on reimbursement of medical expenses as a specific application of its

---

[46] ECJ, case C-204/90, *Bachmann* v. *Belgium*, ECR [1992] I-249.

[47] Vanbraekel, paragraph 51.

[48] Geraets, paragraph 69; Vanbraekel, paragraph 45.

[49] On the various judge-made justifications to restrictions to the fundamental freedoms, see Hatzopoulos (1998).

[50] ECJ, case C-55/94, *Gebhard*, ECR [1995] I-4165. For justifications to restrictions to the free movement of healthcare services, see *infra* Section III.

own case law on the fundamental freedoms. By the same token the Court renders almost superfluous[51] these very provisions[52].

III. Exceptions to the Treaty Freedoms

Despite all the developments presented above, the principle that "Community law does not detract from the powers of the Member States to organise their social security systems"[53] remains. These systems are based on the principle of solidarity and embody the State's choices in the field of social policy.

This is why the Court, in Poucet and Pistre and, before that in Duphar[54], has avoided the application of free market and/or competition principles to issues that obey a completely different logic[55]. In all subsequent cases, the social security schemes scrutinised by the Court, both under the Internal Market and the competition rules, have been examined as to the degree of solidarity they embody. Hence, in Poucet and Garcia[56] the Court found the competition rules to be inapplicable to the organisation of some compulsory insurance schemes, while in cases FFSA, the "trilogy" and Pavlov cases the Court found to the contrary, since in the schemes examined "the principle of solidarity is extremely limited in scope"[57].

Similarly, in the Sodemare case the Court was ready to refrain from the application of the internal market rules to a "system of social welfare [...] based on the principle of solidarity"[58]. In an era where, in the vast majority of internal market cases, the ECJ immediately identifies restrictions and only then looks for eventual justifications[59], the rea-

---

[51]   However, there are still several reasons why one may prefer to rely on the Regulation rather than directly on the Treaty rules, see Chapter by Jorens in this volume.

[52]   An explanation thereof may be that the Regulation did constitute a considerable advance at the date of its adoption, but the subsequent case law of the Court has developed in such a way that it has become outdated. However, it is all but certain that if the Court annulled the Regulation and the Member States were to renegotiate it, they would adopt an approach as liberal as the one put forward by the Court.

[53]   Poucet paragraph 6.

[54]   ECJ, case C-238/82, *Duphar*, ECR [1984] 523.

[55]   On the apparent conflict between competition rules and social security rules see Kessler (1998: 421).

[56]   ECJ, case C-238/94, *Garcia*, ECR [1996] I-1673, an extremely "laconic" judgement.

[57]   See *e.g.* FFSA, paragraph 19. For the criteria embodying the principle of solidarity which, in turn, exclude the qualification of an entity as undertaking, see *infra* Section V.

[58]   Sodemare, paragraph 29.

[59]   On the single interpretation, by the Court, of all four fundamental freedoms and of justifications thereto, see Hatzopoulos (1998).

soning in this judgement is striking. The Court stopped at an earlier stage of the reasoning and did not examine whether the contested measure was restrictive (which it clearly was). The ECJ reasoned in two stages. First, it found that "a Member State may, in the exercise of the powers it retains to organise its social security system, consider [what] a social welfare system necessarily implies" (paragraph 32 of the judgement). Then it was satisfied that the contested measure did not entail any discrimination on the basis of the place of establishment of the various companies (paragraph 33 of the judgement). Hence, the Court concluded that there was no infringement of Articles 52 and 58 (now 43 and 48) EC.

This judgement should be read in conjunction with the more recent judgements of the ECJ where it has consistently held that

> the special nature of certain services does not remove them from the ambit of the fundamental principle of freedom of movement, so that the fact that the national rules at issue in the main proceedings are social security rules cannot exclude application of Articles 59 and 60 (now 49 and 50) of the Treaty.[60]

It has reached the same conclusion in relation to the applicability of Article 28 (then 30)[61].

One way of reading the two series of cases is to accept that the most recent judgements have overturned or partially invalidated the earlier Sodemare judgement. An alternative reading is that when in the presence of "core" solidarity activities, restrictively defined[62], the internal market rules are only infringed by discriminatory measures, not mere hindrances.

If the second reading was accepted, then the existence of "core" solidarity activities would function as yet another "overriding reason", justifying non-discriminatory measures. The only difference, which may simply be to one of drafting style, would be that the existence of "core" solidarity activities is taken into account at an earlier stage of the reasoning, before any restrictions are identified.

The main overriding reason that the member States have put forward and the ECJ has admitted as a possible justification to barriers to the fundamental freedoms, is that of maintaining the "social security system's balance"[63]. This points directly to the "coherence of the fiscal

---

[60] Kohl, paragraph 21; Vanbraekel, paragraph 42 and Geraets, paragraph 54.

[61] Decker, paragraph 25.

[62] Following the judgements of the Court in the FFSA, the "trilogy" and Pavlov cases.

[63] Kohll, paragraph 41; Geraets, paragraph 73 and Vanbraekel, paragraph 47.

system" justification introduced by the Court in the Bachmann cases[64]. Both obey the same logic and satisfy the same need: that factors disturbing the difficult equation between contributions received and moneys paid are circumscribed. However, in more recent tax cases the "coherence" argument has been given less weight in comparison with other more precise reasons for exceptions[65].

A second overriding reason put forward by the member States is the need to "maintain a balanced medical and hospital service open to all". Here the reasoning of the ECJ has been somehow trickier: the ECJ acknowledges that this is a valid objective but denies that it may constitute an overriding reason of general interest. It reasons that this objective is intrinsically linked to the method of financing the social security system and (implicitly) recalls that economic aims may not constitute overriding reasons of general interest[66]. Nevertheless, the Court considers that this objective "may *also* fall within the derogations on grounds of public health under Article 56 of the Treaty, in so far as it contributes to the attainment of a high level of health protection"[67].

Hence, the Court opts for a broad interpretation of the Treaty exception concerning public health (Article 46). In contrast, however, the Court is unwilling to follow the Member States in accepting that receipt of health care services (or goods) in another Member State may entail dangers for public health. The Court gives an excellent illustration of how harmonisation of the legislation may enhance the functioning of the Internal Market. It considers that, where the medical professions have been harmonised[68], professionals "established in other Member States must be afforded all guarantees equivalent to those accorded to [professionals] established on national territory"[69]. It thus becomes, apparent that the harmonisation Directives, aimed at achieving the free movement and establishment of professionals, may also be used to enhance the free provision of cross-border services[70].

---

[64] ECJ, case C-204/90, *Bachmann*, ECR [1992] I-249 and case C-300/90, *Commission v. Belgium*, ECR [1992] I-305.

[65] See *e.g.* ECJ, case C-250/95, *Futura Participations*, ECR [1997] I- 2471 and its annotation by Hatzopoulos (1998b).

[66] See *e.g.* ECJ, case C-398/95, *SETTG* v. *Ypourgos Ergasias*, ECR [1997] I-3091 and its annotation (in Greek) by Hatzopoulos (1998c).

[67] Kohll, paragraph 50; Geraets, paragraph 73; Vanbraekel, paragraph 48. The world "also" is highlighted by the present author, since it is a source of uncertainty as to the existence of an overriding reason of general interest.

[68] On this issue see above Section I.

[69] Kohll, paragraph 48.

[70] This point is quite controversial; see for some criticisms Jorens (2001).

Hence, the Court proceeds to an "alternative" reading of the notion of public health, completely distinct from that described in Directive 64/221 (Council of the European Communities, 1964). The Court leaves to one side issues directly relating to contagious diseases and turns to structural considerations of a macroeconomic nature, pertaining to the continuity of the service of general interest consisting of a "balanced medical and hospital service open to all"[71].

This interpretation of the notion of public health has a further consequence. It is established that, in certain circumstances, derogations from the internal market rules may also originate in the application of Article 86(2) of the Treaty[72]. This provision allows for derogations from the application of the Treaty rules where their application could "obstruct the performance, in law or in fact, of the particular tasks assigned to [undertakings entrusted with the operation of services of general economic interest]"[73]. That is, Article 86(2) permits taking into account, when assessing the compatibility of national measures with the Treaty, considerations of an economic nature. However, especially in relation to health care services, no room is left for the application of Article 86(2), since the pursuit of the financial viability of the service of general interest, consisting of a balanced medical and hospital service, is ensured by the broad interpretation of Article 46 EC and the concept of public health.

IV. Rules on Public Procurement and State Aid

The above discussion indicates that the provision of health care services falls within the ambit of the internal market and that, in principle, it has to comply with the relevant Treaty rules. This section now turns to two specific sets of rules to see how these affect the provision of health care services. It will focus on the rules on public procurement and on state aid. Both sets of rules have, as their recipients, the public authorities of Member States. The common aim of these rules is to make sure that Governments may neither foreclose national markets nor falsify competition between undertakings operating within the internal

---

[71] This directly refers to the extremely vivid debate of what is a service of general interest and how it can be assured in times of divestiture of the State and generalised deregulation. On this issue the French literature is extremely rich, see, among others a multi-dimensional analysis of the issue in Kovar and Simon (1998); Kovar (1994 and 1996: 215 and 493).

[72] ECJ, case C-266/96, *Corsica Ferries France*, ECR [1998] I-3949.

[73] There is much more in Article 86(2) and there is an important body of case law and doctrine on this issue. For an article which is considered to be a "classic" – although not the most recent one – on the field, where the most important cases of the Court are discussed, see Kovar (1996).

market. Therefore, both direct state action, through the allocation of subsidies and indirect action, through the preferential award of procurement contracts, is prohibited.

Yet the Member States, in order to ensure the proper functioning of their health care systems and to promote general social policy objectives, need to inject moneys to entities operating in the relevant sector. In order to ascertain whether this is compatible with the rules on procurement and on state aid, the legal qualification of the entities concerned is of crucial importance.

The rules on state aid are only applicable when some public authority, public body or other entity managing public moneys offers direct or indirect financial advantages to some *undertaking i.e.* an entity pursuing some commercial activity. In this respect the qualification of the various entities that are involved in the provision and the funding of health care services is crucial.

This qualification is also relevant for the application of the rules on public procurement. The relevant rules impose obligations upon "contracting authorities", which are under the direct or indirect control of the State and pursue some activity in the general interest, and thus of a non-commercial nature.

It is therefore necessary to examine the criteria according to which an entity may be considered to be an undertaking before inquiring more specifically into the application of the rules on state aid and public procurement.

V. The Notion of Undertaking

The term "undertaking" has been defined by the Court as "a single organisation of personal, tangible and intangible elements, attached to an autonomous legal entity and pursuing a given long term economic aim"[74]. More recently the Court broadened its definition of an undertaking, stating that it includes "any entity engaged in an economic activity, regardless of its legal status and the way in which it is financed"[75]. From the *broad* and *functional* definitions given by the

---

[74]   See *e.g.* ECJ, case C-19/61, *Mannesman* v. *High Authority of the ECSC*, ECR [1962] 357.

[75]   ECJ, case C-41/90, *Höfner and Elser*, ECR [1991] I-1979, paragraph 21; joined cases C-159/91 and C-160/91, *Poucet and Pistre*, ECR [1993] I-637, paragraph 17; case C-244/94, *FFSA*, ECR [1995] I-4013, paragraph 14.

Court[76], it is clear that the crucial element is the pursuance of an independent economic activity bearing economic risk[77].

A. Doctors and Other Health Care Providers

It seems to be quite clear that self-employed doctors and, more generally, health care providers are undertakings in the sense of Articles 81 ff. According to the extensive case law of the Commission[78] and the Court[79] on this issue, any natural person exercising an economic activity is an undertaking in the sense of Article 81 of the Treaty.

The ECJ took a position in relation to doctors in the recent judgement in the Pavlov case[80]. There, the decision of the Dutch authorities to render membership of an occupational pension fund compulsory, on the request of the representative body of doctors, was scrutinised under competition rules. To reply to the questions of the referring jurisdiction, the Court had to examine whether the representative body may be qualified as an "association of undertakings" and, hence, whether doctors are themselves undertakings. In this respect the judgement of the Court is unambiguous. Having found that self-employed medical specialists offer services in the market for medical services for remuneration and that they bear the financial risks attached to their activity, the Court held that they clearly constitute undertakings. It further specified that "the complexity and technical nature of the services they provide and the fact that the practice of their profession is regulated cannot alter that conclusion"[81]. More recently, the Court held to exactly the same reasoning and reached the same conclusion in relation to lawyers[82].

---

[76] For the notion of undertaking in relation with health services see Pieters (1998: 603, spec. 604 ff.). The characteristics of the Court's definition of undertakings as broad and functional are his.

[77] Hence the case law of the Court on the application of Article 50 EC, which is expressly linked to the pursuance of an economic activity provided for remuneration, is relevant.

[78] See *e.g.* AOIP *v.* Beyard , OJ (1976) L 6/8.

[79] See *e.g.* ECJ, case C-35/83, *BAT v. Commission*, ECR [1985] 363.

[80] ECJ, joined cases C-180-184/98, *Pavlov*, ECR [2000] I-6451.

[81] Pavlov, paragraph 77 *in fine*.

[82] ECJ, case C-35/99, *Arduino*, ECR [2002] I-1529 and case C-309/99, *Price Waterhouse*, ECR [2002] I-1577.

B. Hospitals and Clinics

There is no doubt that private clinics or semi-private hospitals are undertakings in the sense of Articles 81 ff. EC. These are economic entities providing health services for remuneration. The fact that they are contracted into a social security scheme, whereby patients may recover part or all of the expenses incurred, has no bearing whatsoever on the economic nature of the activity pursued[83].

A slightly different question may arise where the clinics or hospitals participate in a social security scheme in such way that they treat patients "for free" while obtaining the relevant fees directly from a social security fund. In the Geraets and the Vanbraekel cases the Court found that the fact that the expenses were paid by a third party (*i.e.* the fund), and that they were only indirectly linked to the actual value of services provided, did not affect the economic nature of the services offered. Therefore, even in this case clinics and hospitals are to be considered as undertakings.

The position is less clear with regard to public hospitals, where health services are genuinely offered for free, being financed directly from the State budget and where staff have the status of civil servants. According to the broad definition of "undertaking" put forward by the Court, whereby any activity pursued or susceptible of being pursued for profit is to be considered as an economic activity[84], even these public hospitals should be treated as undertakings. This conclusion is not universally accepted. In his opinion in the Geraets case, Advocate General Colomer took the clear position that "systems [...] where [health care] institutions have their own means and proper personnel directly recruited by them, working on a pre-established timetable and receiving a salary"[85] are outside the scope of the Treaty. His analysis was reminiscent of the judgement in Humbel, where the Court recognised the right of the Member States to organise their public education system without being subject to the Treaty rules. Yet, the rule in Humbel has been considerably narrowed by the judgements of the Court in the cases Geraets and Vanbraekel and Advocate General

---

[83] See the underlying reasoning of the Court in Kohl, as it has been broadened to include treatment in hospitals by the judgements of the Court in cases Geraets and Vanbraekel, where it has been held that there is "no need to distinguish [...] between care provided in a hospital environment and care provided outside such an environment", Vanbraekel, paragraph 41; Geraets, paragraph 52.

[84] See on this issue case Albany, paragraph 84; case Brentjens, paragraph 84 and case Drijvende, paragraph 74.

[85] Opinion of Advocate General Colomer in case C-157/99, Geraets, paragraph 46, as translated from the French by the present author (official translation not available).

Colomer's opinion has not been followed on this point, and indeed on any point. Therefore, it would seem likely that, even public hospitals may be considered as undertakings[86].

However, in the very recent "lawyer" cases[87] the Court stated clearly that a body would not qualify as an undertaking where a) it pursues aims genuinely linked to the public interest and b) its board includes representatives of public authorities[88]. Up till now, nevertheless, the Court has only applied these criteria to professional associations and has always found that the bodies concerned *were* undertakings. Therefore, it is unclear how and to what extent these two criteria could apply to public hospitals.

There is a different question, not yet examined, whether in each case public hospitals may be exempted from the application of competition rules by virtue of Article 86 paragraph 2, as engaged in the pursuit of some service of public interest[89].

C. Medical Aid Associations

The same logic prevails in relation to emergency care associations. In the recent case Glöckner[90] the Court had to judge on the compatibility with the competition rules of the German legislation concerning ambulance services. According to this legislation, private undertakings wishing to engage in this activity should obtain an authorisation. This was granted by the public authorities of the Länder, after consultation with the medical aid associations, which were already present in the market for ambulance services.

One of the first issues that the Court had to settle was whether the medical aid associations which a) were organised as non-profit associations, b) had been entrusted by law with the operation of the public ambulance service and had set up staff, central control units and ambulance stations to this effect and c) were financed partly through

---

[86] See in the same sense Pieters (1998: 605).

[87] ECJ, case C-35/99, *Arduino*, ECR [2002] I-1529 and case C-309/99, *Price Waterhouse*, ECR [2002] I-1577.

[88] The same criteria had already been used, albeit in a less clear way, in the Pavlov case in relation to a medical association as well as in case C-35/96, *Commission* v. *Italy*, CNSD, ECR [1998] I-3851, in relation to an association of custom agents.

[89] In this respect Advocate General Leger's opinion in the Price Waterhouse Case is directly relevant, since he follows the same logic: the Advocate General refuses to limit the scope of Article 81(1) by applying some "rule of reason" encompassing extra-competitive criteria, while he relegates this function to Article 86(2). It would seem, however, that in the very judgement the Court declined to follow this part of the Advocate General's analysis.

[90] ECJ, case C-475/99, *Glöckner*, ECR [2001] I-8089.

direct public funding (for their infrastructure) and partly through user charges (for their operational costs), were undertakings in the sense of the Treaty. The Court, taking into consideration that "such activities have not always been, and are not necessarily, carried on by such organisations or by public authorities"[91], found in the affirmative. The Court further reasoned that

> public service obligations may, of course, render the services provided by such an organisation less competitive than comparable services rendered by other operators not bound by such obligations, but that fact cannot prevent the activities in question from being regarded as economic activities.[92]

D. Professional Associations

In the Royal Pharmaceutical Society case[93] it was established that, under certain circumstances, professional associations may be considered as exercising public authority and, hence, be subject to the Treaty rules on the Internal Market. This was also implicitly admitted in the Klopp case[94], which dealt with the single-practice rule for lawyers stipulated by the internal rules of the Paris Bar[95].

It is a different question whether professional associations may be viewed as undertakings under Articles 81 and 82 of the Treaty or, alternatively, as associations of undertakings under Article 81 alone. For one thing, the professional association may not be considered as an undertaking itself unless it is engaged in an economic activity distinct from that of its members[96]. This being easily ascertainable, the most delicate issue is whether a professional association that is not itself an undertaking is nevertheless an association of undertakings in the sense of Article 81.

The Commission has, on several occasions treated professional associations under the rules of Article 81 (European Commission, 1993,

---

[91] Glöckner, paragraph 20.

[92] Glöckner, paragraph 21. The Court finally concluded to the compatibility of the contested legislation with Article 82 of the Treaty, precisely on grounds of securing the financial viability of public service obligations, by virtue of Article 86(2).

[93] Joined cases C-266/87 and 267/87, *The Queen* v. *Royal Pharmaceutical Society of Great Britain,* ex parte *Association of Pharmaceutical Importers and others*, ECR [1989] 1295.

[94] ECJ, case C-107/83, Klopp, ECR [1984] 653; see on this case Watson (1985).

[95] Although, the same rule also resulted from a ministerial decree.

[96] See joined cases C-209-215 and C-218/78, *van Landewyck* v. *Commission*, ECR [1980] 3125, paragraphs 87 and 88; joined cases C-96-102, 104, 105, 108 and 110/82, *IAZ* v. *Commission*, ECR [1983] 3369, paragraphs 19 and 20.

1995 and 1999). In the same line of reasoning, the ECJ, in CNSD[97] identified two criteria to decide whether an association of professional custom agents in Italy should be dealt with as an association of undertakings: one pertaining to the *composition* and the other to the *legal framework* of the organisation's activities. Where the members of the association are the representatives of the professionals concerned and there is nothing in the national legislation preventing them from acting in the exclusive interest of the profession, then Article 81 applies. Or, as Advocate General Leger put it in his opinion in the pending Price Waterhouse[98] case:

> a body will not be classified as an association of undertakings within the meaning of Article 85(1) (now 81(1)) of the Treaty where, on the one hand, it is composed of a majority of representatives of the public authorities and, on the other, it is required by national legislation to observe various public interest criteria when taking its decisions.

Applying and further clarifying these criteria, Advocate General Leger, followed by the Court, finding the Dutch Bar Association to be an association of undertakings. According to the Advocate General, the existence of regulatory powers does not preclude the association from being treated as an association of undertakings. Moreover, the existence of a vague and unenforceable obligation to act in the general interest does not alter this qualification.

The Court also used these criteria in its judgement in relation to the Dutch professional body of medical specialists, in the Pavlov case[99]. In a very laconic recital the Court held that the professional body was not to be exempted from the rules on competition since "it was composed exclusively of self-employed medical specialists, whose economic interests it defended"[100].

However, in the recent "lawyers" cases the Court seems to go beyond the mere examination of the characteristics (composition, aim) of the association. It seems that, where the association qualifies *prima facie* as an undertaking, the Court will further examine the nature of every specific measure it adopts. The aim of the Court is to ascertain whether, when adopting the contested measure, the association has acted as an economic agent promoting the interests of the profession or as an independent expert for the State. In order to ascertain this the Court will take into consideration a) the very object (economic or other) of the

---

[97] ECJ, case C-35/96, *Commission v. Italy, CNSD*, ECR [1998] I-3851.
[98] Opinion of the Advocate General Leger delivered on 10 July 2001, paragraph 70.
[99] Joined cases C-180/98 to C-184/98, *Pavlov*, ECR [2000] I-6451.
[100] Case Pavlov, paragraph 88 *in fine*.

measure and b) the extent to which the association, when adopting the measure, was bound by public interest considerations.

The above criteria do not offer hard and fast solutions. Therefore the issues must be examined on a case-by-case basis as to what extent they are fulfilled in order to ascertain whether a particular association will be subject to competition rules.

E. Health Insurance Funds

Whether health insurance funds are to be considered as undertakings has been debated at length by the Court. In the famous Poucet and Pistre cases[101] the Court held that a compulsory sickness and old-age insurance scheme, pursuing a social objective and embodying the principle of solidarity does not fall within the ambit of the competition rules of the Treaty. In this judgement the Court provided some criteria concerning the existence of "solidarity", which have been subsequently narrowed down by the judgements in the FFSA case and, more recently, in the "trilogy" judgements in cases Albany, Brentjens and Drijvende. Subsequently, the Pavlov case consolidated this case law. More recently, however, in the Batisttello case[102], the Court, in a reversal of its previous approach, found that the Italian fund for occupational accidents and diseases embodies "enough" solidarity and does not fall under the competition rules.

From these cases it appears that no single criterion but a group thereof *(faisceau d'indices)*, are to be used to ascertain, on a case by case basis, whether a health insurance fund is an undertaking[103].

A *first* criterion, and a rather general one, is the objective pursued by the scheme. In order to avoid the qualification as an undertaking, the objective pursued by the organisation should be of a social nature. This was established in Poucet and Pistre but was found inadequate in subsequent cases[104]. The requirement that the activity (or the body carrying it out) be non-profit-making, expressed in the same judgement, was expressly abandoned in subsequent ones and is henceforth irrelevant[105].

---

[101] ECJ, joined cases C-159/91 and C-160/91, *Poucet and Pistre*, ECR [1993] I-637.

[102] ECJ, case C-218/00, *Battistello*, ECR [2002] I-691 and its brief commentary by Idot (2002: comm. 109).

[103] For a slightly different – and more authoritative – enumeration of the relevant criteria see the remarkable opinion of Advocate General Jacobs in the "trilogy" cases, paragraphs 333 ff.

[104] See *e.g.* case FFSA, paragraph 20.

[105] See in that sense Advocate General Jacobs in his opinion in the "trilogy" cases, paragraph 336. The learned Advocate General thinks that also the social aim is irrelevant.

A *second* criterion, but not an absolute one, is the compulsory character of the scheme. In Poucet and Pistre this was considered to be an important factor pointing towards a "non-undertaking", while in FFSA the Court pointed to the absence of such a character, in order to conclude on the existence of an undertaking. This criterion, however, was not conclusive in the "trilogy" judgements, where the Court found that, notwithstanding the mandatory character of the scheme, the funds were undertakings.

A *third* criterion is related to the way that contributions and benefits are calculated. There is a strong likelihood that, where benefits are not related to contributions but rather to the personal needs of the insured person, this is dictated by solidarity, not economic considerations. In this respect the judgements in FFSA and the "trilogy" cases are relevant.

From the same set of cases stems a *fourth* criterion involving examining whether the amount of contributions is freely determined by the entity itself, which is a strong indicator of economic activity, or by some regulatory instrument. In addition, the degree of state control that the decision-making of the entity is subject to must be considered[106].

A *fifth* criterion is whether the entity operates according to the principle of capitalisation and is involved in some active management of the funds received, or whether it is limited to the redistribution of the contributions received. In other words, where the amount of benefits distributed depends on the financial results of the entity, we are clearly in the presence of economic activity. In this respect the FFSA and the "trilogy" cases, as well as Pavlov are explicit.

A final criterion indicating the exercise of economic activity may be the existence of schemes offered in competition to private insurance companies[107]. In this regard, schemes that are economically self-sufficient could be considered to constitute economic activity that might be pursued by an undertaking, while schemes that need to be (cross) subsidised, as in Pistre, imply solidarity[108].

None of these criteria is conclusive by itself, but in combination they are decisive. The most recent case law points towards a restrictive interpretation of the principle of solidarity, treating most funds as undertakings[109]. In any event it would seem that the test followed by the Court is a "functional" and not a "structural" one so the judgement may

---

[106] See Poucet and Pistre, paragraph 14 in comparison/contradiction with Pavlov, paragraph 114.

[107] See the "trilogy" cases, *e.g.* Brentjens, paragraph 84. See also Pavlov, paragraph 115.

[108] See Kessler (1998: 430) where reference to other critical commentators.

[109] See Kessler (1998: 430) where reference to other critical commentators.

depend on the activity in question, not merely the structure of the entity[110]. Moreover, once the public (*i.e.* non undertaking) nature of the activity or entity has been established, the fact that the exercise of the activity is carried out by private undertakings contracted by the social security fund does not alter the qualifications[111]. In addition, all agreements and contracts entered into, by the entity, in relation to the non-economic activity, are treated in the same way, irrespective of whether they are central or ancillary to the pursuit of that activity.

F. Health Authorities of Central Government

Central or regional health authorities of any State will *prima facie* not be considered as undertakings. Where public authorities are themselves involved in the pursuance of some economic activity, they will qualify as undertakings in this respect, but still fall outside the scope of the competition rules, in as much as they exercise official authority. As Advocate General Jacobs has put it "the notion of undertaking is a relative concept in the sense that a given entity might be regarded as an undertaking for one part of its activities while the rest fall outside the competition rules"[112]. Official authorities may, however, be subject to competition rules by virtue of the combined application of Articles 3, 10 and 81 (ex 3, 5, 85) EC[113].

VI. Application of the Rules on State Aid and Public Procurement

A. State Aid

Rules on state aid could, under certain circumstances, be an obstacle to money transfers between entities involved in the provision of health care services. In this respect, some of the traditional aspects of the Commission's and the Court's case law on state aid is of particular

---

[110] See the opinion of Advocate General Jacobs in the "trilogy" cases C-67/96, C-115-117/97 and C-219/97, paragraphs 207 and 311 ff.; also Pieters (1998: 605); on a more critical tone Kessler (1998: 430).

[111] See, by analogy, ECJ, case C-222/98, *van der Woude*, ECR [2000] I-7111, paragraph 26, concerning the inapplicability of competition rules on a private undertaking managing a healthcare insurance scheme established within the framework of collective bargaining between employers and employees.

[112] Opinion of Advocate General Jacobs in ECJ, case C-475/99, *Glöckner*, ECR [2001] I-8089, paragraph 72.

[113] See ECJ, case C-2/91, *Meng*, ECR [1993] I-5751, case C-185/91, *Reiff*, ECR [1993] I-5801, case C-245/91, *Ohra*, ECR [1993] I-5851 and case C-266/96, *Corsica Ferries France*, ECR [1998] I-3949 and more recently case C-475/99, *Glöckner*, ECR [2001] I-8089.

importance. First, it must be recalled that the notion of state aid is broadly interpreted. Thus, "measures which, in various forms, mitigate the charges which are normally included in the budget of an undertaking and which, without therefore being subsidies in the strict meaning of the word, are similar in character and have the same effect are considered to constitute aid"[114]. Consequently, not only direct transfers, but also alleviations of debts or of charges due by undertakings are to be considered as aid. What is necessary is that the relevant funds be public and that they confer an unjustified advantage to a specific (category of) undertaking(s).

Second, the test of whether the advantage conferred with public moneys is unjustified, is that of the "private investor"[115] or, if the aid consists of the alleviation of a debt, that of the "private creditor"[116]. This test consists of the examination, in each set of circumstances, of whether a private investor would reasonably have invested money, or a private creditor would have granted more generous payment facilities, to the undertaking in question. If, under normal market conditions, the undertaking was unlikely to obtain such benefits, then aid is present.

Third, and in relation to the previous point, these issues must be resolved by reference to purely economic criteria, which may include the pursuance of a structural policy, guided by prospects of profitability in the medium or longer term. In contrast, social policy considerations do not justify the selective transfer of financial benefits. The Court has consistently held that "the social character of such State measures is not sufficient to exclude them outright from classification as aid for the purposes of Article 92 [now 87] of the Treaty"[117].

The ECJ has given two judgements touching on the organisation of the national welfare and health care systems that apply these well-established principles. In *Belgium v. Commission, Maribel*, the Belgian system of applying reduced tariffs for social security contributions to selected industrial sectors "exposed to fierce international competition" was found by the Court, to constitute a state aid, confirming the Commission's previous decision. The Court was ready to accept that such a measure would foster employment, but held that it should, never-

---

[114] ECJ, case C-200/97, *Ecotrade*, ECR [1998] I-7907, paragraph 34 and case C-75/97, *Belgium v. Commission, Maribel*, ECR [1999] I-3671, paragraph 23.

[115] See, for instance, ECJ, case C-42/93, *Spain v. Commission*, ECR [1994] I-4175, paragraph 14.

[116] *Spain v. Commission*, paragraph 46.

[117] See ECJ, case C-241/94, *France v. Commission*, ECR [1996] I-4551, paragraph 21; case C-342/96, *Spain v. Commission*, ECR [1999] I-2459; case C-75/97 *Belgium v. Commission, Maribel*, ECR [1999] I-3671.

theless, be regarded as state aid, since it distinguished arbitrarily between beneficiaries and non-beneficiaries and "it [was] not justified by the nature or general scheme of the social welfare system"[118].

The same logic was followed by the EFTA Court in the Norway *v.* EFTA Surveillance Authority case[119]. According to the Norwegian National Insurance Act, undertakings were subject to social security contributions according to five different tariff-scales, corresponding to five different geographical zones. The EFTA Court acknowledged, "the Norwegian scheme is purposeful, effective and proportionate when assessed in relation to its objectives"[120]. This did not prevent the Court, from considering that "the system of regionally differentiated social security contributions must be seen as favouring certain undertakings [...] unless it can be shown that the selective effect of the measures is justified by the nature or general scheme of the system itself". The Court further added that any such justification "must derive from the inherent logic of the general system and result from objective conditions within that general system"[121].

On the basis of these cases, a very fine line is to be drawn between, on the one hand, fund transfers or other facilities that form part of a general and coherent system of social benefits and, on the other hand, measures that are aimed at some arbitrarily determined sectors or undertakings. The former will be compatible with the rules on state aid, while the latter will, in principle, be illegal. This does not, however, preclude States from invoking policy considerations in order to uphold such measures under Article 87(3) EC[122].

The judgement of the ECJ in the DMT case[123] provides yet another illustration of state aid linked to the organisation of the social system of Member States. This case concerned the qualification as state aid of the very important payment facilities (deferral for eight years) granted by the Belgian National Social Security Office (ONSS) to a Belgian transport company that was going bankrupt. The Court found that "where a public body with responsibility for collecting social security contributions tolerates late payment of such contributions, its conduct undoubtedly gives the recipient undertaking a significant commercial

---

[118] Case Maribel, paragraph 34 *in fine.*

[119] EFTA Court, case E-6/98, *Norway* v. *EFTA Surveillance Authority*, published in <www.efta.int/ docs/court/Publications/Decision/1999/E-98-06.html>.

[120] Norway v. EFTA Surveillance Authority, paragraph 30.

[121] Norway v. EFTA Surveillance Authority, paragraph 38.

[122] See in that sense the EFTA Court's judgement, *supra,* paragraph 39 *in fine.*

[123] ECJ, case C-256/97, *Déménagements-Manutention Transport SA (DMT)*, ECR [1999] I-3913.

advantage by mitigating, for that undertaking, the burden associated with normal application of the social security system"[124]. Moreover, the Court found that the eventual "interest or penalties for late payment [...] cannot wholly undo the advantage gained by that undertaking"[125]. The same argument would seem to apply to late payment of contributions to a tax based health care scheme. It is unclear, however, what the position would be in relation, say, to a mutual system of health care services, where no state expenditure is involved.

VII. Public Procurement

As far as the application of public procurement rules is concerned, there are no hard and fast answers covering all of the entities involved in the provision and funding of health care services. It would seem, however, that health professionals and private hospitals fall outside the scope of the relevant Directives, while the public hospitals and national authorities are, in principle, covered by them. Doubt remains in relation to social funds and to hospitals that although not public, rely heavily on social security funds for their survival.

In this respect it should be recalled that the Directives are addressed not only to State, regional and local authorities but also "bodies governed by public law". The legal form (public scheme, company etc.) of the latter is irrelevant[126], as long as three conditions are met: they must have legal personality; they must be financed or controlled by the State (or an emanation thereof), and they must be "established for the specific purpose of meeting needs in the general interest, not having an industrial or commercial character". The Court has made it clear that these are cumulative conditions[127]. Member States have been invited to enumerate, in the regularly updated Annexe I of the Directive 93/37, national "bodies" that fall in the above category.

However, this enumeration is not exhaustive and the Court has been called upon on several occasions to interpret these three conditions. Unsurprisingly, the most controversial condition has been the question of whether activities are in the pursuance of general interest or are of an industrial or commercial character. From the judgements of the Court in

---

[124] Case Belgium v. Commission, *supra*, paragraph 19.

[125] Case Belgium v. Commission, *supra*, paragraph 21.

[126] ECJ, case C-360/96, *BFI Holding*, ECR [1998] I-6821, paragraph 53.

[127] See *e.g.* ECJ, case C-44/96, *Mannesmann Anlangebau Austria*, ECR [1998] I-73 and case C-360/96, *BFI Holding*, ECR [1998] I-6821.

the Mannesmann, the BFI Holding and, more recently, the Agorà and Excelsior cases[128] two sets of conclusions may be drawn.

First, that some activity serves the general interest does not, in itself, exclude an industrial or commercial character. Or, to use the Court's wording, there is "a distinction between needs in the general interest not having an industrial or commercial character and needs in the general interest having an industrial or commercial character"[129].

Second, in order to ascertain in which of the above categories an activity falls, the Court uses a group of criteria *(faisceau d'indices)* which may be summarised as follows: the absence of considerable competition in providing the same activity; the existence of decisive State control over the activity[130]; pursuance of the activity and satisfaction of the relevant needs in a way different from what is offered in the market place; and the absence of financial risk. These factors all indicate an absence of industrial and commercial character (Synodinos, 2001: 72 ff.).

These criteria are very similar to those used by the Court to ascertain whether social security, pension and health care funds are to be viewed as "undertakings"[131]. Thus, it would seem that, to the extent that the two series of criteria are applied consistently, co-ordination of the two sets of rules is perfectly workable[132]: an entity that is not an undertaking will, more often than not, be considered to be a contracting authority. Hence, any entity operating in the field of health care services will be subject either to competition or to public procurement rules – but not both. This is a satisfactory result, both from a legal/systematic point of view, since the EC rules are applied in a coherent and complementary way and from an economic point of view, since the same entities are not simultaneously subject to the restrictive rules on procurement and to competition from other undertakings.

However, this idyllic view is disturbed by Annex 1 of the Directive 93/37[133], which contains an extensive enumeration of entities that are considered, by the States to fall within the meaning of "bodies governed

---

[128] For the two first cases see the notes above; see also joined cases C-223/99 and C-260/99, *Agorà and Excelsior*, ECR [2001] I-3605.

[129] Agorà, paragraph 32.

[130] Not the entity providing it, this is a distinct condition directly enumerated in the Directives, see *supra*.

[131] See above Section V.E.

[132] However, such a consistent approach is lacking. See below, the two last paragraphs of the present section.

[133] Although this list is annexed to Directive 93/37/EC, all other public procurement directives refer to it (Council of the European Union, 1993b).

by public law". In this Annex many States, such as Belgium and France, have included a multitude of social funds, some of which are likely to constitute "undertakings" under the criteria set out above. Needless to say, that the fact that they are enumerated in this Annex does not preclude them from being judged under the basic Treaty provisions and, hence, find themselves also subject to competition rules[134].

In this respect, it should be kept in mind that, an entity that is listed in Annex 1 of the Directive 93/37, or any other entity that fulfils the criteria set out above and is considered to be a contracting authority, will be dealt as such even in respect of activities that are of a commercial nature and may be offered within a competitive environment[135]. This is also true in the field of health care services, as it is clearly illustrated in the Tögel case[136]. The "Sickness Insurance Fund for Lower Austria" had concluded contracts with two private undertakings for the provision of ambulance services in Austria. Under the terms of these contracts the Fund would reimburse insured persons for fees paid to the two undertakings for any sort of emergency transport. A third ambulance operator, Mr. Tögel, who sought a similar contract, was turned down by the Fund. Mr. Tögel brought an action before the Austrian Courts alleging the direct effect and the violation of Directive 92/50, on the procurement of services. The Court ruled that most of the Directive's provisions are sufficiently clear to be directly effective, but specified that direct application is possible only after the expiration of the transposition period. Therefore, the Court concluded that the Directive could not be invoked in order to challenge the validity of agreements concluded before that date, not to mention agreements, such as the ones at stake, concluded before the accession of Austria in the EU. All these findings are perfectly in line with previous case law. What is interesting, however, is the fact that nowhere in its judgement does the Court pay any attention to the nature of the transport activities and to the fact that they could be offered, and indeed were offered, by private undertakings within a competitive environment. Despite the fact that Annex 1 of the Directive 93/37 does not contain any list of Austrian "contracting authorities", the Court took it that the Fund was such an authority and did not distinguish between the various activities it undertakes.

---

[134] The current renegotiation of the Directives on public procurement gives the occasion for reconsidering the content of Annex 1.

[135] ECJ, case C-44/96, *Mannesmann Anlangebau Austria*, ECR [1998] I-73 and case C-360/96, *BFI Holding*, ECR [1996] I-6821.

[136] ECJ, case C-76/97, *Tögel*, ECR [1998] 5357.

This case should be compared with the most recent case on ambulance services. In the Glöckner case[137] the Court had to judge on the compatibility of the German legislation on ambulance services, with the EC competition rules and Directive 92/50/EC on the procurement of services (Council of the European Communities, 1992b). The legislation in question made the initiation of ambulance services subject to prior authorisation by the local authorities. No system of public tendering was established. The plaintiff, Glöckner, whose authorisation was not renewed, complained that the system of prior authorisation was contrary both to the rules on competition and those on public procurement. The Court, following the terms of the preliminary question and the opinion of Advocate General Jacobs, limited its answer solely to the applicability of the competition rules. It found that ambulance services did constitute economic activity and, therefore, the entities offering them did qualify as undertakings for the application of the competition rules. On the other hand, the authorities giving the relevant authorisation did not constitute undertakings, since they were exercising official authority.

Despite the arguments put forward by the parties involved, both the Advocate General and the Court avoided the difficult question of whether the absence of a tendering system was altogether compatible with the Treaty rules on free movement of services and the procurement Directives[138]. The Advocate General, followed implicitly by the Court, contended, "the procedure for obtaining such an administrative authorisation is very different from the award of a public service contract and is therefore not covered by the rules on public procurement"[139].

It is not very easy to reconcile this case with the judgement in Tögel. In this earlier case the Court seemed to imply that contracts to provide ambulance services should be awarded to undertakings by public tendering, according to Directive 92/50/EC. In the Glöckner case, on the other hand, the Court took it for granted that such a public tendering system was out of the question. One way of reading the two cases together is to accept that the Court does not intervene directly in the precise way the States organise health care services, but ensures that the system chosen by each State is applied in accordance with the Treaty rules.

Alternatively, it could be put forward that the Court uses a different approach, depending on whether it applies the rules on competition or

---

[137] ECJ, case C-475/99, *Glöckner*, ECR [2001] I-8089.

[138] The decision keeps, nevertheless, its importance, since it gives a number of precisions to the application of Article 86(2) on services of general economic interest, thus enriching the Corbeau case law; see in this respect Idot (2001: comm. 372).

[139] Opinion of Advocate General Jacobs, paragraph 99 *in fine*.

the ones on public procurement. In the first case, the Court is ready to distinguish between non-commercial and commercial activities by the same entity and to submit the latter to the rules on competition. In contrast, where application of the rules on public procurement is at stake, the Court refuses to attach any importance to the commercial character of some activities, thus extending the scope of application of the procurement rules. Hence, the commercial activities of an entity offering services of general interest are likely to be subject simultaneously to the rules on competition and to those on public procurement[140].

Under such circumstances it seems appropriate, in the Directive modifying the public procurement rules (European Commission, 2000: Annex III), to draft the relevant annex taking into account the case law of the Court concerning the definition of undertakings.

Conclusion

Even though the EC has limited powers in relation to health care services, it exerts considerable influence on the way they are organised by Member States. This is due to the existence, within the Treaty, of the rules on free movement and on competition, subsequently operationalised by the case law of the ECJ. First it was established that health care services are, above all *services* liable to be offered on market conditions on a cross-border basis. Then it was held that this analysis is only exceptionally altered by the fact that such services are provided within a social security scheme. Moreover, it has been judged that social security funds may, in certain circumstances, be considered as undertakings and, hence, be subject to the rules on competition. Most of these funds are already subject to Community rules on public procurement. Furthermore to the extent that such entities often manage public moneys, the various transfers they effect may, under certain circumstances, qualify as state aid.

This case law is directed to the effective application of internal market rules. It eventually leads, nonetheless, to a confusing situation, where three different sets of rules may apply simultaneously to the same situation. The rules on competition, on public procurement and on state aid pursue complementary aims, present some similarities, but also have some fundamental differences. What all three sets of rules have in common is that, contrary to the rules on free movement, they tend to regulate the provision of health care services even in the absence of

---

[140] However, this is not necessarily an insurmountable constraint for the entity concerned, since the specific nature of medical goods and services and the "asymmetry of information" that prevails in this field will often allow for recourse to be made to the "closed procedure", thus giving more leeway to the entity.

direct cross-border activity. In other words, the rules on competition, on state aid and on public procurement have more to do with the way in which health care services are organised *internally* within each Member State, than with the way such services are exchanged across the borders of Member States.

The fact that the conditions for the application of these rules have been established by the case law of the Court does not add to legal certainty. First, the Court decides on a case-by-case basis, mainly in preliminary rulings that retain some degree of abstractness. Moreover, the very delicate nature of the issue, touching on national social policies, explains the lack of consensus within the Court and thus the lack of clear and unambiguous reasoning. In addition, the fact that in some cases the Court is called upon to apply competition principles to the organisation of social security schemes which are explicitly designed to compensate for inequalities created by competition, is highly controversial.

The current situation is not completely satisfactory. It is believed that free movement of both professionals and patients is an irreversible *acquis*, which should be encouraged further. This necessitates the adoption of secondary legislation co-ordinating, on the lines set by the recent case law of the Court, the conditions under which health care services are to be organised within Member States. Such legislation should run parallel to the rules of Regulation 1408/71. It is questionable whether such legislation could have as its sole legal basis the internal market rules, or whether recourse should also be made to the provisions of Title XI of the Treaty on Social policy[141] etc.

Moreover, the application of the general rules on competition to entities administering social security schemes may not be satisfactory. The ECJ has exercised great caution in this respect, by excluding altogether from the scope of the rules specific categories of entities and agreements. However, in an era of deregulation and "privatisation" of activities that were traditionally reserved for the State, respect of competition principles by entities involved in administering the social security system may be useful. These rules should, however, be clear,

---

[141] It is recalled that Title XIII on Public Health recognises very limited legislative powers to the Community. Moreover, it should be borne in mind that even if a double legal basis were required, the measures would be adopted according to the procedures laid down in Title III, on free movement, since they provide for a fuller participation of the European Parliament than mere "consultation" and they do not require unanimity like Article 137, for the adoption of measures in the field of social security. On the issue of the double legal basis see ECJ, case C-45/86, *Commission* v. *Council (generalised preferences)*, ECR [1987] 1493 and case C-242/87, *Commission* v. *Council (Erasmus)*, ECR [1989] 1425.

known in advance and sector-specific. Consequently, the adoption of some secondary legislation, which could eventually take the form of a block exemption regulation, seems necessary. From the judgements of the Court in the "trilogy" cases it seems that such an action would necessitate recourse, except for Article 81 itself, to Article 134 EC.

Lastly, entities caught by the rules on competition should unequivocally be exempted from observance of the rules on public procurement, while some guidelines should be drawn in order to avoid a rigid and counter-productive application of the rules on state aid to the organisation and functioning of national health care systems.

Bibliography

COUNCIL OF THE EUROPEAN COMMUNITIES (1964), Council Directive 64/221/EEC on the approximation of 25.02.64 on the co-ordination of special measures concerning the movement and residence of foreign nationals which are justified on grounds of public policy, public security or public health, OJ L 56, 4 April 1964, pp. 0850-0857.

COUNCIL OF THE EUROPEAN COMMUNITIES (1975a), Council Directive 75/362/EEC of 16 June 1975 concerning the mutual recognition of diplomas, certificates and other evidence of formal qualifications in medicine, including measures to facilitate the effective exercise of the right of establishment and freedom to provide services, OJ L 167, 30 June 1975, pp. 0001-0013.

COUNCIL OF THE EUROPEAN COMMUNITIES (1975b), Council Directive 75/363/EEC of 16 June 1975 concerning the co-ordination of provisions laid down by law, Regulation or administrative action in respect of activities of doctors, OJ L 167, 30 June 1975, pp. 0014-0016.

COUNCIL OF THE EUROPEAN COMMUNITIES (1977a), Council Directive 77/452/EEC of 27 June 1977 concerning the mutual recognition of diplomas, certificates and other evidence of the formal qualifications of nurses responsible for general care, including measures to facilitate the effective exercise of this right of establishment and freedom to provide services, OJ L 176, 15 July 1977, pp. 0001-0007.

COUNCIL OF THE EUROPEAN COMMUNITIES (1977b), Council Directive 77/453/EEC of 27 June 1977 concerning the coordination of provisions laid down by Law, Regulation or Administrative Action in respect of the activities of nurses responsible for general care, OJ L 176, 15 July 1977, pp. 0008-0010.

COUNCIL OF THE EUROPEAN COMMUNITIES (1978a), Council Directive 78/686/EEC of 25 July 1978 concerning the mutual recognition of diplomas, certificates and other evidence of the formal qualifications of practitioners of dentistry, including measures to facilitate the effective exercise of the right of establishment and freedom to provide services, OJ L 233, 24 August 1978, pp. 0001-0009.

COUNCIL OF THE EUROPEAN COMMUNITIES (1978b), Council Directive 78/687/EEC of 25 July 1978 concerning the coordination of provisions laid down by Law, Regulation or Administrative Action in respect of the activities of dental practitioners, OJ L 233, 24 August 1978, pp. 0010-0014.

COUNCIL OF THE EUROPEAN COMMUNITIES (1978c), Council Directive 78/1026/EEC of 18 December 1978 concerning the mutual recognition of diplomas, certificates and other evidence of formal qualifications in veterinary medicine, including measures to facilitate the effective exercise of the right of establishment and freedom to provide services, OJ L 362, 23 December 1978, pp. 0001-0006.

COUNCIL OF THE EUROPEAN COMMUNITIES (1978d), Council Directive 78/1027/EEC of 18 December 1978 concerning the coordination of provisions laid down by Law, Regulation or Administrative Action in respect of the activities of veterinary surgeons, OJ L 362, 23 December 1978, pp. 0007-0009.

COUNCIL OF THE EUROPEAN COMMUNITIES (1980a), Council Directive 80/154/EEC of 21 January 1980 concerning the mutual recognition of diplomas, certificates and other evidence of formal qualifications in midwifery and including measures to facilitate the effective exercise of the right of establishment and freedom to provide services, OJ L 033, 11 February 1980, pp. 0001-0007.

COUNCIL OF THE EUROPEAN COMMUNITIES (1980b),Council Directive 80/155/EEC of 21 January 1980 concerning the coordination of provisions laid down by Law, Regulation or Administrative Action relating to the taking up and pursuit of the activities of midwives, OJ L 033, 11 February 1980, pp. 0008-0012.

COUNCIL OF THE EUROPEAN COMMUNITIES (1985a), Council Directive 85/432/EEC of 16 September 1985 concerning the coordination of provisions laid down by Law, Regulation or Administrative Action in respect of certain activities in the field of pharmacy, OJ L 253, 24 September 1985, pp. 0034-0036.

COUNCIL OF THE EUROPEAN COMMUNITIES (1985b), Council Directive 85/433/EEC of 16 September 1985 concerning the mutual recognition of diplomas, certificates and other evidence of formal qualifications in pharmacy, including measures to facilitate the effective exercise of the right of establishment relating to certain activities in the field of pharmacy, OJ L 253, 24 September 1985, pp. 0037-0042.

COUNCIL OF THE EUROPEAN COMMUNITIES (1986), Council Directive 86/457/EEC of 15 September 1986 on specific training in general medical practice, OJ L 267, 19 September 1986, p. 0026.

COUNCIL OF THE EUROPEAN COMMUNITIES (1989), Council Directive 89/48/EEC of 21 December 1988 on a general system for the recognition of higher-education diplomas awarded on completion of professional education and training of at least three years' duration, OJ L 19, 24 January 1989, pp. 0016-0023.

COUNCIL OF THE EUROPEAN COMMUNITIES (1992a), Council Directive 92/51/EEC of 18 June 1992 on a second general system for the recognition of professional education and training to supplement Directive 89/48/EEC, OJ L 209, 24 July 1992, pp. 0025-0045.

COUNCIL OF THE EUROPEAN COMMUNITIES (1992b), Council Directive 92/50/EEC of 18 June 1992 relating to the co-ordination of procedures for the award of public service contracts, OJ L 209, 24 July 1992, pp. 1-24.

COUNCIL OF THE EUROPEAN UNION (1993a), Council Directive 93/16/EEC of 5 April 1993 to facilitate the free movement of doctors and the mutual recognition of their diplomas, certificates and other evidence of formal qualifications, OJ L 165, 7 July 1993, pp. 0001-0024.

COUNCIL OF THE EUROPEAN UNION (1993b), Council Directive 93/37/EEC of 14 June 1993 concerning the co-ordination of procedures for the award of public works contracts, OJ L 1999, 9 August 1993, pp. 54-83.

COUNCIL OF THE EUROPEAN UNION (1996), Consolidated version: Council Regulation 118/97/EC of 2 December 1996 amending and updating Regulation 1408/71/EEC on the application of social security schemes to employed persons, to self-employed persons and to members of their families moving within the Community and Regulation 574/72/EEC laying down the procedure for implementing Regulation 1408/71/EEC, OJ L 28, 30 January 1997, pp. 0001-0229.

EUROPEAN COMMISSION (1993), Commission Decision 93/438/EEC of 30 June 1993 relating to a proceeding pursuant to Article 85 of the EEC Treaty (IV/33.407 CNSD) (Only the Italian text is authentic), OJ L 203, 13 August 1993, pp. 0027-0033.

EUROPEAN COMMISSION (1995), Commission Decision 95/188/EC of 30 January 1995 relating to a proceeding under Article 85 of the EC Treaty (IV/33.686 Coapi) (Only the Spanish text is authentic), OJ L 122, 2 June 1995, pp. 0037-0050.

EUROPEAN COMMISSION (1998), Commission Directive 98/63/EC of 3 September 1998 amending Council Directive 93/16/EEC to facilitate the free movement of doctors and the mutual recognition of their diplomas, certificates and other evidence of formal qualifications (Text with EEA relevance), OJ L 253, 15 September 1998, pp. 0024-0026.

EUROPEAN COMMISSION (1999), Commission Decision 99/267/EC of 7 April 1999 relating to a proceeding pursuant to Article 85 of the EC Treaty (IV/36.147 EPI code of conduct) (Text with EEA relevance) (notified under document number C(1999) 494), OJ L 106, 23 April 1999, pp. 0014-0027.

EUROPEAN COMMISSION (2000), Proposal for a Directive of the European Parliament and of the Council on the coordination of procedures for the award of public supply contracts, public service contracts and public works contracts, COM (2000) 275 final, COD 2000/0115, 30 August 2000 (http://europa.eu.int/eur-lex/en/com/pdf/2000/en_500PC0275.pdf).

EUROPEAN PARLIAMENT and COUNCIL OF THE EUROPEAN UNION (1997), Directive 97/50/EC of the European Parliament and of the Council of 6 October 1997 amending Directive 93/16/EEC to facilitate the free movement of doctors and the mutual recognition of their diplomas, certificates and other evidence of formal qualifications, OJ L 291, 24 October 1997, pp. 0035-0037.

HATZOPOULOS, V. (1998a), "Exigences essentielles, impératives ou impérieuses : une théorie, des théories ou pas de théorie du tout ?", *Revue trimestrielle de droit européen*, Vol. 34, No. 2, pp. 191-236.

HATZOPOULOS, V. (1998b), "Note on ECJ Case C-250/95, *Futura Participations*, ECR [1997] I-2471", *Common Market Law Review*, Vol. 35, No. 2, April 1998, pp. 493-518.

HATZOPOULOS, V. (1998c), "Note on ECJ Case C-398/95, *SETTG* v. *Ypourgos Ergasias*, ECR [1997] I-3091", *Nomiko Vima*, Vol. 46, No. 2, pp. 421-431.

HATZOPOULOS, V. (1999), *Le principe communautaire d'équivalence et de reconnaissance mutuelle dans la libre prestation de services*, Sakkoulas/Bruylant.

HATZOPOULOS, V. (2000), "Recent Developments of the Case Law of the ECJ in the Field of Services", *Common Market Law Review*, No. 43.

HUGLO, J.-G. (1988), « Note on ECJ Case C-158/96, *Kholl*, ECR [1998] I-1931", *Revue trimestrielle de droit européen*, pp. 584-589.

IDOT, L. (1999), "Droit Social et droit de la concurrence: confrontation ou cohabitation (A propos de quelques développements récents)", *Europe*, Vol. 9, No. 11, November 1999, pp. 4-8.

IDOT, L. (2001), "De l'application de l'article 82 CE à un service public de santé" *Europe*, Vol. 11, No. 12, pp. 21-23, comm. 372.

IDOT, L. (2002), "Nouvelle prise de position de la Cour sur la notion d'entreprise dans la ligne de l'arrêt *Poucet*", *Europe*, Vol. 12, No. 3, p. 18, comm. 109.

KESSLER, R. (1998), "Droit de la concurrence et régimes de protection sociale : un bilan provisoire", in KOVAR, R. and SIMON, D. (eds.), *Service public et Communauté Européenne: entre l'intérêt général et le marché*, Vol. I, La Documentation française, Paris, pp. 421-446.

KOVAR, R. (1994), "La Cour de justice et les entreprises chargées de la gestion d'un service d'intérêt économique général. Un pas dans le bon sens vers une dérégulation réglée", *Europe*, Vol. 4, No. 7, pp. 1-5 and Vol. 4, No. 8-9, pp. 1-3.

KOVAR, R. (1996), "Droit communautaire et service public, esprit d'orthodoxie ou pensée laicisée", *Revue trimestrielle de droit européen* (two parts), pp. 215 ff. and 493 ff.

KOVAR, R. and SIMON, D. (1998), *Service public et Communauté Européenne: entre l'intérêt général et le marché*, Vol. I and II, La Documentation française, Paris.

MAVRIDIS, P. (1988), "Libéralisation des soins de santé en Europe : un premier diagnostic", *Revue du marché unique européen*, No. 3, pp. 145-196.

SYNODINOS, H. (2001), *Application of the Competition Rules during the Conclusion and Execution of Public Procurement Contracts* (in Greek), Nomiki Vivliothiki, Athens.

PIETERS, D. (1998), "The Consequences of European Competition Law for National Health Policies", in KREJCI, H., MARHOLD, F., SCHRAMMEL, W., SCHRANK, F. and WINKLER, G. (eds.), *Rechtsdogmatik und Rechtspolitik im Arbeits- und Sozialrecht*, Festschrift T. Tomandl, Wien, Manz, pp. 603-621.

VAN RAEPENBUSCH, S. (1988), "Note on ECJ Case C-158/96, *Kholl*, ECR [1998] I-1931", *Cahier de droit européen*, pp. 683-697.

WATSON, P. (1985), "Note on ECJ Case C-107/83, *Klopp*, ECR [1984] 653", *Common Market Law Review*, pp. 743-751.

CHAPTER 6

Competition Law and
Health Care Systems

Beatrix KARL

Introduction

In recent years, the ECJ has made clear in a series of decisions that social security does not enjoy a general exemption from the scope of application of competition law. This chapter investigates the extent to which European competition law applies to the activities pursued by institutions within health care systems (for the present purposes health care institutions include health care financing and organising institutions) with particular reference to Articles 81, 82 and 86 of the Treaty (Appendix). It begins by asking whether, and to what extent, these institutions are undertakings within the meaning of European competition law. Then, forms of prohibited conduct are explored. Even if a health care institution does qualify as an undertaking and does infringe European competition law, there is still the possibility that it may be exempt from competition law if the conditions set out in Article 86 (2) of the Treaty apply. Accordingly, the conditions for exemption are examined for their applicability to health care.

I. The Status of Health Care Institutions as Undertakings

The EC Treaty does not define the term "undertaking". It is, however, the general practice of Community institutions[1], supported by the available literature[2], to base the definition of an undertaking on func-

---

[1] ECJ, case C-41/90, *Höfner and Elser*, ECR [1991] I-1979, paragraph 21; case C-159/91 and case C-160/91, *Poucet and Pistre*, ECR [1993] I-637; case C-364/92, *SAT Airlines*, ECR [1994] I-43, paragraph 18; case C-244/94, *FFSA*, ECR [1995] I-4019, paragraph 14; case C-55/96, *Job Centre*, ECR [1997] I-7119; case C-67/96, *Albany*, ECR [1999] I-5751, paragraph 77; joined cases C-115/97 to C-117/97, *Brentjens*, ECR [1999] I-6025, paragraph 77; case C-219/97, *Bokken*, ECR [1999] I-6121, paragraph 67; Commission, 1994-07-13, Carton, OJ 1994 L 243/1 (45) and 1994-07-27, PVC, OJ 1994 L 239/14 (28).

[2] Schröter (1999: preliminary remarks on Articles 85 to 89, margins 16 ff., notably 21); Stockenhuber (2001: Article 81 EC, margin 51); Grill (1999: preliminary

tional criteria. Accordingly, an undertaking within the meaning of European competition law is any entity that engages in an economic activity, regardless of its legal status and the way it is financed[3].

The ECJ has held that a profit-making intention is not necessary to qualify as an undertaking[4], so that non-profit and charitable organisations may be undertakings under competition law (Schröter, 1999: preliminary remarks on Articles 85 to 89, margin 22). Nor does an institution's legal person, the circumstances of ownership, its legal form or its incorporation under public or private law play a role (Schröter, 1999: preliminary remarks on Articles 85 to 89, margin 36). Hence, the term undertaking applies to publicly owned enterprises as well as to public corporations or associations engaged in commercial activities. It follows that the status of an undertaking is not restricted to benefit providers, such as physicians, (public) hospitals, pharmacists and manufacturers of drugs and equipment; health care institutions and their umbrella organisations, can also be undertakings despite their public-law structure.

A. Exemptions from Health Care Institutions' Status as Undertakings

European competition law does not apply if the activity carried out by a health care institution is not considered to be economic, but is social, sovereign or purely to cover need. This author considers that the basis for an exemption from competition law is that an activity is non-economic rather than the principle that the organisation of social security systems lies within the jurisdiction of Member States[5]. This principle merely establishes that there are no European regulations specifying a particular form of social security organisation. This area is

---

remarks on Articles 81-86, margin 33); Emmerich (2001: margin 62) and Ebsen (2000: 33).

[3] ECJ, case C-41/90, *Höfner and Elser*, ECR [1991] I-1979, paragraph 21; case C-159/91 and C-160/91, *Poucet and Pistre*, ECR [1993] I-637; case C-244/94, *FFSA*, ECR [1995] I-4019, paragraph 14; case C-55/96, *Job Centre*, ECR [1997] I-7119; case C-67/96, *Albany*, ECR [1999] I-5751, paragraph 77; joined cases C-115/97 to C-117/97, *Brentjens*, ECR [1999] I-6025, paragraph 77; case C-219/97, *Bokken*, ECR [1999] I-6121, paragraph 67.

[4] ECJ, case C-244/94, *FFSA*, ECR [1995] I-4019, paragraph 21; case C-67/96, *Albany*, ECR [1999] I-5751, paragraph 85; joined cases C-115/97 to C-117/97, *Brentjens*, ECR [1999] I-6025; case C-219/97, *Bokken*, ECR [1999] I-6121.

[5] Taking a different view: Benicke (1997: 377) and Ebsen (2000: 35). Regarding this principle, see ECJ, case 238/82, *Duphar*, ECR [1984] 523, paragraph 16; case C-159/91 and C-160/91, *Poucet and Pistre*, ECR [1993] I-637, paragraph 6; case case C-238/94, *García*, ECR [1996] I-1673, paragraph 15; case C-70/95, *Sodemare*, ECR [1997] I-3395, paragraph 27; case C-120/95, *Decker*, ECR [1998] I-1831, paragraph 21; case C-158/96, *Kohll*, ECR [1998] I-1931, paragraph 17.

subject to the principle of co-ordination; harmonisation only applies within the narrow bounds of Article 137 (3) EC. Each Member State is free to determine how to organise its social security system. Whether and to what extent it structures its system according to the principle of solidarity, whether or not it requires compulsory membership, how benefits are provided and so forth are decisions for the Member State. This does not imply, however, that social security systems are beyond the reach of Community law. The ECJ, in recent decisions, clearly states that the Member States are required to observe Community law as it applies to their social security systems[6]. Consequently, it is appropriate to assume that rules governing competition do apply, except where a Member State structures its system in such a way that the activities by its constituent institutions are classed as non-economic.

The next section examines how this can be achieved: how should the activity of a health care institution be organised to be regarded as not being economic.

1. Sovereign Activity

Competition law does not apply if, and in so far as genuine sovereign tasks are performed (Hochbaum, 1999: Article 90, margin 14 with further substantiation).

In the Höfner and Elser case[7], the Court of Justice regarded the employment procurement services of the German Federal Employment Office as an economic activity, even though the Federal Office is a public undertaking subject to public law. The Court held that, just because placement services are normally entrusted to public bodies, that activity was not automatically non-economic. Employment procurement was not always, and need not necessarily be carried out by public entities.

The German Federal government, referring to Article 45 EC argued that the term "official authority" included all activities involving an institution acting under State authority interacting administratively with citizens[8]. The European Commission[9] pointed out that the exercise of official authority was a legal term that did not depend on whether some Member States reserved particular activities for public agencies. As it was accepted that recruitment of executives could be private, employment procurement could not involve the exercise of sovereign power.

---

[6]   ECJ, case C-120/95, *Decker*, ECR [1996] I-1831, paragraph 23; case C-158/96, *Kohll*, ECR [1996] I-1931, paragraph 19; case C-18/95, *Terhoeve*, ECR [1999] I-345, paragraph 34; 2000-11-23, case C-135/99, *Elsen*, paragraph 33.

[7]   ECJ, case C-41/90, *Höfner and Elser*, ECR [1991] I-1979.

[8]   Report for the Hearing in case Höfner and Elser, ECR [1991] I-1979, No. 29.

[9]   Report for the Hearing in case Höfner and Elser, ECR [1991] I-1979, No. 30.

Advocate General Jacobs took a similar view, questioning whether the Federal Employment Office exercised official authority when performing its statutory duties. He was certain that private undertakings, if allowed to provide placement services, would not be exercising official authority:

> Neither the plaintiffs themselves exercise official authority, nor would an undertaking established in another Member State do so if it availed itself of its vested right to provide services pursuant to Article 59 of the EC Treaty (now Article 49 EC). If, therefore, certain undertakings are entitled under the general provision of Article 59 of the EC Treaty (now Article 49 EC) to operate employment procurement services in Germany, they cannot forfeit this right through the exceptional provision of Article 55 of the EC Treaty (now Article 45 EC).[10]

This view, shared by the Commission and Advocate General Jacobs, is, also significant for competition law.

The Court's statement[11] that employment procurement is not inevitably carried out by public entities implies that it need not necessarily involve exercise of official authority, but could be provided by private undertakings as an economic activity, and so cannot be regarded as a sovereign activity. The exercise of official authority was not a necessary requirement for the employment procurement activity carried out by the German Federal Employment Office as it offered the service on the employment market in the same way as a private undertaking. Competition law was therefore applicable.

The judgement in Höfner and Elser implies that health care institutions are not automatically exempt from competition law just because they are holders of sovereign rights (Schulz-Weidner and Felix, 1997: 1123). If an activity is to qualify as being sovereign, the decisive criterion is whether that activity must necessarily be carried out through the exercise of official authority. From the point of view of competition law, a sovereign body cannot assert where they supply or demand products or services in the market alongside other undertakings. In such a case, the public interest underlying the exercise of official authority does not manifest itself any differently from ordinary individual interests and so does not call for any special treatment in terms of competition law. Exemption from the application of competition rules requires that the public has an interest in the performance of a particular task within the meaning of Article 86 (2) EC (see later under "Exemption from

---

[10] Opinion of Advocate General Jacobs in case, *Höfner and Elser*, ECR [1991] I-1979, No. 23.

[11] ECJ, case C-41/90, *Höfner and Elser*, ECR [1999] I-6025.

competition law in respect of services of general economic interest pursuant to Article 86 (2) EC").

The distinction between sovereign and economic activity is thus reduced to the question of whether the activity involved in the exercise of official authority could be carried out, at least in principle, by a private undertaking intending to make a profit[12]. In other words, does the holder of sovereignty functionally engage in commercial operations in the same way as a private undertaking? Haverkate and Huster (1999: margin 595 ff. and 601) take the view that European competition law is applicable because, and in so far as, sovereign institutions operate as business enterprises (as it were, despite the sovereignty of their actions).

This competition-oriented understanding of sovereign activity means the question of whether performance of every public service can be regarded as a sovereign act ceases to be relevant. The decisive issue is the effect of such an action in terms of competition, rather than its legal form (Haverkate and Huster, 1999: margin 595 ff. and 601). It is unimportant whether or not a Member State defines a certain activity as being sovereign. What matters is whether the sovereign institution acts in the market place in the same way as a private undertaking. If it does, the activity in question cannot escape competition law simply on account of its sovereign nature or by the organisation's integration in the sovereign administration[13].

In Germany, for example, the relationship between health insurance institutions and benefit providers is predominantly structured under public law. German health insurance funds have a statutory duty to provide benefits-in-kind, which means that health benefits are provided to the insured through health care providers, paid for by the funds. Benefit provision at the cost of health insurance funds can, as in Austria, be ensured on a contractual basis. The German legislator, in contrast, has opted for the granting of admissions by an autonomous administration involving both health insurance funds and federal associations of panel doctors. That the selection of physicians is decided by an administrative procedure should not obscure the fact that, in functional terms, this constitutes a demand-oriented activity on the part of the funds or the panel doctors' associations. The physician is obliged by an administrative act to provide benefits to the insured within a specific scope and at a specific price. Although the insurance funds and panel doctors' associations conduct an admission procedure under public law, they actually place a demand for medical services on the market. Thus they act as

---

[12]   Advocate General Tesauro, ECR [1993] I-661, No. 8, and Advocate General Jacobs, ECR [1999] I-5751, No. 311; see also Langer (1999: 67).

[13]   Taking a different view: Bieback (1999: 367).

private undertakings and, consequently, should be treated as such, that is, be subject to competition law. That they work under public law does not alter this fact[14].

In cases where health care institutions act not to demand benefits but to supply them, the decisive issue is again whether or not they operate as private undertakings. Private insurance companies also provide cover against the risk of illness. Health care institutions do not, however, act as private undertakings if the activities they are engaged in are not economic, but geared to social objectives.

2. Social Activity

Central to the assessment of whether a health care institution is an undertaking is the distinction between economic and social activity.

In the Poucet and Pistre case[15], the ECJ defined the insurance function of compulsory insurance institutions, organised on the basis of solidarity; as an exclusively social task. The criteria determining the social nature of the activity, were: the social function; the principle of solidarity, the provision of insurance coverage irrespective of the insured persons' financial situation and their health condition at the time of enrolment; State control; the statutory regulation of benefits; the fact that benefits are granted regardless of contributions paid; and the performance of tasks in conformity with legal provisions. Such institutions are unable to influence the level of contributions, the use of funds or the scope of benefit provision. In the Court's view, solidarity exists when contribution payments are geared to income, but benefits are the same for all. As a result, redistribution of income takes place between the well-off and those who, for financial, health or other reasons, would otherwise lack necessary social protection.

In contrast the Court refuses to acknowledge a social character where social insurance institutions perform an economic activity in competition with private insurance companies. It took this view in the Fédération française des sociétés d'assurance (FFSA) case[16], which provided insurance within a system of voluntary supplementary pension insurance. Moreover, it also deemed the work of compulsory supplementary pension funds, based on insurance principles, to be economic in the

---

[14] Regarding procurement activities of German health funds in the health aid sector, see Boecken (2000: 272).

[15] ECJ, case C-159/91 and case C-160/91, *Poucet and Pistre*, ECR [1993] I-637; see also ECJ, case C218/00, *Cisal di Battistello Venanzio & C. Sas*, ECR [2002] I-00691.

[16] ECJ, case C-244/94, *FFSA*, ECR [1995] I-4019, paragraph 17.

Albany[17], Brentjens[18], Bokken[19] and Pavlov[20] cases. The key issue for the Court was the fact that all these systems functioned according to the capitalisation principle. It also noted that qualification as an economic activity was unaffected by the pursuit of a social objective, individual aspects of solidarity, or by restrictions or controls on investments by the social insurance establishment. In the FFSA case, it saw only very limited solidarity because of the voluntary nature of the insurance.

With regard to the criterion of economic efficiency, the ECJ also pointed out, in both the judgements Höfner and Elser[21] and Job Centre[22], that the existence of genuine or potential competition was decisive.

As the previous paragraphs show, health care institutions cannot simply assume that they will not be regarded as undertakings. Instead, their individual activities must be assessed to determine whether they are social or economic. This will depend on the goal of the activity and the manner in which it is carried out.

The ECJ has taken the view that a health care institution operates economically if it competes with private insurance undertakings. However, competition law may apply even when there is no competition between social security establishments and private health insurance companies. Competition law not only safeguards competition between undertakings operating on the same economic level; an undertaking that itself does not compete can still act in a way that makes it subject to competition law. This applies in the event of the prohibited abuse of a dominant position on the market. Article 82 EC seeks to identify monopoly undertakings whose dominant position is expressed not by economic power *vis-à-vis* competitors, but solely by their control over other trading partners (Schröter, 1999: Article 86, margin 101). Consequently, "to be engaged in competition" is not an appropriate criterion for distinguishing between economic and social activity.

Instead, such a distinction must be based on whether the activities and configurations of a health care institution differ so much from those of private undertakings that a private company working on that basis could not, in principle make a profit. It is thus irrelevant whether the health care institution intends to make a profit. The decisive issue is whether such an activity could, at least in principle, be conducted by

---

17   ECJ, case C-67/96, *Albany*, ECR [1999] I-5751, paragraphs 81 ff.
18   ECJ, joined cases C-115/97 to C-117/97, *Brentjens*, ECR [1999] I-6025, para-
      graphs 81 ff.
19   ECJ, case C-219/97 to C-117/97, *Bokken*, ECR [1999] I-6121, paragraphs 71 ff.
20   ECJ, joined cases C-180/98 to C-184/98, *Pavlov*, paragraphs 114 ff.
21   ECJ, case C-41/90, *Höfner and Elser*, ECR [1991] I-1979, paragraph 22.
22   ECJ, case C-55/96, *Job Centre*, ECR [1997] I-7119, paragraph 22.

private undertakings with the purpose of making a profit[23]. An economic activity is defined as one that can be carried out to make a profit, even if this does not actually happen. An activity that is only possible on a non-profit-making basis is not an economic operation because it is not guided by economic motives. Such activities are conducted in the public interest usually performed by government agencies.

The criteria that require activities of a health care institution to be non-profit-making, and so divest it of its economic character, are the principles of solidarity and of social protection (Haverkate and Huster, 1999: margin 502 f). Social protection is expressed by a statutory insurance obligation and the disregard of individual risks. These are the essential features of a social activity. The more pronounced the principles of solidarity and social protection, the greater the manifestation of an activity's social character. The decisive issue is whether the social or the economic criteria predominate.

Social elements, if emphasised, create a product that differs from that from private suppliers, not only from the point of view of private insurance undertakings but also from that of persons demanding benefits. From the latter viewpoint, the crucial difference arises from the principles of solidarity and social protection; from the perspective of private undertakings, it emerges from the resultant "hostility to profit-making", which excludes private companies from performing social activities.

These social principles are encountered not only in insurance schemes, but also in tax-financed national health services. The latter must additionally take into account that, according to the prevalent view, remuneration is a qualifying feature of business activity[24]. In the Höfner and Elser case[25], the Court of Justice held that an economic activity existed although the cost of employment placement was not borne by the job seeker (Eichenhofer, 1991: 2859). Consequently, it is irrelevant whether payment for the benefit is by its recipient or a third party[26]. The only issue is that the activity is not offered completely free of charge. Free activities do not constitute a service within the meaning of Article 50 EC. In the Humbel and Wirth cases, the Court took the view that public education in state schools and universities was not for remunera-

---

[23] Advocate General Tesauro, ECR [1993] I-661, No. 8; Advocate General Jacobs, ECR [1999] I-5751, No. 311.
[24] Eichenhofer (1991: 2859); Marhold (1993: 649); Roth (1990: 1318); Stockenhuber (2001: Article 81, margin 57); taking a different view: Benicke (1997: 376).
[25] ECJ, case C-41/90, *Höfner and Elser*, ECR [1991] I-1979.
[26] Regarding the freedom to provide services, see ECJ, case C-352/85, *Bond van Adverteeders*, ECR [1988] 2085, paragraphs 14 and 16.

tion[27]. It argued that, by establishing and maintaining a national education system, the State did not intend to establish a profit-making activity, but merely fulfilled its duties towards its citizens in the social, cultural and educational sphere, with a system essentially financed from public funds.

In its judgement in Smits and Peerbooms[28] the ECJ confirmed the remunerative character of services provided under the benefit-in-kind system. This view is based on two facts: first that an insured patient receiving medical treatment abroad must pay for this service. The existence of remuneration is obvious and is not changed even if the health insurance fund, which normally provides benefits-in-kind, reimburses the costs. Secondly, the ECJ clearly considers payment for medical services on the basis of contractual agreements made in advance by health insurance fund as remuneration in the sense of Article 50 EC.

As a consequence of this court ruling, the interpretation arising from the judgements in Humbel and Wirth, namely that the provision of health care benefits by tax financed national health services are not remunerative activities, cannot be maintained any more. If a patient covered by a tax-financed national health service receives medical services in another Member State, he/she has to pay for it. This, the ECJ qualifies as remunerability.

The social elements discussed above only apply to the supply of insurance benefits, but not the demand for health care benefits. The relationship between health care institutions and benefit providers, in most cases, is linked to the insurance/benefit relationship existing between the institution and the insured or beneficiaries, respectively. This linkage between the various activities of health care institutions' does not, however, imply that just because an insurance activity is assessed as social, benefit procurement will likewise be exempted from the scope of competition law[29]. Such a view is contrary to the functional definition of an undertaking. The question of whether an institution qualifies as an undertaking relates not to the institution as a whole, but only to each of its individual activities (Ebsen 2000: 33; see also Pieters, 1998: 605).

---

[27] ECJ, case 263/86, *Humbel*, ECR [1988] 5365, paragraphs 14-20; case C-109/92, Wirth, ECR [1993] I-6447, paragraphs 15-19.

[28] ECJ, case C-157/99, *Geraets-Smits and Peerbooms*, ECR [2001] I-5473, paragraphs 55-58.

[29] For a separate view on insurance activity and benefit provision, and an exemption from the scope of application of competition law limited to insurance activity, *cf.* Zechel (1995: 89); Langer (1997: 320); Benicke (1998; 30 f.); Marhold (1995: 454 ff.); Marhold (1999: 48 and 2001: 237 ff.). Regarding a general exemption including benefit provision, *cf.* Knispel (1998: 563); Ebsen (2000: 35 f.); Hailbronner (1991: 123 ff); Schulz-Weidner and Felix (2001: 445 f).

If a health care institution demands benefits on the health care market, such activities will primarily follow economic and not social principles. Their goals are geared to economic considerations; social elements merely play a subordinate role. It does not matter that the purpose of these activities is to achieve socio-political objectives[30]. The decisive point is only whether the health care institution engages in an economic activity in the same way as a private undertaking. Since this is usually the case when health care institutions demand benefits, the deciding factor will be whether or not the exception pursuant to Article 86 (2) EC can be invoked.

3. The Mere Coverage of Need by the Public Sector

The public sector is considered to participate in the market only if it purchases benefits in order to distribute these to others (Bieback, 1999: 365 f. with further substantiation). If, however, these activities merely meet its needs, the public sector does not constitute an undertaking with the meaning of European competition law (Bieback, 1999: 365). The State merely takes part in the economy as consumer; its demand for products and services is solely to satisfy its own requirements and does not entail any further economic processes (Müller-Graff and Zehetner, 1991: 39 and Hochbaum, 1999: Article 90, margin 13 f. with further substantiation). This exemption from competition law applies to both public and private undertakings.

The next question is to what extent should the demand for health care benefits be regarded as pure coverage of need on the part of health care institutions? Ebsen (2000: 34) argues that this applies in the case of tax-financed national health systems in which health care benefits are provided by State authorities as genuine benefits-in-kind. He compares this with the procurement of learning material by schools to distribute them to pupils in lessons. However, he argues that this does not apply to the benefit-in-kind system in the German health insurance scheme, for two reasons, which at least when taken together justify this assessment. Firstly, he says, the "benefit-in-kind" has been "watered down" by the insurance funds to form a legal construct in which economic process of benefit providers supplying services and products to the insured has become a triangular benefit relationship. Secondly, argues that statutory health insurance schemes are organised as provident-provision systems.

---

[30] In case C-155/73, *Sacchi*, ECR [1974] 409, paragraph 14, the European Court of Justice ruled that although a Member State may have granted, for non-economic reasons of public interest, one or several broadcasting establishments the exclusive right to broadcast television and radio programmes, these establishments are nevertheless subject to competition rules in performing their task if that task involves activities of an economic nature.

The insurance obligation and financing by contributions means that insurance funds act, in economic terms, as mediators between the benefit providers and the ultimate recipients. Thus Ebsen correctly takes the view that the German health insurance funds cannot be considered simply to be public consumers[31].

Differentiation must be made not between national health services and health insurance systems but between two types of demand. It is mere coverage of need when health care institutions make purchases for their own purposes, such as establishment and equipment of buildings. If a health care institution operates its own health care facilities, the purchase of, medical equipment and other goods is subject to procurement law, not competition law (Köck, 2000: 55 ff). This does not apply where health care institutions conclude contracts with providers of medical services on behalf of patients entitled to benefits-in-kind. The Sodemare[32] case dealt with a social assistance carriers' demand for health services. The ECJ did not discuss the status of the social assistance carrier as an undertaking, but still applied the law on competition to the legal regulation of the demand. If the Court abides by this ruling, obtaining goods and services demanded by health care institutions that provide benefits-in-kind, must be ruled in accordance with competition law. This applies to both health insurance systems and national health services. Demand for health services is, however, also subject to procurement law. In the Tögel[33] case the ECJ applied procurement law to the purchase of ambulance services by a health insurance carrier.

II. Prohibited Conduct

European competition law prohibits cartels (Article 81 EC) as well as abuse of a dominant position on the market (Article 82 EC). Both issues may co-exist.

A. Cartel Prohibition

Pursuant to Article 81 (1) EC, an anticompetitive cartel may be characterised by the following features: prohibited forms of co-operation between undertakings, restraint of competition, restraint of trade between Member States and perceptibility. Prohibited cartel agreements are automatically void pursuant to Article 81 (2) EC.

---

[31] Taking a different view: Schulz-Weidner and Felix (2001: 446).
[32] ECJ, case C-70/95, *Sodemare*, ECR [1997] I-3395, paragraphs 41 ff.
[33] ECJ, case C-76/97, *Tögel*, ECR [1998] I-5357.

1. Prohibited Co-operation

Article 81 (1) EC prohibits all agreements between undertakings, decisions by associations of undertakings and concerted practices that may interfere with competition. Common to all three elements is conscious and deliberate co-operation between several legally independent undertakings, which in this way strive for, or bring about, co-ordination of their competitive conduct (Schröter, 1999: Article 85, margin 40). The term "agreement" also pertains to legally non-binding arrangements (so-called "gentlemen's agreements") (Stockenhuber, 2001, margin 97 and Schröter, 1999: Article 85, margin 42). Decisions by associations of undertakings include recommendations made by such associations to their members which bind them, in law or in fact, or which are observed by them (Grill, 1999: Article 81, margin 4; Stockenhuber, 2001: Article 81, margin 104 and Schröter, 1999: Article 85, margin 42 and 57). "Concerted practices" is a collective term (Schröter, 1999: Article 85(1), margin 41) intended to cover agreements and decisions that are not legally and factually binding, as well as other forms of conscious and deliberate co-operation among undertakings (Schröter, 1999: Article 85, margin 59).

2. Restraint of Competition

For restraint of competition to exist, agreements must "have as their object or effect the prevention, restriction or distortion of competition within the Common Market". This means that competition, which would exist in the absence of co-operation between the parties to a cartel agreement, must be impaired by restriction of the economic freedom of action of one or more of these parties (Grill, 1999: Article 81, margin 10 and Emmerich, 1999: 415 f). Article 81 EC protects competition in all its manifestations. It seeks to prevent not only restrictions and distortions of competition between parties to such agreements, but also of competition between each of these parties and third parties. Thus cartel prohibition applies both to "horizontal" agreements that restrict competition between undertakings at the same stage in the economic process and to "vertical" agreements between undertakings which operate at different stages of that process and therefore do not compete with each another (Schröter, 1999: Article 85, margin 83). It is contested whether an impairment of third parties' freedom to compete constitutes a sufficient ground (Schröter, 1999: Article 85, margin 84, note 322). The prohibition applies to distortions of both supplier and demand competition (Schröter, 1999: Article 85 (1), margin 88 and Stockenhuber, 2001: Article 81, margin 127), and covers product as well as service markets (Schröter, 1999: Article 85 (1), margin 88). Agreements that restrain demand competition are examined primarily as to whether the supplier's economic scope of action is restricted (Schröter, 1999: Article 85 (1), margin 108). A restraint of competition has to be caused, at least partly, by the agreement in question. That other factors, such as government measures, play a part does not exclude the application of Article 81 (1) EC (Schröter, 1999: Article 85, margin 116).

Article 81 (1) EC also lists examples of prohibited modes of conduct. These include actions that "directly or indirectly fix purchase or selling prices or any other trading conditions" (Article 81 (1) (a) EC). Prohibited price agreements include the arrangement of fixed prices or of minimum or maximum prices (Emmerich, 1999: 423 and Schröter, 1999: Article 85, margin 131 and 139). Moreover, actions which "limit or control production, markets, technical development, or investment" are expressly prohibited (Article 81 (1) (b) EC). These disparate elements share a restriction of competition in terms of quantity and quality (Schröter, 1999: Article 85, margin 146). The definitional elements expressed by actions which "limit or control production" pertain primarily to quota fixing (Schröter, 1999: Article 85, margin 147 and Stockenhuber, 2001: Article 81, margin 184).

In assessing whether a restraint of competition exists, the ECJ attaches particular importance to the market share of the parties to an agreement (Stockenhuber, 2001: Article 81, margin 221). Its rulings imply that it considers the necessary threshold for market share (achieved jointly or individually) to be about 5%[34].

3. Restraint of Trade between Member States

Article 81 (1) EC also establishes that trade between Member States can be affected by the formation of cartels. This so-called intra-Community clause is broadly construed and is thus of only minor significance (Stockenhuber, 2001: Article 81, margin 206 f. and Grill, 1999: preliminary remarks, Articles 81-86, margin 13-19). Agreements involving only undertakings in one Member State may, however, also impact cross-border trade[35].

4. Perceptibility

The ECJ has consistently recognised perceptibility, both as regards restraint of competition and restraint of intra-Community trade, as an unwritten definitional element of Article 81 (1) EC (Emmerich, 1999:

---

[34] See judicial references by Grill (1999: Article 81, margin 19) and Stockenhuber (2001: Article 81, margin 221).

[35] ECJ, joined cases 240-242/82 *et al.*, *SSI*, ECR [1985] 3831, paragraph 49; case 246/86, *Belasco*, ECR [1989] 2117, paragraphs 33 ff.

417 f.; Grill, 1999: Article 81, margin 17-19; Stockenhuber, 2001: Article 81, margin 215 ff. and Eilmansberger, 2000: 50 f.). In this way it seeks to exempt minor cartels.

The European Commission has issued an, albeit non-binding, notice concerning minor cartels (European Commission, 1997). Thus, cartels will, as a rule, be permitted if the aggregated market shares of all parties to the agreement do not exceed 5% in any of the given market (in the case of horizontal agreements) or 10% (in the case of vertical agreements). However, if specific restraints of competition are considered especially grave, exemption may not be permitted. In horizontal agreements, such serious restraints would be price-fixing agreements, market partitioning arrangements, and restrictions on markets or production; for vertical agreements this would apply to agreements fixing reselling prices and territorial protection arrangements (Eilmansberger, 2000: 50 f.).

It should also be noted that the Court considers even a potentially perceptible restraint to be relevant[36].

5. Exemptions from the Cartel Prohibition

a. Exemption Pursuant to Article 81 (3) EC

Agreements, decisions and concerted practices potentially prohibited under Article 81 (1) EC can be exempted by virtue of Article 81 (3) EC. Such exemption may apply to an individual case or entire groups of agreements. The prerequisite is that the agreement in question contributes to improving the production or distribution of products or to promoting technical or economic progress. Consumers must receive a fair share of the resultant benefit. In addition, restriction of competition must be necessary to attain the objectives envisaged and the agreement may not allow the parties the possibility to eliminate competition from a substantial share of the products concerned

b. Lack of an Autonomous Scope of Action

Article 81 EC applies only to anticompetitive conduct pursued by undertakings on their own initiative[37]. If sovereign measures adopted by Member States preclude the possibility of autonomous market activity or if competitive actions on the part of undertakings are obstructed or rendered impossible, the resulting restraint of competition cannot be attributed to the conduct of the undertakings as their scope of action is constrained (Stockenhuber, 2001: Article 81, margin 118 with numerous

---

[36] ECJ, case 19/77, *Miller*, ECR [1978] 131, paragraphs 14 f.

[37] ECJ, joined cases C-359/95 P and C-379/95 P, *Ladbroke Racing*, ECR [1997] I-6265, paragraph 33.

judicial references). This occurs when national legal provisions dictate anticompetitive conduct or if there is a legal framework that rules out any possibility of competitive conduct on the part of undertakings[38].

It is not only government measures that may constrain autonomous action; it may also arise from associated undertakings. The ECJ consistently takes the view that market and competition related co-operation between members of an association of undertakings or of a group (of companies) does not constitute a cartel. This is justified by the fact that competition between individual group members cannot be restricted as they lack economic autonomy (Stockenhuber, 2001: Article 81, margin 165). The deciding factor is thus whether the parties are free to take independent economic decisions that could be restricted by the agreement in question (Schröter, 1999: Article 85, margin 97 and Stockenhuber, 2001: Article 81, margin 165). If not, the charge of anticompetitive conduct is levelled not at the individual undertakings, but at the association of undertakings or the group, with anti-competitiveness in the absence of a prohibited cartel, arising only from the abuse of a dominant position on the market.

c. Other Exemptions Recognised by the Courts

In a series of decisions that dealt with price fixing by statutory compulsory associations, the ECJ held that a cartel agreement within the meaning of Article 81 (1) EC did not exist because the members of those associations could not be viewed as being empowered by the undertakings or associations of undertakings to negotiate and conclude price agreements. This happens if the members of an association are legally obliged, when fixing prices to consider not only the interests of the undertakings in the sector they represent, but also the interests of the general public and of undertakings in other sectors or of the persons using the service[39]. The Court also accepts exemptions from considerations of prohibited cartels where the majority of the association's members are representatives of public bodies[40].

In several cases the ECJ has not blocked arrangement that restrain competition or freedom of action on grounds of cartel prohibition

---

[38] ECJ, joined cases C-359/95 P and C-379/95 P, *Ladbroke Racing*, ECR [1997] I-6265, paragraph 33.

[39] ECJ, case C-153/93, *Delta*, ECR [1994] I-2517, paragraphs 17 f.; case C-185/91, *Reiff*, ECR [1993] I-5801, paragraphs 18 f.; case C-96/94, *Centro Servizi Spediporto*, ECR [1995] I-2883, paragraphs 24 f.; case C-38/97, *Librandi*, ECR [1998] I-5955, paragraphs 30 and 34; case C-35/96, *Commission* v. *Italy*, ECR [1998] I-3851, paragraphs 41-44.

[40] ECJ, case C-153/93, *Delta*, ECR [1994] I-2517, paragraphs 16 and 18; case C-185/91, *Reiff*, ECR [1993] I-5801, paragraph 17; case C-96/94, *Centro Servizi Spediporto*, ECR [1995] I-2883, paragraphs 23 and 25.

because of their ability to foster market penetration and integration (Stockenhuber, 2001: Article 81, margin 152). This applies, for example, if restricting parties' or third parties' economic freedom of action is required for the emergence of new forms of competition.

In the cases Albany, Brentjens and Bokken, the Court ruled that agreements concluded between the social partners in the context of collective bargaining with a view to the social policy objectives of the EC Treaty did not come under Article 81 (1) EC by virtue of their nature and purpose[41].

B. Abuse of a Dominant Position on the Market

The definitional prerequisites set out in Article 82 EC include the dominant position of one or more undertakings, the abuse of a dominant position on the market and the restraint of trade between Member States.

1. Dominant Position of One or More Undertakings

The application of Article 82 EC requires that one or several undertakings hold a dominant position within the Common Market or in a substantial part of it. The Community institutions consider a dominant position to exist if an undertaking's economic position enables it to prevent enduring and effective competition by allowing it to act on an appreciable scale, independently of its competitors, its customers and, ultimately, consumers[42]. In the case of legal or *de facto* monopolies the Commission and the Court of Justice, as a rule, regard a dominant position as existing within the meaning of Article 82 EC[43].

Several undertakings may jointly occupy a dominant position on the market if they are so closely affiliated that they can proceed in the same way on that market[44]. Several companies of one group fulfil this definitional criterion, for example, if they are in a position to prevent effective competition in a substantial part of the market in question (Schröter,

---

[41] ECJ, case C-67/96, *Albany*, ECR [1999] I-5751, paragraph 60; joined cases C-115/97 to C-117/97, *Brentjens*, ECR [1999] I-6025, paragraph 60; case C-219/97, *Bokken*, ECR [1999] I-6121, paragraph 50.

[42] See numerous judicial references by Schröter (1999: Article 86, margin 58, note 191).

[43] Schröter (1999: Article 86, margin 55 with further substantiation, 72 and 77); ECJ, case C-41/90, *Höfner and Elser*, ECR [1991] I-1979, paragraph 28; case 311/84, *CBEM*, ECR [1985] 3261, paragraph 16; case C-179/90, *Merci convenzionali porto di Genova*, ECR [1991] I-5889, paragraph 14; case C-18/88, *GB-Inno-BM*, ECR [1991] I-5491, paragraph 17; case C-67/96, *Albany*, ECR [1999] I-5751, paragraph 91; joined cases C-115/97 to C-117/97, *Brentjens*, ECR [1999] I-6025, paragraph 91; case C-219/97, *Bokken*, ECR [1999] I-6121, paragraph 81.

[44] ECJ, case C-393/92, *Almelo*, ECR [1994] I-1477, paragraphs 41-43; case C-96/94, *Centro Servizi Spediporto*, ECR [1995] I-2883, paragraph 33.

1999: Article 86, margin 67). A jointly held dominant market position can also result from a cartel agreement between undertakings (Grill, 1999: Article 82, margin 21).

To be able to assess the market position of undertakings it is necessary to ascertain where, when and in what products they compete with one another. To this end, the relevant market is differentiated in material and territorial terms (Schröter, 1999: Article 86, margin 103). The definition of the materially relevant market is based on the exchangeability of the product or service from the perspective of the respective market counterpart (Jung, 2001: Article 82, margin 30). The Community institutions define the territorially relevant market as the region in which the particular product or service is offered and in which competitive conditions are sufficiently homogenous (Jung, 2001: Article 82, margin 42; Grill, 1999: Article 82, margin 7).

2. Abuse of a Dominant Position on the Market

Article 82 EC prohibits the abuse of a dominant position on the market by one or several market-dominating undertakings (Grill, 1999: Article 82, margin 22).

The examples of abusive conduct listed in Article 82 EC are chiefly restricted to different forms of exploitation of trading partners (so-called exploitative abuse) (Jung, 2001: Article 82, margin 2 and Emmerich, 1999: 456). Thus, for instance, it is prohibited to impose, directly or indirectly, unfair purchase or selling prices or other unfair trading conditions (Article 82 (a) EC) or to apply dissimilar conditions to equivalent transactions with other trading parties, so placing them at a competitive disadvantage (Article 82 (c) EC).

The very broad scope of protection set out under Article 82 EC also covers individual interests of the consumer. The ECJ consistently emphasises that the prohibition of abuse is aimed "both at practices through which consumers are prejudiced directly and at conduct which places them at an indirect disadvantage by distorting a state of effective competition within the meaning of Article 3 (g) of the Treaty" (Schröter, 1999: Article 86, margin 138). The examples of abuse listed also take account of the individual interests of consumers. For instance, limiting of production, markets or technical development to the prejudice of consumers is expressly prohibited (Article 82 sent. 2 (b) EC). Production, sales and rendering of services are treated in the same way (Schröter, 1999: Article 86, margin 159).

Article 82 EC also prohibits the abuse of a dominant market position to obstruct competitors (so-called obstructive abuse) (Emmerich, 1999: 456). Such abusive conduct is seen if (domestic) suppliers or their associations set quality standards or take part in setting them, so as to place other (typically foreign) suppliers at a disadvantage, without convincing reasons. Such concerns can be reduced if quality standards are laid down by neutral agencies that act independently of market participants[45].

The ECJ also sees an infringement of Article 82 EC in cases where an undertaking attempts to extend the monopoly it enjoys on a particular market to other markets without objective justification[46].

If several undertakings abuse the dominant position they have established jointly by way of a cartel agreement, both Articles 81 and 82 EC become applicable. The same applies if the abuse takes the form of competition-restricting agreements between the dominant undertaking and its suppliers, customers or competitors (Schröter, 1999: Article 86, margin 37).

3. Restraint of Trade between Member States

In order for the abuse of a dominant market position to exist, it must also be possible to affect trade between Member States. The intra-Community clause embodied in Article 82 EC is analogous to the provision set out in Article 81 EC (see "Restraint of trade between Member States").

4. Exemptions from the Prohibition of Abuse

Article 82 EC applies only to anticompetitive modes of conduct which undertakings display on their own initiative[47]. It follows that they must have the scope of action to determine their competitive conduct (see section on "Lack of an autonomous scope of action"). This precondition is considered to be lacking if anticompetitive conduct is required of undertakings because of national legal provisions or where there is a legal framework that rules out any possibility of competitive conduct on the part of undertakings[48].

Conduct by market-dominating undertakings not covered in the examples set out under Article 82 EC, but covered by the general clause (*e.g.* the refusal to do business) is deemed abusive only if further definitional elements come to bear. These include lack of objective grounds for justification, infringement of the principle of proportionality,

---

[45] Hänlein and Kruse (2000: 169); ECJ, case C-202/88, *France* v. *Commission*, ECR [1991] I-1223, paragraph 51; case C-18/88, *GB-INNO-BM*, ECR [1991] I-5941, paragraph 25.

[46] ECJ, case C-18/88, *GB-INNO-BM*, ECR [1991] I-5941, paragraph 24.

[47] ECJ, joined cases C-359/95 P and C-379/95 P, *Ladbroke Racing*, ECR [1997] I-6265, paragraph 33.

[48] ECJ, joined cases C-359/95 P and C-379/95 P, *Ladbroke Racing*, ECR [1997] I-6265, paragraph 33.

employment of unfair or non-performance-related means, as well as substantial obstruction of remaining competition (Schröter, 1999: Article 86, margin 142). In part, the different forms of discrimination prohibited under Article 82 EC are also recognised as possible justifications (Jung, 2001: Article 82, margin 130 f).

C. The Responsibility of the State

Articles 81 and 82 EC are addressed to undertakings. However, the ECJ has consistently inferred from Articles 10 (2) and 86 (1) in connection with Article 3 (g) and Articles 81 and 82 EC that Member States are required not to adopt or maintain in force any measures that could destroy the practical effect *(effet utile)* of competition rules[49].

A Member State violates this requirement if it requires or favours agreements that are incompatible with Article 81 EC or reinforces their effects[50]. However, this only applies if an agreement that contravenes rules on cartel prohibition exists. In the case of peremptory State measures that leave undertakings no freedom of decision or action, for example the official fixing of prices, the Court does not consider the State to have infringed Articles 10 (2) and 86 (1) in connection with Article 3 (g) and Article 81 EC[51]. In the decisions described earlier concerning price fixing by statutory compulsory associations (see "Other exemptions recognised by the courts"), the Court rejected the responsibility of the State since a prohibited cartel agreement, whether required, favoured or reinforced by the State did not exist. Notwithstanding the absence of a prohibited cartel agreement, the Court, however, did examine whether the State deprived any of its own regulations of their State character by delegating the responsibility for decisions affecting the economic sphere to private undertakings. [52] It did not take this view in the Reiff and Delta cases on the grounds that the competent

---

[49] ECJ, case C-66/86, *Ahmed Saeed*, ECR [1989] 804, paragraph 48; case C-41/90, *Höfner and Elser*, ECR [1991] I-1979, paragraph 26; case C-55/96, Job Centre, ECR [1997] I-7119, paragraph 28; case C-320/91, Corbeau, ECR [1993] I-2533, paragraph 11.

[50] ECJ, case C-66/86, *Ahmed Saeed*, ECR [1989] 804, paragraph 48; case 229/83, *Leclerc* v. *Au Blé Vert*, ECR [1985] 1, paragraph 14; case 231/83, *Cullet* v. *Leclerc*, ECR [1985] 305, paragraph 16.

[51] ECJ, case C-38/97, *Librandi*, ECR [1998] I-5955, paragraphs 30 and 34; case C-185/91, *Reiff*, ECR [1993] I-5801, paragraphs 15-19; case C-153/93, *Delta*, ECR [1994] I-2517, paragraphs 15-18; case C-96/94, *Centro Servizi Spediporto*, ECR [1995] I-2883, paragraphs 22-25; Schröter (1999: Article 85, margin 121).

[52] ECJ, case C-38/97, *Librandi*, ECR [1998] I-5955, paragraph 26; case 267/86, *Van Eycke*, ECR [1988] 4769, paragraph 16; case C-185/91, *Reiff*, ECR [1993] I-5801, paragraph 14; case C-153/93, *Delta*, ECR [1994] I-2517, paragraph 14; case C-96/94, *Centro Servizi Spediporto*, ECR [1995] I-2883, paragraph 21).

public authorities ensured that the fixing of tariffs was geared to the general welfare and, if necessary, decided these on their own[53]. In the Centro Servizi Spediporto and the Librandi cases it based its decisions on the fact that the competent public authorities sought the opinions of other public and private institutions prior to their approval of proposals, or even fixed the tariffs *ex officio*[54].

In the case of the abuse of a dominant market position by public undertakings, the ECJ infers from Article 86 (1) in connection with Article 82 EC, that Member States are not only prohibited from adopting measures that lead to an infringement of competition law by market-dominating undertakings[55], but they are also not allowed to take any measures that would, as business measures, violate Article 82 EC (Giesen, 1999: 117 f.). It is thus irrelevant whether or not the under-taking concerned was a party to the abuse through an autonomous business act.

D. Do Health Care Associations Form Cartels?

In many health care systems the competent institutions form associations entrusted with widely differing tasks. For example, they decide on the admission of benefit providers or make arrangements with providers' associations. In addition, many set out standard business conditions for their institutions. Hence the question arises as to how far the prohibition of cartels is applicable to these institutions.

To assess the applicability of the cartel prohibition to decisions by associations of health care institutions, the decisive factor is whether or not such associations, or their affiliated institutions, enjoy a scope of action that may be limited by self-determined economic acts. For health care systems, the absence of such a scope of action will primarily result from statutory measures. If statutory provisions go so far as to leave no scope for autonomous business action, cartel prohibition will not apply. This will be the case, for example, if a national provision establishes how an association should decide on the admission of benefit providers, thereby stipulating the admission criteria in a binding and conclusive manner, so that the association merely enforces the statutory regulations

---

[53] ECJ, case C-185/91, *Reiff*, ECR [1993] I-5801, paragraphs 21-23; case C-153/93, *Delta*, ECR [1994] I-2517, paragraphs 20-22.

[54] ECJ, case C-96/94, *Centro Servizi Spediporto*, ECR [1995] I-2883, paragraphs 27-30; case C-38/97, *Librandi*, ECR [1998] I-5955, paragraphs 31 and 35.

[55] ECJ, case C-66/86, *Ahmed Saeed*, ECR [1989] 804, paragraph 48; case C-41/90, *Höfner and Elser*, ECR [1991] I-1979, paragraph 26; case C-55/96, *Job Centre*, ECR [1997] I-7119, paragraph 28; case C-387/93, *Banchero*, ECR [1995] I-4663, paragraph 51; Schröter (1999: Article 85, margin 120).

without having any scope to influence the selection decision. If, in contrast, anticompetitive co-operation is permitted, or even desired by State authorities, or even if it is merely facilitated by State influence, cartel prohibition will apply (Stockenhuber, 2001: Article 81, margin 119). It follows that an association's decision concerning the prices of health services will be attributed to that association even if these prices are subsequently sanctioned by sovereign measures and declared generally binding[56].

The Cartel prohibition will not apply to decisions by health care associations, even where the law allows for a certain freedom of action if that freedom can only be utilised by the associations but not by the institutions themselves, or where the health care system is structured in such a way that the respective association and its institutions form an economic unit which deprives the institutions of the possibility of autonomous market conduct. In such cases, the institutions involved lack the economic autonomy needed to enter into a prohibited cartel agreement. Their co-operation is not deemed a "decision by an association of undertakings". Although the health care association with which they are affiliated cannot be accused of contravening the cartel prohibition, the abuse of a dominant position on the market may exist if the prerequisites set out under Article 82 EC are fulfilled (see under Section B). Institutions will lack sufficient autonomy if, for example, the health care system is structured in such a way that these institutions operate only as a single customer on the health care market. If admission requirements, scope of benefits, quality and price are determined not at the level of the individual institutions, but jointly and uniformly, then a resolution adopted by an association on the admission of benefit providers or on the price of medical products and services does not constitute a decision by an association of undertakings within the meaning of Article 81 (1) EC (also see Schulz-Weidner and Felix, 2001: 447).

Conversely, if the individual institutions, and not only the association, have the possibility of making autonomous decisions, this will constitute a cartel, provided the pertinent decisions are legally or factually binding on these institutions, or observed by them.

Finally, a resolution adopted by a health care association cannot be deemed a prohibited cartel agreement if the representatives of the institutions affiliated with that association and called upon to pass the resolution cannot be regarded as representatives of those institutions. This will be the case if, upon adoption of the resolution, not only the interests of the institutions, but also those of other undertakings and the

---

[56] ECJ, case 123/83, *BNIC* v. *Clair*, ECR [1985] 391, paragraph 23.

general public need to be taken into account[57]. The same will apply if the institutions' representatives are independent of their institutions or if representatives of public authorities are a majority in the decision-making body[58].

The question of the State's responsibility remains. Any national regulations that require health care associations to conclude prohibited agreements favour such agreements or reinforce their effects are not compatible with Articles 10 (2) and 86 (1) in conjunction with Articles 3 (g) and 81 EC. If, however, the association concerned cannot be accused of concluding an agreement in violation of Article 81 EC, the State only infringes its obligations if it deprives its own regulations of its State character by transferring the responsibility for intervening in economic processes to the association. Consequently, the State is not allowed to delegate sovereign powers of economic regulation to an association (Schröter, 1999: Article 85, margin 123).

Agreements and decisions are often made between health care associations and benefit providers. Here too, associations are considered not to infringe Article 81 (1) EC if the statutory provisions are so far-reaching as to allow no scope for autonomous business conduct. As regards State responsibility, the remarks above also apply in this context.

To assess the nature of agreements between associations, it is irrelevant whether the particular health care association is considered an undertaking because it comprises an "association of undertakings" or because its affiliated institutions form an economic unit. Associations that are parties to such an agreement must, however, enjoy a scope of action that may be limited by self-determined economic acts, and the agreement must be binding on their members or observed by them. In addition, it must be possible to regard the associations' members, which are parties to the agreement, as representatives of the health care institutions or as representatives of the relevant professional group of benefit providers. This implies that they may not be subject to any statutory obligation that takes account of the interests of the public and undertakings of other sectors, or benefit recipients; moreover, they may not assume the function of independent experts (see *supra* (II.A.5.c.)).

---

[57] ECJ, case C-153/93, *Delta*, ECR [1994] I-2517, paragraphs 17 f.; case C-185/91, *Reiff*, ECR [1993] I-5801, paragraphs 18 f.; case C-96/94, *Centro Servizi Spediporto*, ECR [1995] I-2883, paragraphs 24 f.; case C-38/97, *Librandi*, ECR [1998] I-5955, paragraphs 30 and 34; case C-35/96, *Commission* v. *Italy*, ECR [1998] I-3851, paragraphs 41-44.

[58] ECJ, case C-153/93, *Delta*, ECR [1994] I-2517, paragraphs 16 and 18; case C-185/91, *Reiff*, ECR [1993] I-5801, paragraph 17; case C-96/94, *Centro Servizi Spediporto*, ECR [1995] I-2883, paragraphs 23 and 25.

E. Restrictions on the Admission of Panel Doctors – Abuse of a Dominant Market Position?

If health care institutions operate as demanders of health care benefits, as a rule, as demand monopolists, they meet the criteria defining a joint dominant position on the market within the meaning of Article 82 EC. The resulting question is whether an abuse of this dominant market position exists if not all physicians are admitted as providers. If restricted admission is based on the decision of an association of health care institutions or on an agreement between such an association and an association of benefit providers, this may constitute an infringement of the cartel prohibition (see previous section).

Concerning restrictions on admission of physicians, Marhold (1999: 50 f. and 1995: 457 f.)[59] sees as unlawful both limiting of supply to the prejudice of the insured, pursuant to Article 82 sent. 2 (b) EC, and exclusion of non-admitted physicians from the health care market, without them being subject to economic competition based on the quality of their performance. This is an accurate appraisal. If medical treatment is provided as a benefit-in-kind, physicians are largely dependent in economic terms on health care institutions due to a lack of other potential markets, and thus to a lack of effective demand competition (Schröter, 1999: Article 86, margin 61). As demand monopolists, health care institutions are obliged to conclude contracts with physicians. A failure to meet this obligation constitutes an infringement of the prohibition of abuse pursuant to Article 82 sent. 1 EC, unless a factual justification exists[60]. Accordingly, a system of restricted admission of physicians will be inadmissible if the procedure for selection is arbitrary or abusive. As Steinmeyer (2000: 48) rightly remarks: the greater the market power, the stricter the requirements. Justification for a refusal of contract includes both subjective criteria relating to the physician, such as capability or reliability, and market circumstances (Schröter, 1999: Article 86, margin 209).

Restrictions on admission of panel doctors also have adverse effects on patients as consumers, since it leads to a shortage of services rendered by panel doctors at the expense of health care institutions. In particular, these institutions violate Article 82 sent. 2 (b) EC if the limitation on the number of doctors admitted is obviously insufficient to satisfy the demand for medical services and if recourse to non-admitted

---

[59] Fundamentally in agreement, Köck (2000: 50).

[60] See Jung (2001: Article 82, margin 156); Schröter (1999: Article 86, margin 204 ff.) and Grill (1999: Article 82, margin 36).

physicians causes financial disadvantages to patients[61]. Whether a refusal of business can in fact be construed as a "limiting [of own] markets" pursuant to Article 82 sent. 2 (b) EC or merely constitutes an infringement of the general clause stipulated in Article 82 sent. 1 EC is nevertheless contested (Schröter, 1999: Article 86, margin 168; Jung, 2001: Article 82, margin 252).

Limiting markets to the prejudice of consumers pursuant to Article 82 sent. 2 (b) EC can, also result from setting budgets for pharmaceuticals etc, since the consequent pressure exerted on panel doctors' fees if they exceed their budgets is passed on to patients by them. Capped budgets lead to rationing. If this is to the detriment of medical progress, the criterion of limiting technical development to the prejudice of consumers (Article 82 sent. 2 (b) EC) may be fulfilled.

III. Exemption from Competition Law in Respect of Services of General Economic Interest Pursuant to Article 86 (2) EC

Article 86 (2) EC provides an exemption from the scope of application of the EC Treaty for undertakings entrusted with the operation of services of general economic interest. The Treaty provisions, in particular the rules governing competition, apply only in so far as their application does not obstruct the performance, in law or in fact, of the particular task assigned to them. This does not, however, permit interference with the development of trade to such an extent as would be contrary to the interests of the Community.

A. *Entrusting Health Care Institutions with Services of General Economic Interest*

The first prerequisite for a sectoral exemption pursuant to Article 86 (2) EC is that the undertaking in question is entrusted by the State with services of general economic interest. The criteria for determining "general interest" are defined in accordance with Community law,[62] thus encompassing health and social protection (European Commission, 1996: paragraphs 69 and 73 and Schulz-Weidner and Felix, 1997: 1125). The activities pursued by health care institutions are very closely related to public welfare. If, in addition, these institutions also become active in economic terms, their activity can be said to consist of providing services of general "economic" interest.

---

[61] ECJ, case C-41/90, *Höfner and Elser*, ECR [1991] I-1979, paragraphs 30 f.

[62] ECJ, case 41/83, *Italy* v. *Commission*, ECR [1985] 873, paragraph 30; Schulz-Weidner and Felix (1997: 1125) with further substantiation; Steinmeyer (2000: 59).

The term "services of general economic interest" is found not only in Article 86 (2) EC, but also in the newly established Article 16 EC and in Article 36 of the Fundamental Rights Charter. These provisions clearly show that services of general economic interest occupy a special position within the framework of the European Union.

B. Obstructing Health Care Institutions from Performing the Particular Task Assigned to Them

To meet this precondition, the application of competition rules must obstruct the performance, in law or in fact, of the particular task assigned to health care institutions.

Since Article 86 (2) EC is a regulation that limits the application of Treaty provisions to undertakings, this provision must be construed restrictively[63]. Accordingly, it does not suffice if, say, the task assigned to a social insurance institution is merely hampered or impeded by its observance of competition law[64]. Its task must be "obstructed", with "obstruction" strictly defined (Hochbaum, 1999: Article 90, margin 63). In the cases of Sacchi[65] and Höfner and Elser[66], the ECJ established that application of the provisions must be shown to be incompatible with the performance of the particular task. In the cases of Albany[67], Brentjens[68] and Bokken[69], the Court held that it is not necessary, in order for the exceptional provision set out under Article 86 (2) EC to be fulfilled, that the economic viability of the undertaking entrusted with the operation of a service of general economic interest should be threatened. Rather, it suffices that, without the rights in question, it would not be possible for the undertaking to perform the particular tasks assigned to it, or that possession of those rights is necessary for the performance of the tasks under economically acceptable conditions. In the author's view, reliance on the term "endangering" of task performance, as in the German translation of the Commission v. France case[70], is not justified as the

---

[63] Hochbaum (1999: Article 90, margin 49 and 62 f.); Grill (1999: Article 86, margin 27); see also Schulz-Weidner and Felix (1997: 1125).
[64] Schulz-Weidner and Felix (1997: 1125); Grill (1999: Article 86, margin 27) and Gassner (2000: 121 (p.141).
[65] ECJ, case C-155/73, *Sacchi*, ECR [1974] 409, paragraph 15.
[66] ECJ, case C-41/90, *Höfner and Elser*, ECR [1991] I-1979, paragraph 24.
[67] ECJ, case C-67/96, *Albany*, ECR [1999] I-5751, paragraph 107.
[68] ECJ, joined cases C-115/97 to C-117/97, *Brentjens*, ECR [1999] I-6025, paragraph 107.
[69] ECJ, case C-219/97, *Bokken*, ECR [1999] I-6121, paragraph 97.
[70] ECJ, case C-159/94, *Commission* v. *France*, ECR [1997] I-5815, paragraph 59; case C-157/94, *Commission* v. *Netherlands*, ECR [1997] I-5699, paragraph 43.

English and French judgement versions use the terms "not be possible" and *"faire échec à"* (Gassner, 2000: 141).

The particular task assigned to health care institutions, as a rule, embraces the provision of widespread, high-quality and low-cost, equal medical care for all persons eligible for benefits, with different degrees of emphasis placed on the social criteria governing eligibility. The question of whether a health care institution can only perform this particular task if it contravenes European competition rules cannot be asked in relation to all the institution's activities, but must be considered separately for each individual activity. Such an examination must take account of the specific situation of health care institutions and the special features of the health care market.

1. The Specific Situation of Health Care Institutions

The specific situation of health care institutions results from their inherent social nature. If these social elements are so strong that they divest the institution's activities of its economic character, its status as an undertaking will already be lacking, as will the precondition for the applicability of competition law. Yet those activities not classed as "social" are, as a rule, not completely free of social elements. These elements can impair health care institutions' ability to compete with private undertakings. In its decisions concerning supplementary pension schemes, the ECJ recognised that such constraints could justify the exclusive right of these funds to manage the supplementary schemes[71].

Social elements have a formative influence on the activity of health care institutions as suppliers of insurance or health care benefits. As a rule, the impact of these elements on the institutions' demand conduct *vis-à-vis* benefit providers is not so strong as to divest benefit procurement activities of their economic character , nor to justify an exemption pursuant to Article 86 (2) EC. Demand conduct, however, can be influenced significantly if an absolute obligation to provide benefits-in-kind is imposed on health care institutions. Such an obligation makes their demand conduct less competitive compared to private insurance undertakings, since their relationship with benefit providers leaves them less scope for negotiations. In financial terms, their margin for negotiations is frequently restricted by the requirement to safeguard contribution stability.

---

[71]   ECJ, case C-67/96, *Albany*, ECR [1999] I-5751, paragraphs 109 f.; joined cases C-115/97 to 117/97, *Brentjens*, ECR [1999] I-6025, paragraphs 109 f.; case C-219/97, *Bokken*, ECR [1999] I-6121, paragraphs 99 f.

2. The Special Features of the Health Care Market

The health care market does not adhere to the image of pure competition. In merchandise markets that function under competitive conditions, the demander usually bears the financial consequences of his decision based on need. This differs in the case of the health care market: depending on how national health care systems are organised, the insured, as demanders of health care benefits, bear none, or only a certain portion, of the cost of benefits they receive. In addition: the insured patient is not a classic demander. As a rule, she/he makes only the first decision to consult a physician and subsequently "consumes" a benefit that is prescribed by the doctor and ultimately funded by the health care institution. Wille (1999: 106) therefore rightly speaks of a "splitting of functions", since, unlike with most products purchased on the market, different persons act as demander, spending unit and consumer.

As the cost is borne by the health care system, patients may demand medical benefits that are not needed, while physicians may use their information advantage to maximise profit and, through their advisory function, will seek to create additional demand, which may be harmful to health (Kletter, 1994: 28). Health care systems counter this so-called "moral hazard" primarily by means of admission restrictions, fixed prices and limits on benefit provision (Kletter, 1994: 28 and 2000: 707 f.). The aim is to avoid an increase in the quantity of benefits and the concomitant rise in expenditure, both of which pose a threat to health systems' financial efficiency.

The ECJ has repeatedly recognised the financial viability of social security schemes as a ground for exemption from internal market regulations. Thus, for example, in the Duphar case[72] it held that Community law did not affect the power of Member States to adopt measures to regulate drug consumption in order to maintain the financial balance of their health insurance schemes. In the cases Kohll[73], Decker[74], Smits and Peerbooms[75] as well as Vanbraekel[76], the Court acknowledged the considerable threat to the financial balance of social security schemes as a compelling reason of general interest that could justify a restriction of the free movement of goods and services. Finally, in the Albany[77],

---

[72] ECJ, case C-238/82, *Duphar*, ECR [1984] 523, paragraph 16.

[73] ECJ, case C-158/96, *Kohll*, ECR [1998] I-1931, paragraph 41.

[74] ECJ, case C-120/95, *Decker*, ECR [1998] I-1831, paragraph 39.

[75] ECJ, case C-157/99, *Geraets-Smits and Peerbooms*, ECR [2001] I-5473, paragraph 72.

[76] ECJ, case C-368/98, *Vanbraekel*, ECR [2001] I-5363, paragraph 47.

[77] ECJ, case C-67/96, *Albany*, ECR [1999] I-5751, paragraph 107.

Brentjens[78] and Bokken[79] cases, it considered the exceptional provision of Article 86 (2) EC to be fulfilled if maintenance of the rights at issue was necessary to enable their holder to perform its tasks of general economic interest under economically acceptable conditions.

Yet the threat to the financial balance of health care schemes is not the only criterion that could obstruct the performance of the particular task; another important factor is the threat to health.

Arguments to the effect that health care institutions can only perform the particular task assigned to them if they recourse to anticompetitive price fixing and/or restrictions on admission presuppose that the means employed are appropriate and do justice to the principle of proportionality. Limitations on the applicability of Treaty provisions may not go beyond that which is necessary for the performance of the task (European Commission, 1976). The burden of proof is imposed on Member States only in respect of the obstruction of performance of the particular task within the meaning of Article 86 (2) EC[80]. They need to provide evidence that there is no other possibility to ensure performance of the task. In proceedings under Article 226 EC for failure to fulfil an obligation, it is incumbent upon the Commission to prove the allegation that the obligation has not been fulfilled[81].

Consequently, as long as, and to the extent that, performance of the particular task is possible without infringing the EC Treaty, health care institutions will be bound by the Treaty. Moreover, if a health care institution is unable, or unwilling, to perform the task assigned to it, there will be no scope for the application of Article 86 (2) EC[82]. It follows that a Member State will not be able to invoke Article 86 (2) EC to justify its system of restricted admission of panel doctors if health care institutions are obviously not in a position to meet beneficiaries' demand for medical services, whether because the medical care provided by panel doctors does not ensure blanket coverage or quality is lacking. This confirms that the assessment, within the scope of Article 86 (2) EC, of State measures taken in the health care market, must consider not only cost, but also quality of, and access to health care. In this regard, the existence of waiting lists could be significant.

An exemption from the application of Article 81 EC also demands that the possible exceptions set out under Article 81 (3) EC have been

---

78 ECJ, joined cases C-115/97 to C-117/97, *Brentjens*, ECR [1999] I-6025, paragraph 107.

79 ECJ, case C-219/97, *Bokken*, ECR [1999] I-6121, paragraph 97.

80 ECJ, case C-159/94, *Commission* v. *France*, ECR [1997] I-5815, paragraph 101.

81 ECJ, case C-159/94, *Commission* v. *France*, ECR [1997] I-5815, paragraph 102.

82 ECJ, case C-41/90, *Höfner and Elser*, ECR [1991] I-1979, paragraphs 25 ff.

exhausted (Emmerich, 2001: margin 161; Müller-Graff and Zehetner, 1991: 154).

C. Taking Account of the Development of Trade

Finally, as a last prerequisite, Article 86 (2) EC demands that the development of trade must not be affected to such an extent as would be contrary to the interests of the Community[83].

An impairment of the development of trade is prohibited only if it reaches a scale that runs counter to the interests of the Community. This creates a balance between the national interests of the Member State in performing the particular task through a service institution, on the one hand, and the interests of the European Union, on the other (Hochbaum, 1999: Article 90, margin 66; Emmerich, 2001: margin 166). The interests of the Union are inferred from the objectives and principles of the Treaty, in particular Articles 2, 3, 12, 14, 25, 28, 43, 49, 81 and 82 EC (Emmerich, 2001: margin 166; Müller-Graff and Zehetner, 1991: 152 f.).

Weighty interests on the part of the Community counterbalance the interest in the performance of the particular task assigned to health care institutions. Thus, for example, restrictions on the admission of panel doctors are questioned not only by competition law, but also by the freedom of establishment and the freedom to provide services[84]. It is therefore necessary to examine carefully whether restrictions on admission of benefit providers are compatible with the fundamental freedoms. Clarification is also needed as to whether the conditions for filling panel doctors' posts also allow applicants from other EU Member States to gain access (Pitschas, 1996: 26). A conflict of interest will arise, for example, if the possibility of concluding contracts with benefit providers is subject to territorial limits. This can imply both a restriction of the passive freedom to receive services on the part of the insured and an indirect restriction of the active freedom to supply services on the part of benefit providers resident in another EU Member State (Karl, 2002: 26 ff.).

Should a system of restricted admission of benefit providers or a price fixing scheme prove to violate one of the fundamental freedoms, a weighing of interests will produce a result in favour of Community interests (Hochbaum, 1999: Article 90, margins 68 ff.; Emmerich, 2001: margin 166). This would mean that, so far, an exemption from the scope of application of competition rules does not exist.

---

[83] In part, the view is taken that the barrier established in Article 86 (2) sent. 2 EC should not be observed as long as the Commission has not provided a more precise definition of this provision through secondary legislation. See Ehricke (1998: 746 f.).

[84] Regarding the staffing and fee cartel of the Austrian panel doctor scheme, see Pitschas (1996: 25 f.) and Kopetzki (1999: 57 f.).

Bibliography

BENICKE, C. (1997), "Zum Unternehmensbegriff des Europäischen Wettbewerbsrechts", *Europäisches Wirtschafts- und Steuerrecht*, No. 11, pp. 373-379.

BENICKE, C. (1998), "EG-Wirtschaftsrecht und die Einrichtungen der freien Wohlfahrtspflege", *Sozialrecht in Deutschland und Europa*, No. 1, pp. 22-35.

BIEBACK, K. J. (1999), "Die Kranken- und Pflegeversicherung im Wettbewerbsrecht der EG", *Europäisches Wirtschafts- und Steuerrecht*, No. 10, pp. 361-372.

BOECKEN, W. (2000), "Rechtliche Schranken für die Beschaffungstätigkeit der Krankenkassen im Hilfsmittelbereich nach der Publizierung des Vertragsrechts – insbesondere zum Schutz der Leistungserbringer vor Ungleichbehandlungen", *Neue Zeitschrift für Sozialrecht*, No. 6, pp. 269-277.

EBSEN, I. (2000), "Öffentlich-rechtliches Handeln von Krankenkassen als Gegenstand des Wettbewerbsrechts? Probleme materiellrechtlicher und kompetenzrechtlicher Koordinierung", in IGL, G. (ed.), *Das Gesundheitswesen in der Wettbewerbsordnung*, Verlag Chmielorz, Wiesbaden, pp. 22-38.

EHRICKE, U. (1998), "Zur Konzeption von Artikel 37 I und Artikel 90 II EGV", *Zeitschrift für Europäisches Wirtschaftsrecht*, No. 24, pp. 741-747.

EICHENHOFER, E. (1991), "Anmerkungen zu EuGH 17.2.1993, Rs C-159/91 und C-160/91 (Poucet und Pistre)", *Neue Juristische Wochenschrift*, No. 40, p. 2859.

EILMANSBERGER, T. (2000), *Europarecht II. Das Recht des Binnenmarkts: Grundfreiheiten und Wettbewerbsrecht*, Orac-Verlag, Wien.

EMMERICH, V. (1999), *Kartellrecht* (8th edition), CH Beck-Verlag, München.

EMMERICH, V. (2001), "Wettbewerbsregeln. Artikel 81 und 82 EGV", in DAUSES, M. A. (ed.), *Handbuch des EU-Wirtschaftsrechts*, Volume 2, loose-leaf edition, CH Beck-Verlag, München.

EUROPEAN COMMISSION (1976), Commission Decision 76/684/EEC of 26 July 1976 relating to a proceeding under Article 85 of the EEC Treaty (IV/28.980 Pabst & Richarz/BNIA) (Only the French text is authentic), OJ L 231, 21 August 1976, pp. 0024-0029.

EUROPEAN COMMISSION (1996), Notice from the Commission on "Services of General Interest in Europe" (COM (96) 443, final version), OJ C 281, 26 September 1996, pp. 0003-0012.

EUROPEAN COMMISSION (1997), Commission Notice on the definition of relevant market for the purposes of Community competition law, OJ C 372, 9 December 1997, pp. 0005-0013.

GASSNER, U.M. (2000), "Nationaler Gesundheitsmarkt und europäisches Kartellrecht", *Vierteljahresschrift für Sozialrecht*, No. 2, pp. 121-148.

GIESEN, R. (1999), *Die Vorgaben des EG-Vertrages für das Internationale Sozialrecht*, Nomos-Verlag, Baden-Baden.

GRILL, G. (1999), "Artikel 81 und 82", in LENZ C. O. (ed.), *EG-Vertrag* (2nd edition), Bundesanzeiger, Helbing & Lichtenhahn, Ueberreuter, Köln, Basel, Genf, München, Wien.

HAILBRONNER, K. (1991), *Rechtsstellung und Tätigkeitsbereich der öffentlich-rechtlichen Pflicht- und Monopolversicherungsanstalten in der Europäischen Gemeinschaft*, Nomos Verlagsgesellschaft, Baden-Baden.

HÄNLEIN, A. and KRUSE, J. (2000), "Einflüsse des Europäischen Wettbewerbsrechts auf die Leistungserbringung in der gesetzlichen Krankenversicherung", *Neue Zeitschrift für Sozialrecht*, No. 4, pp. 165-176.

HAVERKATE, G. and HUSTER, S. (1999), *Europäisches Sozialrecht*, Nomos Verlagsgesellschaft, Baden-Baden.

HOCHBAUM, I. F. (1999), "Artikel 90", in GROEBEN, H., THIESING, J. and EHLERMANN, C. D. (eds.), *Kommentar zum EU-/EG-Vertrag*, Volume 2/I (5th edition), Nomos Verlagsgesellschaft, Baden-Baden.

JUNG, C. H. A. (2001), "Article 82 EGV", in GRABITZ, E. and HILF, M. (eds.), *Das Recht der Europäischen Union*, Volume I: EUV/EGV (Amsterdam version), loose-leaf edition, CH Beck-Verlag, München.

KARL, B. (2002), "Die Auswirkungen des freien Waren- und Dienstleistungs-verkehrs auf die Kostenerstattung", *Das Recht der Arbeit*, No. 1, pp. 15-29.

KLETTER, M. (1994), "Kostenerstattung und Sachleistungsvorsorge", *Soziale Sicherheit*, No. 1, pp. 27-37.

KLETTER, M. (2000), "Das VfGH-Erkenntnis zur Kostenerstattung", *Soziale Sicherheit*, No. 7/8, pp. 704-714.

KNISPEL, U. (1998), "Krankenkassen als Adressaten des Kartellrechts", *Neue Zeitschrift für Sozialrecht*, No. 12, pp. 563-566.

KÖCK, S. (2000), "Die Auswirkungen des EG-Wettbewerbsrechts auf die öster-reichische Sozialversicherung", in TOMANDL, T. (ed.), *Der Einfluß europäischen Rechts auf das Sozialrecht,* Braumüller Verlag, Wien, pp. 27-60.

KOPETZKI, C. (1999), "Rechtsfragen der vertragsärztlichen Stellenplanung in Österreich", in JABORNEGG, P., RESCH, R. and SEEWALD, O. (eds.), *Der Vertragsarzt im Spannungsfeld zwischen gesundheitspolitischer Steuerung und Freiheit der Berufsausübung*, Manz-Verlag, Wien, pp. 31-58.

LANGER, R. (1997), "Konsequenzen der Privatisierung für die Koordinierung der Systeme der sozialen Sicherheit in der Verordnung (EWG) 1408/71: Probleme und Lösungen", *Zeitschrift für ausländisches und internationales Arbeits- und Sozialrecht*, No. 4, pp. 314-332.

LANGER, R. (1999), "Probleme der Koordinierung beim Public/Private-Mix von Gesundheitsleistungen", in IGL, G. (ed.), *Europäische Union und gesetzliche Krankenversicherung*, Chmielorz, Wiesbaden, pp. 60-78.

MARHOLD, F. (1993), "Europäisches Wettbewerbsrecht für öffentliche Unter-nehmen", in ENZINGER, M., HÜGEL, H.F. and DILLENZ, W., *Aktuelle Probleme des Unternehmensrechts*, Festschrift G. Frotz, Wien, Manz, pp. 645-659.

MARHOLD, F. (1995), "Europäischer Wettbewerb im Gesundheitswesen", in TOMUSCHAT, C., KÖTZ, H. and VON MAYDELL, B. (eds.), *Europäische Integration und nationale Rechtskulturen*, Carl Heymanns Verlag, Köln, Berlin, Bonn, München, pp. 451-462.

MARHOLD, F. (1999), "Das europäische Wirtschaftsrecht und die Gesundheitsleistungen – Auswirkungen", in PALM, W. (ed.), *Gesundheitsleistungen ohne Grenzen in der Europäischen Union?*, Association Internationale de la Mutualité (AIM), Brussels, pp. 48-54.

MARHOLD, F. (2001), "Auswirkungen des Europäischen Wirtschaftsrechts auf die Sozialversicherung", in THEURL, E. (ed.), *Der Sozialstaat an der Jahrtausendwende*, Physica-Verlag, Heidelberg, pp. 234-246.

MÜLLER-GRAFF, P. C. and ZEHETNER, F. (1991), *Öffentliche und privilegierte Unternehmen im Recht der Europäischen Gemeinschaften*, WISO, Linz.

PIETERS, D. (1998), "The Consequences of European Competition Law for National Health Policies", in KREJCI, H., MARHOLD, F., SCHRAMMEL, W., SCHRANK, F. and WINKLER, G. (eds.), *Rechtsdogmatik und Rechtspolitik im Arbeits- und Sozialrecht*, Festschrift T. Tomandl, Wien, Manz, pp. 603-621.

PITSCHAS, R. (1996), "Heilberufe im Europäischen Gesundheitsrecht. Der Einfluß des Gemeinschaftsrechts auf die Ausübung von Heilberufen in Österreich", in TOMANDL, T. (ed.), *Sozialrechtliche Probleme bei der Ausübung von Heilberufen*, Braumüller Verlag, Wien, pp. 1-28.

ROTH, W.-H. (1990), "Versicherungsmonopole und EWG-Vertrag", in BAUR, J. F., HOPT, K. J. and MAILÄNDER, K. P. (eds.), *Festschrift für E. Steindorff*, Walter de Gruyter, Berlin and New York, pp. 1313-1332.

SCHRÖTER, H. (1999), "Artikel 85-89", in GROEBEN, H., THIESING, J. and EHLERMANN, C.D. (eds.), *Kommentar zum EU-/EG-Vertrag*, Volume 2/I (5th edition), Nomos Verlagsgesellschaft, Baden-Baden.

SCHULZ-WEIDNER, W. and FELIX, F. (1997), "Die Konsequenzen der europäischen Wirtschaftsverfassung für die österreichische Sozialversicherung", *Soziale Sicherheit*, No. 12, pp. 1120-1160.

SCHULZ-WEIDNER, W. and FELIX, F. (2001), "Die Bedeutung des europäischen Wettbewerbsrechtes für die österreichische Sozialversicherung", *Soziale Sicherheit*, No. 5, pp. 435-464.

STEINMEYER, H. D. (2000a), "Kassen sind kein Kartell", *Gesundheit und Gesellschaft* , No. 5, pp. 44-49.

STEINMEYER, H. D. (2000b), *Wettbewerbsrecht im Gesundheitswesen. Kartellrechtliche Beschränkungen in der gesetzlichen Krankenversicherung*, Erich Schmidt Verlag, Berlin.

STOCKENHUBER, P. (2001), "Artikel 81 EGV", in GRABITZ, E. and HILF, M. (eds.), *Das Recht der Europäischen Union*, Volume I: EUV/EGV, loose-leaf edition, CH Beck-Verlag, München.

WILLE, E. (1999), "Auswirkungen des Wettbewerbs auf die gesetzliche Krankenversicherung", in WILLE, E. (ed.), *Zur Rolle des Wettbewerbs in der gesetzlichen Krankenversicherung*, Nomos Verlagsgesellschaft, Baden-Baden, pp. 95-156.

ZECHEL, S. (1995), *Die territorial begrenzte Leistungserbringung der Krankenkassen im Lichte des EG-Vertrages, Erich Schmidt, Berlin.*

Appendix

The main EC Treaty articles referred to in this chapter are:

Article 81

1. The following shall be prohibited as incompatible with the Common Market; all agreements between undertakings, decisions by associations of undertakings and concerted practices which may affect trade between Member States and which have as their object or effect the prevention restriction or distortion of competition within the Common Market, and in particular those which:

   (a) directly or indirectly fix purchase or selling prices or any other trading conditions;

   (b) limit or control production, markets, technical development, or investment;

   (c) share markets or sources of supply;

   (d) apply dissimilar conditions to equivalent transactions with other trading parties, thereby placing them at a competitive disadvantage;

   (e) make the conclusion of contracts subject to acceptance by the other parties of supplementary obligations which, by their nature or according to commercial usage, have no connection with the subject of such contracts.

2. Any agreements or decisions prohibited pursuant to this Article shall be automatically void.

3. The provisions or paragraph 1 may, however, be declared inapplicable in the case of:

   − any agreement or category of agreements between undertakings;

   − any decision or category of decisions by associations of undertakings;

   − any concerted practice or category of concerted practices;

   − which contributes to improving the production or distribution of goods or to promoting technical or economic progress, while allowing consumers a fair share of the resulting benefit, and which does not:

      (a) impose on the undertakings concerned restrictions which are not indispensable to the attainment of these objectives;

      (b) afford such undertakings the possibility of eliminating competition in respect of a substantial part of the products in question.

Article 82

Any abuse by one or more undertakings of a dominant position within the Common Market or in a substantial part of it shall be prohibited as incompatible with the Common Market in so far as it may affect trade between Member States. Such abuse may, in particular, consist in:

(a) directly or indirectly imposing unfair purchase or selling prices or unfair trading conditions;

(b) limiting production, markets or technical development to the prejudice of consumers;

(c) capplying dissimilar conditions to equivalent transactions with other trading parties, thereby placing them at a competitive disadvantage;

(d) making the conclusion of contracts subject to acceptance by the other parties or supplementary obligations which, by their nature or according to commercial usage, have no connection with the subject of such contracts.

Article 86

1. In the case of public undertakings and undertakings to which Member States grant special or exclusive rights, Member States shall neither enact nor maintain in force any measure contrary to the rules contained in this Treaty, in particular to those rules provided for in Article 12 and Articles 81 to 89.

2. Undertakings entrusted with the operation of services of general economic interest or having the character of a revenue-producing monopoly shall be subject to the rules contained in this Treaty, in particular to the rules on competition, in so far as the application of such rules does not obstruct the performance, in law or in fact, of the particular tasks assigned to them. The development of trade must not be affected to such an extent as would be contrary to the interests of the Community.

3. The Commission shall ensure the application of the provisions of this Article and shall, where necessary, address appropriate directives or decisions to Member States.

CHAPTER 7

Voluntary Health Insurance and EU Insurance Directives: Between Solidarity and the Market

Willy PALM

Introduction

National authorities have always intervened in the health sector, either as regulator, provider and/or funder of health care. Regulation of the health sector can fulfil several functions:

- It can ensure access to necessary health care for all within reasonable time, either by organising health care provision itself or by funding health care services provided by private or contracted providers. This can be considered as social protection regulation.
- It can ensure good quality health care. This function generally encompasses activities such as regulating training standards for providers, supervising entry to the market and planning the supply of medical goods and services, monitoring clinical activities, and empowering patients. These can be considered as public health regulation.
- It can ensure a stable and transparent voluntary health insurance market. This mainly relates to controlling and supervising the financial soundness of insurers, their state of solvency and standards for market entry. It can also include rules to protect policyholders against malpractice. This can be considered as consumer protection regulation.

The European Community has concentrated on the last of these functions when creating the legal framework for an integrated European market for insurance activities. The first two types of regulation have been guarded almost exclusively as areas of national competence. This situation leads to certain discrepancies. Co-ordination between the different policy areas is needed especially since Article 152 (1) of the EC Treaty, introduced by the Amsterdam Treaty (1997), obliges all Community policies *"to ensure a high level of health protection"*.

I. Voluntary Health Insurance in the European Union

A. The Predominance of Solidarity-based Statutory Health Care Protection

Voluntary health insurance only plays a secondary role in the European Union. In all EU Member States comprehensive public systems of social health care protection have been established to cover the risk of injury and illness, guaranteeing access to a comprehensive set of health care services and goods. On average 75% of health expenditure in the European Union is covered publicly (Table 7.1).

Table 7.1: Public Health Expenditure as a Percentage of Total Health Expenditure in the European Union (1960-1998)

	1960	1970	1980	1990	1998
Austria	69.4	63.0	68.8	73.5	70.5
Belgium	61.6	87.0	83.4	88.9	89.7
Denmark	-	-	87.8	82.6	81.9
Finland	54.1	73.8	79.0	80.9	76.3
France	57.8	74.7	78.8	76.9	76.4
Germany		72.8	78.7	76.2	74.6
Greece	48.8	42.6	55.6	62.7	56.8
Ireland	76.0	81.7	81.6	71.7	75.8
Italy	83.1	86.9	80.5	78.1	68.0
Luxembourg	-	88.9	92.8	93.1	92.3
The Netherlands	-	-	71.1	68.7	70.4
Portugal	-	59.0	64.3	65.5	66.9
Spain	58.7	65.4	79.9	78.7	76.9
Sweden	72.6	86.0	92.5	89.9	83.8
UK	85.2	87.0	89.4	84.2	83.7

Source: Copyright OECD Health Date (2000).

Health systems are funded through compulsory income-based financial contributions from all citizens covered, either through taxes or social contributions. Essentially two separate models dominate, the first one based on compulsory social insurance, instituting a set of relationships managed jointly by the social partners and the State, the second based on the universality principle, ensuring access to a national health service run by the State.

Despite the important differences among European health systems, all Member States, including candidate Member States, affirm the fundamental objective of ensuring access to necessary health care for the whole population, irrespective of individual health and financial status. A key feature is solidarity, with contributions according to capacity to pay (vertical dimension) and benefits according to need (horizontal dimension). This solidarity principle is applied in different ways:

– in terms of integration into the system
  - through inclusion of all citizens (universality);
  - through mandatory affiliation for the citizen (prohibition of opting-out), implying his or her financial participation in the public system;
  - through mandatory acceptance in the administering bodies (pro-hibition of exclusion);
– in terms of funding
  - through a progressive income-related contribution;
  - through contributions independent of individual risk factors (medical history, age, sex etc.);
  - through contributions independent of the size of the family;
  - through cross-subsidising among schemes;
– in terms of benefits
  - through equivalent cover (equal treatment);
  - through a progressive cover according to needs (positive selec-tion for the benefit of deprived categories or categories at risk).

Solidarity does not implement equality in absolute terms. The level of solidarity applied in the different public health care protection systems varies according to:

– application of a ceiling on contributions;
– limitation of the scope for levying contributions;
– exemption of certain categories from contributions;
– application of individual and/or nominal (not income-related) premiums;
– restriction of funding – and hence solidarity – to the level of a specific scheme, a specific sickness fund, a region;
– exclusion of certain categories from compulsory protection (per-sonal scope);
– requirement for payments by patients;
– limitation of services covered (material scope).

Influenced by the principle of universal protection enshrined in national health systems and the increasing funding by the State, social health insurance systems have gradually extended compulsory cover to other professional categories. Except for Germany and the Netherlands, where larger parts are excluded or exempt from compulsory social insurance (respectively 9% and 31% of the population), all Member

States cover nearly the entire population, Recently, both France and Belgium passed legislation that closed the final gaps (Table 7.2).

Since 1 January 1998, all persons legally residing in Belgium for a sufficient period of time and not entitled to claim coverage under another Belgian or foreign system, are integrated under the general statutory health insurance scheme[1]. If income is under the subsistence level[2] no contributions are due.

The French *"couverture maladie universelle" (CMU de base)* guarantees each person who has a stable and regular residence on French territory and is not entitled to health care benefits by any other approved health insurance scheme coverage under the general health insurance scheme[3]. This integrated some 150,000 people into statutory health insurance (Volovitch, 1999). Only those exceeding a certain level of income pay a contribution[4].

Table 7.2: Share of the Population Covered by Public Health Care Protection (1960-1997)

	1960	1970	1980	1990	1997
Austria	78.0	91.0	99.0	99.0	99.0
Belgium	58.0	97.8	99.0	97.3	99.0
Denmark	95.0	100.0	100.0	100.0	100.0
Finland	55.0	100.0	100.0	100.0	100.0
France	76.3	95.7	99.3	99.5	99.5
Germany	85.0	88.0	91.0	92.2	92.2
Greece	30.0	55.0	88.0	100.0	100.0
Ireland	85.0	85.0	100.0	100.0	100.0
Italy	87.0	93.0	100.0	100.0	100.0
Luxembourg	90.0	100.0	100.0	100.0	100.0
The Netherlands	71.0	86.0	74.6	70.7	72.0
Portugal	18.0	40.0	100.0	100.0	100.0
Spain	54.0	61.0	83.0	99.0	99.8
Sweden	100.0	100.0	100.0	100.0	100.0
UK	100.0	100.0	100.0	100.0	100.0

Source: Copyright OECD Health Data (2000).

---

[1] Belgian Royal Decree of 25 April 1997 instituting measures to generalise and ease the access to statutory health insurance, especially for socially and economically deprived groups, Belgisch Staatsblad/Moniteur belge, 19 June 1997.

[2] For a family this is a gross yearly income of € 8,803.62 (2001).

[3] Article 3 of the French Act No. 99-641 of 27 July 1999 instituting a universal health coverage, *Journal Officiel*, 28 July 1999, pp. 11229-11249.

[4] A fiscal reference income of € 7,317.55 per year for a single person, € 15,366.86 for a couple with two children (2001).

B. Different Types of Voluntary Health Insurance

The existence of public health protection and the way it is organised strongly influence the demand for private voluntary health insurance in Member States. For this reason the scope and nature of voluntary health insurance is very different from one country to another, as it is essentially filling the gaps left by public provision in terms of personal and material scope of application as well as choices. Direct competition between public and private coverage only exists where people can choose between both alternatives and opt out of the public system.

Figure 7.1: Voluntary Protection in the EU

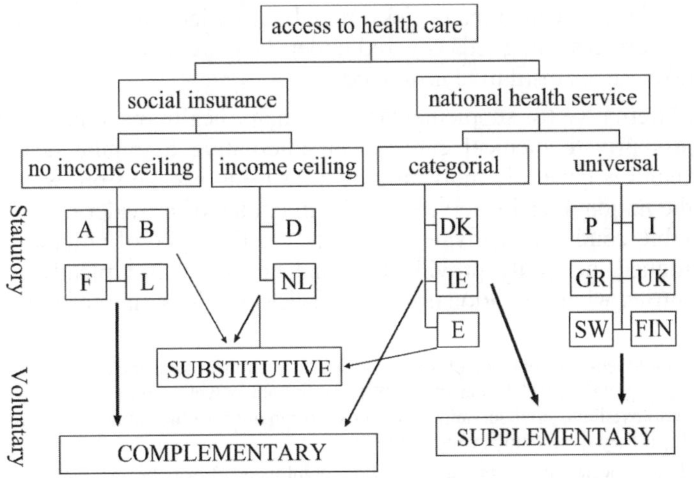

Generally a distinction can be made between three types of private voluntary health insurance (Hermesse *et al.*, 1992).

- substitutive cover: private voluntary health insurance to cover medical expenses for persons excluded or exempted from statutory protection;
- complementary cover: private voluntary health insurance to cover out-of-pocket payments charged to patients for medical services and goods not or only partially covered under statutory protection;
- alternative or supplementary cover: private voluntary health insurance to cover health care services delivered by private health care providers outside the scope of statutory protection.

Substitutive private health insurance is offered in Germany and the Netherlands. In Germany high earners, the self-employed and civil servants are eligible for private health insurance and can actually choose between statutory and private health insurance[5]. But once they have left the statutory system they cannot return[6]. In the Netherlands, the entire population is covered for long-term and chronic care under the AWBZ (first compartment)[7]. For regular health care (second compartment), high earners[8] and the self-employed are excluded from statutory cover and can take out private health insurance. At 65, the privately insured whose taxable household income drops under a certain level[9] can opt back into the statutory system. In Spain only civil servants can opt out of the national health service and take private health insurance (MUFACE, MEGEJU and ISFAS) to which the employer (the State) contributes[10]. In Belgium self-employed workers are only compulsory insured for so-called major risks, mainly in-patient care. For minor risks, other services and goods covered under the general scheme they are free to take out a substitutive insurance[11].

Alternative (or supplementary) voluntary health insurance is taken to access private medical care, as an alternative to public health care. Demand is generally motivated by a desire to escape from waiting lists in the national health service, to obtain choice of provider or more comfortable conditions (private rooms etc.)[12]. This type of voluntary health insurance, generally providing a dual coverage, is typically found in countries where a national health service provides statutory protection,

---

[5] Employees can opt out of statutory health insurance once their salary exceeds the ceiling of € 40,034.15 per year (2001) for the old as well as for the new *Länder*. Self-employed and civil servants can choose to remain into the statutory system (opting-in) if they were statutory insured before.

[6] It is reported that more than 75% of employees above the income level actually prefer to stay in statutory health insurance. Those opting out are generally young, single or couples with double income. Also civil servants can easily opt out as their policies are highly subsidised up to 80%. Also the new *Länder* are underrepresented in voluntary health insurance (see Busse, 2000).

[7] Including hospital care after one year, mental care, nursing care.

[8] Employees whose annual salary exceeds € 30,700 (2002); small self-employed € 19,650; pensioners € 19,550.

[9] In 1999 it was € 18,559.61.

[10] About 85% of civil servants are estimated to have chosen for substitutive health insurance.

[11] About 77% of all self-employed and their family members take out this voluntary insurance with their mutual health fund, which already administers the compulsory scheme. Recently, a working party looking into the social security status of self-employed in Belgium, proposed to generalise the minor risk cover for this category, either by integrating it into the compulsory insurance (social security) or by imposing a legal obligation on self-employed to take out (private) insurance for minor risks (Report working group Cantillon, January 2001).

[12] In Ireland about 40% of the population has alternative health insurance.

but it could in principle also appear in social insurance systems, where statutory protection is provided in kind via contracted providers[13].

Complementary voluntary health insurance is more often associated with social health insurance systems, where patients generally are required to share the cost of treatment. However, it can also be found in countries with a national health service, especially where user fees have been introduced. Furthermore, cover under the national health service is not always equivalent. In Denmark, 3% of the population claim free choice of doctors and so opt for "group 2" statutory coverage, exempting them from the obligation to register with an approved GP and to have a referral from their GP when consulting a specialist. In return, they have to pay for the extra costs. In Ireland only those on lower incomes who are eligible for a medical card (category I: 32% of the population) are actually entitled to the full range of public medical care. Higher incomes, in category II, are required to pay co-payments and even cover the full cost for some public health care services (*e.g.* dental services).

C. Growing Demand for Voluntary Health Insurance

1. Decline of Public Cover

Statutory health care protection not only determines the types of voluntary health insurance, but also the need for it. In that respect, the potential market for voluntary health insurance has been growing over the last decade. Indeed, over the period 1987-1998, public expenditure on health has not managed to keep pace with total health expenditure, which in most Member States has grown at a higher rate than GDP (Table 7.3).

---

[13] In Austria the statutory health insurance also covers services delivered by non-contracted providers (in Austria and abroad), although to a lesser extent (80% of the fee paid for contracted provider).

Table 7.3: Average Annual Growth Rate
of Health Expenditure in Selected EU Member States
Compared to Gross Domestic Product (1987-1998)

	GDP %	Total Health Expenditure %	Public Health Expenditure %
Austria	5.2	6.7	6.0
Belgium	4.9	6.6	7.3
Denmark	4.6	4.2	4.0
Finland	5.2	4.6	4.2
France	4.3	5.5	5.5
Germany	6.0	7.4	7.0
Ireland	9.7	8.2	8.5
Italy	6.8	8.0	6.7
Luxembourg	9.0	7.9	7.8
The Netherlands	5.3	5.5	5.4
Spain	8.3	10.4	10.1
Sweden	5.3	4.8	4.1
UK	6.6	7.8	7.7

Source: Copyright OECD Health Data (2000).

National governments' cost containment policies have shifted costs to households. In social health insurance systems, capped budgets and limits to growth in public expenditure were introduced, co-payments were increased, cover for new techniques or drugs was postponed and insurance packages were, on some occasions, even reduced. This has clearly increased the need for complementary health insurance to cover the growing bill paid by patients. In national health services the problem has mainly been the under funding of public health care, reducing quality and increasing waiting lists, which forces people to seek care in the private sector, which in turn also increases the need for insurance cover.

In a globalising economy, where governments are urged to strengthen competitiveness of business by reducing public expenditure, this process of reducing or stabilising public cover is likely to be exacerbated by the prospect of an ageing society with increasing medical needs, especially in the field of long-term care, as well as the growing scope of technology, introducing new but costly treatments.

It is increasingly argued that rationalising health care delivery is not sufficient, but that choices will have to be made in terms of what services will be covered under statutory protection. In several countries the definition of a core package of medical services to which all citizens should be guaranteed access is being debated.

Since 1992, to be eligible for statutory coverage in the Netherlands, interventions must be shown to be cost-effective and requiring collective funding[14]. On these criteria, some interventions have been removed from cover by compulsory health insurance, or reduced in scope (*e.g.* dental care for adults, physiotherapy, certain pharmaceuticals). However, early optimism that it would be possible to reduce drastically the scope of coverage has been misplaced, since it seems impossible to designate large parts of health care as "unnecessary" and any dichotomy created would stimulate undesired substitution. As complementary health insurance would only provide cover for what falls outside the scope of "necessary" health care, the need for regulating this sector is considered low (Ministerie van Volksgezondheid, Welzijn en Sport, 2001: 53).

In France, given the high level of co-payments charged to patients, the debate on defining a basic package of medical goods and services also extends to the field of complementary insurance.

2. Generalising Complementary Health Insurance

Increased cost sharing by patients, has led some governments to introduce special protection for lower income and high risks groups. These statutory arrangements seek to guarantee access to health care, either directly, by limiting user charges (*e.g.* guaranteed cap on co-payments in Belgium) or indirectly, by guaranteeing access to voluntary health insurance (*e.g.* free-of-charge complementary health insurance in France).

The social and health problems resulting from increasing user charges, especially in deprived groups of the population, compelled the French government to introduce, on 1 January 2000, universal health coverage, the *"couverture maladie universelle"* (CMU)[15]. Besides ensuring affiliation to statutory health insurance by all residents, this new law also provides free access to complementary health insurance for about six million persons (10% of the population) who have an income under a fixed level[16]. CMU beneficiaries are granted free benefits-in-kind, including exemption from payment in advance (direct payment by the sickness fund) and coverage of co-payments for hospital stay, and supplementary charges for dental care and spectacles (up to a certain level). Providers delivering care to CMU must adhere to the agreed tariffs and cannot charge any supplementary fees. In the comple-

---

[14] The used method and criteria form the so-called "hopper of Dunning" named after the chairman of the Commission on choices in health care (Commissie Keuzen in de zorg, Kiezen en delen, Den Haag, November 1991).

[15] French Act No. 99-641 of 27 July 1999 instituting a universal health coverage, *Journal Officiel*, 28 July 1999, pp. 11229-11249.

[16] A fiscal reference income of € 7,317.55 per year for a single person, € 15,366.86 for a couple with two children (2001).

mentary CMU, beneficiaries are free to choose between either the statutory sickness fund or the traditional complementary insurers (mutual benefit societies, provident institutions and commercial insurance companies). Funding for this free-of-charge insurance comes from a 1.75% contribution on premiums of all participating complementary health insurers, supplemented by a state subsidy to balance the account.

For several reasons the French CMU is a remarkably novel step in health protection. It has instituted complete, free-of-charge cover for low-income groups by extending complementary health insurance to those who could normally not afford it. At the same time it has created an opening for statutory sickness funds to enter this field, competing with private operators, not-for-profit as well as for-profit[17]. Clearly, it takes a hybrid form between social security and voluntary health insurance (Beau, 2001). Finally, even if the CMU restores solidarity between subscribers to complementary health insurance and those unable to afford it, at the same time it serves as a legitimation for developing a fully-fledged (second) branch of collective complementary health insurance in France. Article 21 of the CMU Act amends the labour code by requiring employers to engage yearly in negotiations with employees on the modality of a health scheme, if no agreement has been reached at a company or sector level.

In general, employers seem keen to integrate collective health insurance schemes as a new element in negotiating collective labour agreements with their employees. Where there are waiting lists they have a direct interest. In the health insurance market, group health insurance contracts have become most promising. Moreover, transaction costs are lower and exclusion practices are less pronounced.

To conclude, for the time being, apart from in a few Member States like France[18], decreasing levels of public coverage have generally not led to a sustained growth in demand for voluntary health insurance. Slow overall market growth (5.4% annually between 1994 and 1999) is to a great extent explained by premium increases. High prices are considered by some as one of the main deterrents for consumers to buy private health insurance (Mossialos and Thomson, 2001: 9-11, 24-26, 46-47 and 57-58).

---

[17] It is important to note in this respect that under the so-called Juppé experiments, private insurance companies formerly offered to "privatise" statutory health insurance, by administering at the time compulsory and complementary health insurance in return for a capitation payment by social security.

[18] In France, increased cost sharing complementary health insurance has grown from 69% in 1980 to 85% in 1999, before the introduction of CMU.

D. Different Approaches to Voluntary Health Insurance

The type of actors offering it to a great extent, influences the level of demand and access to voluntary health insurance. Historically, the first models of organised protection against the risk of illness were developed by mutual aid and provident societies during the process of industrialisation in the second half of the 19th century. They were initially aimed at compensating for loss of work capacity in the event of illness or restoring it as quickly as possible through ensuring access to health care (Von Stillfried, 1996). Organised on a non-profit basis as spontaneous initiatives by localities, professional organisations and other social groupings, premiums were community-rated as individual health risks were pooled across the members of the mutual society. Often mutual health funds also became involved in organising health care provision through their own providers in order to control prices and quality of care.

In most European countries these mutual health funds have formed the basis of statutory health care protection (Table 7.4). In several countries they were invited to administer statutory health insurance. In other cases they continued to complement public cover (see Dreyfus and Gibaud, 1995; van der Linden, 1996; Duranton *et al.*, 2001).

Table 7.4: Involvement of Mutual Health Funds in Health Insurance in the EU

	Compulsory	Substitutive	Alternative	Complementary
Austria	-	-	-	-
Belgium	yes	yes (1)	-	yes
Denmark	no	-	yes	yes
Finland	-	-	-	-
France	yes (2)	-	-	yes
Germany	yes	No	-	no
Greece	no	-	yes	yes
Ireland	no	-	yes	yes
Italy	no	-	yes	yes
Luxembourg	no	-	-	yes
The Netherlands	yes	yes (3)	-	yes (4)
Portugal	no	-	yes	Yes
Spain	no	yes	yes	yes
Sweden	-	-	-	-
UK	no	-	yes	yes

(1) Self-employed scheme for minor risks;
(2) Schemes for civil servants, students, self-employed and the agricultural sector
(3) The Dutch social sickness funds created own private corporate entities to cover members exceeding the income limit for statutory health insurance.
(4) Since 2000 these forms of cover are legally transferred to separate private entities.

Based upon this historic role, mutual health funds remain an impor-tant actor in the field of voluntary health insurance[19]. However, their role extends beyond the sole scope of insurance, which distinguishes them from private commercial insurers. Generally, mutual health funds can be characterised as personal non-profit associations, based on indi-vidual affiliation (membership), providing social services and protect-tion, democratically defined by their members[20] and financed on the basis of solidarity, with a view mutually to improving social conditions. Accordingly, they are typically committed to open enrolment, lifelong affiliation and non-selection of risks. In return for their social mission and their specific commitments towards their members, mutual health funds are often granted a specific legal status. These national laws explicitly refer to their more comprehensive role, including their involvement in activities related to prevention and health education, social cohesion, solidarity and reducing social inequalities in health.

For-profit health insurers became involved at a later stage, essen-tially in offering group contracts and products designed for higher income classes. They apply a logic of pure insurance, based on com-monly used commercial techniques of risk rating, segmentation of policyholders and exclusion of risks. Aimed at producing profit for the company's shareholders, their interest is essentially to provide selective products for attractive markets. Thus they do not aim to cover more deprived groups, nor do they cover the full range of health care, generally excluding long-term disorders, such as mental health and chronic diseases[21].

Although for-profit and non-profit providers of voluntary health care protection traditionally operated in different segments of the market, the newly emerging demand for complementary or alternative cover as well as the progressive creation of a European single market for insurance creates increasing conflicts. The open, unregulated confrontation by entities pursuing these different approaches is detrimental to solidarity-

---

[19]   In France mutual health funds cover about 50% of the population and represent a market share of 59% of the insurance branch health care costs. In the UK the British United Provident Association (BUPA) holds nearly 40% of the market. In Ireland, VHI provides cover to 95% of the 1.5 million with voluntary health insurance.

[20]   As personal societies, mutual health funds operate essentially according to the principle of self-governance, where stakeholders or their representatives directly take part in defining the funds' policy. This feature is regarded important for creating a specific dynamic essentially driven by patients' interests, adapting the services to actual needs.

[21]   In the Netherlands, substitutive health insurance is limited to the second compartment of basic health care services, while long-term is organised through a universal statutory insurance (AWBZ).

based insurance, as so-called good risks would be drained from the common pool by risk-rating insurers, which would therefore lead to premium increases for those remaining who are at higher risk. By being put on the same footing as "classic" commercial insurers, a real threat exists of *"cannibalisation"* of mutual health funds (see Hélary-Olivier, 2000) and a forced drift towards lowest common denominator market practices[22]. This could have serious consequences for patients, especially those facing higher health risks.

II. An Integrated European Market for Voluntary Health Insurance

A. Principles of the Third Non-Life Insurance Directive

A range of national regulations generally ensures consumer protection in the field of insurance. These include measures to secure a stable and transparent market, controlling and supervising the financial solvency of insurers, and ensuring that existing institutions and new entrants are sound.

Previously there were two main models for the supervision of insurance operations in Member States: contract control or prudential control (Freeman, 1996: 120-22). Contract control is based on the premise that if insurers are sufficiently regulated in the type of contracts they offer and the level of premiums charged, there should be no question of insolvency. This model applied in Germany, where the supervisory body scrutinised policies before they were offered for sale, restricted price competition by enforcing compulsory tariffs and only permitted insurers who specialised in health care to operate in the field of voluntary health insurance. Prudential control, as practised in the United Kingdom, is concerned with the general ability of the insurance company to meet its obligations; the regulatory body's role is not directly concerned with types of contract and premium levels.

Since the 1970s, however, supervision and regulation of insurance companies has been progressively harmonised, so as to promote a single market for life and non-life insurance. The Directives have aimed to provide the necessary legal framework to ensure the development of private insurance in an integrated European market, while stimulating competition, increasing choice for consumers and protecting them against financial loss. The focus of Community regulation has conse-

---

[22] In this respect, it may be reminded that a similar process occurred in the USA when the so-called Blue Cross organisations entered open competition with commercial insurers (see Light, 1996).

quently moved from contract to prudential control (CEA, 1999). The only distinction made is that between life and non-life insurance, for which rather different frameworks have been agreed.

The single market for voluntary health insurance, as a part of the non-life insurance branch, came into effect in the second half of 1994. It took nearly twenty years and three generations of Directives to harmonise insurance regulation with the intention of liberalising the direct non-life insurance market. The first generation (Council of the European Communities, 1973) of Directives allowed insurance companies to establish a branch office or an agency in another Member State. By co-ordinating legal and financial conditions, an authorisation could be obtained more easily. The second generation (Council of the European Communities, 1988) extended free provision of services, allowing insurance companies to cover a risk located on the territory of another Member State without having to set up a branch or agency in that Member State. However, the application was limited to policyholders whose status, size or the nature of the risk to be insured did not require special protection. Hence, health insurance was excluded from the right freely to provide a service. The third Non-Life Insurance Directive (Council of the European Communities, 1992) completed the economic integration process by extending the principle of free movement of insurance services to all risks and all policyholders.

Henceforth, private insurers were in principle allowed to freely

- establish a branch or agency in another Member State, without the need to receive authorisation by the competent national authorities of that State;
- provide insurance services in another Member State without the need to establish a branch office or agency;

This was realised through:

- the introduction of a single licensing and financial control system for insurance activities throughout the EU, led by the Member State where the head office is situated (home country control);
- the mutual recognition of authorisation and prudential control systems on the state of solvency, the establishment of adequate technical provisions and coverage of those provisions by matching assets;
- the abolition of contract and price controls by risk-based Member States and of any prior notification of policy conditions and tariffs[23].

---

[23] For some compulsory classes the right to systematic – but not prior – notification may remain.

This whole legal framework is based on a logic of free Community-wide competition among insurers in which solvency is supervised and guaranteed by the competent authorities of the home Member State, based upon a harmonised set of business conditions and minimal prudential rules. Basically, governments are no longer allowed materially to regulate prices and conditions of insurance products, as this could impede fair competition among European insurers and could jeopardise the financial health of insurance undertakings. Consequently, consumer protection is essentially reduced to financial safeguards against the negative consequences of insolvency of insurance companies[24].

However, the competence of Member States to control or regulate the conditions of insurance offered on their territory is not fully abolished. Such intervention can be justified if insurance conflicts with legal provisions protecting the general good in the Member State where the risk is situated (Article 28 third Non-Life Directive). As this general good concept is rather vague and not defined by law, the European Commission tried to shed more clarity on its application in an interpretative communication (European Commission, 2000a). This document essentially recalls the different criteria defined by the jurisprudence of the ECJ[25]. To justify the general good exemption, a national measure by the host Member State must satisfy all following criteria:

- not have been the subject of prior Community harmonisation;
- not be discriminatory;
- be justified for reasons imperative to the general good (*e.g.* consumer protection, prevention of fraud, cohesion of the tax system and worker protection, including social protection);
- be objectively necessary;
- not duplicate home-country rules;
- be proportionate to the objective pursued.

B. Application to Voluntary Health Insurance

Despite the fact that the third Non-Life Insurance Directive concluded a long process that started more than twenty years earlier, its implementation in the field of voluntary health insurance is not self-evident, mainly because it has to confront a complex and diverse situation in the Member States.

---

[24] Article 31 of the third Non-Life Insurance Directive guarantees a prior information by the insurer on the law applicable to the contract and the arrangements for handling policyholders' complaints.

[25] These criteria are partially already mentioned in recital 19 of the third Non-Life Insurance Directive.

1. The Intersection Between Social Security and Voluntary Health Insurance

Health insurance "forming part of a statutory system of social security" is explicitly left outside the scope of the insurance Directives (Article 2 (1) (d) Directive 73/239/EEC). Since different definitions of social security exist, there is room for confusion.

From the settled case law of the ECJ, it seems that solidarity-based activities performed by social security bodies are only considered as non-economic if compulsory affiliation is involved. Referring to the Poucet and Pistre rulings[26], the ECJ recalled in Garcia and others[27] that social security schemes excluded from the scope of the insurance Directives require compulsory contributions in order to ensure that the principle of solidarity is applied and that their financial equilibrium is maintained.

In this respect, some doubts are raised about the status of voluntary statutory health insurance (Hamilton, 2000: 39), as exists for high-income earners in Germany who reject opting out. This statutory health insurance for voluntarily insured persons is administered by the same social security institutions (Krankenkassen) and follows precisely the same rules as in their compulsory counterpart. As voluntary statutory health insurance is subject to competition with substitutive private insurance, some would regard it as an economic activity, irrespective whether it is operated for profit or not (Mossialos and Thomson, 2001: 18).

Furthermore, in a recent judgement, Commission v. Belgium, the ECJ specified that the exclusion of social security schemes from the insurance Directives only applies to public social security institutions[28]. If a compulsory statutory scheme of social security is administered by private insurance undertakings operating at their own risk with a view to profit – as is the case for the Belgian social security scheme for accidents at work – it is subject to the third Non-Life Insurance Directive. This case is specifically provided for in Article 55, which allows Member States to require that private insurance companies offering compulsory insurance against accidents at work and operating at their own risk comply with specific national provisions, except for those concerning financial supervision.

The question remains whether the same reasoning could apply to compulsory health insurance, especially if public or non-profit social

---

[26] ECJ, joined cases C-159/91 and C-160/91, *Poucet and Pistre*, ECR [1993] I-637.

[27] ECJ, C-238/94, *Garcia*, ECR [1996] I-1673.

[28] ECJ, C-206/98, *Commission* v. *Belgium*, ECR [2000] I-3509.

security institutions are operating in a more market-oriented context, as has arisen from certain social security reforms in several Member States, or if they compete directly with private commercial insurers offering substitutive forms of protection to those authorised to opt out of social security.

This issue directly influences the current debate on the future reform of the Dutch health insurance system. The basis for reform is the goal of a more efficient and demand-driven health care system in which accessibility and solidarity prevails. On the insurance side, the idea is to integrate the different schemes into one compulsory basic insurance scheme, based on mandatory acceptance by the insurer and uniformity of premiums. In a previous opinion, the Dutch social-economic council (SER), a tripartite advisory body, promoted the idea of private health insurance with social safeguards and administered by private insurance companies (SER, 2000). However, the Dutch government in its reform plan (Ministerie van Volksgezondheid, Welzijn en Sport, 2001) finally chose a public model of health insurance. This was inspired by a more recent opinion from a special government commission, which warned against a private model, as it would entail application of the European insurance Directives (ICER, 2001).

2. Substitutive Health Insurance and the General Good Exception

Substitutive health insurance, providing private cover for persons excluded or exempted from statutory protection, seems to be included in the scope of application of EU insurance law. Given its importance, governments have traditionally intervened in this area to ensure that no one is excluded from coverage.

In 1986, Dutch voluntary statutory health insurance was abolished, shifting 700,000 people to private insurance. In order to guarantee access to private health insurance, a standardised package policy was introduced under the Medical Insurance Access Act (WTZ), a publicly designed private substitutive insurance with a legally defined scope of benefits (comparable to statutory cover) and a legally fixed maximum premium[29]. All Dutch health insurers are obliged to provide this policy to any applicant meeting the legal criteria. Some 14% of all of those privately insured have opted for this standard package. The financial risk for these WTZ subscribers is, however, shared among all insurers through a risk pooling system financed out of a special contribution paid by all private policyholders[30].

---

[29] In 1999 the premium for an adult was € 1306.88 (€ 1202.51 for a person over 65).
[30] In 1999 this contribution was € 185.14 for an adult.

In Germany a similar regulation was introduced, requiring health insurers to offer standard policies to persons over 55 who have been privately insured for at least ten years, covering the same range of benefits under the statutory health insurance scheme at a price comparable to the average statutory health insurance contribution[31]. Traditionally, substitutive health insurance in Germany has been based on life insurance rules. Health insurers are prohibited from cancelling their contracts or increasing premiums according to age[32]. However, this has been by-passed by insurers creating new policies, and hence, reconstituting risk pools.

Since these kinds of regulation are likely to hinder the entrance of foreign competitors to the market, such measures need to be justified in the light of the general good principle (Article 28 third Non-Life Directive).

Indeed, when establishing rules for integrating insurance markets, the European legislator has recognised the particular nature and social consequences of health insurance contracts, serving as a partial or complete alternative to health cover provided by the social security system. Therefore, to protect the general good, it was made possible for Member States to adopt or maintain legal provisions that would ensure that policyholders have effective access to health cover taken out on a voluntary basis regardless of their age or risk profile. Measures that might be justifiable on this basis include open enrolment, community rating, lifetime cover, legally fixed standard policies as well as participation in loss compensation schemes. Such measures may, however, not unduly restrict the right of establishment or the freedom to provide services and must apply in an identical manner whatever the home Member State of the undertaking may be (recitals 22-24 third Non-Life Insurance Directive).

For the same purpose, Member States are justified in requiring systematic notification of general and special policy conditions in order to verify that such contracts are a partial or complete alternative to health cover provided by the social security system. However, prior communication of the general and specific insurance conditions does not imply prior authorisation for the marketing of the products (European Commission, 2000a: 33).

---

[31] At the same time, the social health insurance reform law 2000 prohibits private substitutive insured over 55 to return to statutory health insurance, even if their earnings fall below the income ceiling.

[32] Premium level at entry has to contain a reserve for age-related cost increase *(Altersrückstellung)*. However, if real health care cost deviate too much from calculated health care cost, an adaptation clause allows insurers to increase premiums.

The exemption based on the general good, found in Article 28 of the third Non-Life Insurance Directive, was specified with regard to private health insurance in Article 54 (Withers, 1996: 91-97). Where private insurance partially or completely substitutes for health cover provided by the statutory social security system, a Member State might require compliance with its specific legal provisions to protect the general good. It could also demand prior communication of the general and special conditions of that insurance (Article 54 (1) third Non-Life Insurance Directive). For the German regulation, Article 54 (2) allows a Member State to require substitutive health insurance to be operated on a technical basis similar to life assurance, implying specific provisions for premium calculation, establishing age reserves, contract cancellation etc. In that case, the home Member State shall receive all relevant statistical data to control the calculation basis of premiums (Article 54 (2) 2).

It seems obvious that national regulation of substitutive health insurance could meet these criteria. Even though the option of requiring insurers to offer "standard policies in line with the cover provided by statutory social security schemes at a premium rate at or below a pre-scribed maximum and to participate in loss compensation schemes" was explicitly mentioned as a possible means to protect the general good (recital 24 third Non-Life Directive)[33]. The sustainability of the Dutch WTZ, with its mixed public-private character, was questioned in advice to the Minister of Health (Dutch Council of Public Health and Care, 1999: 39). Nevertheless, given the absence of any financial risk in providing standard policies it could be questioned whether this should be considered as an economic insurance activity[34]. As long as the obligation to offer WTZ policies is limited to insurers based in the Netherlands[35], it would not constitute a barrier to the free provision of services[36].

---

[33] During the drafting of the third Non-Life Directive the Dutch government intervened to preserve this piece of legislation.

[34] In that respect, only doubt would seem justified for one category of insured persons eligible for the standard package policy: private insured who pay a higher premium than the maximum WTZ-premium. They can enter the WTZ but the insurer is individually accountable for the financial risk, as they are excluded from the pooling system. Therefore, any intervention from the State could be regarded in this context as harmful for the financial health of insurance activities (Hamilton, 2000: 42).

[35] The Minister of Health can even exempt Dutch insurers from the obligation to offer the WTZ policies. Exemptions are generally awarded to insurers concentrating on employees of a particular company or a group of undertakings.

[36] The same report also criticised the obligation for holders of a private substitutive health insurance contract, to pay a special contribution, compensating for the over-representation of elderly in the statutory health insurance (the so-called MOOZ contribution). However, this could be regarded as an earmarked tax imposed on

3. The Limits of Article 54

The extent to which Member States can rely upon the provisions of Article 54 to justify national regulation in the field of voluntary health insurance is far from clear. It is hard to predict the view that the ECJ might take in particular circumstances. The interpretative Communication issued by the European Commission on the concept of general good in insurance business (European Commission, 2000a) did not add much in this respect.

Sustainability becomes especially hazardous when moving from substitutive health insurance to complementary or supplementary health insurance, which covers services or providers excluded fully or partially from the ambit of social protection. Although the wording of Article 54 seems to refer to substitutive forms of voluntary health insurance[37], it seems that the concept should be interpreted broadly. This is clearly the position of the Irish authorities.

Traditionally, Ireland has complemented its national health service with a publicly regulated system of voluntary health insurance for higher income groups (category II), who do not fully benefit from free access to public health care services. This complementary health insurance is provided mostly by mutual health funds, of which the semi-public Voluntary Health Insurance (VHI Health Care) is the biggest. In order to preserve its open system of community-rated, complementary health insurance in the face of EU insurance liberalisation, Ireland became one of the main advocates of a general good exemption during the drafting of the third Non-Life Insurance Directive. It was under this condition that it accepted opening of the Irish market to other competitors and on this basis, it adopted the 1994 Health Insurance Act, establishing a regulatory framework that sought to promote a level playing field for voluntary health insurance, in Ireland[38]. This Act, which came into effect on 28 March 1996, sets out three main principles for voluntary health insurance to be respected by all insurers: community rating, open enrolment, and life time cover.

In support of these principles, the government announced the creation of a risk equalisation scheme based on age, gender and prior utilisation, to compensate for the possible effects of risk selection (Department of Health and Children, 1999). The first competitor in the

---

private health insurance policies, falling under the fiscal competence of the Member States.

[37] Article 54 actually speaks of "a partial or complete alternative to health cover provided by the statutory social security system".

[38] To this end, the State owned VHI is soon to be converted to a public limited company with full commercial freedom.

newly liberalised market is questioning the necessity and proportionality of this approach (Kinsella and Cully, 2001, see also Light, 1998: 745-748). The participation in loss compensation schemes is mentioned as one of the regulatory measures that could fall under the general good exemption (recital 24 of the third Non-Life Directive). Under the Health Insurance (Amendment) Bill 2000, the new Health Insurance Authority is given the discretion to advise the Minister of Health as to whether or not to invoke the risk equalisation process, based upon the observed differences in risk profiles between insurers[39].

C. The Transposition of the Third Non-Life Insurance Directive

1. The German Speciality Criterion

The transposition of the insurance Directives in the field of voluntary health insurance can hardly be considered a smooth process. Although the problems only emerged in the 1990s this reflects how the process of economic integration had, until then, only a marginal impact on the market for private health insurance, which was then beginning to develop. Indeed, under the first Non-Life Insurance Directive, Germany was allowed to maintain its speciality criterion (Council of the European Communities, 1973: Article 7 (2) b), prohibiting voluntary health insurers from operating in other insurance sectors. This principle has, for a very long time, prevented opening up one of the biggest markets for voluntary health insurance[40].

Even if this privilege was limited to a four-year transitional period, it required the third Non-Life Insurance Directive finally to abolish the German speciality criterion (Council of the European Communities, 1992: Article 5; see also recital 25). Even now, this case is still not settled. The rule of specialisation still applies for insurers based in Germany. Under German social law, employees can only rely on employer contributions if the insurer specialises in health care. The European Commission has sent a reasoned opinion to Germany for infringement of the Directive.

---

[39] New insurers can choose to exempt themselves from participating in risk equalisation arrangements for a period of three years from the start of trading in Ireland (extended from the eighteen months originally envisaged in the White Paper).

[40] In Germany the branch health insurance accounts for 14,5% of total insurance premium income (1996). More than 99% of this market is held by the 54 German health insurance companies grouped under the German association of private health insurance (PKV).

2. *The French* Code de la Mutualité

More fundamental, however, are the problems related to the "personal scope" of the insurance Directives. Besides the differing "material scope" of the insurance Directives, as described above. There are also uncertainties about the types of operators to whom they might apply. Every undertaking developing an economic activity of insurance, "normally provided for remuneration"[41] is presumed to be within the internal market for insurance services. It seems as if the legal status of the operator, as well as its non-profit or profit orientation, are not relevant in deciding the Directive's application. However, the activity of insurance is not further defined. All this is likely to lend uncertainty to the application of the insurance Directives, especially for mutual health funds.

The difficulty in integrating mutual health activities into the narrow concept of insurance, while preserving the specific nature of mutuality, has been demonstrated by the troublesome application of the insurance Directives to the French *Code de la mutualité*. In 1992 the French government took the initiative of inserting the *mutualité* as one of the legal forms an insurance undertaking can adopt to be authorised to provide insurance services throughout the European Union[42]. Whereas transposition of the third Non-Life Insurance Directive did not present any particular problems for the other operators, the insurance companies and the provident institutions[43], the European legal provisions appeared to be incompatible with the specific nature of the French mutuality concept, as enshrined in the French *Code de la mutualité*[44].

Besides the more general problem for individual mutual health funds in meeting the financial requirements of provisions and solvency margins, several issues arose that were, likely to put the specific character of French mutual health funds at risk, including their democratic functioning and their commitments to solidarity:

- the contractual relation between insurer and insured, which is not at all defined, much less harmonised at European level, differs

---

[41] Definition of a service governed by the freedom of movement for services (Article 50 EC Treaty).

[42] Article 8 (1) a Directive 73/239/EEC as modified by Article 6 Directive 92/49/EEC (Council of the European Communities, 1973 and Council of the European Union, 1992).

[43] The *institutions de prévoyance* are company-based non-profit organisations, administered by employer and employee representatives, providing complementary employee benefits, mainly in the field of old age and disability. The are subject to the French Social Security Code (Article L. 931-1).

[44] This Act celebrated its 100 anniversary in 1999.

quite profoundly from membership in a democratically structured society;

- the speciality principle: under the Non-Life Insurance Directives, every insurance undertaking is obliged to "limit its objects to the business of insurance and operations directly arising therefrom, to the exclusion of all other commercial business"[45]. This obligation to specialise in insurance activities would prohibit the French mutual health funds from managing their own social and health care facilities, through which they provide services in kind to their members within the same legal structure.

- the freedom of reinsurance: as many small-scale mutual health funds would not individually meet the prudential criteria, they would need to reinsure their risks. However, the Non-Life Insurance Directives would not allow confining reinsurance for mutual health funds only to other mutual health funds, unless this could be justified by imperatives of general interest. This could seriously affect the autonomy of mutual health funds in defining guarantees and preserving their specific mutuality principles.

- the free transfer of portfolios: under the Non-Life Insurance Directives, transfer of a portfolio of contracts to another operator established within the Community can be submitted only to the control and certification of the solvency margin[46]. Limiting transfer of portfolio for mutual health funds or imposing on the accepting office the specific supplementary commitments of the mutual health fund towards its members would be contrary to the principle of free movement, unless it could be justified by imperatives of general interest.

To solve the deadlock created by the conflicting objectives of establishing an internal market for voluntary health insurance and preserving the specificity of mutual health funds, the French government charged former Prime Minister Michel Rocard with the mission of proposing arrangements for transposition of the Directives into French law that would incorporate and respect mutuality principles. In his mission report (Rocard, 1999) Rocard concluded that, by integrating mutual health funds into the scope of the third Non-Life Insurance Directive, France had already recognised that at least part of their acti-

---

[45] Article 8 (1) b Directive 73/239/EEC as modified by Article 6 Directive 92/49/EEC (Council of the European Communities, 1973 and Council of the European Union, 1992).

[46] Article 11 (2) – (7) Directive 88/357/EEC (as modified by Article 12 Directive 92/49/EEC) (Council of the European Communities, 1988 and Council of the European Union, 1992).

vities were insurance activities. However, a transposition of the Community Directives could be realised without jeopardising the mutuality principles.

The insurance Directives allow insurance services to be provided in kind through an insurer's own facilities. If, however, these services would be extended to persons other than members[47], the speciality principle would require organisation within a separate legal structure. Meanwhile, the ECJ has confirmed that French mutual health funds are permitted to establish a separate legal structure for organising other activities, as long as the capital subscribed to that body does not exceed the value of their free assets and that society's liability is limited to the value of its capital contributions[48].

To preserve mutuality principles, the "Rocard" report concluded that EU law would not oppose any voluntary commitments from the parties involved or the submission of decisions on reinsurance and transfer of portfolios for special approval by the general assembly of the mutual benefit society.

On the other hand, Rocard agreed that the transposition should be embodied in a wider exercise of modernising the French Mutuality Code. He found that the specific nature of the French mutual health funds relies on their own statutory rules rather than on national law. If any derogation or preferential treatment for mutual health funds could be justified under Community law, it would at least require the enactment of the fundamental mutuality principles in national law.

The incomplete transposition of the third Non-Life Insurance Directive into French law during the period defined by the Directive finally led to a ruling against France in the ECJ[49]. In the meantime, a revised *"Code de la Mutualité"* has been adopted[50]. The new Code strengthens the prudential obligations for mutual health funds and increases powers of the supervising body[51]. Insurance activities are separated from other business (*e.g.* the management of social and health care facilities), unless the latter are of minor importance and only accessible to their own members or those of a contracted organisation. To link activities of different legal structures, the concept of "twinning organisations" *(mutuelles et unions soeurs)* has been instituted, with

---

[47] These services in kind can also be provided to insured of another insurance operator with which a contract was concluded to this end.

[48] ECJ, case C-109/99, *Association basco-béarnaise des opticiens indépendants*, ECR [2000] I-7247.

[49] ECJ, case C-239/98, *Commission v. France*, ECR [1999] I-8935.

[50] Ordonnance de réforme du Code de la Mutualité, *Journal Officiel*, 22 April 2001.

[51] Commission de contrôle des mutuelles et des institutions de prévoyance (CCMIP).

partially overlapping boards of administrations and limited financial commitments towards each other. The general assemblies are entrusted, among other things, with decisions on transfer of portfolio and reinsurance. The specific (contractual) relationship between the member and his or her mutual health fund is designated by a signature in an affiliation booklet. Also the status (rights and duties) of the elected administrator is clarified. Finally, the law institutes the specific mutuality principles: absence of medical selection, non-individualisation of premiums according to health status and lifetime cover.

Whilst the difficult transposition seems to have reached a final settlement in France, the discussion on EU conformity is only emerging in other countries. In that respect, it should be recalled that the insurance Directives do not distinguish between profit and non-profit insurers. The non-profit orientation of an operator and its activities do not exclude it from the scope of economic integration. Commercial insurance business is likely to be interpreted by the Commission as services in the broadest way, as all activity that is potentially engaged in competition with other "classic" insurers.

D. Competition among Voluntary Health Insurers

The establishment of an integrated health insurance market raises an even wider debate on equal treatment and fair competition. The application of the freedom to establish and provide insurance services in the Community almost automatically activates EU competition law. Any practice or preferential treatment, likely to distort competition and affect trade between Member States is, in principle, outlawed (Articles 81-89 EC Treaty). Anti-competitive behaviour can, however, be justified if they serve a higher cause (Articles 81 (3) and 87 (2)-(3) EC Treaty[52]) or if they are deemed to be necessary for preserving a specific task of general economic interest entrusted to public undertakings and undertakings to which Member States grant special or exclusive rights (Article 86 (1-2) EC Treaty). The relevance of the latter exemption for the health sector is acknowledged, especially for certain activities performed by sickness funds (Kapteyn and Verloren van Themat, 1995).

---

[52] Of particular importance could be:
- Article 87 (2) (a): aid having a social character, granted to individual consumers, provided that such aid is granted without discrimination related to the origin of the products concerned;
- Article 87 (3) (e): such other categories of aid as may be specified by decision of the Council acting by a qualified majority on a proposal from the Commission.

1. State Aid

Differential treatment, especially with respect to taxes, is increasingly challenged as a market distortion or unfair competition. Member States are under increasing pressure to justify any advantages they permit.

In 1993, the French Federation of Insurance Companies (FFSA) lodged two complaints against the French authorities for favouring mutualities and provident institutions with respect to company and premium taxes. These reliefs are essentially based on the non-profit status of the operator[53]. The FFSA argued that the exemption of a 7% premium tax and other fiscal advantages were in conflict with free competition rules, and likely to discourage foreign insurers, as all operators performed comparable activities. Foregoing tax income, consequent upon these exemptions, could be regarded as state aid.

After several years of silence, the European Commission's DG Competition, acting on a default notice by the plaintiff, instituted a procedure against the French authorities in February 2001 urging them to take all appropriate measures to abolish tax advantages granted to the mutual health funds and provident institutions.

It accepted, however, selective company tax provisions for non-profit organisations, as this is considered a normal element of the tax system. As to preferential treatment with respect to other taxes[54], the Commission, although recognising the specific role of mutual health funds in providing services of general good, considered that the advantages granted are disproportionate to the burden borne by undertaking services of general interest, which it considers represents only a minor fraction of their activities. This confirms the Commission's practice to place services of general economic interest within clearly circumscribed activities.

Whereas preferential tax treatment can be considered as disguised subsidies, direct state aid can also be challenged. In Belgium, the self-employed generally take out a voluntary minor risk insurance with mutual health funds, which also administer their compulsory cover for major risks. This voluntary health insurance is funded by nominal premiums (80%) and complemented by state subsidies (20% or

---

[53] In 1994 the French Confederation of social providence associations joined the complaint as its member organisations were also subject to the 7% premium tax, even if they – formally – also have a non-profit status. However, they often were created by insurance companies in an attempt to benefit of tax exemptions.

[54] Besides the 7% tax on individual health insurance contracts, also other tax exemptions are concerned, *e.g.* on registration rights for real estate, on commercial vehicle tax etc.

€ 49,578.705) for which only mutualities are eligible. Since 1997 these subsidies have been distributed among mutualities according to patterns of risk. Mutualities are obliged to cover the same services and apply the same reimbursement rules as under the general scheme of compulsory health insurance. Even if state subsidies would not be justified by simply referring to the national competence in social security[55], they clearly fulfil a function of general interest, *i.e.* equalising risks and discouraging risk selection, which may justify the award of exclusive rights and exemption from competition rules. However, the argument would stand a better chance if all insurers were offered the benefit of subsidies as long as they respect the same rules as mutual health funds. At present, private insurers compensate for the competitive disadvantage of a lack of state subventions by risk selection, mainly by excluding or limiting cover for services essential for chronically ill patients and the elderly (pharmaceuticals, stay in nursing homes etc.) (Diels, 2000: 15-20; Avalosse, 2000: 3-12).

2. Abuse of Dominant Position

It is not only preferential treatment of non-profit institutions that is challenged under competition law. It is also the position of social security institutions. The participation of the French public sickness funds (CPAM) in administering free complementary CMU health insurance was the subject of a complaint to the European Commission. Some complementary insurers[56] claimed unfair competition as the public sickness funds are guaranteed full recovery of claims paid for under the CMU, whereas the other complementary actors only receive a capitation payment from the CMU fund. Furthermore, the sickness funds are exempt from co-funding the CMU scheme so they do not pay the 1.75% contribution on premium incomes. Finally, the CPAMs benefit from a dominant position due to their role in the compulsory health insurance scheme[57]. The European Commission (DG Competition) rejected this complaint. Basically, it defines the CMU as a public non-contributory service of social aid, as an almost mandatory right to complementary cover for a deprived group of the population. The fact that complementary insurers can participate voluntarily in the CMU does not alter its non-economic nature. Since the CPAMs do not provide any other

---

[55]   ECJ, joined cases C-159/91 and C-160/91, *Poucet and Pistre*, ECR [1993] I-637.

[56]   Fédération nationale de la mutualité indépendante (FNIM) and Fédération française des sociétés d'assurance (FFSA).

[57]   At the time nearly 92% of all CMU beneficiaries are registered with the public sickness funds.

complementary insurance services, there is no competition with other institutions[58].

Where sickness funds have a double function, in both compulsory and complementary health insurance, as in Belgium under the specific legal status of mutual health funds, the private insurance sector may use competition rules to claim a larger share and to repel non-profit mutual health funds. One of the leading Belgian mutual health funds, administering compulsory health insurance for 10% of the population, introduced a new complementary hospital insurance service for all its members at the beginning of 2000, guaranteeing full cover of patient payments in excess of a certain amount[59]. This service, in response to the ever rising direct cost of hospital stays, is based on principles of solidarity; all members affiliated to this mutual health fund are automatically enrolled, no medical screening or any age or illness restrictions are applied, and an identical compulsory community-rated premium[60] funds the service.

The main commercial health insurers[61] in Belgium have attacked this service, labelling it as unfair competition. They claim unequal treatment and unfair commercial practice, based upon the mutual health fund's specific legal status and its (dominant) position in statutory health insurance. In reality, commercial health insurers fear an undermining of their position, given the low premium level of the new mutual health service and its open structure in the field of both individual and group insurance contracts.

Another question is whether the challenged service is to be considered as an economic one. The Belgian Arbitrage Court, ruling on a referral from the President of the Brussels' commercial tribunal, has classified the service offered by the mutual health funds as not commercial[62]. It completely fits within the mutual health funds' statu-

---

[58] This statement also seems particularly relevant for the Flemish care insurance that was recently introduced to compensate for non-medical expenses of care-dependant persons. This new compulsory insurance is administered by the mutual health funds, two private insurance companies and a public fund. It is primarily funded by a nominal premium (€ 10).

[59] A front-end deductible applies of € 247.89 per hospitalisation (€ 123.95 for a minor and € 49.58 for day hospitalisation) and annually € 495.79 per family. Fee and room supplements connected to a stay in a private single room (20% of hospital stays) are excluded from cover. For covering these supplements or the front-end deductible, members can subscribe to two optional insurances.

[60] The monthly premium is € 2.85 per family.

[61] DKV, AG Fortis, AXA Royale Belge and the Belgian Professional Union of insurance companies (UPEA).

[62] Cour d'Arbitrage, Arrêt No. 102/2001 of 13 July 2001.

tory mission of providing services in the field of health, in addition to compulsory health insurance, based on providence, mutual assistance and solidarity, and aimed at promoting health and well-being of its members[63]. The Court confirmed the legitimacy and specificity of the mutualist action in ensuring access to health care. It is, however, very likely that this case will end up before the ECJ on a question of competition law.

3. Exclusive Rights

The question as to what activities in the field of health care protection must be considered as economic and to which Community competition rules therefore apply cannot be answered unambiguously (see Chapters 5 and 6). The question is not only whether the organisation acts as an undertaking, but also in which circumstances and for what objective the activity is pursued.

In the area of insurance the ECJ has traditionally applied a quite broad concept of "undertaking", irrespective of the organisation's legal status and the way in which it is financed[64]. It excludes a compulsory social security scheme, based on solidarity principles such as income-related contributions, with pay-as-you-go funding, cross subsidies between schemes and benefit entitlements that are not proportional to the contributions paid[65]. However, this does not mean that all other activities are automatically subject to competition law or cannot be counterbalanced by other Treaty objectives.

In its Albany International[66] judgement, the ECJ laid down that mandatory membership of a pension fund that manages a supplementary pension scheme, established by collective agreement between the social partners in a sector of industry is not covered by Article 81 (1) (ex Article 85 (1)) of the EC Treaty prohibiting any agreement between undertakings likely to affect intracommunity trade and intended to hamper, restrain or distort competition.

Although the Court defined the pension fund as an undertaking[67] and it admitted that competition was restricted by both the collective agree-

---

[63] Article 3 of the Belgian Act of 6 August 1990 concerning mutualities and national unions of mutualities.

[64] ECJ, case C-41/90, *Höfner and Elser*, ECR [1991] I-1979 ; ECJ, case C-244/94, *FFSA*, ECR [1995] I-4013.

[65] ECJ, joined cases C-159/91 and C-160/91, *Poucet and Pistre*, ECR [1993] I-637.

[66] ECJ, case C-67/96, *Albany*, ECR [1999] I-5751.

[67] Even if the sector pension fund is non-profit-making and its operation based on the principle of solidarity, its activity is considered economic since it determines itself the amount of the contributions and benefits. Furthermore, the Fund operates in accordance with the principle of capitalisation.

ment instituting a single pension fund and the decision of the public authorities to make affiliation to such a fund compulsory, it held that the nature and purpose of the agreement justified its exclusion from the scope of Article 85(1) of the Treaty. Indeed, as collective agreements are the outcome of negotiations between social partners aimed at improving their working conditions, they contribute to the objective of achieving a high level of employment and social protection, set out in Article 2 of the Treaty. Consequently the ECJ recognises the fund's particular social task of general interest, which may justify the awarding of exclusive rights if the application of competition rules would seriously undermine the social policy objectives (Article 86 (2) EC Treaty). Noting that the supplementary pension scheme managed exclusively by the fund displayed a high level of solidarity[68], the Court qualified the exclusivity as justified to prevent the progressive departure of "good" risks, leaving the sectoral pension fund with responsibility for an increasing share of "bad" risks. This would increase the cost of pensions for workers, particularly those in small and medium-sized undertakings with older employees engaged in dangerous activities, to which the fund could no longer offer pensions at an acceptable cost.

The Albany decision was later confirmed for substitutive health insurance based upon a collective labour agreement[69]. The fact that the insurance activity was contracted to a private health insurance institution (instead of a foundation as in Albany) was considered irrelevant.

In connection with this, it is relevant to consider the ECJ's Sodemare judgement[70]. In this case, the ECJ had to rule on an Italian provision that prevented local health authorities from contracting with for-profit providers. Noting that Community law does not affect the power of Member States to manage their social security scheme[71], the Court concluded that a Member State may indeed require that, in order to achieve the social objectives of its social assistance system, it is necessary to limit the scope of contracting to non-profit-making private operators.

---

[68] Contributions not reflecting the risk, obligation to accept all workers without a prior medical examination, exemption from the payment of contributions in the event of incapacity for work, discharge by the Fund of arrears of contributions due from an employer in the event of insolvency, indexing of the amount of pensions in order to maintain their value.

[69] ECJ, C-222/98, *van der Woude*, ECR [2000] I-7111.

[70] ECJ, C-70/95, *Sodemare*, ECR [1997] I-3395.

[71] ECJ, 238/82, *Duphar*, ECR [1984] 523.

In the light of the broader concept of social tasks of general interest, the granting of exclusive rights to non-profit institutions may also be justified in the field of voluntary health care protection.

III. Towards a Broader Social Concept of General Interest in Voluntary Health Insurance

A. The Need for Another Definition of "Fair Competition"

The strategy for European economic integration is essentially based on the assumption that a competitive market economy is the ideal instrument for generating best quality services, with goods at the lowest price. However, this assumption is not always valid in certain sectors nor is it always compatible with the specific policy objectives pursued.

An insurance market could remain relatively unregulated, on a for-profit basis, if the insurable risk is unpredictable and equally distributed among the population (Schieber, 1997). However, in health care, these conditions do not apply.

- Health care risk is highly concentrated. 20% of the population generate over 80% of health care expenses. A small minority, typically 5%, is responsible for 60% of all costs. This concentration is even greater for hospital care, where nearly 90% of the population incurs no cost at all, and the remaining 10% incurs nearly all costs.

- The risk of needing health care is to some extent predictable. The high-risk minority can, to some extent, be identified in advance on the basis of risk factors, such as age, sex, medical (history), social situation etc. (AIM, 1995). New developments in genetics introduce ever more possibilities (Fischer, 2001).

In an unregulated environment, profit-oriented insurers are likely to attract subscribers by offering low premiums, which they can only provide if high financial risks are avoided. This can be done by excluding or delaying cover for pre-existing conditions, limiting or excluding cover for costly modes of care or diseases, risk rating or cream skimming. Older people and those with pre-existing medical conditions will face high insurance premiums or simply be excluded from cover.

If fundamental social principles underlie the health system, aiming to provide access to health care irrespective of financial or health status, appropriate regulation is needed to prohibit these practices, to discourage their use or to remedy their effects. In Europe the existence of comprehensive systems of statutory health care protection, ensuring access to a comprehensive package of health care services, has traditionally limited the need for regulation in the field of voluntary health insurance. Also the fact that voluntary health insurance was mainly conducted by not-for-profit organisations reduced the danger of opportunistic practices. Only in the field of substitutive health insurance, have legislators so far intervened to ensure that no one would be excluded from coverage.

However, discussion on regulation in other fields of voluntary health insurance has attracted renewed interest in some countries, mainly because it is seen as playing an increasingly important role in complementing the statutory health care system. Public restrictions in some countries, designed to contain the steep rise in health care expenditure, together with increased interest by private insurance companies to develop activities in the health care sector, have given impetus to this debate. Further regulatory developments have been suggested to ensure that the EU market for voluntary health insurance works efficiently and allocates resources in a more equitable manner (Mossialos and Thomson, 2001: 20).

In this context, allegations of unfair competition, addressed essentially against non-profit operators organising cover according to solidarity principles, are counter productive to the objective of achieving a high level of social and health protection. Thus, the debate on the concept of "fair competition" should rather be reversed, inviting all operators to observe commonly agreed rules of general interest that rule out practices of selection and exclusion. Only by creating a level playing field for solidarity-based insurance can fair competition among all health insurers be based on performance and quality services.

B. Ensuring Access to Voluntary Health Insurance

In his mission report Michel Rocard advocated the idea of common European rules for meeting the cost of medical treatment in accordance with ethical principles, which should apply to all operators in the field of voluntary health insurance. On his initiative, once elected as an MEP, the European Parliament adopted in December 2000 a resolution on supplementary health insurance (European Parliament, 2000) calling on the Commission to examine the possibility of establishing a framework for supplementary health insurance schemes, to preserve solidarity and accessibility in the field of health care.

The resolution starts from the observation that all Member States are facing growth in health care costs and problems of financing statutory health systems, which has lead to increasing charges for patients. This may force a growing number of European citizens to postpone necessary treatment for financial reasons. Under these circumstances, supplementary health insurance has become almost indispensable for realising the fundamental right of access to quality health care within reasonable time limits.

Although the European Parliament insist on maintaining the state social security model as the cornerstone for social solidarity in the European Union, it draws attention to the increasing importance of voluntary health insurance in complementing the statutory health care system. Consequently, the resolution promotes the idea of an active private sector commitment, applying ethical principles (*e.g.* codes of good conduct), and insists on a constructive dialogue between public and private actors to develop a common view of universal services in the light of the Amsterdam Treaty.

The European Parliament calls on the Commission to present a green paper on Member States' policies in this field. This should serve as a basis for proposing appropriate legislative initiatives at Community level. The resolution suggests setting out guiding principles for public policy on "supplementary" health insurance schemes, preferably through a recommendation, including:

- the recognition of a common concept of basic service, based on the Community principle of general interest;
- the guarantee of community-rating and non-discrimination on health, age and financial grounds;
- the organisation of a system of pooling funds to cover the cost of serious diseases or clinical conditions;
- the participation of private insurers in public policies for monitoring contagious diseases and developing preventive measures.

On the other hand, the resolution proposes harmonising, preferably through a directive, common minimum rules to be observed by all "supplementary" health insurers, whether non-profit or for-profit, including:

- a prohibition on the use of personal medical data, such as genetic profiles, preferably subject to a transitional period;
- a prohibition on prior medical screening, except for the requirement of completing a medical questionnaire, subject to certain restrictions;
- an obligation by the insurer to provide lifelong insurance;
- a guarantee of transparency, especially with regard to foreseeable changes in premiums;
- the introduction of a mediation procedure.

Although the European Parliament recognises the primary role of the Member States in this area, it justifies the need for Community action on account of differences between health insurance systems, public and private, creating serious obstacles to the free movement of persons. Consequently, it emphasises the need to ensure retention of entitlements in supplementary health insurance schemes when staying or residing in another Member State, as well as to adopt a more flexible approach by private health insurers towards refunding health care provided throughout the EU. Now that the ECJ has widened the possibility for patients to receive health care services in another Member States while obtaining reimbursement from their own social security system[72], voluntary health insurance is generally considered to be exempt from these rulings except where national legislation governing voluntary health insurance provides for restrictions to free movement, where private health insurers are responsible for carrying out public policies on behalf of the State, or if they acted in concert so as to hinder the principle of free movement.

C. Services of General Interest

The uncertainty that faces the health sector, with increasing economic integration, also applies to the debate on services of general interest. This notion covers market and non-market services that public authorities class as being of general interest and subject to specific public service obligations (European Commission, 2000b: Annex II). Since the insertion in the Amsterdam Treaty of a special provision on services of general economic interest (Article 16 EC Treaty)[73], the fundamental values underpinning these services are recognised and placed on an equal level with the Community's economic principles.

While the debate primarily focuses on the economic sectors that are being liberalised (energy, telecommunication, transport etc.), clearly the concept is relevant to social sectors. Its aim is to counterbalance competition and internal market rules, where these might jeopardise universal access, high quality and affordability of the service. All services that intend to ensure the exercise of fundamental rights[74] would automatically be treated in the same way.

---

[72] ECJ, C-120/95, *Decker*, ECR [1998] I-1831; ECJ, C-158/96, *Kohll*, ECR [1998] I-1931; ECJ, C-157/99, *Geraets-Smits and Peerbooms*, ECR [2001] I-5473.

[73] Article 16 – without prejudice to Articles 73, 86 and 87, and given the place occupied by services of general economic interest in the shared values of the Union as well as their role in promoting social and territorial cohesion, the Community and the Member States, each within their respective powers and within the scope of application of this Treaty, shall take care that such services operate on the basis of principles and conditions which enable them to fulfil their missions.

[74] Including the right to medical treatment contained in Article 35 of the Charter on fundamental rights of the European Union.

In its updated Communication on services of general interest in Europe (European Commission, 2000b: 8), the European Commission states:

many activities conducted by organisations performing largely social functions, which are not profit-oriented and which are not meant to engage in industrial or commercial activity, will normally be excluded from the Community competition and internal market rules. [...] However, whenever such organisation, in performing a general interest task, engages in economic activities, application of Community rules to these economic activities will be guided by the principles in this Communication respecting in particular the social and cultural environment in which the relevant activities take place. Moreover, where Community law would apply to these activities, the Commission will also examine, in the light of a more general reflection on the use of its discretionary powers, whether the interests of the Community require to proceed with regard to these cases, subject to its legal obligations established in the EC Treaty.

Even if the Commission shows some reluctance in its approach to social services and notes that non-economic services are excluded from the application of competition and internal market rules, this does not create greater legal certainty for the actors involved, especially those being threatened because of their specific role or status.

This was also recognised by the Economic and Social Committee in a recent own-initiative opinion on private not-for-profit social services in the context of services of general interest in Europe (ESC, 2001). This opinion addresses the specific position of "private not-for-profit organisations [...] that are active in the health and social spheres, though where necessary conducting economic activities that are subordinate to their primary social functions". Referring to the contribution to the general interest of "organised civil society" in protecting the most vulnerable groups in the population and generating social cohesion and solidarity among citizens, the Committee advocates that a legitimate place should be reserved in the EU for social services that strikes a balance between those that are entirely public and those that are entirely profit-driven. In order to create more certainty with regard to the application of European competition law, the opinion suggests two options. The first is introducing a general exemption principle for categories of social services provided by private not-for-profit operators in Article 16 of the EC Treaty. The other is to draw up more detailed criteria for competition rules with areas that should be exempted from them.

The latter suggestion could find support in the proposal for the structure of a framework Directive determining the general principles according to which services of general interest are to be delivered and operated. It is suggested that sectoral Directives elaborating on the specific characteristics of each sector would complement this framework Directive[75]. Along the same line, some suggest developing a fourth generation of insurance Directives, creating a wider regulatory environment for human and social risk insurance, binding on all insurers, in order to prohibit any selection of risks and to rule out the possibility of cancellation of contracts due to age or state of health (Hamilton, 1999: 1-3).

Conclusion

Integration of the market for insurance has created uncertainties regarding Member States' scope to create policies basing voluntary health insurance on solidarity principles. Even if Article 54 of the third Non-Life Insurance Directive introduces the possibility of exemption based on the general good, it is unclear whether this would meet the regulatory needs of different Member States. Furthermore, the ambit of the Community regulatory framework, in terms of what activities and what operators are concerned, is somewhat obscure, creating legal uncertainty for the different actors involved in this sector. And finally, competition rules tend to discourage the principle of solidarity.

Consequently, a more differentiated approach is needed for several reasons, taking into account the existing diversity and complexity of voluntary health care protection in the EU. The concept of general interest could serve as a basis to develop a more comprehensive framework for voluntary health insurance, integrating social and public health interests.

Between public statutory health protection and private commercial medical insurance, social services of a voluntary nature exist, in which principles of general interest are considered necessary to guarantee accessibility to care irrespective of financial or health status. In that respect not only the demarcation line between economic and non-economic activities needs to be defined, but clarification of the concept of services of general interest in the field of voluntary health care protection also seems desirable.

The European social model is not confined to state systems of solidarity. Many actors contribute to development of a coherent social policy in an integrated Europe, promotion of social cohesion and achievement of a high level of social and health protection.

---

[75] See discussion document by the CEEP (Centre européen des entreprises à participation public et des entreprises d'intérêt économique général) and ETUC (European Trade Union Confederation) presented on 4-5 October 2001.

Bibliography

AIM (1995), "Risk Structure Compensation. Financing Health Care: Sharing Risks, Preserving Solidarity", Proceedings of an AIM workshop, 11 October 1995.

AVALOSSE, H. (2001), "Verzekering kleine risico's voor zelfstandigen", *CM-Informatie*, No. 197, pp. 3-12.

BEAU, P. (2001), "La CMU est-elle une prestation complémentaire concurrentielle?", *Espace social européen*, 23 February 2001.

BUSSE, R. (2000), *Health Care Systems in Transition: Germany*, European Observatory on Health Care Systems, Madrid.

CEA (1999), *Annual Report 1999*, Comité européen des assurances, Paris.

COUNCIL OF THE EUROPEAN COMMUNITIES (1973), First Council Directive 73/239/EEC of 24 July 1973 on the co-ordination of laws, Regulations and administrative provisions relating to the taking-up and pursuit of the business of direct insurance other than life assurance, OJ L 228, 16 August 1973, pp. 0003-0019.

COUNCIL OF THE EUROPEAN COMMUNITIES (1988), Second Council Directive 88/357/EEC of 22 June 1988 on the co-ordination of laws, Regulations and administrative provisions relating to direct insurance other than life assurance and laying down provisions to facilitate the effective exercise of freedom to provide services and amending Directive 73/239/EEC, OJ L 172, 4 July 1988, pp. 0001-0014.

COUNCIL OF THE EUROPEAN COMMUNITIES (1992), Council Directive 92/49/EEC of 18 June 1992 on the co-ordination of laws, Regulations and administrative provisions relating to direct insurance other than life assurance and amending Directives 73/239/EEC and 88/357/EEC (third Non-Life Insurance Directive), OJ L 228, 11 August 1992, pp. 0001-0023.

DEPARTMENT OF HEALTH and CHILDREN (1999), White Paper, Private Health Insurance, Dublin.

DIELS, J. (2000), "Risicoverevening in de vrije verzekering. Hefboom tot solidariteit", *CM-Informatie*, No. 190, January 2000, pp. 15-20.

DREYFUS, M. and GIBAUD, B. (1995) (eds.), *Mutualités de tous les pays. Un passé riche d'avenir*, Mutualité française, Paris.

DURANTON, M., ZOUAQ, A. and PILON, J. (2001), "Mutual Benefit Societies: Solutions in Europe, North-Africa and Latin America", in RON, A. and SCHEIL-ADLUNG, X. (eds.), *Recent Health Policy Innovations in Social Security*, International Social Security Series, Vol. 5, ISSA, Transaction, London, pp. 253-266.

DUTCH COUNCIL OF PUBLIC HEALTH and CARE (1999), *Europa en de gezondheidszorg*, Dutch Council of Public Health and Care, Zoetermeer.

ESC (2001), "Own-initiative opinion of the Economic and Social Committee on private not-for-profit social services in the context of services of general interest in Europe", CES 1120/2001, 12 September 2001.

EUROPEAN COMMISSION (2000a), "Freedom to Provide Services and the General Good in the Insurance Sector", Commission Interpretative Communication,

C(1999)5046 of 2 February 2000 (http://www.europa.eu.int/comm/internal_market/en/finances/insur/5046en.pdf).

EUROPEAN COMMISSION (2000b), Communication from the Commission. "Services of General Interest in Europe", COM (2000) 580 final (http://europa.eu.int/comm/consumers/policy/developments/serv_gen_int/serv_gen_int05_en.pdf).

FISCHER, A. (2001), "Die Gentechnik: Gefahr für ein solidarisches Gesundheitssystem?", *Die BKK*, No. 10, October 2001, pp. 465-471.

FREEMAN, S. (1996), "Health Care Provision in the EC", *AIDA Information Bulletin*, No. 47, pp. 120-122.

HAMILTON, G. J. A. (1999), "Towards a Fourth Generation of European Insurance Directives", *AIMS*, No. 5, March 1999, pp. 1-3.

HAMILTON, G. J. A. (2000), "Interne markt en (aanvullende) ziektekostenverzekeringen", *Tijdschrift voor Gezondheidsrecht*, No. 1/2000.

HÉLARY-OLIVIER, C. (2000), "Les mutuelles ont-elles encore une raison d'exister?", *Droit Social*, No. 9/10, pp. 878-883.

HERMESSE, J., LEWALLE, H. and PALM, W. (1992), "Private Complementary Health Schemes in the EC", presented at the EC Seminar "Complementary Health Schemes in the European Union", Prien and Chiemse (Bavaria), 14-16 October 1992. Published by ed. Basys in 1995, pp. 47-80.

ICER (2001), *Werkgroep zorgstelsel*, eindrapport, Interdepartementale Commissie Europees Recht, 3 April 2001.

KAPTEYN P.J.G. and VERLOREN VAN THEMAT P. (1995), *Inleiding tot het recht van de Europese Gemeenschappen, Na Maastricht*, Kluwer Academic Publishers, Deventer.

KINSELLA, R. and CULLY, A. J. (2001), "Risk Equalisation – The Health Insurance (Amendment) Bill 2001 and the Irish PMI Market", *Irish Financial Services Law Journal*, Vol. II, No. 2, pp. 5-10.

LIGHT, D. (1996), "Does Medical Care Have to be Rationed?", AIM International Conference, "Paying for Health: The New Partnership", 3-4 October 1996, May 1997, pp. 11-22.

LIGHT, D. (1998), "Keeping Competition Fair for Health Insurance. The Irish Beat Back Risk-rated Policies", *American Journal of Public Health*, No. 88, pp. 745-748.

MINISTERIE VAN VOLKSGEZONDHEID, WELZIJN EN SPORT (2001), Vraag aan bod. Hoofdlijnen van vernieuwing van het zorgstelsel, Tweede Kamer, 2000-2001, 27855, No. 1-2 (http://www.zorgaanzet.nl/materiaal/Vraag_aan_bod.pdf).

MOSSIALOS, E. and THOMSON, S. (2001), "Voluntary Health Insurance in the European Union", *LSE Health Discussion Paper*, No. 19, May 2001.

ROCARD, M. (1999), "Mission mutualité et droit communautaire", Rapport de fin de mission, Paris, May 1999.

SCHIEBER, G. J. (1997) (ed.), "Innovations in Health Care Financing", *World Bank Discussion Paper*, No. 365, Proceedings of a World Bank Conference, 10-11 March 1997.

SER (2000), "Naar een gezond stelsel van ziektekostenverzekeringen", Sociaal-Economische Raad, Den Haag, December 2000.

VAN DER LINDEN, M. (1996), *Social Security Mutualism. The Comparative History of Mutual Benefit Societies*, International and Comparative Social History, Vol. 2, Peter Lang, Bern.

VOLOVITCH, P. (1999), "Egalité devant les soins, égalité devant la santé: quel rôle pour l'assurance-maladie?", *La Revue de l'IRES*, No. 30, Paris, pp. 149-171.

VON STILLFRIED, D. (1996), *The Reconcilability of Solidarity and Competition in the Health Care Sector, Competition and Solidarity*, AIM, pp. 7-25.

WITHERS, S.D. (1996), "The Concept of General Good in European Jurisprudence, in Competition and Solidarity. Can they Co-exist in Europe's Health Care Systems?", AIM symposium, pp. 91-97.

CHAPTER 8

The Pharmaceuticals Market: Competition and Free Movement Actively Seeking Compromises

Leigh HANCHER

Introduction

The key issue is to achieve a Single Market that both ensures a high level of protection of public health and promotes competitiveness, growth and employment – whilst recognising the legitimate right of Member States to control their health care expenditure. Considerable progress has been made in licensing and in intellectual property – although there is [...] work to be done on the market side (Liikanen, 2001a: 19).

This chapter is divided into two main parts: first, the evolution of the harmonisation of regulatory procedures for medicines for human use, and second, competition and free movement issues. The application of EC law and in particular the rules on competition and free movement to the pharmaceutical sector have been the subject of considerable commentary and analysis in recent years. This is partly due to the intrinsic importance of the subject from a practical as well as a more theoretical or academic perspective, but can perhaps also be attributed to the fact that the organisation and practices of the pharmaceutical industry have produced a rich seam of European legal problems, often raising many novel issues. This chapter cannot attempt to cover all the many and varied aspects of the application of EC competition law to this complex sector. Instead it focuses on the interconnection between regulatory issues and the evolution of European secondary legislation, and recent developments in the case law of the European Courts and the practice of the Commission in relation to competition and free movement issues. Important matters relating to the development and gradual harmonisation of the Community authorisation procedures[1], as well as advertising and marketing are now subject to increasingly complex bodies of

---

[1] For an overview, see the series of volumes entitled "The Rules Governing Medicinal Products, the European Union" (http://dg3.endra.org/endralex/index.htm).

secondary law. In this respect, the chapter will look in some detail at the development of recent case law, particularly with respect to the application of the regulatory framework to generic products and parallel imports.

This contribution further examines the legal and policy dimensions of Community intervention in industry pricing strategies as well as national regulatory controls. It examines the link between these issues and the relevant findings of the recent report by expert economists on the competitiveness of the European pharmaceutical industry. The report, entitled, "Global Competitiveness in Pharmaceuticals: A European Perspective" commissioned by DG Enterprise (Gambardella *et al.*, 2000) confirmed that the European industry has declined in competitiveness as compared to the USA, albeit that there are large differences and trends across the Member States. The report puts forward a number of explanations to support its finding that, as a whole, Europe is lagging behind the USA in its ability to generate, organise and sustain innovation processes that are increasingly expensive and organisationally complex. Significantly, the Report stresses that many European national markets are not sufficiently competitive, and that the nature and intensity of competition in final markets is too weak to nurture efficiency and innovation.

It is self-evident that the publication of this report, coinciding with the Commission's review of the current legal procedures for marketing or licensing products put on to the European market, raises many complex issues. Furthermore, the publication of this latest report coincides with important legal challenges to the Commission's powers to regulate the activities of pharmaceutical firms who seek to impose dual-pricing systems or other methods of blocking competition from low-priced markets. This paper concludes with some suggestions on the options open to the Commission to move forward the pressing but perplexing problems that the Community faces at the beginning of the twenty-first century.

A. The Changing Community Pharmaceutical Market

The pharmaceutical market differs in several important respects from the market for most consumer goods. Medicinal products cannot be put on the market of the European Union without a product licence, also known as a marketing authorisation. Demand for prescription products is filtered through the prescribing physician and to a certain extent, through health payers: the consumer/patient rarely selects the product or pays, or is even aware of the full price that the manufacturer receives. Nor can the supplier usually set its own price: in the majority of Member States prices are regulated through a bewildering variety of techniques ranging from direct price control to complex profit control schemes. At the risk of generalising, government intervention is more stringent, resulting in tougher price controls, where the volume of demand is traditionally high. Prices for medicines, especially prescription medicines, continue to diverge dramatically across the Member States – with some market leaders costing up to 50% more in the high price Northern markets as compared to the Southern European markets.

The eventual accession of the Eastern European countries now lined up to join the European Union will undoubtedly lead to wider divergence in prices across the Union. In addition, the increasingly heated debate as to whether major pharmaceutical companies should supply essential medicines at "discounted prices" to developing countries can only fuel this long running debate. As is well known, price divergences within Europe fuel the process of parallel importation – that is the re-exportation of branded medicines from low priced markets to high-priced markets. Growth in re-exportation and parallel trade from beyond the expanding European borders cannot totally be excluded (EFPIA, 2001)[2]. On patent expiry, the lucrative market position enjoyed by leading branded products increasingly comes under threat from generic substitutes. Patent protection for pharmaceuticals has traditionally been weak in many Eastern European companies, and their thriving generic manufacturing sector is gearing up for full integration into the European Union[3]. Further, several of the so-called accession countries – *i.e.* the ten East European countries, as well as Cyprus and Malta – are contemplating the introduction of so-called "Roche-Bolar"-type provisions in their domestic intellectual property laws to allow generic manufacturers to develop versions of patented pharmaceuticals before the patents expire. The European Parliament in its recent opinion on the Commission's proposal for a Community action programme in the field of public health has lent its support to this approach[4]. The Commission has now included a Roche-Bolar provision in its recent proposals on revising the current product authorisation regulations, as discussed below. Added to this cocktail is the impact of e-commerce and the spread of campaigns by patient advocates and health care and insurance

---

[2]   See further, the report of the meeting between the Commission and six major companies on 29 May 2001, *Agence Europe*, No. 7978, page 16, 6 June 2001 and the proposals put forward by the European Parliament to reduce the duration of patents on vital medicines, reported in the same issue.

[3]   See further "Accession States Start Driving the EU Agenda", *Scrip Magazine*, February 2001, pp. 13-15.

[4]   *Scrip Magazine*, No. 2638, page 2, 27 April 2001. The Commission has, however, supported the research based industry in its concerns to limit prepatent expiry development work for commercial purposes.

companies for more efficient medicine purchasing procedures – and hence direct access to information about medicines as well as eventually to the medicines themselves – all of which will put pressure on the margins enjoyed by traditional pharmaceutical wholesalers.

B. Competition, Parallel Trade and Generic Products

Parallel trade – or intra-brand competition – in pharmaceuticals is well established as a phenomenon, although it seems difficult to quantify with any degree of precision. For some it has its origins in the fact that it is a product of national regulations on pricing and profit controls and/or controls on reimbursement through social security schemes. Thus the process is driven by the ease of exporting certain products from low-priced countries into higher priced countries, thereby undercutting existing suppliers of the same products in the Member State of importation. For others it is attributable to the practices of an industry that seeks to maximise the benefits of national regulatory divergence: parallel importing therefore promotes overall efficiency by curbing excessive profits. It is probably fair to say that the truth of the matter lies somewhere between these two poles. The industry must continue to live with a scattergram of national policies on pricing and profit controls, but is of course able to react to this situation in a number of ways, even if it cannot necessarily control it. Currency movements have further fuelled price divergences. Exchange rate movements alone account for a 40% price gap between Germany and Italy for SmithKline Beecham's (SKB) Sorxat (paraxotine), even although the brand was introduced at a common launch price in 1993. Obviously the introduction of the euro has tempered the impact of currency fluctuations, at least between those Member States that have adopted it, or are fixed to it. However, some countries that are not members remain net importers of parallel products.

The recent case law reviewed here indicates that the ECJ has been unwilling to reverse its traditional pro-internal market and hence pro-parallel import approach, especially in the field of intellectual property law. Intellectual property rights are of vital importance to the research-based industry. At the risk of oversimplification, the Court has taken the attitude that once the holder of a patented product or the owner of a trademark or copyright puts its product on the market of Country A as well as Country B, its rights are "exhausted" in the sense that it cannot rely upon these rights to prevent trade in the products between Country A and B, or in the case of trademark rights to prevent further trade within the European Economic Area[5].

Generic or inter-brand competition between products whose patent protection has lapsed is or ought to be another important source of price competition. Barriers to increased market entry for generics abound, however. These include not only difficulties in obtaining market authorisation without generating all the requisite data but may also relate to the workings of national price and profit control regimes. The report on Global Competitiveness, submitted to DG Enterprise in late 2000, concludes that, in countries that rely on administered price regimes, prices and market shares do not vary substantially after patents expire. Companies may be awarded a guaranteed price on the introduction of a new product into a national health system and this price does not usually vary over time, hence reducing the incentive for further innovation by the company in question, which is content to benefit from a protected market share. Although cost saving measures might realise short-term savings for governments they have in their turn introduced new distortions in final markets (Jacobzone, 2000). The leading research-based companies in their turn blame the slower uptake of innovative medicines and lower prices in Europe for the lack of incentive and reward for innovation – there can be as much as four years between patients having access to innovative medicine in the first and last Member State (Edmonds *et al.*, 2000).

C. The Legal and Policy Framework

The processes of intra-brand (*i.e.* parallel trade) and inter-brand competition (*i.e.* generics) are considered generally by the European Commission, and particularly the Directorate-General for Competition (DG Comp), as essential if not inevitable for the eventual realisation of a single market across the European Union. The Commission as legal guardian of the Treaty on European Union must safeguard these processes. In particular, it must guarantee the proper enforcement of the Treaty rules on free movement of goods and competition – two of the major pillars on which the single market edifice is constructed. For example, if the original manufacturer attempts to protect a high-priced market from parallel importation, through seeking to enforce its intel-

---

[5]   This paper will not, however, examine in full the implications of the Court's judgements in case C-355/96, *Silhouette International Schmied* v. *Hartlauer Handelsgesellschaft*, ECR [1998] I-4799 and in case C-173/98, *Sebago*, ECR [1999] I-4103 for the future of the doctrine of international *versus* European exhaustion. The relevant issues are discussed further in Advocate General Stix-Hackl's Opinion in joined cases C-414/99 to C-416/99, *Zino Davidoff SA* v. *A & G Imports and Levi Strauss and Co.* v. *Tesco Stores*, ECR [2001] I-8691, 5 April 2001.

lectual property rights, it may well find that it has infringed the Treaty rules on free movement. Attempts to reach contractual agreements with wholesalers/distributors to restrict supplies to a particular territory and cut off the source of parallel trade may also infringe the Treaty's competition rules. It should be stressed that the Commission itself does not have the monopoly on enforcement of these provisions – all these Treaty principles, enshrined in the directly effective Articles 28, 30, 81 and 82 EC, can be enforced by the party claiming injury through local courts in each Member State.

D. Commission Competence

An important dilemma which besets the Community pharmaceutical market – which has both policy as well as legal connotations – is the nature of the Commission's executive competence to launch policy initiatives and eventually propose binding rules to promote intra and interbrand competition: is this to be dealt with as an industrial policy issue, as a health policy issue or as a social security and consumer protection issue? The choice of policy focus is not merely of political importance but has a definite legal dimension. The division of legal competences between Member States and the Community differs depending on whether industrial policy, public health or social security is at stake. The latter areas remain, from a legal as well as a political perspective, very much the preserve of the Member States[6]. Article 152 of the EC Treaty, as amended by the Treaty of Amsterdam, extends Commission competence on health care only to a limited extent. At the same time, it must be acknowledged that, even prior to the introduction of a specific Treaty competence on health, the Community was able to advance complex and advanced pharmaceutical regulation on the basis of its general powers under Articles 100 and 100A (now 95). The challenge ahead for the Commission in particular is to achieve a better integration of its many health related policies. And how should such policy choices be reconciled with the Commission's related legal duties to uphold and enforce the principles of European law? This could be a key focus for the newly created high-level group on competitiveness in the industry, and its attendant "issue groups" although the first Consultation Paper, issued in

---

[6] In its recent judgement in Case C-157/99, *Geraets-Smits and Peerbooms*, of 12 July 2001, the Court recalled that "according to settled case law, Community law does not detract from the power of the Member States to organise their social security systems. In the absence of harmonisation at Community level it is therefore for the legislation of each Member State to determine the conditions concerning the right or duty to be insured with a social security scheme. Nevertheless, the Member States must comply with Community law when exercising that power" (paragraphs 44-46 of the judgement).

early October 2001 does not directly touch on this issue, as noted below (European Commission, 2001a).

As already noted, the Commission may effectively protect intra-brand competition via parallel importation through a judicious enforcement of the Treaty competition rules. It can and has ruled that companies that seek to impose export bans or other restrictions on wholesalers operating in low priced countries to supply their products to higher price markets infringe Article 81(1) EC, which outlaws cartels and agreements restricting competition[7].

These Treaty provisions are of course equally applicable to the demand side of the market, with the added proviso that national regulatory measures may be justified on grounds of social solidarity. Much can depend on the mechanics of the national scheme in question and whether responsibility for setting prices or drawing up reference lists rests with governmental authorities or is entrusted to market actors such as health care or insurance funds. The German Federal Association of sickness funds was initially involved actively in the national reference pricing system, as amended in 1999, and set the upper price limits for certain products. This system was estimated to lead to savings of on average DM 3 billion per year – almost 9% of the total pharmaceutical expenditure of the sickness funds. Early in 1999, however, a German court ruled that price setting by the sickness funds violates Article 81 EC resulting in a reference for a preliminary ruling to the ECJ from the German Federal Court on 4 July 2001[8].

Although Commission intervention by virtue of the powers of competition law is on an *ad hoc* basis, usually as a result of a complaint by a parallel trader, the Commission can use these occasions to give clear guidance as to how it interprets the Treaty rules in individual cases. This in turn can provide guidance to national courts and authorities entrusted with the enforcement of both national and European competition law. As discussed in greater detail below, the Commission's interpretation of its competition-based powers to prevent dual pricing regimes and export bans is now under direct legal challenge before the ECJ.

The importance of the application of the basic Treaty principles on free movement and competition are not only apparent in relation to parallel trade or intra-brand competition. They have played an important role in the evolution of the case law of the ECJ in interpreting secondary

---

[7] The judgement of the Court of First Instance in case T-41/96, *Bayer*, 26 October 2000 illustrates the limits of its powers in this respect, however, see below.

[8] In early 2001 the German health ministry put reference prices on a new legal footing by means of an ordinance.

legislation on product licensing, as well as trademarks. The Court's interpretation of the former body of law, particularly with regard to the availability of the so-called abridged licensing procedures for generic products, has been strongly influenced by these principles.

Finally, the Commission, as the executive arm of the Community, and the institution entrusted with formulating legislative proposals to the Council and the Parliament, is constantly forced to seek compromise positions between potentially competing, if not conflicting interests of industrial and health policy, and Community competence and Member State power. It is the European Court that acts as final arbiter of the validity of such compromises under European law. How have these compromises been struck and do they remain valid in an environment which is rapidly changing in both technological and social terms?

E. Product Authorisations

Considerable progress has been made towards the harmonisation of product authorisation (or registration and licensing procedures) throughout the Community since the adoption of the very first framework Directive 65/65 in 1965 which provided that Member States must ensure basic requirements for premarketing authorisation at national level in relation to the proven quality, efficacy and safety of the product in question (Council of the European Communities, 1965). No medicinal product, as defined in Article 1 of the Directive, can be "put on the market" or otherwise distributed in any Member State without prior approval based upon these three criteria. Subsequent Directives (Council of the European Communities, 1975a and b) have fleshed out the requirements for the national evaluation of medicines, focusing on the authorisation process as such, as well as expanding on the various procedures to be followed by applicants in establishing that their products meet these criteria. Further measures have provided for the harmonisation of the procedures for inspection and pharmacovigilance as well as manufacturing authorisations. As the Court of Justice has confirmed in several rulings, as the process of harmonisation has evolved, Member States, despite retaining ultimate sovereignty in most matters relating to health care, have little scope to deviate from the strictures of the Directives – given the level of harmonisation of the common criteria for the evaluation of medicines that has now been achieved[9].

As the process of completing the "internal market" progressed through the late 1980s, towards the target date of 1992, the body of Community pharmaceutical regulation expanded rapidly, especially with

---

[9]   Case C-440/93, *The Queen* v. *The Licensing Authority,* ex parte *Scotia Pharmaceuticals*, ECR [1995] I-2851, and see further Dodds-Smith (2000).

the adoption of the so-called "rational use package" of measures covering all industrially produced medicines, including vaccines, blood and plasma products and homeopathic remedies. The rational use package also established the Summary of Product Characteristics (SPC) as the basis not only for reference information to be provided to health professions for each medicine, but also as the basis from which all other advertising and information for patients was to be derived. Information for patients was introduced in some Member States and harmonised for all. Steps were also taken to improve the co-ordination of decision-taking procedures, which remained national, with the adoption of legislation concerning biotechnology and other high-technology medicinal products in 1987. Three points can be stressed in the context of this chapter, however, with respect to the current system of product authorisation.

F. Parallel Procedures

Firstly, only a limited degree of centralisation of the regulatory process has been achieved: the process of harmonisation of the procedures for product authorisation was, at least until 1993, centred upon the concept of decentralised procedures, based on voluntary, mutual recognition between Member States. In 1993 the Council and Parliament adopted Regulation 2309/93 that introduced a centralised authorisation procedure, administered and managed by a newly created agency – the European Agency for the Evaluation of Medicinal Products (EMEA) – that commenced operation in 1995 (Council of the European Union, 1993). The centralised procedure as it currently stands, is compulsory for all medicines derived from biotechnology and is optional for other innovative new medicines. On the basis of the EMEA's opinion, which is in turn dependent upon assessment by various scientific committees, the European Commission takes a Decision on the granting of the Community-wide marketing authorisation. All other products subject to Directive 65/65 are covered by the mutual recognition procedures and, in accordance with the procedures introduced in the Directive, a marketing authorisation granted by one Member State (the Reference country) is extended to one or more other Member States as selected by the applicant (Selected Member States). If a Member State cannot recognise the original marketing authorisation, the points in dispute are then referred to the EMEA for arbitration. The Commission adopts the final Decision. The role of the EMEA and the centralised and mutual recognition procedures have recently been subject to detailed review, as required under Article 71 of Regulation 2309/93, and recommendations for further reform to the system were published on 18 July 2001. These will be discussed in greater detail below. The recent review as well as the latest proposals illustrate the conflicting interests in, on the one hand, ensuring a Community-wide process of regulation which allows firms access to the entire European market and, on the other hand, preserving the legitimate interests of Member States in seeking to protect the health and well-being of their population, as well as allowing the industry itself a degree of choice in where and how it markets its products.

G. Generics

Secondly, with regard to generic products, the Community regulatory regime has tried to strike a compromise between the interests of innovative companies in protecting their research data and the process of intra-brand competition. Directive 87/21 (Council of the European Communities, 1987)[10], amending Directive 65/65, stipulates that such products may qualify for a so-called abridged or shortened licensing procedure at national level, which in effect allows the person putting such a product on the market to qualify for a less burdensome procedure by piggy-backing on the evaluative data submitted by the first holder of a marketing licence. This procedure is obviously of considerable importance to generic producers who are seeking to market products as soon as they are out of patent. Considerable savings can be made if most of the testing requirements do not have to be repeated. At the same time, the Commission was concerned to strike a balance between the competing interests of public health, with access to low priced medicines and the need to protect innovation. Hence, Directive 87/21 also provided that Member States could only use data lodged by the innovator after a certain period of time (usually six, but up to ten, years) had elapsed, during which the innovator had additional possibilities to recoup its costs of research.

Unfortunately, the relevant rules are not clearly drafted and this is an area of European pharmaceuticals law that has been heavily litigated. The Court, as well as the Commission, has been anxious to recognise that the process of applying for market authorisations is both costly and time-consuming for original manufacturers and that the data produced in the process is itself of considerable commercial value: hence, generic products are only allowed to benefit from a "short cut" under certain restrictive conditions as set out in Article 4.8 of the amended Directive 65/65. The Court has interpreted the scope of the relevant rules in such a way that many critics believe it has erred too far in favour of the interests of generic competition. In order to qualify for the abridged

---

[10] For the history of this measure and the Commission's rationale for introducing greater protection of research data, see European Commission (1984 and 1987).

procedures, generic producers must (a) have obtained the consent of the original licensor to allow the national authority to use the existing data on the file, or (b) they must present detailed references to published scientific literature demonstrating the efficacy and safety of the product as stipulated in detailed testing requirements – the so called published literature exemption, or (c) the generic producer must await the expiry of the national protection period granted pursuant to Article 4.8(a)(iii) and then require the competent authority to cross-refer to existing data on file from the original product in order to establish that the generic version is "essentially similar" to the authorised product – the essentially similar exemption[11]. Disputes have arisen, however, as to how essential similarity is to be established, and whether or not published literature must provide a similar level of information that would have been obtained from original evaluations. In a 1995 case the European Court interpreted the published literature test very strictly and held that the published literature must yield the same degree of detail. Obviously, this will occur only very rarely, and many commentators believe that the effect of the 1995 ruling has killed the published literature exception altogether[12]. As the originator will only rarely give consent to use the original test and trial data, generic applicants will have to wait for the six/ten-year period to expire.

But what happens in a case where the original manufacturer has added new therapeutic indications to its original product – does the six/ten-year protection period run from the date these new indications were added or from the date the original product was first marketed? Many of the leading companies face patent expiration of some of their most lucrative products and are anxious to delay the inevitable sales losses after patent expiry. Adding new indications to existing products and claiming data protection for additional ten-year periods can be a useful delaying tactic. The relevant case law illustrates how multiple disputes can arise on the finer points of Community secondary legislation and at the same time illustrates the difficulties that beset the Commission in drafting compromise provisions. The UK Medicines Control Authority (MCA) has taken the line that the 10-year period will only be extended in cases where a new marketing authorisation is required. If the original authorisation is only varied to include the new indications, then no additional period of data protection will be granted.

---

[11]   That is essentially similar to a product which has been authorised in the Community for not less than six years and is marketed in the Member State where the application is made. This period can be extended to ten years for so-called high-technology products (Council of the European Communities, 1987).

[12]   ECJ, case C-440/93, *The Queen* v. *Licensing Authority*, ex parte *Scotia Pharmaceuticals*, ECR [1995] 1-2851.

In Case C-368/96 Generics (UK) Ltd.[13], the Court of Justice was asked to rule on a reference submitted by the English High Court concerning the UK MCA's refusal to grant a marketing authorisation to Generics for products which had originally been licensed by research-based companies in 1981 but for which new indications had been subsequently developed. The licensing authority had, however, granted an authorisation for two other products that were subsequently marketed by the original license holder in different dosages and routes of administration. These licenses were subsequently challenged. The innovative pharmaceutical companies considered that the so-called abridged procedure may be applied only if the applicant can show that the composition of the product for which it has applied for a marketing authorisation is comparable to the original product, which has been authorised for not less than ten years, but also that each therapeutic indication, dose etc. for which the marketing authorisation has been applied for has been authorised for not less than ten years. Generics took the opposite view, arguing that the abridged procedure may be applied as long as the composition of the product for which a marketing authorisation is requested is essentially similar to the original product.

The Court focused its appraisal on the concept of "essentially similar" in Article 4.8(a)(iii) and ruled that, having regard to the purpose of the Directive, which was to safeguard public health, the concept of an "essentially similar" medical product could not be interpreted in such a way that the abridged procedure could amount to a relaxation of the requirements of safety and efficacy that must be met by medicinal products. The Court took notes of the minutes of the meeting of the Council at which Directive 87/21 was adopted, and of the criteria to be applied in determining the concept of essential similarity. On the basis of these criteria, it followed that, as long as essential similarity could be demonstrated, the applicant could receive an authorisation for all therapeutic indications concerned, including any such indications added subsequently by the original licence holder. The Court rejected the argument, put forward by the innovative companies and the Commission, that any major therapeutic innovation should be given independent protection. In any event, the Court found that not only did the actually wording of the Directive preclude such an interpretation, but also that the concept of a major therapeutic innovation was too imprecise to guarantee legal certainty. It further rejected the argument that the tests laid down in the Directive were themselves invalid on the grounds that they infringed the principles of protection of innovation, non-discrimination, proportionality and respect to the right of property.

---

[13] ECJ, case C-368/96, *Generics (UK) Ltd.*, ECR [1998] 1-7967.

With regard to the last of these principles, the Court observed that the principle of a right to property was not absolute, but must be viewed in relation to its social purpose. The provisions at issue were in accordance with the objectives of general public importance pursued by the Community. This judgement was hailed as a significant victory for generic companies but inevitably criticised by the research based sector. The Court's reasoning has also been criticised in that the Court failed to recognise that adequate protection was necessary to protect clinical data generated for significant therapeutic innovations, a concept which, it is argued, is implicit although not explicit in Article 4.8(a)(iii) (Stuys and Ainger, 2001)[14]. Nor has the 1998 ruling entirely resolved the issue. Several cases are now pending before the ECJ, including separate appeals lodged by respectively, Novartis (for Captopril), Glaxo Wellcome (for Ranitidine) and Wellcome (for Acyclovir), against decisions of the UK MCA to allow their generic competitors to use the abridged procedures for products that had been granted marketing authorisations for new indications and dosages[15].

H. Parallel Imports

Thirdly, the present Community regulatory system does not extend to the licensing of parallel imports. Unless the medicinal product in question has been authorised in accordance with the centralised European procedure and has obtained a European marketing authorisation, its introduction into the markets of the individual Member States still requires authorisation. Products that have already obtained an authorisation in one Member State may not automatically be placed on the market of another Member State: in the interests of public health and as recognised by Article 30 EC (ex 36), Member States are still entitled to impose a licensing requirement for medicinal products. At the same time, and in the light of previous case law, the Commission in its Communication of 6 May 1982 (European Commission, 1982) encouraged Member States to adopt a "simplified" licensing procedure for parallel imports so that products already licensed elsewhere in the

---

[14]   It may be noted that in the Generics case both the Commission and the Advocate General took the position that where the original product has been subsequently authorised for a new purpose, then the period of data protection should run for an additional period from the granting of that authorisation.

[15]   ECJ, case C-106/01, *The Queen* ex parte *Novartis Pharmaceuticals UK* v. *The MCA*, pending. Case (OJ, 2001 C173/23) – this reference for a preliminary ruling from the Court of Appeal raises the problem of whether in considering a product authorisation for a new product under Article 4.8(a)(iii) referencing a product (A) authorisied more than 6/10 years ago a national authority can cross-refer, without consent, to data submitted in support of a product (B) which was authorised within the last six-ten years, and product B was authorised under the hybrid abridged procedure.

European Community could subsequently benefit from a form of "fast-track" licensing when introduced into a particular Member State market and would not need to produce the normal documentary evidence required to satisfy a full licensing application. A parallel importer can invoke a simplified licensing procedure if it can establish that the product in question is identical to the product authorised and marketed in the country of importation. This will usually be fairly straightforward where the same manufacturer has produced the parallel product, albeit in a different country. But this is not the only possibility and, unfortunately, due to the absence of harmonisation there is no clear definition of a parallel imported product. The ECJ has, however, established that in order to be treated as a parallel import a product had to be manufactured according to the same formulation as the original. In the Smith & Nephew case the UK MCA had revoked a parallel import licence upon discovering that the product sourced by the importer, Primecrown in Belgium, had not been manufactured by the original product approval holder for the UK market, Smith and Nephew. The European Court ruled that it was not necessary for the purposes of the parallel licensing procedure for the parallel product to be identical in all respects. The national licensing authority need only establish that the product is effective and not harmful. This will be demonstrated by evidence that the parallel product is manufactured according to the same formulation, using the same active ingredients and has the same therapeutic effects as the original product[16]. This ruling has been criticised on the grounds that the Court seems to have applied a quasi-exhaustion approach to the data involved: once the product has been put on the market, the first marketer can no longer prevent the data from being used by others (see generally Kon and Schaeffer, 1997: 123).

Alleged obstacles to parallel importation caused by manufacturers withdrawing their original products from a national market and then introducing them again in slightly varied forms were examined in the recent case of Rhône-Poulenc Rorer (RPR). In 1989 and 1993 May and Baker had obtained marketing authorisations in the UK for their insomnia treatment, "Zimovane". RPR, a member of the same group of companies, was appointed as agent to manufacture and market the product and, subsequently developed its own version of Zimovane using a different manufacturing process. RPR subsequently obtained marketing authorisations for its new version of Zimovane in the United Kingdom and, in 1996, it requested the UK authorities to revoke the authorisations under which the old version of Zimovane had been marketed. RPR

---

[16]   ECJ, case C-201/94, *The Queen* v. *The Medicines Control Agency*, ex parte *Smith and Nephew Pharmaceuticals Ltd and Primecrown Ltd* v. *The Medicines Control Agency*, ECR [1996] 1-5819.

continued, however, to market the *old* version in several other Member States. In the meantime and prior to the revocation of the authorisation for the old Zimovane, several companies obtained parallel import licences in the UK for this product in accordance with relevant national procedures[17]. Once the authorisation for the old Zimovane had been revoked these companies were informed by the UK authorities that if they wished to maintain their licences they would have to apply for so-called variations in those licences in order to determine a new appropriate reference product. The UK authorities accepted the new Zimovane as the reference product for these variations, and declared that the existing parallel licences were still valid. Both May and Baker and Rhône-Poulenc challenged this decision and argued that the products were no longer parallel imports within the meaning of Community and United Kingdom law as there were no longer any valid marketing authorisations current for the old version of Zimovane in the UK: the parallel imported products were not identical to the new version. However, the UK authorities took the view that if it had treated the two versions of Zimovane as different products and required the parallel importers to apply for a full marketing authorisation, it would have created an unjustifiable restriction on imports, contrary to Article 28 (ex 30) EC. The English High Court referred detailed questions to the ECJ, seeking clarification of the definition of a parallel import in these circumstances.

Advocate General La Pergola based his opinion on a careful legal analysis of the application of the principles laid down in the Court's earlier rulings in de Peijper[18] and in Smith and Nephew[19] to the present case. He cautioned the Court against applying its earlier case law too rigidly in its quest to strike a delicate balance between the opposing requirements of free movement of goods and protection of public health. The 1976 de Peijper case, as interpreted by La Pergola, rests on the implicit assumption by the Court that where the mere existence of national variations without therapeutic effect are at issue there is a refutable presumption that the manufacturer intended to divide markets. It is up to the manufacturer to demonstrate to the full satisfaction of the competent national authorities that the difference in formulation is a response to genuine and objective concerns for public health. A national licensing authority, on the other hand, should not consider the de Peijper ruling as laying down an irrefutable presumption that where two

---

[17] On the basis of the Commission Communication, the UK authorities issued a document entitled "Notes on Application for Product Licences (Parallel Importing) (Medicines for Human Use) ("MAL 2 (PI)")" in 1984.

[18] ECJ, case 104/75, *de Peijper*, ECR [1976] 613.

[19] *Loc. cit. Note.*

variants of a product have the same therapeutic effect, it must treat these as one and the same product and apply the simplified licensing procedures accordingly[20]. In the Advocate General's view the requirement to protect public health must be seen as overriding considerations of free movement of goods. Hence in his view, the "proportionality" test applies not to the measures in question, but the ultimate goal of the measure.

The Court held that notwithstanding the Treaty rules on free movement of goods, no medicinal product may be placed on the market in a Member State unless a marketing authorisation has been issued in accordance with the Directive 65/65, as amended. It recognised, however, that there were two exceptions to this requirement, that is where the abridged "procedure" discussed above is applicable, or on the basis of the Court's case law, and in particular the de Peijper ruling.

The RPR case raised four particular sets of circumstances that might cast doubt on the compliance of the decisions of the UK authorities with Community law. These included the fact that product authorisations for the old version of the product were no longer in force in the Member State of importation, having been voluntarily revoked. Furthermore, there were some variations in the formulation of the two versions of the product. In addition, and as reflected in the observations put forward by the Commission, as well as those submitted by the French government, there was concern that the Community pharmacovigilance system would not work because once the parent marketing authorisation had been revoked the holder of the marketing authorisation is no longer obliged to submit information regularly in relation to the old version of the product. Finally, there was the issue of whether the particular benefit to public health that is provided by the new version of the product as compared with the old version could be achieved if both versions were available on the UK market at the same time.

According to the Court (at recital 45 of its judgement), national authorities are required to authorise a medicinal product imported as a parallel product in accordance with the rules relating to parallel imports where they are convinced that a product, in spite of differences relating to the excipients (inactive ingredients), does not pose a problem for public health. They must ensure that, even if the product is not identical in all respects to the product already authorised by them, that it has the same active ingredient and the same therapeutic effect and does not pose a problem of quality, efficacy or safety. As to pharmacovigilance, the

---

[20] If the variations in the formulation are proved to be intended to protect public health then any refusal by a competent national authority to refuse to licence the product under a simplified procedure would be justified under Article 30.

Court found that the concerns raised could be met through co-operation between national authorities. Furthermore, it is possible to compel the holder of the marketing authorisation for the new product, who belongs to the same group of companies in possession of the marketing authorisations for the old version in the other Member States, to supply the necessary information. Finally, the Court summarily dismissed the public health interest arguments as essentially spurious: after all both products were still on the Community market. Even if those arguments had been well founded, national authorities would not be compelled to require parallel importers to follow the full licensing procedure if they were convinced that the parallel import did not pose a risk to quality efficacy or safety. Hence, the Court ruled that the competent licensing authority need not comply with all the requirements of the Directive even if the manufacturing process was different, as long as that authority was able to verify that the product complied with the requirements relating to quality, efficacy and safety in normal conditions of use and is in a position to ensure normal pharmacovigilance.

The RPR case therefore offered the Court a number of useful opportunities; that is: to define the scope of "Community law" with respect to parallel imports fairly and squarely in terms of the principles laid down in the relevant Directives, and at the same time to establish some important differences between the procedures to be applied to parallel as opposed to generic products. In parallel import cases considerations of data protection do not enter the picture at all.

The Court's approach to what it qualified as the second, judge-made exception to the requirements laid down by the Directive, is more liberal than that which it has developed in the context of generic products: the parallel import product does not have to be essentially similar in every respect to the version of the product on the market of the Member State of import. In this respect, however, the Court adds an important qualification to the older de Peijper judgement: given that the primary purpose of any system of rules concerning the production and distribution of medicines must be to safeguard public health, even if it follows from Article 28 (ex 30) and 30 (ex 36) of the Treaty that national authorities must not obstruct parallel imports by requiring parallel importers to satisfy the same requirements as those that are applicable to undertakings applying for the first time for a marketing authorisation for a medicinal product "that principle is subject to the condition that the exception of that kind to the rules normally applicable to marketing authorisations for medicinal products does not undermine the protection of public health" (recital 40).

It remains for the individual Member States to decide upon relevant procedures given the absence of harmonisation in this area and to strike a suitable balance between the need to protect the interests of the original manufacturer and holder of a full marketing authorisation who has produced the complex data, and the free movement of goods. Unlike the Court, the Advocate General was anxious to stress the importance of the precautionary principle and the increased importance of pharmacovigilance or adverse reaction monitoring – something which barely existed in the de Peijper days. Article 29a of Directive 75/319, amending Directive 65/65, puts considerable stress on the importance of the duties for national licensing authorities to exert the necessary supervisory controls on the actual use of medicines. In the view of the Advocate General, and in the submissions of the French authorities, these duties must be interpreted in the light of the precautionary principle and the principle of preventative action[21]. The competent authorities may take restrictive measures without having to wait until the nature and scale of any risk to health have become fully apparent. The Court, on the other hand, did not make any link with the precautionary principle or the principle of preventative action.

This latest ruling confirms that the ECJ is not averse to reviewing the decisions of national licensing authorities in cases involving complex and often sensitive public health issues and is prepared to strike its own balance between free movement and public health objectives. Nevertheless, parallel importers still claim that manufacturers are continuing to de-register products and introduce new formulations in order to secure the cancellation of authorisations for both parallel and generic products that have used the deregistered product as their reference product[22]. In the meantime, the Commission has recently revised its "Notice to Applicants" which explains the Community registration procedures in detail, so that a national regulator should be able to grant generic authorisation even when the originator's authorisation has been

---

[21] Although the Advocate General acknowledges that these principles apply under the Treaty to the actions of the Community authorities, analogous principles apply to national authorities. Thus a competent authority or the national courts of the importing Member State, in analysing the level at which the protection of human life and health is to be ensured in national law, is required to establish whether these principles are applicable case C-157/96, *The Queen* v. *MAFF*, ECR [1998] 1-2211 and case C-180/96, *UK* v. *Commission*, ECR [1998] 1-2265.

[22] The Finnish Medicines Agency recently withdrew a licence awarded to Paranova to declare its marketing authorisation to parallel import Losec, one of the best selling prescription drugs in the world, automatically void. Paranova challenged the decision before the Finnish Supreme Administrative Court which has in turn referred questions to the European Court of Justice concerning the right of the national agency automatically to declare void a parallel licence in these circumstances (*Scrip Magazine*, No. 2658, 6 July 2001, page 4).

withdrawn provided the withdrawal was not due to concern about public health[23].

I. The 2000 Review and the Reform of Community Pharmaceutical Regulation

As indicated above, the current European system of pharmaceutical regulation for product authorisation for human (as well as veterinary) use has been recently subjected to an extensive review. On 18 July 2001, the Commission proposed a series of wide reaching reforms. The review examined to what extent the current system should be reformed with a view to securing certain intrinsically linked goals, including:

- guaranteeing a high level of health protection for European citizens and in particular by making safe, innovative products available to patients as quickly as possible;
- guaranteeing tighter surveillance of the market, in particular by strengthening pharmacovigilance procedures;
- completing the internal market for pharmaceuticals while taking globalisation into account;
- setting up a legal framework which fosters the competitiveness of European industry;
- meeting the challenges of EU enlargement;
- taking the opportunity to rationalise and improve the system of regulation especially the transparency of decision-making procedures.

The report covered not only an evaluation of the two parallel Community authorisation systems but also touched on issues relating to transparency, information production, access to medicines and data protection, enlargement and pharmacovigilance.

The Commission was presented with a number of fundamental choices as to how it can ensure the benefits of the centralised system that has allowed larger firms scope to reach the entire Community market with their biotechnology and innovative products and at the same time guarantee a proper place for national regulation, as well as to allow those companies who wish to market their products on a less than Community-wide basis a suitably flexible set of procedures. As the independent evaluation report noted:

> there are relatively few areas where the different participants in the regulatory process agree on the extent of any shortcomings in these systems, let alone the solutions. Decisions on what changes to make to the systems will,

---

[23] *Scrip Magazine*, No. 2657, 4 July 2001, page 2.

as ever, involve the Commission and legislature in balancing different considerations, all of which are important but often conflicting.[24]

Although the centralised procedures and the work of the EMEA received a highly favourable review, the report criticised the amount of time taken for the Commission's own decision-making procedures, which has sometimes amounted to a third of the total time required for the entire authorisation procedure. The administrative structure of the EMEA had in any event to be modified to deal with new tasks resulting from future enlargement, to be in line with more recent proposals for the creation of similar regulatory agencies, to provide sufficient guarantees that the interests of civil society and industry are represented, and any possible extension of the centralised system to new categories of medicines.

The report suggested that the Commission could consider three options for modification of the scope of the centralised procedure: (a) partial optionality – so that it would be left to the firms to decide whether to follow centralised or decentralised procedures for any product not included in list "A" (*i.e.* biotechnology products); (b) full optionality whereby both central and decentralised procedures are in full competition and it is up to the firm itself to select the procedure; and (c) to extend the competence of the EMEA to cover all new molecules, thereby establishing a Community approach to all new innovative medicinal products.

Little consensus appears to exist between the Member States on these options. Obviously the acceptance of full or partial optionality would depend upon substantial modifications and improvements to the mutual recognition procedure (MRP). This procedure was found not to have functioned optimally as many Member States continued to re-evaluate each case so that there is in fact no mutual recognition worthy of the name. Although additional checks insisted upon by the second Member State may well have ensured a high degree of safety for patients, the report suggested that these concerns are more directly related to national preferences and cultural traditions than to serious health concerns. Nevertheless, if there is a real choice to be made between the two parallel procedures, the MRP must be perceived to be as scientifically efficient as the centralised procedure for reasons of both credibility and public health, and it must generate the same level of harmonisation for the authorisation of medicinal products.

---

[24] See paragraph 1.7 of the report by CMS Cameron McKenna and Andersen Consulting (2001).

A major issue has proved to be the modification of the procedures for the authorisation of generic versions of products that have been granted a Community authorisation. As explained above, generic products must currently be authorised under the same procedure and by the same authority that authorised the medicinal product of which they are copies (reference product). The consultant's report commented that neither the centralised system nor the mutual recognition system currently meets the needs of manufacturers of generics or products for self-medication. As from 2005 it will potentially be possible to produce generic versions of any medicinal product authorised under the centralised procedure[25]. However, some Member States oppose the use of the centralised procedure for generic medicinal products, and argue that this procedure should be reserved for new products. Nevertheless, Member States have expressed general support for a compromise proposal to progressively harmonise generic medicinal products by product class through a process of agreeing upon "core" SPCs.

J. The Reform Proposals

The package of reforms published on 18 July 2001 includes changes to the role and structure of the EMEA as well as to the two main systems of product registration[26]. It also introduces greater transparency into the process of decision-making at Community as well as national level. The form and composition of the scientific committees and the Management Board of the EMEA will be reformed. An Advisory Board is to be created, composed of representatives of the national authorities that will have a consultative role in respect to all authorisation procedures. The Management Board will be restructured to include representatives from patients and industry. The Agency will also be given a clearer role as scientific adviser to small and medium companies and, in particular, biotechnology companies before they embark on all the trials and tests necessary for authorisation. It will also be given the power to impose financial sanctions directly on companies infringing the Com-

---

[25] It was first proposed by the Commission that future generic versions of products could be authorised either at central level or under the decentralised procedure, the choice being left to the generic firm. A provision could be introduced to ensure that national authorisations of generic versions of products under the decentralised procedure are similar in every way to the reference centralised authorisation. The Commission does not, however, propose to extend the current system of "conventional arbitration" under the MRP to automatic arbitration in the case of generic products. See generally European Commission (2001b).

[26] Modifications of Council Regulation 2309/93 concern the centralised procedure; Modifications of Directive 2001/83/EC on the Community Code relating to medicinal products for human use concern the decentralised and national procedures (European Commission, 2001c).

munity rules. Finally the EMEA will have the task of ensuring that the conditions laid down in Community legislation are observed in the case of parallel distribution authorised under the centralised procedure.

The centralised procedure, which will be accelerated, will be mandatory for all new active substances (*i.e.* any substance which has not been part of an authorised medicinal product in any Member State), but will be available on an optional basis to any other product which the applicant demonstrates constitutes a significant innovation or that there is a community interest for patients, as well as for generic versions of centrally authorised medicinal products. Fast-track procedures are foreseen for major breakthrough products, as is the possibility for conditional, one-year authorisations and for co-ordinated procedures to encourage Member States to allow compassionate use of medicinal products not yet available under license. An authorisation will be valid for an indefinite duration (as opposed to five years under the current regime) and at the same time periodic safety reporting is strengthened.

The decentralised procedure will be subject to a major overhaul to meet the criticisms reflected in the independent report. The duration of a national procedure should not exceed 150 (as opposed to 210) days. The Commission now proposes to further remedy the delays caused by Member States failing to recognise products which are accepted for authorisation elsewhere, by providing for a greater role for a Community decision directly granting a Community authorisation if recognition is refused or if an application is withdrawn by a firm preceded by automatic arbitration involving all the Member States covered by an application. In addition, at the behest of certain Member States, the new proposals further clarify the public health criteria for justifying a refusal of mutual recognition. Improved control and co-ordination of national decisions to withdraw products will also be introduced.

The package of reforms will also improve the data protection periods discussed above: generic firms will only be able to rely on data submitted by the original manufacturer to obtain a licence after ten years has elapsed from the first date of marketing. An extension of one year will be allowed if a medicinal product covered by the normal data protection provisions has developed a new therapeutic indication with an important benefit for patients.

Greater transparency will be introduced into the registration process, for the benefit of patients as well as the potential benefit of generic companies. In particular, it is proposed to allow "interested parties" a right of access to European Public Assessment Reports – or EPARs as they are also known, and to ensure the wider dissemination of SPCs[27]. Furthermore, the proposals include a "Roche-Bolar" provision allowing scientific tests to be carried out on products which are still subject to patent protection on the basis of the so-called supplementary protection certificate (Council of the European Communities, 1992). It is estimated that this alone could speed up the introduction of generics onto the market by up to two years.

Controversially the proposals also aim to allow direct patient access to patient orientated and controlled information for three specific diseases: AIDS, asthma and chronic bronchitis and diabetes. Such information will be subject to a new Community Code of Good Practice and this pilot project will be reviewed after five years[28]. The EMEA will draw up this Code in co-operation with industry, patient groups and Member States. Information to be directed to patients mainly through the Internet must be notified to the EMEA, which will have one month to raise objections[29]. The development of e-Health was a priority of the 2001 Belgian[30] presidency. US studies indicate that health related web sites are among the most frequently accessed sites on the Internet and it is estimated that there are currently over 40,000 sites worldwide that offer health related information. It may be noted that this limited experiment for legalising direct patient access is only one of the possible reforms proposed in a comprehensive report on the impact of electronic commerce on the European pharmaceutical sector in November 1998[31].

Finally it should be noted that, although the review itself[32], as well as the Commission's reflection document, does not deal with greater har-

---

[27] For a critique of ongoing lack of transparency see *International Society of Drugs Bulletins Newsletters* (ISDB), 2001, Vol. 15, No. 1, pp. 11-13.

[28] For the results of American experiments with direct information provision to patients see Buchner *et al.* (1998).

[29] See further the EU's "e-Europe" Action Plan. The "Health Online" Chapter of the Action Plan outlines four actions at EU level: Best practices in e-Health will be identified and disseminated in order to assist purchasing departments in decision-making. A series of data networks will be established to assist with informed health care planning in Member States. A communication on legal aspects of e-Health will be drafted which will clarify which existing legislation has an impact on e-Health; a set of quality criteria for health websites will be developed to boost consumer confidence in the use of such sites and foster best practice in the development of sites. See generally speech by Liikanen (2001b) available on the europa web site.

[30] See further the Belgian Presidency website <www.eu2001.be>.

[31] See the report prepared by Ashurst Morris Crisp and Executive Perspective S.A., Brussels, November 1998.

[32] See paragraph 5.6.11 of the review on Parallel Trade which concludes that there seems little support for a specific legal framework for parallel trade in medicinal products.

monisation of parallel import products, some Member States have suggested this as a topic for further debate in the context of the proposed amendments to the centralised and decentralised systems.

The proposals have met with general approval from the research-based as well as the generic industry, albeit that both parties see room for further improvement and furtherance of their respective sets of interests. Consumers and patients are likely to welcome improved transparency, stricter pharmacovigilance procedures as well as the fast-track procedures. The major source of resistance is likely to come from those Member States who are less than enthusiastic about a further transfer of competence to the European institutions, particularly in the context of the decentralised procedures. It may, however, be added that the proposals may not necessarily result in any greater transparency in the complex "comitology" procedures surrounding the adoption of decisions on individual products. These types of procedures which allow extensive, hidden bargaining between the Commission and the Member States on many regulatory issues across most areas of shared Community/Member State competence are the subject of considerable criticism and are seen as a major contributor to the so-called "demo-cratic deficit" which attends much of Community decision-making.

K. Harmonisation of Pricing Regulation

The conclusions of the report on Global Competitiveness, as well as the future work of the new high-level group which has been set up by the Commission to examine the issues raised by the report, may also provide renewed stimulus for Community action on the national price regimes which can insulate the sector from competitive forces. National price and profit regulation was criticised in the report on Global Com-petitiveness as having insulated European industry and reduced the incentive to innovate. Following from the December 2000 Competitive-ness Round Table, the newly established High Level Group, which will comprise health and industry ministers, pharmaceutical company and patient representatives, is to report by April 2002 to Commission President Romano Prodi on how to reconcile the needs of patients and industry. The Commission has expressed the hope that the group will be able to agree on policy approaches that do not necessarily require the Commission to take legislative action[33].

Indeed, Commission attempts to tackle the issue of price divergence at source by seeking to harmonise national rules and regulations on pricing and profit controls have not found much favour from either the

---

[33] See Commission Press Release IP/01/444 for list of members of the new group (European Commission, 2001d).

Member States, who regard this as a matter of health policy and therefore of national competence, or from the research-based industry, which distrusts attempts to set average "European" prices for their products. Previous efforts to reach consensus under the auspices of the three Bangemann "round tables" failed to deliver[34]. The subsequent Commission's Communication of 25 November 1998 on the Single Market in Pharmaceuticals confirmed that, despite the fact that the various parties involved, the Member States and the Commission, have deliberated at length on the issue of pricing in three round tables, little real consensus has been reached. The Commission's suggested compromise was to advance a "market segments" approach and to promote deregulation in the over the counter (OTC) market as well as to stimulate competition in the generic market. As far as "in-patent" medicines are concerned, the main thrust of policy would be to guarantee adequate incentives for the research-based industry. The Communication was widely criticised by the industry, generic as well as research-based, and by the pharmacy profession. No further concrete action resulted.

The only existing measure in this field, the so-called Price Transparency Directive in 1989 (Council of the European Communities, 1989a) was originally intended as a first, but in retrospect can perhaps be seen as the last, step in the direction of Community regulation of national price and profit control. Despite subsequent reviews of its impact and effectiveness, the Commission has not established sufficient consensus among the Member States to move towards a stricter Community regime. The 1989 measure is limited in its aims: it does not harmonise the levels at which national price controls or profit caps are fixed, but merely endeavours to ensure that the national procedures are efficient, transparent and fair[35]. Moreover, if the process of setting prices and profit caps becomes more transparent it becomes easier for the Commission as well as stakeholders to establish whether or not the Treaty rules on free movement and competition are being properly respected, particularly if these processes favour domestic production over and above imports. The recent attempt by the UK parallel trade organisation for judicial review of the modulation provision in the UK Pharmaceutical Price Regulation Scheme (PPRS) is a case in point[36].

---

[34] For a further discussion of the Bangemann round and the Commission's policy response see European Commission (1998).

[35] For a fuller discussion of the Directive, see Hancher (1990: 170-175).

[36] Parallel importers claim that this scheme allows manufacturers to introduce deep discounts for prices of products under competition from parallel trade while maintaining high prices for other products. See further *Scrip Magazine*, No. 2627, page 5. The research based industry has also used the Directive to challenge national schemes

The key policy questions facing the High Level Group will be whether the Commission can succeed in convincing national governments to accept intervention, even in the form of "soft law" such as guidelines, not only in industrial policy matters but also for sensitive health policy issues. There are a number of possible avenues to explore depending on the strategic approach chosen. The group has been set up to deal with competitiveness, not social solidarity as such. The underlying presumption appears to be that a fully competitive industry should deliver on Europe's health care goals. In this respect its proposals may well be directed at ensuring the primacy of the first goal with certain trade-offs to guarantee the ability of national governments to manage health care budgets. A more vigorous promotion of generic competition is certainly one avenue, and the new legislative proposals on marketing authorisations offer scope for trade-offs. Generic companies may have access to the centralised procedure but will have to live with a 10-year data protection period that will apply at Community as well as Member State level. Another option would be to adopt the current American experiment and seek to move more prescription products into the over the counter (OTC) market. This might well appeal to budget conscious governments but not necessarily to pharmacists. It should be noted, however, that Member States remain in principle free to determine selling methods of pharmaceutical products pursuant to Article 28, provided that imported products are not discriminated against[37].

Those countries seeking to promote themselves as a preferred location for research and development may look to different trade-offs[38]. The industry itself would like to draw a further distinction between reimbursable and non-reimbursable prescription products, with no price control of the latter. A certain relaxation of the current Community prohibition on advertising or the provision of direct information on prescription products to the public, as put forward in the July 2001 package of proposals, is another candidate for review in the trade-off game.

---

which use imported product prices as a benchmark – thus in their view discriminating against domestic products – see the complaint filed by the Danish pharmaceutical industry association, LIF, *Scrip Magazine*, No. 2612, 16 January 2001, page 3. The Commission has also launched infringement proceedings against the Greek government in relation to its so-called confirmation price system and with regard to its failure to respect the timetables for price approval as imposed in the Directive, *Scrip Magazine*, No. 2589, 3 November 2000, page 7. Infringement proceedings were also reported to have been initiated against Finland for its failure to provide for reimbursement procedures for certain categories of drugs. See *Scrip Magazine*, No. 2558, 19 July 2000, page 6.

[37] ECJ, case C-391/92, *Commission* v. *Greece*, ECR [1995] I-1621.

[38] See in this respect UK Department of Health (2001).

Undoubtedly, in the era of anti-globalisation, the Commission must be careful to ensure that it has the right pressure groups lined up on its side. The debate on how to tackle pricing can no longer be safely confined to privileged dialogues between industry, governments and European bureaucrats. Nevertheless, it remains to be seen to what extent the Commission can ensure broad stakeholder involvement in detailed issues. One of the much-heralded outcomes of the British Pharmaceutical Industry Task Force Report, for example, is a commitment to develop an internationally comparable set of competitiveness performance indicators. These benchmarks are designed to enable industry and government to assess progress on the goals that the Task Force has set. It is unlikely that consumers or health care providers could be closely involved in this assessment process. The recent Consultation Paper published by the High Level G10 group lists benchmarking as a possible way forward but does not touch on this latter issue at all.

I. The Treaty Principles on Competition and Free Movement

A. Competition Law (Articles 81-82)

Even if the parallel trader can take advantage of weak patent protection to obtain supplies of imitation products in some countries, the more usual source of this trade is from wholesalers supplied through official distribution channels by the original manufacturers in low-priced Member States. The most obvious defensive strategy for such manufacturers is to try to limit supplies to the volumes required to serve the relevant national markets or to attempt to persuade wholesalers not to supply parallel traders. Both these tactics can involve the risk of infringement of the Community competition rules, and the risk of a heavy fine. In this respect, pleas to the effect that the internal market is divided along national lines as a result of national pricing rules, and that original manufacturers should be able to defend their position accordingly, have fallen on deaf ears at DG Competition guardian. This argument was pursued without success, by Organon in 1995 to defend its attempts to limit supplies of cheap contraceptive drugs from the UK into the Netherlands[39]. The Spanish competition authorities have similarly rejected an attempt by Glaxo Wellcome.

A similar fate befell Bayer in its attempts to stem the flow of parallel imports of its product "Adalat", which could be purchased on the French market at up to 50% less than the UK market price. A straightforward

---

[39] Case IV/M.555, *Glaxo/Wellcome*, OJ C-65, 16 March 1995, p. 4.

ban on export by wholesalers can lead to breach of Article 81(1) – which prohibits, *inter alia*, anti-competitive agreements between manufacturers and distributors. Bayer's approach was subtler. Wholesalers were requested to provide regular information on their onward supplies. No contractual agreements were entered into, however. The Commission took action against this strategy, claiming that a quasi-contractual agreement existed between Bayer and the suppliers, and that these bilateral arrangements infringed Article 81(1). It should be noted that the Commission could not have condemned Bayer's apparent plan to control supplies as an abuse of a dominant position under Article 82, as it found that Bayer only held a relatively small share of the relevant market (European Commission, 1996). Bayer challenged the Commission's decision on the ground that its behaviour was purely unilateral, and so could not be caught by Article 81(1).

The President of the European Court agreed with Bayer and suspended the Commission decision in interim proceedings in 1996. The Court of First Instance has now confirmed that the Commission had erred in law in its interpretation of Article 81(1) and has quashed the Commission's decision. The Conference of First Instance ruled that the Commission cannot hold that apparently unilateral conduct on the part of a manufacturer adopted in the context of the contractual relations which he maintains with his dealers in reality forms the basis of an agreement between undertakings within the meaning of Article 81(1) if it does not establish the existence of an acquiescence by the other partners, express or implied, in the attitude adopted by the manufacturer. The Court appears to have imposed a high standard of proof on the Commission (paragraph 72), especially as the Commission will usually not have access to documentary evidence to support the conclusion that there is agreement or acquiescence on limiting or reducing exports. Much of the circumstantial evidence put forward by the Commission to support its claim that parties had agreed to an export ban was held to be irrelevant. Importantly, the Court ruled that

> the right of a manufacturer faced, as in this case, with an event harmful to his interest, to adopt the solution which seems to him to be the best is qualified by the Treaty provisions on competition only to the extent that he must comply with the prohibitions referred to in Articles 85 (now 81) and 86 (now 82). Accordingly, provided he does so without abusing a dominant position, and there is no concurrence of wills between him and his wholesalers, a manufacturer may adopt the supply policy which he considers necessary, even if, by the very nature of its aim, for example, to hinder parallel imports, the implementation of that policy may entail restrictions on

competition and free trade between the Member States (see paragraph 176).[40]

Contrary to the assertions of the Commission, the Court has never recognised in its jurisprudence that parallel imports must be protected in all circumstances. The Commission has lodged an appeal against this ruling, not least because the approach of the Court of First Instance now appears to offer manufacturers numerous possibilities of hindering parallel imports through restricting supply volumes on low-price markets and has effectively deprived the Commission of a meaningful way of dealing with them.

Its recent decision of 8 May 2001 prohibiting Glaxo Wellcome from maintaining a dual-pricing scheme indicates that the Commission is not yet prepared to accept the research-based industry's argument that it should be entitled to take appropriate action to respond to differences in national price control regimes[41]. Glaxo Wellcome had notified the Commission of new conditions for the sale of all its products to wholesalers in Spain (where maximum regulatory prices prevail). These wholesalers would have to pay higher prices for products that they would export than for products that they would resell for consumption on the domestic market. Glaxo Wellcome's dual pricing system was found to limit parallel trade from Spain to other Member States for the vast majority of its products, therefore interfering with the Community's objectives of integrating national markets, and restricting price competition for Glaxo Wellcome products to a significant extent. The Commission was not convinced by the "consumer welfare" claims that losses incurred by Glaxo Wellcome due to parallel trade would seriously affect Glaxo Wellcome's research and development budget with consequences for its ability to develop innovative drugs. This argument was not corroborated by the facts presented.

Many saw Glaxo Wellcome's dual pricing scheme as an important test case. The Commission was confronted for the first time with a set of agreements that explicitly sought to restrict parallel trade but which the company sought to justify on economic grounds[42]. The policy implications are clear: the Commission considers that companies will have to continue to live with national regulatory diversity. Importantly, the Commission stressed that the research and development budget of most

---

[40] Court of First Instance, case T-41/96, *Bayer*, 26 October 2000.

[41] The European Court of Justice had already made it eminently clear that divergent national price regulations in the pharmaceutical sector do not exclude the operation of the Treaty rules on free movement – Merck and Primecrown 1996.

[42] Glaxo Wellcome has recently announced its intention to appeal this decision to the Court of Justice.

pharmaceutical companies only represents around 15% of their total budget: losses stemming from parallel trade could equally be deducted from the companies' other budget items such as marketing costs (European Commission, 2001e).

The findings of the recent report on "Global Competitiveness in Pharmaceuticals: A European Perspective" commissioned by DG Enterprise (Gambardella *et al.*, 2000) may have encouraged the Commission's competition authorities to make such a bold statement. Parallel trade, as the Commission emphasises in the Glaxo Wellcome decision, is the only source of competition for products still in patent. Glaxo Wellcome has announced that it will challenge this decision before the Court of First Instance, confronting the European courts to address the legitimate scope available to companies to deal with disparities arising from national price regulatory schemes. In its earlier ruling in Merck and Beecham[43] the ECJ had ruled that such divergence did not justify any derogation from the principle of free movement of goods and the possibility of preventing parallel imports entailed an undesirable partitioning of national markets. In the recent Bayer case, the Court of First Instance noted that the Merck judgement confirms that

> it is not open to the Commission to achieve a result, such as the harmonisation of prices in the medicinal products market, by enlarging the scope of the … (competition rules), especially since the Treaty gives the Commission specific means of seeking such harmonisation where it is undisputed that large disparities in the prices of medicinal products in the Member States are engendered by the differences between the state mechanisms for fixing prices […] (paragraph 179).

It went on to note that the case law of the Court indirectly recognises the importance of safeguarding free enterprise when applying competition rules, where it expressly acknowledges that even an undertaking in a dominant position may change its supply policies without falling under the prohibition of Article 82.

The question now before the Court is whether private enterprise is entitled to deal with disparities in national laws to protect its legitimate commercial interests. In this context, the actual scope available to the Commission to address the national disparities in question, which do not appear in themselves to conflict with the principles of free movement, appears limited[44].

---

[43]   ECJ, joined cases C-267/95 and C-268/95, *Merck and Beecham*, ECR [1996] I-6285.

[44]   The Commission can and of course does institute proceedings against Member States who fail to comply with the requirements of the Transparency Directive in so far as the requisite time limits for approving drugs for reimbursement have not been

B. Article 28 EC and Industrial Property Rights

Article 28 prohibits all measures that have equivalent effect to quantitative restrictions on the free movement of goods, including, in principle, national laws on intellectual or industrial property rights. Nevertheless, Article 30 provides that Article 28 shall not preclude prohibitions or restrictions on imports that are justified by the protection of industrial and commercial property rights as long as these rights do not constitute a means of arbitrary discrimination or a disguised restriction on trade between Member States. Intellectual or industrial property rights are of course nationally constituted rights and are of unquestionable importance in the pharmaceutical sector.

The early case law of the Court firmly established the principle that the owner of an industrial or commercial property right could not invoke it in order to prevent the importation and sale of goods that had been placed on the market with his consent in another Member State. That principle was first laid down in Deutsche Grammophon v. Metro[45] in relation to copyright, in Centrafarm v. Winthorp[46] in relation to trademarks and in Centrafarm v. Sterling[47] in relation to patents. The so-called principle of exhaustion of rights was prompted by the desire to eliminate any risk of the use of intellectual property rights to establish artificial divisions within the Common Market. The principle balanced the idea that the owner could hold or enjoy the national rights in question, *i.e.* that the rights in question continued to exist in national law, against the idea that the exercise of those rights was controlled by Community law. As with any principle, its limits were quickly put to the test.

In Merck v. Stephar[48] the Court upheld a strict interpretation of the principle of exhaustion and found that even where a Member State did not provide patent protection, the mere consent to placing of the product on that market was sufficient to establish exhaustion. In 1996 the Court was offered the opportunity of reversing this judgement, and to reconsider the issue of consent in Merck v. Primecrown[49]. Merck argued that pharmaceutical companies did not choose where to market their products, but that they were under an ethical and sometimes even a legal

---

adequately transposed into national law – see most recently case C-424/99, *Commission* v. *Austria*, ECR [2001S I-9285.

45   ECJ, case C-78/70, *Deutsche Grammophon* v. *Metro*, ECR [1971] 487.

46   ECJ, case C-16/74, *Centrafarm* v. *Winthrop*, ECR [1974] 1183.

47   ECJ, case C-15/74, *Centrafarm* v. *Sterling*, ECR [1974] 1147.

48   ECJ, case C-187/80, *Merck* v. *Stephar*, ECR [1981] 2063.

49   ECJ, joined cases C-267/95 and C-268/95, *Merck* v. *Primecrown*, ECR [1996] I-6285.

obligation to supply their products to a market. They could not discontinue existing supplies to a market and were forced to accept national price controls. The Advocate General strongly recommended that the Court should reconsider the earlier Merck *v.* Stephar judgement and that the patent holder should be able to prevent parallel imports from Member States (Spain and Portugal) where the patent holder could not have obtained protection. The Court maintained its approach to the matter of consent in the Primecrown case, and ruled that the original manufacturers had "consented" voluntarily to putting their products on the market in the knowledge that full patent protection could not be obtained. While acknowledging the problems created by national price differentials as the driving force for parallel trade, as discussed above, the Court firmly placed responsibility for resolving them with the Commission and the Council. It resolutely refused to water down the rights of free movement as guaranteed by the Treaties. The judgement has, however, been criticised as failing to take on board the realities of the situation confronting the industry, which are, of course, that national price regulation still divides the Common Market. As already noted, this issue is now before the Court of First Instance in the Glaxo Wellcome appeal.

The Court's insistence on a strict application of the exhaustion doctrine has led the research-based industry to lobby for strict safeguards in the accession treaties with the Eastern European countries, which have traditionally denied strong patent protection to pharmaceuticals. The precedent of such safeguarding measures in the earlier accession agreements with Spain and Portugal indicate that a transitional period preventing importation of non-patented products is possible, but that these safeguard measures must be properly drawn up to be effective in practice.

C. Trademarks

Complex litigation has also arisen with respect to trademarks, and the rights of the original manufacturer to defend its trademark where parallel importers have repackaged a product sold under a particular trademark in Country B to resell it under the trade mark used in Country A. Once again the doctrine of exhaustion is of importance here although the problem is further complicated by the fact that trademarks are subject to a certain degree of harmonisation as a result of the adoption of secondary legislation in 1989. Has the manufacturer exhausted his trademark rights by putting the product on the Common Market under different trademarks in the first place? The answer to this question lies in the nature of the specific subject matter of the trademark right. The Court has recognised that trade marks have, as an essential function, a guarantee to the consumer or end user of the identity of the trademarked product's origin[50]. Hence, the Court has recognised that a trademark owner can oppose any use of the trademark that is liable to impair the essential function of the trademark. Nevertheless, in its early case law, the Court added an important proviso: it was still necessary to consider whether the exercise of that right could constitute a disguised restriction on trade within the meaning of the second sentence of Article 28 (ex 30) EC[51].

Three cases decided in 1996, Paranova[52], Eurim-Pharm[53] and Rhône-Poulenc,[54] raised the issue of whether the trademark holder could rely upon the First Trade Marks Directive (Council of the European Communities, 1989b) to prevent importation of repackaged parallel-imported products. Article 7 (1) of the First Trade Mark Directive en-shrines the principle of exhaustion of rights, but Article 7 (2) introduces an exception so that the owner of the trademark may oppose further marketing of a repackaged product "where there exist legitimate reasons for the proprietor to oppose further commercialization of the goods, especially where the condition of the goods is changed or impaired after they have been put on the market". The Directive has led to a number of competing interpretations, ranging from a narrow concept of exhaustion, where only if the imported product was in the very form in which it had been marketed could the trade mark owner not oppose its use, to a broader approach, whereby the trade mark owner could only oppose the use if the product was put on the market and was substantially changed.

In the three cases decided in 1996 the parallel importers had repack-aged the goods, either by removing the blister packs from their original outer packaging and placing them in new packs or by severing the blister strips and repackaging them. The key issue before the Court in these "repackaging cases" was whether any of these actions impaired or changed the conditions of the products. However, the Court was also asked to address the relevance of the trademark owner's intention to partition markets. In essence, it was asked to determine whether this test should be a subjective or an objective one: was it necessary to demon-strate that the trade mark owner actually planned this result, or was it sufficient to demonstrate that this was the inevitable result of its action in using different marks in the first place?

---

[50]   ECJ, case C-3/78, *American Home Products*, ECR [1978] 1823.
[51]   ECJ, case C-102/77, *Hoffmann-La Roche*, ECR [1978] 1139.
[52]   ECJ, joined cases C-427/93, C-429/93 and C-436/93, *Bristol-Myers Squibb* v. *Paranova*, ECR [1996] 1-3457.
[53]   ECJ, joined cases C-71/94, C-72/94 and C-73/94, *Eurim-Pharm*, ECR [1996] 1-3603.
[54]   ECJ, case C-232/94, *MPA* v. *Rhône-Poulenc*, ECR [1996] 1-3671.

The Court took a strict approach to the question of intention[55]. The trademark owner could not oppose repackaging of the product in new external packaging when the size of packet in the country of origin cannot be marketed in the Member State of importation because of a rule authorising packaging in only a certain size, or where there is a national practice that has the same effect. The power of the owner of trade mark rights protected in a Member State to oppose the marketing of repackaged products under the trade mark should be limited only in so far as the repackaging undertaken by the importer is necessary in order to market the product in the Member State of importation. It was not up to the importer to demonstrate that the trademark owner had deliberately sought to partition the markets between Member States. The Court held that an "adverse effect on the original condition of the pro-duct" refers to the condition of the product inside the packaging. Only if the action of the parallel importer affected or was likely to affect the product itself could the trademark owner oppose the repackaging as an infringement of his legitimate trademark rights. It expressly stated that "trade mark rights are not intended to allow their owners to partition national markets and thus promote the retention of price differences which may exist between Member States" (paragraphs 42 to 45 of the Paranova ruling).

There will be no artificial partitioning where action by the trademark owner is needed to safeguard the essential function of the trademark. In this sense the Court reformulated the requirement of intention: where reliance by the owner of the trade mark right was justified by the need to safeguard the essential function of the trade mark, the resulting par-titioning could not be regarded as artificial. Article 7(2) had the same effect as Article 28 (ex 30) EC. Hence, subjective intention is irrelevant.

The Court did, however, seek to ensure that the trademark owner could exercise some degree of control over how products were repack-aged. The parallel importer must indicate who has repackaged the product; he must indicate on the packaging who manufactured the product and he must not wrongly attribute any responsibility for any additional articles added to the packaging to the trademark owner. He must give the trademark owner advance notice of the product being put on sale, and the owner can require that he be supplied in advance of sale with a specimen of the repackaged product[56].

---

[55] For a discussion of the earlier case law and the question of subjective *versus* objective intention, see Castillo de la Torre (1997).

[56] ECJ, joined cases C-427/93, C-429/93 and C-436/93, *Bristol-Myers Squibb* v. *Paranova*, ECR [1996] 1-3457.

Numerous disputes before national courts have arisen as a result of these rulings and in particular there appears to be considerable variation as to how national courts apply the "necessity" test that the Court introduced in Paranova. Glaxo challenged the repackaging undertaken by a parallel importer, Dowelhurst, before the English courts, contending that this was not necessary at all. The English judge felt that further clarification from the Court was needed as, in his view, cases where it was necessary for importers to repackage in order to market the product in the Member State of importation would be rare. He therefore referred nine detailed cases to the Court[57]. In two recent rulings the Court of Justice has provided some further clarification on the question of when repackaging is deemed necessary and has confirmed that parallel importers must give notice to the original manufacturer of their intentions to repackage. In case C-143/00 Boehringer Ingelheim *et al.* the Court once again considered the scope of Article 7(2) of the First Trademarks Directive. The Court confirmed that a trade mark proprietor may not oppose repackaging if this contributes to artificial portioning of the markets between Member States, and where in addition the repackaging is done in such a way that the legitimate rights of the proprietor are respected. Thus the repackaging must not adversely affect the original condition of the product and must not be such as to harm the reputation of the mark. A proprietor may oppose repackaging if it is based solely on the parallel importer's attempt to secure a commercial advantage. If, however, such repackaging is necessary to deal with local requirements regarding packaging then this may constitute a justification but it would seem that a mere resistance to foreign products is not sufficient – there must be such strong resistance from a significant proportion of consumers to relabelled products that there must be held to be a hindrance to effective market access. This will inevitably be a question of proof. If repackaging is indeed required then the original proprietor must be given at least fifteen days notice to examine the proposed repackaging[58]. A further issue has arisen as to whether products licensed under the central Community procedures may also be repackaged. In case C-433/00 Aventis, the Advocate General has suggested that where a product is subject to two separate central marketing authorisations each of which relate to different packaging conditions, then the relevant products cannot be repackaged[59].

---

[57] Glaxo Group and Others *v.* Doelhurst Ltd. [2000] ETMR 415. See now the ruling of the Court of Justice in case C-143/00, discussed below.

[58] Judgement of 23 April 2002. See also case C-443/99, *Merck, Sharp & Dohme and Paranova*, of the same date, where the Court took the same approach to the question of when repackaging could be justified.

[59] Opinion of the Advocate General of 7 March 2002 under case C-433/00, Aventis.

D. Rebranding

A further development in this line of case law concerns the right of a parallel importer to affix different trademarks to parallel imported products. Once again, the original trademark owner may have been compelled for reasons of national law to register its product under different marks in different Member States. This may be because certain similar marks had already been registered at national level or because of simple language differences. Again the basic question arises, should the trademark owner be allowed to take advantage of a situation that has arisen as result of circumstances outside his control and rely on his trademark in order to exclude parallel imports even though the exclusion of such imports is not necessary on grounds of trademark protection. The Advocate General concluded in case C-379/97 Upjohn *v*. Paranova that a similar approach should be taken where the affixing of different trademarks is an issue. The factors that led the trademark owner to use different marks in the importing and exporting States are not relevant. Nevertheless, the Advocate General also examined the question of when it might be necessary for parallel importers to rebrand products in order to lawfully import and market them in another Member State. In principle, if various practices or rules in the Member State of import prevent the importer from marketing the products under the mark they bear in the State of export, the trademark owner will not be able to rely on the trademark rights to prevent importation of identical goods. Indeed, there may be an even greater necessity for the importer to rebrand in order to avoid confusion with other marks currently used in the state of import.

The circumstances that led the original trademark owner to use different marks should be regarded as historical and there is no good reason for the Court to use them as defining criteria for determining the lawfulness of subsequent conduct. The decisive test, according to the Advocate General, who based his view squarely on the Court's approach in the repackaging cases, is whether, in a given case, prohibiting the importer from rebranding would constitute an obstacle to effective access to the markets of the importing Member State. The Court followed this approach in its subsequent ruling handed down on October 1999[60].

---

[60] ECJ, case C-379/97, *Upjohn* v. *Paranova*, ECR [1999] I-6927 at recital 43.

E. Non-EEA Goods

Finally, with regard to the possibility of imports of trade marked products being put on the market outside the EEA countries, the ECJ recognised in its judgement in the Silhouette case[61] that the concept of exhaustion is European and not international. Thus trade market owners could, in principle, take action to prevent goods entering the EEA without their consent. Doubts as to what amounted to "consent", however, have caused another spate of legal action. The Court did not address the question in Silhouette of whether it would be sufficient for a manufacturer of goods put on the market outside the EEA to state in contracts with third parties that the goods may not be sold within the EEA or whether the goods themselves must be marked in some way to show that the proprietor of the mark has not consented to their sale within the EEA. In the Sebago[62] case the Court accepted that it was not sufficient to establish consent for the claimant merely to have sold within the EEA goods of the type imported by the defendant; consent must relate to each individual item or product in respect of which exhaustion is pleaded, but the Court did not go as far as to say that express consent to sale in the EEA was a prerequisite. This issue is now before the Court in the Davidoff and Tesco cases. The Advocate General who handed down his Opinion in April 2001 appears to favour an implied consent approach.

Conclusion

The questions of whether the European Commission and indeed the Courts should take a positive or negative attitude to intra-brand competition through the promotion of parallel importing as well as fostering generic or inter-brand competition is much debated. In general, in the past, the Commission has appeared equivocal, accepting to a certain extent that the practice of parallel imports is an important stimulus to intra-brand competition, but at the same time expressing a certain sympathy towards the claims of the research-based industry that it must continue to receive adequate rewards to fund expensive research into new forms of treatment. At the same time, in so far as the cause of parallel imports is to be attributable to national divergence in price regulation, the Commission has little political or legal means, or even hope of either, to attack the problem at source. Parallel imports continue to proliferate and so do the legal issues, most notably on matters of intellectual property law protection but also with regard to issues of pro-

---

[61]   ECJ, case C-355/96, *Silhouette International Schmied v. Hartlauer Handelsgesellschaft*, ECR [1998] 1-4799.

[62]   ECJ, case C-173/98, *Sebago*, ECR [1999] I-4103.

duct registration or authorisation. The various cases which have come before the Court in recent years were often seen as offering the Court the possibility of reassessing its hitherto somewhat narrow, if not strict, approach to the use of patent, copyright and trademark protection by an industry attempting to curtail the flux of low priced drugs into higher priced markets. It was argued by some that this was an outdated approach, governed by the dictates of market integration as opposed to the recognition of the legitimate role of intellectual property law. Given the relative success of the single market exercise, it was anticipated that the Court might change direction and give more weight to the latter factors. The Court did not react as some had clearly hoped, and confirmed its existing approach. Its more recent case law on the application of the Community rules on marketing authorisation to parallel imports indicates that, although it is at pains to give prominence to public health issues, it will still exercise great care to protect parallel and generic trade. In the interests of legal certainty, as well as market access, it will not tolerate any special exemptions from the fundamental principles of free movement and competition. Parallel trade is therefore likely to remain protected by the "passive tolerance" of both the Commission and the European Courts.

It now remains to be seen whether the Community institutions should or could take a firmer, more pro-active position on generic or inter-brand competition as the way to reconcile the competing objectives inherent in its industrial and health care delivery policies and to overcome the fragmentation caused by different market structures in each of the Member States. This chapter has reviewed some of the potential avenues now open to the Community institutions to encourage the supply of generics to the European market and to ensure their more widespread availability across the Union. The potential reforms under active consideration include the relaxation of data exclusivity measures and the reforms to the Community market authorisation procedures. But differences in market structures also reflect differences in the way Member States organise and fund their health care services. Demand side measures, including pricing and reimbursement rules, and incentives, both financial and by way of encouragement, are also relevant to the use of generics. It is perhaps here that the most important challenges and opportunities lie ahead. The growth of the information society and increased patient awareness can be used to promote more widespread awareness of generic alternatives at many levels – including the promotion of benchmarks and exchange of good practice between Member States, as well as exchange of comparative information on market access for both branded and generic medicines and wider awareness of differences in distribution systems for medicines. Permitting the advertising of non-prescription medicines to the general public in all Member States may accelerate these processes while stricter Community based pharmacovigilance procedures may contribute to customer confidence with regard to older products as well as new, more innovative products. In summary the current G10 High Level Group Initiative on Innovation and Provision of Medicines may contribute to an important re-evaluation and reorientation of the role of Community law and policy for the pharmaceutical sector and provide the basis for a new and co-ordinated focus on the demand side of pharmaceutical provision in the European Union.

Bibliography

BUCHNER, D.A., BUTT, L. T., DE STEFANO, A., EDGREN, B., SUAREZ, A. and EVANS, R.M. (1998), "Effects of an Asthma Management Program on the Asthmatic Member: Patient Centred Results of a Two-year Study in a Managed Care Organisation", *The American Journal of Managed Care*, Vol. 4, No. 9, pp. 1288-1297.

CASTILLO DE LA TORRE, F. (1997), "Trade Marks and Free Movement of Pharmaceuticals in the European Community: To Partition or not to Partition the Market", *European Intellectual Property Review*, No. 306, pp. 304-314.

CMS CAMERON MCKENNA and ANDERSEN CONSULTING (2001), "Evaluation of the Operation of the Community Procedures for the Authorisation of Medicinal Products", Report produced for DG Enterprise of the European Commission, January 2001.

COUNCIL OF THE EUROPEAN UNION (1965), Council Directive 65/65/EEC of 26 January 1965 on the approximation of provisions laid down by Law, Regulation or Administrative Action relating to proprietary medicinal products, OJ P 022, 9 February 1965, pp. 0369-0373.

COUNCIL OF THE EUROPEAN UNION (1975a) Council Directive 75/318/EEC of 20 May 1975 on the approximation of the laws of Member States relating to analytical, pharmaco-toxicological and clinical standards and protocols in respect of the testing of proprietary medicinal products, OJ L 147, 9 June 1975, pp. 0001-0012.

COUNCIL OF THE EUROPEAN UNION (1975b) Second Council Directive 75/319/EEC of 20 May 1975 on the approximation of provisions laid down by Law, Regulation or Administrative Action relating to proprietary medicinal products, OJ L 147, 9 June 1975, pp. 0013-0022.

COUNCIL OF THE EUROPEAN UNION (1987), Council Directive 87/21/EEC of 22 December 1986 amending Directive 65/65/EEC on the approximation of provisions laid down by law, regulation or administrative action relating to proprietary medicinal products, OJ L 15, 17 January 1987, pp. 0036-0037.

COUNCIL OF THE EUROPEAN COMMUNITIES (1989a), Council Directive 89/105/EC of 21 December 1988 relating to the transparency of measures regulating the pricing of medicinal products for human use and their inclusion in the scope of national health insurance systems, OJ L 40, 11 February 1989, pp. 0008-0011.

Leigh Hancher

COUNCIL OF THE EUROPEAN COMMUNITIES (1989b), First Council Directive 89/104/EEC of 21 December 1988 to approximate the laws of the Member States relating to trade marks, OJ L 40, 11 February 1989, pp. 0001-0007.

COUNCIL OF THE EUROPEAN COMMUNITIES (1992), Council Regulation 1768/92/EEC of 18 June 1992 concerning the creation of a supplementary protection certificate for medicinal products, OJ L 182, 2 July 1992, pp. 0001-0005.

COUNCIL OF THE EUROPEAN UNION (1993), Council Regulation 2309/93/EEC of 22 July 1993 laying down Community procedures for the authorisation and supervision of medicinal products for human and veterinary use and establishing a European Agency for the Evaluation of Medicinal Products, OJ L 214, 24 August 1993, pp. 0001-0021.

DODDS-SMITH, I (2000), "European Drug Regulation", in GOLDBERG, R. and LONBAY, J. (eds.), *Pharmaceuticals Medicine Biotechnology and the Law*, Cambridge University Press, Cambridge, pp. 93-136.

EDMONDS, P., GLYNN, D. and OGLIARLORO, C. (2000), "Access to Important New Medicines", *European Business Journal*, Vol. 12, No. 3, pp. 146-157.

EFPIA (2001), Draft Position on Discounted Pricing, European Federation of Pharmaceutical Industries and Associations, Brussels, January 2001 (http://www.efpia. org/4_pos/legal/discountprice.pdf).

EUROPEAN COMMISSION (1984), Proposal for a Council Directive on the approximation of national measures relating to the placing on the market of high technology medicinal products, particularly those derived from biotechnology; Proposal for a Council Directive amending Directive 75/318/EEC on the approximation of the laws of Member States relating to analytical, pharmaco-toxicological and clinical standards and protocols in respect of the testing of proprietary medicinal products; Proposal for a Council Directive amending Directive 81/852/EEC on the approximation of the laws of the Member States relating to analytical, pharmaco-toxicological and clinical standards and protocols in respect of the testing of veterinary medicinal products; Proposal for a Council Recommendation concerning tests relating to the placing on the market of proprietary medicinal products and Proposal for a Council Directive amending Directive 65/65/EEC on the approximation of provisions laid down by law, regulation or administrative action relating to proprietary medicinal products, COM (84) 437 final.

EUROPEAN COMMISSION (1987), Note from the Services of the Commission on the consequences of the entry into force of the Directive EEC.IIIB/6 of 29 July 1987.

EUROPEAN COMMISSION (1996), Commission Decision 96/478/EC of 10 January 1996 relating to a proceeding under Article 85 of the EC Treaty (Case IV/34.279/F3 ADALAT) (Only the German text is authentic), OJ L 201, 9 August 1996, pp. 0001-0077.

EUROPEAN COMMISSION (1998), Commission Communication on the Single Market in Pharmaceuticals, COM (98) 588 final, 25 November 1998.

EUROPEAN COMMISSION (2001a), Consultation Paper, G10 Medicines, High Level Group on Innovation and Provision of Medicines (http://pharmacos.eudra.org/ F3/g10/docs/g10an1.pdf).

274

EUROPEAN COMMISSION (2001b), "Review of Pharmaceutical Legislation", Discussion Document (Final version), Brussels, 22 January 2001 (http://pharmacos. eudra.org/F2/review/doc/reviewrp_en.pdf).

EUROPEAN COMMISSION (2001c), Proposal for a Regulation of the European Parliament and of the Council laying down Community procedures for the authorisation and supervision of medicinal products for human and veterinary use and establishing a European Agency for the Evaluation of Medicinal Products, Proposal for a Directive of the European Parliament and of the Council amending Directive 2001/83/EC on the Community code relating to medicinal products for human use and Proposal for a Directive of the European Parliament and of the Council amending Directive 2001/82/EC on the Community code relating to veterinary medicinal products, COM (2001) 404 final of 26 November 2001.

EUROPEAN COMMISSION (2001d), "Pharmaceuticals: High Level Group Established to Look at Medicines for Europe", *Commission Press Release*, IP/01/444, 26 March 2001.

EUROPEAN COMMISSION (2001e), "Commission Prohibits Glaxo Wellcome's Dual Pricing System in Spain", *Commission Press Release*, IP/01/661, 8 May 2001.

GAMBARDELLA, A., ORSENIGO, L. and PAMMOLLI, F. (2000), "Global Competitiveness in Pharmaceuticals: A European Perspective", Report prepared for the Directorate-General Enterprise of the European Commission (http://dg3.eudra. org/F2/pharmacos/docs/Doc2000/nov/comprep_nov2000.pdf).

HANCHER, L. (1990), *Regulating for Competition*, Oxford University Press, Oxford.

JACOBZONE, S. (2000), "Pharmaceutical Policies in OECD Countries: Reconciling Social and Industrial Goals", *Labour Market and Social Policy Occasional Papers*, No. 40, OECD, Paris.

KON, S. and SCHAEFFER, F. (1997), "Parallel Imports of Pharmaceutical Products: A New Realism", *European Competition Law Review*, No. 3, pp. 123-144.

LIIKANEN, E. (2001a), "Where Next for Pharmaceuticals in Europe", *Eurohealth*, Vol. 7, No. 2, Summer 2001, pp. 19-20.

LIIKANEN, E. (2001b), "European Aspects of E-Health", Speech at the workshop on "Quality Criteria for Health Related Websites", Speech/01/268, 7 June 2001.

STUYS, M. and AINGER, L. (2001), "ECJ Judgement on Fast-track Generics", *Scrip Magazine*, June 2001, pp. 41-44.

UK DEPARTEMENT OF HEALTH (2001), Final Report 2001, Pharmaceutical Industry Competitive Task Force (http://www.doh.gov.uk/pictf/pictf.pdf).

CHAPTER 9

Regulation of Medical Devices in the EU[1]

Christa ALTENSTETTER

Introduction

The pharmaceutical industry has featured strongly in European and national political debates for quite some time. By contrast, the medical device industry has only recently become visible. Yet while medical devices represent a tiny share of the output of European industry (0.4%), their share of intra-EU trade (2.6%) exceeds that of pharmaceuticals (1.9%). In addition, the medical device sector generates a higher percentage of notifications (5%) than the pharmaceutical sector (2.9%) (Pelkmans *et al.*, 2000). In short, and as will become apparent, medical devices matter (Altenstetter, 2001; 1998a and b).

The time is especially ripe for the study of medical devices. The industry seems to be on the defensive as the proportion of national health spending on medical devices has come to the attention of payers. The long lasting honeymoon between the industry and European health care regulators seems to have ended. For health care payers and purchasers the case is clear: medical technology is a cost-driving force. Thus medical devices and the medical device industry have come under increasing scrutiny and are subject to growing regulation.

It should be noted at the outset that there is no medical device industry *per se*. Instead, there is a cluster of producers that can be subdivided roughly into four sectors: (i) medical-electrical devices; (ii) non-electrical products; (iii) implantables; and (iv) diagnostic products. The medical device industry is relatively small, with about 15,000 manufacturers employing about 611,000 highly skilled and specialised workers worldwide. About 5,000 of these manufacturers are located in the EU, employing around 240,000 persons. The industry includes companies such as Siemens, Hewlett-Packard, Toshiba, Philips, and

[1] The author would like to thank Richard J. Meagher of the CUNY Graduate Center for his assistance in editing and formatting this paper.

GE-Thompson, who dominate the world market in electrical-medical equipment, and others such as Boston Scientific and Medtronic, which dominate the implantables sector. In the *in vitro* diagnostic product sector, seven or eight leading companies hold some 70% of the world market.

Many medical devices are evaluated in terms of their clinical performance over a long life cycle, as well as in the terms of general product quality that are important in other industries. Medical devices must be repeatedly tested and modified; innovation occurs incrementally with each model slightly different from the previous generation. Since the industry depends on teaching hospitals, research physicians, and suppliers for product development, they are highly sensitive to any changes occurring in delivery systems or payment methods and any shifts from inpatient to outpatient care.

Additional features of the medical device industry stand out when compared to the pharmaceutical industry. Unlike pharmaceuticals, and apart from the giants mentioned above, the industry is highly frag-mented, consisting of numerous small, niche markets each with only a few products. Most product groupings serve markets of under $150 million, a figure that is in striking contrast to the pharmaceutical industry, whose US markets alone often exceed billions of dollars. The industry mainly is composed of small and medium-sized enterprises, many of them start-up firms that develop much of the technological "breakthroughs" in today's health care environment. Often these enter-prises have a single product line and have only limited resources to address new regulatory requirements.

Although pharmaceuticals may target different diseases, treatments and organs, they all can be counted as part of the generic family of about 4,000 drugs worldwide. In contrast, medical devices are heterogeneous products (Table 9.1). According to the Emergency Care Research Institute (ECRI), there are 5,000 different generic product types, 2,000 different types of surgical instruments, 450 implants using dif-ferent materials, and over one million different marks, models and sizes worldwide.

Indeed, the term "medical device" is widely used for a host of very different tools. A typical hospital may have a few dozen of one type of medical device (such as imaging and operating room equipment) and huge volumes of others (such as syringes or sutures). Clearly, medical devices in all their various forms, shapes, and sizes are not only tools for addressing major health problems, but are the very stuff of which health care delivery is made.

Table 9.1: Examples of Medical Devices

Anaesthetic and respiratory equipment: – CEN/TC 215 – tracheal and breathing tubes – anaesthetic machines – medical breathing systems – medical gas supply systems – lung ventilators – pressure regulators – flow metering devices – connectors	Implants for surgery: – CEN/TC 285 – cardiac implants – vascular implants – osteosynthesis implants – reconstructive implants – joint replacement tools – mechanical contraceptives
Non-active medical devices: – CEN/205 – urinary and drainage catheters – hypodermic syringes and needles – plasma filters – condoms – extra corporal circuits – blood gas exchangers – transfusion and infusion sets – parenteral devices – medical gloves – clinical thermometers – anti-embolism hosiery – pen injectors – enteral feeding tubes – surgical tapes and gowns TC	**Electrical equipment:** – X-ray equipment – medical electron systems and accelerators – cardiac defibrillators and monitors – ultrasonic therapy equipment – nerve and muscle stimulators – lung ventilators – electro convulsive therapy equipment – endoscopic equipment – baby incubators and radiant warmers – electrocardiography – blood pressure monitoring equipment – external cardiac pacemakers – magnetic resonance equipment – heated pads, blankets and mattresses – electrically operated hospital beds

Source: Adcock *et al.* (1998) with contributions from Cutler and Gropp.

While drugs have been subject to internationally agreed methods of evaluation for some twenty-five years, this is not the case for medical devices; standards, essential requirements, and consensus protocols for clinical investigations are emerging only now. According to European law, a medical device is not an organ, prescription drug, transplant, blood product, nor cosmetic product. These are all subject to different regulatory requirements and underlying philosophies. The difference between medical devices and pharmaceuticals, however, sheds the most light on the complexity of medical device regulation.

The chief difference between pharmaceutical drugs and medical devices as it affects patients is that drugs interact with a patient directly while medical devices typically interact with patients through an intermediary: the health care professional. However, the two product sectors also differ on a number of other dimensions (Table 9.2). The methods used to evaluate the quality, safety and efficacy of pharmaceuticals are not appropriate for testing the quality, safety and performance of most medical devices. Differences such as these justify distinct regulatory regimes.

Table 9.2: Differences in the Nature of Drugs and Devices

Criteria	Drugs	Devices
1. Scientific Background	Based on pharmacology and chemistry	Based on engineering
2. R & D Process	Screening of substances on having desired effects (resource-driven)	Designing devices to perform certain functions (object-driven)
3. Methodology	Effective by absorption in human body	Thorough evaluation during design-phase
4. Safety Precautions	Long-lasting (time-consuming) tests for efficacy and side effects	Thorough evaluation during design-phase
5. Life Cycle	Brand-loyalty to reliable products, extensive research and registration procedures = Long Life Cycle	Permanent innovations and improvements based on new technologies and materials = Short Life Cycle
6. Consequences for Regulation	Individual product registration and control of procedures necessary	Manufacture to prove general reliability of design and production
7. Consequences for Evidence and Payment	Consideration based on individual drug	Assessment based on generic product type

Source: EUCOMED, 1998.

Another significant difference between the two product sectors is the justification for including products from each in a national benefits catalogue. A well-known industry expert argues that the "traditional evidence principles" and "hierarchies" designed for pharmaceuticals are inappropriate for many medical devices. In addition, placebo controls and blinding may be difficult or impossible, and "The affected population may be too small to achieve the sample size used in drug trials". Health care payers demand a higher level of efficiency as well; with medical devices, "Payers care about effectiveness ("does it work?"), not just efficacy ("can it work?")" (Goodman, 2000).

While these issues have become salient in the last few years, the EU drew a legal boundary between medical devices and pharmaceuticals a decade ago. Yet some components of certain medical devices may be covered by pharmaceutical regulation, and the regulatory scope for pharmaceuticals is more extensive than for medical devices. British legal expert Christopher Hodges notes, "Many activities with pharmaceuticals require prior Competent Authority approval, which is not the case with devices" (Hodges, 1999). Although the regulatory regimes are separate, the shadow of the pharmaceutical regime remains long, affecting regulatory activities in the medical devices sector.

EU Directives concerning medical devices introduced procedures for market authorisation across Europe, with the CE mark providing a passport to regional trade. Compared to what has previously existed at the European level, the new regulations were considered an innovative step forward. Still, when the revisions were adopted in 1998, most parties to the negotiations, according to Weiler (Weiler, 1999), realised that revisions were already necessary and criticism of market authorisation for medical devices based on CE-marking increased over time.

Because the pathways to market authorisation for pharmaceuticals and medical devices are very different, regulators, manufacturers, and third party certification bodies are presented with enormous challenges. Under pressure from its membership, the French trade association SNITEM began to sketch out the differences in late 1999. Since it was widely known that the French government planned to reorganise the regulatory process for market approval, the industry grew concerned about how to market their products, especially since France (and other countries) had not met deadlines for implementation of regulations. Table 9.3 outlines the differences between the two sectors; while the market authorisation path is the same for all EU Members, institutional arrangements for enforcement and implementation differ from country to country.

Table 9.3: Market Authorisation for Medical Devices and Pharmaceutical Drugs: A Comparison[2]

Medical devices	Pharmaceuticals AMM
Risk Analysis	
Manufacturers must: – be aware of all potential risks associated with the use of a medical device; – estimate related risks and the acceptability of such risks in light of the intended purpose and the medical benefit; – carry out this analysis according to the standard FN EN 1441	– Tolerance (part of the evaluation of secondary effects, that is, safety and efficacy)
Quality	
Manufacturers must demonstrate conformity with ER's: – Either conformity with harmonised European standards (NF EN); or – Conformity with an organised QAS at the manufacturing site	– Analysis of raw materials according to monographs of the pharmacopoeia – Conformity with good European manufacturing practices – QSA of pharmaceutical companies
Biological Safety	
– Verification of biocompatibility – Verification of biological safety through laboratory tests and/or preclinical trials of animals	– Verification of biocompatibility – Therapeutic action and secondary effects
Efficacy	
– Clinical tests of performance and safety, either by EN 540 and *loi* Huriet-Serusclat or scientific literature – Search for undesirable effects (must be included in promotional materials) – Possible withdrawal/notification	– Phase I: definition of the dose with effect – Phase II: pharmacological safety – Phase III: confirmation of agreement with *loi* Huriet-Serusclat by clinical trials
After Sales	
– Marketing – Materiovigilance – Audit by the notified body – Renewal of market authorisation	– Phase IV: marketing tests – Pharmacovigilance – Pharmacological inspection – Renewal of AMM

I. EU Regulation of Medical Devices

The EU regulatory system for medical devices is quite young; it is twenty-five years behind the regulation of medical devices in the US, and some twenty-five years behind the European regulation of

---

[2] This information provided by Madame Danielle Hanaire, Directeur des Affaires Techniques, SNITEM; and Gerard Brient, Directeur des Affaires Sectorielles et Européennes, SNITEM (translated by the author).

pharmaceuticals. It is embedded in the general policy on the single market (Articles 100 and 100a) and three device-specific Directives. Article 189 of the EEC Treaty outlines four different instruments of regulatory power: regulations, directives, decisions, and recommendations. Regulations are directly binding upon Member States, while directives must be transposed in their entirety into national law, leaving implementation to national governments. Decisions are binding upon specific parties (*e.g.* the decision against the Honeywell merger), and Recommendations are not binding.

- The Council Directive on active implantable medical devices (AIMD) of June 20, 1990, in force in the Member States since 1 January 1993 (Council of the European Communities, 1990);

- The Council Directive on medical devices (MDD), effective since 1 January 1995 (Council of the European Union, 1993) as amended by Directive 2001/104/EC (European Parliament and Council of the European Union, 2001);

- The *In vitro* Diagnostic Devices Directive (IVDD) of the European Parliament and of the Council of 27 October 1998, which was adopted on 8 December 1998, a delay of some eight years after a first draft became available (European Parliament and Council of the European Union, 1998).

Additional Directives affect the medical device sector, including those that deal with such diverse areas as public procurement, general product safety, electro-magnetic compatibility, product liability and, with increasing use of information technology in medical practice and research, the Information Technology Equipment Directive.

By March 1997, the AIMD had been passed into national law in a total of seventeen European countries, including two EFTA countries. These seventeen except for Belgium had transposed the MDD. The IVDD was supposed to come into force on 7 December 1999, but the deadline was extended to 7 June 2000 because most Member States experienced considerable problems in transposition. Of course, the transposition record of IVDD is just beginning.

The delay of almost eight years in adopting the IVDD was due in large part to political and strategic differences between the Commission and the Council and among France, Germany and the UK. There were also conflicts among the companies in the sector; still, there was a widespread resistance to moving away from IVD self-regulation and toward what was perceived as a EU-imposed regulatory approach.

Events beyond the control of the major players also left their mark. Four years after the first draft was available in 1991, a revised draft became embroiled in the application of the new co-decision procedure between the European Parliament and the Council adopted by the Maastricht Treaty of 1992-1993. This procedure gave the Parliament a right of veto over legislation concerning the single market, health care and consumers, and the environment. The European Parliament made full use of its new power by proposing numerous amendments and additions to the draft IVDD. After several rounds of revisions, the Council and the European Parliament finally agreed on a common position in 1998.

The IVDD delay was also related to discord over the issue of medical devices incorporating human tissue and the use of animal tissues and their derivatives. Decisions on these matters were postponed because of seemingly insurmountable controversies among national governments and in particular among health authorities and regulators from France, Germany and the UK, as well as disagreements among the industry and scientific communities. Only by divorcing the issues of human and animal tissues from the Directive was the IVDD able to move forward.

In late December 2000, the European Medical Device Trade Association EUCOMED announced that a draft for a human tissue Directive would be available by mid-2001. It also endorsed a risk/ benefit approach for the Directive, with a level of control commensurate with the risk, and suggested that the Directive should cover "sourcing, procurement and ethical issues, as well as manufacturing and aspects relating to its placing on the market"[3]. In addition, Germany, which had opposed an amendment of the MDD, withdrew resistance in early 2001 and joined France and the UK in their efforts to revise the Directives. Such a Directive would increase the European regulatory scope for medical devices, since human tissues are implicated in medical devices in a variety of ways. For example, wound healing and skin grafts fall under the medical devices category, as do many other recent medical innovations.

A. Defining Medical Devices

The EU Directives define a medical device as:

- Any instrument, apparatus, appliance, material or other article intended by the manufacturer to be used on human beings for the purpose of:
  - diagnosis, prevention, monitoring, treatment or alleviation of disease, or injury or handicap;

---

[3] *Clinica*, No. 936, 27 November 2000, pp. 2-3.

- investigation, replacement or modification of the anatomy or of a physiological process; or
- control of conception;
- and which does not achieve its principal intended action in or on the human body by pharmacological, immunological or metabolic means[4].

The *principal intended action* as declared by the manufacturer is crucial for determining what is included under the rubric of medical devices, and is culled from both the manufacturer's labelling and claims, and scientific data regarding the mechanism of action. For medical devices the intended action is "Fulfilled by physical means (including mechanical action, physical barrier, replace of or support to organs or body functions)", as opposed to the pharmacological, immunological or metabolic means. The Directives further differentiate medical devices that use medicinal products – such as a drug delivery pump – from the medicinal products themselves. Also described are "accessories" such as contact lens care products and disinfectants specifically intended for use with medical devices such as endoscopes.

The new IVDD adds to this catalogue the definition of *in vitro* diagnostic devices, which includes any medical device that is a reagent, reagent product, calibrator, control material, kit, instrument, apparatus equipment, or system, intended by the manufacturer to be used *in vitro* for the examination of specimens, including blood and tissue donations, derived from the human body, solely or principally for the purpose of providing information:

- concerning a physiological or pathological state, or
- concerning congenital abnormality, or
- to determine the safety and compatibility with potential recipients, or
- to monitor therapeutic measures.

In vitro diagnostic devices are a perfect example of the complexity of medical devices. From the above definition it is clear that IVD products can be vastly different, ranging from a reagent to a kit to an instrument to an entire computer-based laboratory system. IVD devices include about 21,000 separate products, representing not even 1% of total health care expenditure in most Member States. Yet laboratory-testing products are vital to prevent, diagnose, treat and monitor disease. Unlike pharmaceuticals, professionals and laboratory technicians are the primary users of IVD products, although the Directive also covers devices for self-testing by patients and consumers.

---

[4]   Language adopted from the MDD.

285

B. The Old versus the New Approach in Legislation

EU regulation of medical devices grew out of the adoption in the mid-1980s of so-called *new approach* legislation, which affected seventeen industrial sectors, including medical devices. The adoption of this new approach was a historic move made at the highest political levels. While not free from conflict, EU members accepted the entire "new approach" legislative package in order to set in motion the single market, which was perceived to be in the national interest of each country. But once the package was enacted, conflict resolution in the medical devices sector shifted from the "high politics" level to highly specialised and technocratic committees, working groups, and issue networks (Peterson and Bomberg, 1999).

Under "old approach" legislation, technical standards and specifications were written into directives. New approach legislation, by contrast, institutionalised a separation between law and technical standards. Instead, directives would rely on essential requirements[5] and the use of voluntary standards. However, at the insistence primarily of France, considerations of technical specifications are again debated for *in vitro* diagnostics and other high-risk products. The irony is that conflicting views among the leading stakeholders about appropriate technical specifications was what caused interminable delays under the old legislative approach.

Many principles inherent in new approach legislation clearly demonstrate that Member States, and not the EU, direct the path of implementation of EU regulations. CE marking[6], for example, serves as a kind of market authorisation but should not be confused with pre market approval of individual products, or with the strict product-testing regime existing in the pharmaceutical sector. More importantly, directives need to be transposed into national law. Essential requirements are specified in highly detailed annexes, and are a precondition for market authorisation. The meaning of the annexes has been the target of conflicts and disagreements among French, German and British experts and policy-makers ever since the debates about medical devices regulation started in the late 1980s. In practice, their disagreements are

---

[5] Essential requirements are outlined for chemical, physical, and biological properties, infection and microbial contamination; construction and environmental properties; devices with measuring function; protection against radiation; requirements for medical devices connected to or equipped with an energy source (including electromagnetic compatibility); and information to be supplied by the manufacturer.

[6] Contrary to a widespread perception, it does not stand for *Communauté européenne*. Rather, it means *Conformité européenne*.

reflected in the extent to which they have resorted to their national prerogative to request additional national regulatory requirements.

Member States also can invoke a safeguard clause (Article 36 of the Treaty of Rome) in the interest of public health when they have reasonable doubt that essential requirements for products have not been respected. So far, France has taken action regarding condoms, breast implants and animal tissues, and has an ongoing query about electrical safety; the UK has taken action in regard to high-risk implantables. The ECJ has not yet provided a clear-cut ruling on the conditions under which Member States can invoke this clause in the interest of public health. The whole notion of a precautionary principle is entangled with political and legal issues, with political considerations sometimes stronger than legal considerations. Unsurprisingly, the ECJ puts a high premium on legal considerations, although its jurisprudence and case law is not without critiques (Weiler, 1999).

Member States have considerable discretion in how they organise their approach to enforcing compliance with European law and endorsing, or not endorsing, the philosophy behind many informal Commission guidance documents. Even though this discretion might be supposed to lead to a loosening of restrictions from the perspective of health and safety, the EU Directives actually intend to strengthen medical vigilance and the reporting of adverse incidents encountered in the delivery of health care.

C. Post-market Surveillance and Medical Device Vigilance Reporting

The two most innovative components of the EU regulatory system are the introduction of post-market surveillance (PMS) measures and the development of a vigilance system, including a safeguard clause for incident reporting. The Commission's guidance documents state:

> The purpose of the Vigilance system is to improve the protection of health and safety of patients, users and others by reducing the likelihood of the same type of adverse incident being repeated in different places at different times. This is to be achieved by the evaluation of reported incidents and, where appropriate, dissemination of information which could be used to prevent such repetition, or to alleviate the consequences of such incidents.[7]

Thus, EU regulations include a direct attempt to affect consumer/ patient safety issues. And this attempt incorporates substantial regulatory reach by extending responsibility to health care professionals and facility managers. The guidelines continue:

---

[7]   MEDDEV 3/93 (rev. 2) on medical vigilance.

An adverse incident is defined as an event which gives rise to, or has the potential to produce, unexpected or unwarranted effects involving the safety of patients, users or other persons. Adverse incidents in medical devices may arise due to shortcomings in: the device itself, instructions for use, servicing and maintenance, locally initiated modifications or adjustments, user practices, including training, management procedures, the environment in which it is used or stored and incorrect prescription.

So health care systems, and not just manufacturers, are also held responsible for the proper functioning of medical devices.

PMS consists of two complementary elements: a performance monitoring system internal to manufacturers, and product field performance (Gropp, 1998). PMS is intended to serve as an early warning system to detect problems with a medical device after it is launched onto the market, and should allow for early corrective action. Manufacturers have multiple obligations, some as a result of being in the business of manufacturing goods and selling them, and some as a result of specific regulations such as the EU Directives. As part of these obligations, manufacturers are responsible for ensuring that information from post-market surveillance complements clinical trials in the premarket phase.

Regulators typically receive reports on medical devices from three sources: manufacturers who report a serious injury or a death; users and other third parties who report the malfunction of a medical device; and competitors who complain about non-compliance with the Directives by another manufacturer. The regulator will decide whether or not the complaint is justified. If it is and non-compliance is confirmed, the regulator has two options: ask the manufacturer to take corrective action, or demand withdrawal and/or replacement of the device. One should note that the goals of both post-market surveillance and vigilance systems are ambitious, and will be difficult to meet. These reporting systems are perhaps the weakest link in the EU integrative process.

D. Political Background and Resources

European regulatory policy shares a number of characteristics with other highly complex and knowledge-based sectors. Policy has evolved over time; it is multifaceted, intersects with many other areas of activities, and is not expressed in one single EU directive. The development of a politically and economically acceptable regulatory approach was relatively quick, starting around 1987 when the Single European Act came into effect, continuing to the present day.

Much of the leadership for strategic and operational policy development in this sector came from ministries of health in France, Germany and the UK, experts from global companies, including US subsidiaries, and European trade associations. How the early promoters of European regulation wrote their own preferences into the new regime, how they are altering or reversing the decisions regarding regulatory policy and channels for implementation inherited from the pre-Community regulatory system, and, finally, how EU Directives shape the new path in the post-Community system, are among a few intriguing issues for future research. But sorting out claims of leadership by one country or countries from facts and actual developments is next to impossible without a step by step review of decision-making on each EU Directive running through the complex multi-layered EU governance.

At this preliminary stage, one only should note that a focus on "scientific decision-making" and consideration of the latest scientific research tends to privilege the larger Member States that have the necessary expertise and resources. Implementation requires highly trained and specialised staff; yet knowledgeable individuals with an understanding of regulatory objectives seem to be in short supply everywhere. Actual resources available for the implementation of the three EU Directives are limited; staff capacity within the Commission is low (between three and five individuals).

Administrative capacity varies greatly across the fifteen EU Member States. In most, it is weak, notably the Mediterranean rim and in Central Europe. Even in the Scandinavian countries, resources are scarce[8]. With a staff of about 150 at the Medical Devices Agency, the UK until recently had been the only EU country with sufficient regulatory manpower capacity and a diversity of professional skills under one organisational roof (specialists, administrators, medical and nursing staff, professionally qualified technologists and scientists including biologists, chemists, engineers, toxicologists, pharmacists and physicists; and specialists in quality assurance). This "head start" was due to the UK's centralised NHS structure and considerable experience in voluntary user reporting of incidents and accidents over the last four decades. However, France has developed an agency for health care product safety (AFSSAPS), which has had responsibility for medical devices since 1998. While they are imitating the US FDA, France may end up moving closer to the UK's MDA.

Resources will likely remain low. Neither the Commission nor national governments seem to have authorised more staff or raised the budget for this purpose, with the noticeable exception of France and Germany in fiscal year 2000. Additional resources are necessary if the

---

[8]   In 1998, Denmark assigned two staff members to the implementation of the MDD; Finland twelve, Norway two, and Sweden five.

claim that patient safety is more important to the EU regulatory regime than free movement and if competitiveness is to be made credible.

E. Boundary Issues

To the extent that medical devices and in particular high-risk devices were regulated in the past in France, Germany and the UK, many regulatory requirements were anchored in pharmaceutical drugs regulation. As a result, the lines between drugs and medical devices were never satisfactorily demarcated. In negotiating these issues, members of different Commission services, business interests and national authorities were pitted against each other. Sometimes the Commission and company experts were pitted against national authorities. At other times coalitions of actors agreed on the need for European legislation at the "high politics and policy" level while disagreeing over specific issues at the technical committee level. For the moment, the thorniest borderline issues between medical devices and medicinal products seem to have been resolved through collective consensus and a shared willingness to address new issues as they arise.

Yet advances in biotechnology (*e.g.* tissue engineered skin, bone cement and fillers, cultured cartilage and tissue engineered wound dressings) create new boundary issues. These advances are increasingly blurring the lines between medicinal products, biological and medical devices. Experts recognise the inadequacy of the existing regimes for regulating drugs and medical devices for coping with emerging technologies. As new medical innovations arise, these boundary lines continue to erode.

Current safety reporting regulations differ depending on the product, whether a drug, a device or a biological entity. Domestic vigilance systems tend to follow these distinctions. The result is a huge procedural and organisational diversity between vigilance systems. Regulatory affairs specialists, company experts and scientists (as well as social scientists interested in learning about the effects of EU directives) face major challenges. The organisational channels and procedures for enforcing compliance with EU directives and national regulation differ across the (product-based) vigilance systems, even in a fairly streamlined system such as that existing in France.

**Table 9.4: Varieties of Medical Device
Vigilance Reporting Systems**

– Medicinal vigilance (pharmacovigilance)
– Medical devices vigilance (called materiovigilance in France)
– Blood product vigilance (haemovigilance)
– Reagent vigilance (reactovigilance)
– Biovigilance (highly probable in the future)

F. The Future: A European Medical Device Agency?

The creation of an independent European regulatory agency is the hallmark of an emerging "European regulatory state" for some scholars (Majone, 1997). Yet in the field of medical devices there is no "European Medical Device Agency" along the lines of the European Medicines Evaluation Agency (EMEA) in London (Pelkmans *et al.*, 2000 and Vos, 1999). EMEA is widely seen as an illustration of an independent regulatory agency modelled after the US FDA; it uses a two-pronged approach, with a centralised procedure managed by EMEA and a decentralised procedure managed by the Member States. Yet in the field of medical devices, enforcement and implementation is only decentralised, with Member States responsible for transposition of directives.

For the last ten years, European governments have not embraced the idea of a European-wide agency, with the exception of France. A "high level" French demand for a European Medical Device Agency was briefly on the European agenda in 1997-1998, but then disappeared for a few years. It has re-emerged as a future option to be decided upon when the review of the EU pharmaceutical regime is completed in 2003[9]. The case can be made that four years ago the time simply was not ripe for a European medical device regulatory agency. With circumstances changing rapidly, and an increasingly strong consensus that stricter requirements for high-risk devices are necessary, the creation of a EU-level agency grows more likely. Still, a separate European agency is less likely than a new organisational unit created within existing structures.

However, industry groups also have not welcomed the idea of a EU-wide agency. The two US trade associations (AdvaMed or Advanced Technology Association, previously HIMA, and NEMA), the Trans-atlantic Business Dialogue (TABD), and American subsidiaries in Europe have been strong advocates of the decentralised EU approach.

---

[9] Interestingly, the UK completed a review in 2000 on whether to merge the Medicinal Control Agency (MPA) with the Medical Device Agency (MDA) but rejected any merger, at least for the time being.

And any enthusiasm for EMEA as a regulatory model for medical devices should be dampened by an examination of other European agencies. Those who have studied them conclude that they have little power to overrule national governments (Dehousse, 1997).

If, on the other hand, "regulation by information" is a defining characteristic of a European regulatory state that aims to end existing information asymmetries in the medical device sector (Pelkmans *et al.*, 2000), then one should note that the Enterprise Directorate-General (previously DG III Industrial Affairs) is endowed with powers to generate, collect and analyse regulatory data through EUDAMED. Other DGs are responsible for surveying the health status of European populations through various European observatories. Whether Unit G4 of the Enterprise Directorate General has more teeth to enforce compliance with EU directives remains to be seen.

It should, however, be noted that EUDAMED suffers from at least two inherent limitations that impact on public health. First, the regulatory databank is only accessible to national regulators, the competent authorities. Second, the information kept by competent authorities on manufacturers and medical devices on the market and on certificates issued by notified bodies are not linked with information on medical vigilance. Information from the market authorisation process cannot be assumed to reach those audiences who secure patient and clinical safety and enforce other aspects of the Directives.

II. Regulatory Responsibilities in the Member States

Member States, under the umbrella of the three EU Directives, have considerable discretion in implementation. Yet the very fact that institutional contexts are country-specific makes it especially difficult to generalise about the implementation paths of individual Member States. Still, an attempt will be made to outline the various roles involved in implementation. The EU Directives assign responsibilities in the regulatory cycle to three organisations: manufacturers, state-based Competent Authorities (CAs), and mostly private third-party certification organisations, or Notified Bodies (NBs).

A. Competent Authorities

While Device Competent Authorities – typically but not exclusively the Ministries of Health – were first introduced in the MDD, their role was unclear. The IVDD clarified that they ultimately are politically and legally responsible for oversight, enforcement and compliance (European Commission, 1994). They are called upon to step out of a traditional bureaucratic role and engage in a number of new activities:

step up the reporting of adverse events by users; improve oversight of notified bodies and ensure a more uniform level of certification by notified bodies. Implementation has not been without problems, including lack of oversight and monitoring of NBs by CAs, different perceptions and interpretations of their responsibilities, and differing enforcement behaviour, laws, and administrative procedures across Member States.

Unlike in the pre-Community regulatory era, CAs are responsible for establishing whether a manufacturer followed up a reported incident, how this was done, and whether the manufacturer took additional actions suggested by a NB. CAs have considerable discretion in what actions they may undertake. Possible corrective action includes:

- device recall;
- issue of advisory notice;
- additional surveillance/modification of devices in use;
- modification to future device design, components or manufacturing process;
- modification to labelling or instructions of use.

Once a remedy has been suggested, hospital administrators, medical practitioners and other health care professionals, and user representatives responsible for the maintenance and the safety of the device should take the necessary steps to correct the problem. Such steps should, where practicable, be taken in co-operation with the manufacturer. Whether the procedures that trigger a reporting of an adverse incident are workable and produce the effects for which they were designed remains to be seen. Triggering depends on many factors but above all relies upon the reporting behaviour of users. Again, there is a great distance between these ideal reporting goals and their actual implementation.

B. Manufacturers

Prior to European market integration, manufacturers in most product sectors were not concerned about marketing and selling their products. In the post-war expansion period from the mid-1960s to the late 1980s, friendly relations with health administrations and public insurers provided them with many advantages and, in many instances, monopoly supplier status. Over time, each manufacturer learned the ropes of heavily regulated markets and adapted sales and marketing strategies to the prevailing regulatory framework existing in each country. After the creation of the single European market, the industry faced challenges from health care reformers and had to reconsider its strategies. Of course, global companies have had less of an adjustment to make than small and medium-sized enterprises. Despite these adjustment costs, observers agree that the opportunities by far outweigh the inconveniences for all manufacturers provided they respect the "ten golden rules" (Table 9.5).

**Table 9.5: The "Ten Golden Rules" for
Medical Device Manufacturers**[10]

1. Classify medical device in accordance with rules in annex IX
2. Identify standards to be used to satisfy the essential requirements in annex I which apply to the device
3. Carry out risk analysis according to EN 1441
4. Ensure that all relevant essential requirements are satisfied
5. Prepare technical documentation, and design dossier if class III
6. Choose conformity assessment route from those allowed by the classification and if applicable choose notified body
7. Comply with conformity assessment annex(s)
8. Prepare EC declaration of conformity (annexes II, IV, V, VI, VII, or, for custom-made devices or devices for clinical investigation, the statement in annex VIII
9. Affix CE marking (not for custom-made or clinical investigation devices)
10. Maintain post-market medical device vigilance system

Manufacturers' responsibilities for post-market surveillance and after sales responsibilities are summarised in the MDD.

Directive 92/43/EEC on medical devices contains the following obligation on the manufacturer in each of the available procedures of conformity assessment:

An undertaking by the manufacturer to institute and keep up to date a systematic procedure to review experience gained from devices in the post-production-phase and to implement appropriate means to apply any necessary action. This undertaking must include an obligation for the manufacturer to notify the competent authorities of the following incidents immediately on learning of them:

- any malfunction or deterioration in the characteristics and/or performance of a device, as well as any inadequacy in the instructions for use which might lead to or might have led to the death of a patient or user or to a serious deterioration in his state of health;
- any technical or medical reason connected with the characteristics or performance of a device leading for the reasons referred to in

---

[10] Courtesy of Peter Styles, President, Oxford Instruments. European Standardisation and Medical Device Regulation. This document had been prepared with Trudy Phelps, BSI, Chris Grishon and was called "CEN/CENELEC/ETSI Healthcare Project. European Standardisation and Medical Device Regulation". It became a victim of European politics.

Subparagraph (i) to systematic recall of devices of the same type by the manufacturer.

This clearly imposes a general post-marketing obligation similar to Article 3.2 of the General Product Safety (GPS) Directive but with two differences. First, the wording differs; second, the status and enforceability of the obligation is also different (Hodges *et al.*, 1996).

C. Notified Bodies

Embedded as they are in the domestic political economy, notified bodies (NBs) are certification organisations appointed by EU Member countries to conduct formal audits of products and quality systems. NBs are primarily private organisations, but they can also include public bodies that accredit NBs to certify and test medical products and inspect manufacturing sites, as they do in Germany. Irrespective of status, NBs act on behalf of the public and work on a fee-based contractual basis.

NBs must be independent, impartial and competent. Independence is defined as having no association with the manufacturer, supplier or installer and being free from financial inducements or pressures. Impartiality of inspection staff is ensured by deliberately severing remuneration from the number of controls or reviews made. Competency is defined as having qualified staff with special training and all necessary evaluation and verification experience; confidential handling of manufacturers' files; the application of appropriate methods and testing equipment; the ability to draw up certificates, records, and reports to demonstrate that the controls have been carried out; and carrying of liability insurance.

In the European Economic Area, most countries have one or two NBs, but can have as many as Germany's 25. In the past, the accreditation and certification practices by about 61 NBs (up from 40 in 1995) in the European Union have been described as lax, too liberal and uneven. Information about which NBs in which countries are engaging in lax practices and which Competent Authorities do not do their job are treated as "state secrets", all under the political rhetoric of "open government" and "transparency". While regulators refuse to talk about these issues, information is publicly available that indicate which NBs have been implicated in the recall of products.

NBs are supposed to co-ordinate their activities Europe-wide by improving the exchange of information and experience among each other and between NBs and the Competent Authorities. They have elaborated non-binding guidance documents, have addressed issues of electro-magnetic compatibility (EMC), and are applying stricter rules for enforcing significant changes relating to quality systems, product ranges and clinical investigations, including clinical evaluations. Representatives of NBs began to meet on a regular basis at a European level in 1997 in order to standardise requirements for internal procedures, gain the necessary expertise and documentation of evaluations carried out by other NBs, and develop recommendations for the collection and presentation of clinical data and guidance documents for the assessment of certain categories of medical devices.

D. Task Force

In recent years, a Task Force comprised of Commission staff, NBs, and the European Manufacturers' Association has been meeting regularly to prepare a recommendation for the evaluation of clinical data in the context of CE marking, as well as to address other outstanding issues aimed at raising standards in the interest of public health. They have addressed:

- general issues of scientific validity of data from both basic science and clinical investigation;
- circumstances in which critical reports should be provided by manufacturers;
- decision-making process including guidance for assessing benefit/risk ratios.

Assessment of particular categories of devices is also ongoing, namely for devices manufactured with animal tissues or derivatives and breast implants. The basis of participation in this Task Force, which resembles the membership in Global Harmonisation Task Force (GHTF) subgroups, undoubtedly conceals an interesting story, although at this point it is unclear whether the story eventually emerging will illuminate the fine lines between law and politics, between law and safety, and between health and commercial interests. It is expected that the Commission will press for tighter mandatory technical requirements in the areas of animal tissues and breast implants.

E. Shared Competence

The Community and the Member States have shared competence over human health and safety [Articles 36 and 100a(4) and 100(5)]. As the legal scholar Ellen Vos explains:

> The ability of the Member States to adopt measures under these provisions depends on the method of harmonisation used and the degree of harmonisation achieved [...] the Court has confirmed its pragmatic approach to preemption, stating that the Member States may validly adopt unilateral measures to ensure human health and safety. Consequently, even where the Community has chosen to pursue partial harmonisation, this is likely to lead

towards a greater degree of harmonisation of health and safety regulation by the Community… However, Article 100a(4) also gives evidence of elements of shared competence between the Community and the Member States on human health and safety (Vos, 1999).

Within the General Product Safety Directive, the Council expressly confirms the competence of the Member States on product safety. For example, Article 5 of the Directive grants the Member States the power to adopt necessary regulatory provisions to make producers and distributors comply with their obligations under the Directive; the States can thus ensure that products placed on the market are safe, can monitor the safety of products brought on the market, and can give the competent authorities the necessary powers to take appropriate measures. Article 6 additionally recognises the power of the Member States to adopt immediate measures to arrange for the withdrawal of dangerous products already placed on the market.

III. Member State Policies and EU Regulation

This final section explores issues related to implementation by Member States of EU regulatory policies. As noted earlier, it is sometimes difficult to differentiate between European and national regulatory responsibilities. The issues discussed are some of the more salient ones in this respect, in Labelling and Instructions for Use.

Labelling and warnings, both on products and equipment and in instructions for use (IFU), are as much a public health issue as they are a free trade issue. The need for effective labels has grown significantly as societies have become increasingly diverse. When warnings about hazards and instructions for use of medical devices are written only in English, some consumers will be unable to comprehend this vital information. The failure to provide non-native warnings can pose serious risks to patients, leading not only to high rates of adverse effects but also increased consultations, thus adding to health care costs.

Labelling and packaging issues have been on the global agenda, and the GHTF has made efforts to move towards globally harmonised standards for medical device labelling and packaging. But it is the EU Directives on medical devices that address most extensively the regulatory provisions for labelling, while also raising the issue of training and knowledge of potential users. As Luc Morisset has noted:

> The objective of labelling is to secure the safe use of medical devices. Each device must be accompanied by the information needed to use it safely and properly, take into account the training and knowledge of the potential users, and identify the manufacturer […] This information includes labels and IFU (Morisset, 2000).

The scope of labelling covers device marking, labels and instructions for use. In addition, labelling can be a cause for medical concern when it is inadequate. Information supplied by the manufacturer includes all written, printed or graphic matter on a medical device or any of its containers or wrappers; or accompanying a medical device; relating to the identification, technical description and use of a medical device, while excluding shipping documentation and promotional material. The information comprises the details on the labels and the data in the instructions for use.

The issue of language is pertinent to the regulatory regime in two ways. First, a Member State may insist that labels and instructions for use must be translated into the national language of the country where the device is used. Second, a manufacturer must provide evidence that the documents are translated when they are submitted to the Competent Authority before placing a product on the market. Thus translation requirements for medical device documentation appear more stringent than general product liability requirements.

Again, one may note that a substantive policy aimed at public health and safety protection is written into the essential requirements on labelling and instructions for use. The Directives provide the evidence for concern for public health in the EU regulatory regime. Thus when analysts complain that human health and safety has been sacrificed to the imperatives of EU market integration, they only present one side of the public health story.

A. Clinical Investigations and Market Approval of Medical Devices

"Globalise the evidence, localise decision-making" is the latest slogan in the international health services community and, lately, the medical device sector. This slogan describes two sides of the same coin: the globalisation of scientific medicine and the continuing importance of local medical practice. The three EU Directives on medical devices do not harmonise rules for clinical investigations, leaving rule making and application entirely up to the Member States. Again, EU-inspired regulatory processes complement national regulatory processes; both unfold simultaneously.

On the European level, France and the UK have insisted on stricter regulatory requirements for high-risk products and have requested a revision of the MDD at the European level. After hesitating, if not blocking action for about three years, Germany has now joined them. A consensus seems to exist on the parameters for the scrutiny that domestic regulators will be looking for when approving products for the

market and when making coverage decisions. Among the pieces of evidence regulators will be looking for are:
- preclinical and clinical data;
- impact of Health Technology Assessment (HTA);
- impact of evidence-based medicine/outcome analysis;
- availability of guidelines and standards;
- depth of guidance;
- review of current guidance and standards.

Clinical investigations can be undertaken with CE-marked devices and non CE-marked devices but the requirements for each differ and the regulatory requirements for clinical investigations with non CE-marked devices are reported to differ considerably across countries, within countries, and across health sectors (Sorrel, 2000a and b).

B. HTA and EBM: Reimbursement and Market Approval

The connection between funding, reimbursement and price-setting issues, and EU Directives on medical devices requires further explanation. A strict legal reading of the Treaty of Rome, as amended by the Treaty of Maastricht of 1992, and again by the Treaty of Amsterdam of 1997, leaves reimbursement and pricing issues under the jurisdiction of the Member States. A close strict reading of the three medical device-specific Directives does not challenge this interpretation. Yet the need to comply with EU medical device-specific Directives provides a "unique window of opportunity" to restructure fundamentally the existing evaluation, reimbursement and accountability processes. How the mix of European and national elements influences French and German decision-makers, and what bearing these will have on the ultimate outcome of EU regulations presents a few puzzles. In time, these will need to be unravelled and explained as will the funding of major capital investment, which is subject to European procurement rules that supersede national regulations (see Chapter 6).

The rising cost of medical technology and its share in national health spending was high on the agenda in the 1970s. As European countries became more successful in containing rising costs the topic slowly disappeared from the agenda. However, it has recently resurfaced with a vengeance. In health care policy-making, the idea that health technology is driving costs is likely to occupy centre stage, with Evidence-Based Medicine (EBM) and Health Technology Assessment (HTA) moving deeper into routine decision-making at all levels. In short, HTA and EBM are major forces in health care regulation and legislation, and will continue to be in the near future.

Experience with HTA and EBM over the last two decades suggests that they are considered to be appropriate tools to optimise the allocation of resources and secure access to innovative treatments. The practice of evaluating medical devices prior to their launch on the market and their diffusion into the health care system is certain to grow in importance even though the parties involved – payers, organised medicine and the medical device industry – do not agree on how to improve health care services.

Everywhere, it can be observed that concerns for EBM are spreading from the macro-policy and macro-structural level down to the delivery of care. Regional decision-makers allocate funds among hospital services, research and education, and among disease types or segments of the population. In many European countries the demand for quality hospital management is politically "in", however, the full impact on local sites is often uncertain.

C. Single Use Devices versus Multiple Use Devices

The issue of single use versus multiple use devices raises many health and safety issues which, while beyond the legal boundaries of the MDD, are highly pertinent in clinical practice. The issue has been debated in the relevant European circles for years, but a satisfactory solution has not been found. In drawing a distinction between "placing on the market" and "putting into service", the MDD has imposed a heightened requirement for product liability; however, it stops short of imposing stricter requirements on Member States out of respect for their jurisdiction over health care. As a result, a serious divide exists between the industry, payers and purchasers, and health care providers. The device industry took a position against the reuse of single-use devices, arguing, that reuse can create unacceptable risks (EUCOMED, 1996). The industry stated: "Reuse is clinically, legally and ethically undesirable. Although reuse supposedly offers economic and environmental benefits, even these benefits are questionable in light of the procedures required to process devices for reuse".

However, budgetary pressures create incentives to adopt multiple use devices. The European Hospital Federation estimates that between 4-15% of all hospitalised patients contract an infection while hospitalised; a similar figure is given by EUCOMED. This serious problem needs addressing, but any attempt faces the hurdles of cost containment and falsely understood economies. There are relatively few studies of the cost of hospital-acquired illness during hospital stays. Table 9.6 below compares the trade-offs between the costs and benefits of single use and multiple use devices.

Table 9.6: Single Use *versus* Multiple Use Devices: A Trade-off in Choices

Actions	+/-	Single Use	Multiple Use
Purchase	+	Lower costs	Higher costs
Sterilisation	-	PrEN 556 Maintenance of the equipment	Quality commitment of the distributor
Collection	-	Specific circuit	Waste circuit
Utilisation	-	Internal guarantee and responsibility	External guarantee and responsibility
Evolution	-	Internal constraints, few distributors	Benefit of R&D of the industrialists
Elimination	+		Necessity of incineration at 1200 C

Source : Fédération hospitalière de France (1997: 441).

The era of looking at funding and reimbursement issues through the lens of domestic politics alone seems to have come to an end. The boundaries between exclusive and shared responsibilities of the EU and Member States over the evaluation of medical devices for market approval on the one hand and reimbursement on the other are eroding. As with medical device regulation in general, European regulatory processes and local decisions aimed at containing the rising costs of medical technology are becoming increasingly intertwined.

Bibliography

ADCOCK, J., SORREL, S. and WATTS, J. (eds.) (1998), *Medical Devices Manual*, Euromed Communications Ltd., Haslemere.

ALTENSTETTER, C. (1998a), "Collective Action of the Medical Devices Industry at the Transnational Level", *Current Politics and Economics of Europe*, Vol. 8, No. 1, pp. 39-60.

ALTENSTETTER, C. (1998b), "Regulating and Financing Medical Devices in the European Union" in LEIDL, R. (ed.), *Health Care and Its Financing in the Single European Market*, IOS Press, Amsterdam, pp. 116-149.

ALTENSTETTER, C. (2001), "Regulatory Regimes in Transition: The Case of Medical Devices and Patient Care", draft manuscript.

COUNCIL OF THE EUROPEAN COMMUNITIES (1990), Council Directive 90/385/EEC of 20 June 1990 on the approximation of the laws of the Member States relating to active implantable medical devices, OJ L 189, 20 July 1990, pp. 17-36.

COUNCIL OF THE EUROPEAN COMMUNITIES (1993), Directive 93/42/EEC of 14 June 1993 concerning medical devices, OJ L 169, 12 July 1993, pp. 1-43.

CUTLER, I. (1998), "The Role of Technical Standards", in ADCOCK, J., SORREL, S. and WATTS, J. (eds.), *Medical Devices Manual*, Euromed Communications Ltd., Haslemere, pp. 6.1-6.14.

DEHOUSSE, R. (1997), "Regulation by Networks in the European Community: The Role of European Agencies", *Journal of European Public Policy*, Vol. 4, No. 2, June 1997, pp. 246-261.

EUCOMED (1996), Position paper, "The Case Against Reuse of Single Use Medical Devices", The European Medical Technology Industry Association, Brussels.

EUCOMED (1998), "Medical Devices: Implementation of the Directives and Future Developments", Document MO 24, 25-26, European Trade Association of Medical Suppliers Industries, London, March 1998.

EUROPEAN COMMISSION (1994), *Guide to the Implementation of Community Harmonisation Directives Based on the New Approach and the Global Approach*, Office for Official Publications of the European Community, Luxembourg (revised second edition in 1999).

EUROPEAN PARLIAMENT and COUNCIL OF THE EUROPEAN UNION (1998), Directive 98/79/EC of the European Parliament and of the Council of 27 October 1998 on *in vitro* diagnostic medical devices, OJ L 331, 7 December 1998, pp. 1-37.

EUROPEAN PARLIAMENT and COUNCIL OF THE EUROPEAN UNION (2001), Directive 2001/104/EC of the European Parliament and of the Council of 7 December 2001 amending Council Directive 93/42/EEC concerning medical devices, OJ L 6, 10 January 2001, pp. 50-51.

FÉDÉRATION HOSPITALIÈRE DE FRANCE (1997), "Usage Unique-Coûts directs et indirects – GEEHP-1995", Revue hospitalière de France, No. 3, May-June 1997.

GOODMAN, C. (2000), "The Lewin Group", Presentation at ISTHAC, The Hague, 18 June 2000.

GROPP, M. (1998), "The Authorised Representative in Europe", in ADCOCK, J., SORREL, S. and WATTS, J. (eds.), *Medical Devices Manual*, Euromed Communications Ltd., Haslemere, pp. 20.1-20.16.

HODGES, C. (1999), "European Regulation of Medical Devices" in O'GRADY, J., SPENCER, M., WALSH, N. and DODDS SMITH, I. (eds.), *Medicines, Medical Devices and the Law*, Greenwich Medical Media Limited, London, pp. 3-24.

HODGES, C., TYLER, M. and ABBOTT, H. (1996), *Product Liability*, Sweet and Maxwell, London.

MAJONE, G. (1997), "The New European Agencies: Regulation by Information", *Journal of European Public Policy*, Vol. 4, No. 2, June 1997, pp. 262-75.

MORISSET, L. (2000), "Medical Device Labelling", IIR-Post Conference Workshop, London, 29 March 2000.

PELKMANS, J., LABORY, S. and MAJONE, G. (2000), "Better EU Regulatory Quality: Assessing Current Initiatives and New Proposals", in GALLI, G. and PELKMANS, J. (eds.), *Regulatory Reform and Competitiveness in Europe, 1. Horizontal Issues*, Edward Elgar, Cheltenham and Northhampton, MA, pp. 461-526.

PELKMANS, J., VOS, E. and DI MAURO, L. (2000), "Reforming Product Regulation in the EU: A Painstaking, Iterative Two-level Game", in GALLI, G. and PELKMANS, J. (eds.), *Regulatory Reform and Competitiveness in Europe, 1. Horizontal Issues*, Edward Elgar, Cheltenham and Northhampton, MA, pp. 238-291.

PETERSON, J. and BOMBERG, E. (1999), *Decision-making in the European Union*, St. Martin's Press, New York.

SORREL, S. (2000a), "Clinical Investigations", Presentation at the conference on Medical Devices Regulation, Euston Hotel, London, 1 December 2000.

SORREL, S. (2000b), "Clinical Evaluation and Investigation of Medical Devices in Europe and Case Study of a Clinical Investigation", presentation at the Conference organised by IBC Conferences Ltd., Strand Palace Hotel, London, 4 December 2000.

VOS, E. (1999), *Institutional Frameworks of Community Health & Safety Regulation: Committees, Agencies and Private Bodies*, Hart Publishing, Oxford and Portland, pp. 251-311.

WEILER, J.H.H. (1999), "Epilogue: 'Comitology' as Revolution – Infranationalism, Constitutionalism and Democracy", in JOERGES, C. and VOS, E. (eds.), *EU Committees: Social Regulation, Law and Politics,* Hart Publishing, Oxford and Portland, pp. 339-349.

Chronological Table of Cases

Rulings by the European Court of Justice and Court of First Instance can be read in full at <www.europa.eu.int/cj/en/jurisp/index.htm>.

European Court of Justice

Case 19/61, Judgement of 13 July 1962, Mannesmann AG *v.* High Authority of the European Coal and Steel Community.

Case 33/65, Judgement of 1 December 1965, Adrianus Dekker *v.* Bundesversicherungsanstalt für Angestellte.

Case 61/65, Judgement of 30 June 1966, G. Vaassen-Göbbels (a widow) *v.* Management of the Beambtenfonds voor het Mijnbedrijf.

Case 78/70, Judgement of 8 June 1971, Deutsche Grammophon Gesellschaft mbH *v.* Metro-SB-Großmärkte GmbH & Co. KG.

Case 155/73, Judgement of 30 April 1974, Giuseppe Sacchi.

Case 8/74, Judgement of 11 July 1974, Procureur du Roi *v.* Benoît and Gustave Dassonville.

Case 15/74, Judgement of 31 October 1974, Centrafarm BV et Adriaan de Peijper *v.* Sterling Drug Inc.

Case 16/74, Judgement of 31 October 1974, Centrafarm BV et Adriaan de Peijper *v.* Winthrop BV.

Case 33/74, Judgement of 3 December 1974, Johannes Henricus Maria van Binsbergen *v.* Bestuur van de Bedrijfsvereniging voor de Metaalnijverheid.

Case 36/74, Judgement of 12 December 1974, B.N.O. Walrave and L.J.N. Koch *v.* Association Union cycliste internationale.

Case 104/75, Judgement of 20 May 1976, Adriaan de Peijper, Managing Director of Centrafarm BV.

Case 5/77, Judgement of 5 October 1977, Carlo Tedeschi *v.* Denkavit Commerciale s.r.l.

Case 19/77, Judgement of 1 February 1978, Miller International Schallplatten GmbH *v.* Commission of the European Communities.

Case 102/77, Judgement of 23 May 1978, Hoffmann-La Roche & Co. AG *v.* Centrafarm Vertriebsgesellschaft Pharmazeutischer Erzeugnisse mbH.

Case 117/77, Judgement of 16 March 1978, Bestuur van het Algemeen Ziekenfonds Drenthe-Platteland *v.* G. Pierik.

Case 3/78, Judgement of 10 October 1978, Centrafarm BV. *v.* American Home Products Corporation.

Joined cases 110 and 111/78, Judgement of 18 January 1979, Ministère public and "Chambre syndicale des agents artistiques et impresarii de Belgique" ASBL *v.* Willy van Wesemael and others.

Case 182/78, Judgement of 31 May 1979, Bestuur van het Algemeen Ziekenfonds Drenthe-Platteland *v.* G. Pierik.

Joined cases 209 to 215 and 218/78, Judgement of 29 October 1980, Heintz van Landewyck SARL and others *v.* Commission of the European Communities.

Case 187/80, Judgement of 14 July 1981, Merck & Co. Inc. *v.* Stephar BV. and Petrus Stephanus Exler.

Case 279/80, Judgement of 17 December 1981, Criminal proceedings against Alfred John Webb.

Joined cases 96-102, 104, 105, 108 and 110/82, Judgement of 8 November 1983, NV. IAZ International Belgium and others *v.* Commission of the European Communities.

Case 238/82, Judgement of 7 February 1984, Duphar BV. and others *v.* The Netherlands State.

Joined cases 240, 241, 242, 261, 262, 268 and 269/82, Judgement of 10 December 1985, Stichting Sigarettenindustrie and others *v.* Commission of the European Communities.

Joined cases 286/82 and 26/83, Judgement of 31 January 1984, Graziana Luisi and Giuseppe Carbone *v.* Ministero del Tesoro.

Case 35/83, Judgement of 30 January 1985, BAT Cigaretten-Fabriken GmbH *v.* Commission of the European Communities.

Case 41/83, Judgement of 20 March 1985, Italian Republic *v.* Commission of the European Communities.

Case 72/83, Judgement of 10 July 1984, Campus Oil Limited and others *v.* Minister for Industry and Energy and others.

Case 107/83, Judgement of 12 July 1984, Ordre des avocats au Barreau de Paris *v.* Onno Klopp.

Case 123/83, Judgement of 30 January 1985, Bureau national interprofessionnel du cognac *v.* Guy Clair.

Case 229/83, Judgement of 10 January 1985, Association des Centres distributeurs Édouard Leclerc and others *v.* SARL "Au blé vert" and others.

Case 231/83, Judgement of 29 January 1985, Henri Cullet and Chambre syndicale des réparateurs automobiles et détaillants de produits pétroliers *v.* Centre Leclerc à Toulouse and Centre Leclerc à Saint-Orens-de-Gameville.

Case 18/84, Judgement of 7 May 1985, Commission of the European Communities *v.* French Republic.

Case 311/84, Judgement of 3 October 1985, Centre belge d'études de marché – Télémarketing (CBEM) *v.* SA Compagnie luxembourgeoise de télédiffusion (CLT) and Information publicité Benelux (IPB).

Case 352/85, Judgement of 26 April 1988, Bond van Adverteerders and others *v.* The Netherlands State.

Case 45/86, Judgement of 26 March 1987, Commission of the European Communities *v.* Council of the European Communities.

Case 66/86, Judgement of 11 April 1989, Ahmed Saeed Flugreisen and Silver Line Reisebüro GmbH *v.* Zentrale zur Bekämpfung unlauteren Wettbewerbs e.V.

Case 246/86, Judgement of 11 July 1989, SC Belasco and others *v.* Commission of the European Communities.

Case 263/86, Judgement of 27 September 1988, Belgian State *v.* René Humbel and Marie-Thérèse Edel.

Case 267/86, Judgement of 21 September 1988, Pascal Van Eycke *v.* ASPA NV.

Case 242/87, Judgement of 30 May 1989, Commission of the European Communities *v.* Council of the European Communities. European Community action scheme for the mobility of university students (Erasmus).

Joined cases 266 and 267/87, Judgement of 18 May 1989, The Queen *v.* Royal Pharmaceutical Society of Great Britain, *ex parte* Association of Pharmaceutical Importers and others.

Case C-18/88, Judgement of 13 December 1991, Régie des télégraphes et des téléphones *v.* GB-Inno-BM SA.

Case C-202/88, Judgement of 19 March 1991, French Republic *v.* Commission of the European Communities.

Case C-322/88, Judgement of 13 December 1989, Salvatore Grimaldi *v.* Fonds des maladies professionnelles.

Case C-154/89, Judgement of 26 February 1991, Commission of the European Communities *v.* French Republic.

Case C-180/89, Judgement of 26 February 1991, Commission of the European Communities *v.* Italian Republic.

Case C-198/89, Judgement of 26 February 1991, Commission of the European Communities *v.* Hellenic Republic.

Case C-260/89, Judgement of 18 June 1991, Elliniki Radiophonia Tiléorassi AE and Panellinia Omospondia Syllogon Prossopikou *v.* Dimotiki Etairia Pliroforissis and Sotirios Kouvelas and Nicolaos Avdellas and others.

Case C-288/89, Judgement of 25 July 1991, Stichting Collectieve Antennevoorziening Gouda and others *v.* Commissariaat voor de Media.

Case C-340/89, Judgement of 7 May 1991, Irène Vlassopoulou *v.* Ministerium für Justiz, Bundes- und Europaangelegenheiten Baden-Württemberg.

Case C-353/89, Judgement of 25 July 1991, Commission of the European Communities *v.* Kingdom of the Netherlands.

Case C-39/90, Judgement of 20 June 1991, Denkavit Futtermittel GmbH *v.* Land Baden-Württemberg.

Case C-41/90, Judgement of 23 April 1991, Klaus Höfner and Fritz Elser *v.* Macrotron GmbH.

Case C-76/90, Judgement of 25 July 1991, Manfred Säger *v.* Dennemeyer & Co. Ltd.

Case C-159/90, Judgement of 4 October 1991, The Society for the Protection of Unborn Children Ireland Ltd. *v.* Stephen Grogan and others.

Case C-179/90, Judgement of 10 December 1991, Merci convenzionali porto di Genova SpA *v.* iderurgica Gabrielli SpA.

Case C-204/90, Judgement of 28 January 1992, Hanns-Martin Bachmann *v.* Belgian State.

Case C-300/90, Judgement of 28 January 1992, Commission of the European Communities *v.* Kingdom of Belgium.

Case C-2/91, Judgement of 17 November 1993, Criminal proceedings against Wolf W. Meng.

Joined cases C-159/91 and C-160/91, Judgement of 17 February 1993, Christian Poucet *v.* Assurances Générales de France and Caisse Mutuelle Régionale du Languedoc-Roussillon.

Case C-185/91, Judgement of 17 November 1993, Bundesanstalt für den Güterfernverkehr *v.* Gebrüder Reiff GmbH & Co. KG.

Case C-245/91, Judgement of 17 November 1993, Criminal proceedings against Ohra Schadeverzekeringen NV.

Case C-320/91, Judgement of 19 May 1993, Criminal proceedings against Paul Corbeau.

Case C-328/91, Judgement of 30 March 1993, Secretary of State for Social Security *v.* Evelyn Thomas and others.

Case C-109/92, Judgement of 7 December 1993, Stephan Max Wirth *v.* Landeshauptstadt Hannover.

Case C-364/92, Judgement of 19 January 1994, SAT Fluggesellschaft mbH *v.* Eurocontrol.

Case C-393/92, Judgement of 27 April 1994, Municipality of Almelo and others *v.* NV. Energiebedrijf Ijsselmij.

Case C-391/92, Judgement of 29 June 1995, Commission of the European Communities *v.* Hellenic Republic.

Case C-42/93, Judgement of 14 September 1994, Kingdom of Spain *v.* Commission of the European Communities.

Case C-153/93, Judgement of 9 June 1994, Bundesrepublik Deutschland *v.* Delta Schiffahrts- und Speditionsgesellschaft mbH.

Joined cases C-358/93 and C-416/93, Judgement of 23 February 1995, Criminal proceedings against Aldo Bordessa and Vicente Marí Mellado and Concepción Barbero Maestre.

Case C-387/93, Judgement of 14 December 1995, Criminal proceedings against Giorgo Domingo Banchero.

Case C-415/93, Judgement of 15 December 1995, Union royale belge des sociétés de football association ASBL *v.* Jean-Marc Bosman, Royal club liégeois SA *v.* Jean-Marc Bosman and others and Union des associations européennes de football (UEFA) *v.* Jean-Marc Bosman.

Joined cases C-427/93, C-429/93 and C-436/93, Judgement of 11 July 1996, Bristol-Myers Squibb *v.* Paranova A/S (C-427/93) and C. H. Boehringer Sohn, Boehringer Ingelheim KG and Boehringer Ingelheim A/S *v.* Paranova A/S (C-429/93) and Bayer Aktiengesellschaft and Bayer Danmark A/S *v.* Paranova A/S (C-436/93).

C-440/93, Judgement of 5 October 1995, The Queen *v.* Licensing Authority of the Department of Health and Norgine Ltd., *ex parte* Scotia Pharmaceuticals Ltd.

Case C-451/93, Judgement of 8 June 1995, Claudine Delavant *v.* Allgemeine Ortskrankenkasse für das Saarland.

Case C-55/94, Judgement of 30 November 1995, Reinhard Gebhard *v.* Consiglio dell'Ordine degli Avvocati e Procuratori di Milano.

Joined cases C-71/94, C-72/94 and C-73/94, Judgement of 11 July 1996, Eurim-Pharm Arzneimittel GmbH *v.* Beiersdorf AG (C-71/94), Boehringer Ingelheim KG (C-72/94) and Farmitalia Carlo Erba GmbH (C-73/94).

Case C-96/94, Judgement of 5 October 1995, Centro Servizi Spediporto Srl v. Spedizioni Marittima del Golfo Srl.

Case C-137/94, Judgement of 19 October 1995, The Queen v. Secretary of State for Health, *ex parte* Cyril Richardson.

Case C-157/94, Judgement of 23 October 1997, Commission of the European Communities v. Kingdom of the Nederlands.

Case C-159/94, Judgement of 23 October 1997, Commission of the European Communities v. French Republic.

Joined cases C-163/94, C-165/94 and C-250/94, Judgement of 14 December 1995, Criminal proceedings against Lucas Emilio Sanz de Lera, Raimundo Díaz Jiménez and Figen Kapanoglu.

Case 201/94, Judgement of 12 November 1996, The Queen v. The Medicines Control Agency, *ex parte* Smith & Nephew Pharmaceuticals Ltd. and Primecrown Ltd. v. The Medicine Control Agency.

Case C-232/94, Judgement of 11 July 1996, MPA Pharma GmbH v. Rhône-Poulenc Pharma GmbH.

Case C-238/94, Judgement of 26 March 1996, José García and others v. Mutuelle de Prévoyance Sociale d'Aquitaine and others.

Case C-241/94, Judgement of 26 September 1996, French Republic v. Commission of the European Communities.

Case C-244/94, Judgement of 16 November 1995, Fédération Française des Sociétés d'Assurance, Société Paternelle-Vie, Union des Assurances de Paris-Vie and Caisse d'Assurance et de Prévoyance Mutuelle des Agriculteurs v. Ministère de l'Agriculture et de la Pêche.

Case 18/95, Judgement of 26 January 1999, F.C. Terhoeve v. Inspecteur van de Belastingdienst Particulieren/Ondernemingen buitenland.

Case C-70/95, Judgement of 17 June 1997, Sodemare SA, Anni Azzurri Holding SpA and Anni Azzurri Rezzato Srl v. Regione Lombardia.

Case C-120/95, Judgement of 28 April 1998, Nicolas Decker v. Caisse de maladie des employés privés.

Case C-250/95, Judgement of 15 May 1997, Futura Participations SA and Singer v. Administration des contributions.

Joined cases C-267/95 and C-268/95, Judgement of 5 December 1996, Merck & Co. Inc., Merck Sharp & Dohme Ltd. and Merck Sharp & Dohme International Services B v. Primecrown Ltd, Ketan Himatlal Mehta, Bharat Himatlal Mehta and Necessity Supplies Ltd. and Beecham Group plc v. Europharm of Worthing Ltd.

Joined cases C-359/95 P and C-379/95 P, Judgement of 11 November 1997, Commission of the European Communities and French Republic v. Ladbroke Racing Ltd.

Case C-398/95, Judgement of 5 June 1997, Syndesmos ton en Elladi Touristikon kai Taxidiotikon Grafeion v. Ypourgos Ergasias.

Case C-35/96, Judgement of 18 June 1998, Commission of the European Communities v. Italian Republic.

Case C-44/96, Judgement of 15 January 1998, Mannesmann Anlagenbau Austria AG and Others v. Strohal Rotationsdruck GesmbH.

Joined cases C-51/96 and C-191/97, Judgement of 11 April 2000, Christelle Deliège v. Ligue francophone de judo et disciplines associées ASBL, Ligue belge de judo ASBL, Union européenne de judo (C-51/96) and François Pacquée (C-191/97).

Case C-55/96, Judgement of 11 December 1997, Job Centre coop. Arl.

Case C-67/96, Judgement of 21 September 1999, Albany International BV v. Stichting Bedrijfspensioenfonds Textielindustrie.

Case C-157/96, Judgement of 5 May 1998, The Queen v. Ministry of Agriculture, Fisheries and Food, Commissioners of Customs & Excise, ex parte National Farmers' Union, David Burnett and Sons Ltd., R. S. and E. Wright Ltd., Anglo Beef Processors Ltd., United Kingdom Genetics, Wyjac Calves Ltd., International Traders Ferry Ltd., MFP International Ltd., Interstate Truck Rental Ltd. and Vian Exports Ltd.

Case C-158/96, Judgement of 28 April 1998, Raymond Kohll v. Union des caisses de maladie.

Case C-160/96, Judgement of 5 March 1998, Manfred Molenaar and Barbara Fath-Molenaar v. Allgemeine Ortskrankenkasse Baden-Württemberg.

Case C-180/96, Judgement of 5 May 1998, United Kingdom of Great-Britain and Northern Ireland v. Commission of the European Communities.

Case C-266/96, Judgement of 18 June 1998, Corsica Ferries France SA v. Gruppo Antichi Ormeggiatori del porto di Genova Coop. arl, Gruppo Ormeggiatori del Golfo di La Spezia Coop. arl and Ministero dei Trasporti e della Navigazione.

Case C-342/96, Judgement of 29 April 1999, Kingdom of Spain v. Commission of the European Communities.

Case C-355/96, Judgement of 16 July 1998, Silhouette International Schmied GmbH & Co. KG v. Hartlauer Handelsgesellschaft mbH.

Case C-360/96, Judgement of 10 November 1998, Gemeente Arnhem and Gemeente Rheden v. BFI Holding BV.

Case C-368/96, Judgement of 3 December 1998, The Queen v. The Licensing Authority established by the Medicines Act 1968 (acting by The Medicines Control Agency), ex parte Generics (UK) Ltd., The Wellcome Foundation Ltd. and Glaxo Operations UK Ltd. and Others.

Case C-38/97, Judgement of 1 October 1998, Autotrasporti Librandi Snc di Librandi F. & C. v. Cuttica spedizioni e servizi internationali Srl.

Case C-75/97, Judgement of 17 June 1999, Kingdom of Belgium v. Commission of the European Communities.

Case C-76/97, Judgement of 24 September 1998, Walter Tögel v. Niederösterreichische Gebietskrankenkasse.

Joined cases C-115/97 to C-117/97, Judgement of 21 September 1999, Brentjens' Handelsonderneming BV. v. Stichting Bedrijfspensioenfonds voor de Handel in Bouwmaterialen.

Case C-200/97, Judgement of 1 December 1998, Ecotrade Srl v. Altiforni e Ferriere di Servola SpA (AFS).

Case C-219/97, Judgement of 21 September 1999, Maatschappij Drijvende Bokken BV. v. Stichting Pensioenfonds voor de Vervoer- en Havenbedrijven.

Case C-256/97, Judgement of 29 June 1999, Déménagements-Manutention Transport SA (DMT).

Case C-379/97, Judgement of 12 October 1999, Pharmacia & Upjohn SA *v.* Paranova A/S.

Case C-173/98, Judgement of 1 July 1999, Sebago Inc. and Ancienne Maison Dubois & Fils SA *v.* G-B Unic SA.

Joined cases C-180/98 to C-184/98, Judgement of 12 September 2000, Pavel Pavlov and Others *v.* Stichting Pensioenfonds Medische Specialisten.

Case C-206/98, Judgement of 18 May 2000, Commission of the European Communities *v.* Kingdom of Belgium.

Case C-222/98, Judgement of 21 September 2000, Hendrik van der Woude *v.* Stichting Beatrixoord.

Case C-239/98, Judgement of 16 December 1999, Commission of the European Communities *v.* French Republic.

Case C-281/98, Judgement of 6 June 2000, Roman Angonese *v.* Cassa di Risparmio di Bolzano SpA.

Case C-368/98, Judgement of 12 July 2001, Abdon Vanbraekel and Others *v.* Alliance nationale des mutualités chrétiennes (ANMC).

Case C-376/98, Judgement of 5 October 2000, Federal Republic of Germany *v.* European Parliament and Council of the European Union.

Case C-411/98, Judgement of 3 October 2000, Angelo Ferlini *v.* Centre hospitalier de Luxembourg, Reference for a preliminary ruling: Tribunal d'arrondissement de Luxembourg - Grand Duchy of Luxemburg .

Case C-35/99, Judgement of 19 February 2002, Criminal proceedings against Manuele Arduino, third parties: Diego Dessi, Giovanni Bertolotto and Compagnia Assicuratrice RAS SpA.

Case C-109/99, Judgement of 21 September 2000, Association basco-béarnaise des opticiens indépendants *v.* Préfet des Pyrénées-Atlantiques.

Case C-135/99, Judgement of 23 November 2000, Ursula Elsen *v.* Bundesversicherungsanstalt für Angestellte.

Case C-157/99, Judgement of 12 July 2001, B.S.M. Geraets-Smits *v.* Stichting Ziekenfonds VGZ and H.T.M. Peerbooms *v.* Stichting CZ Groep Zorgverzekeringen.

Case C-173/99, Judgement of 26 June 2001, The Queen *v.* Secretary of State for Trade and Industry, *ex parte* Broadcasting, Entertainment, Cinematographic and Theatre Union (BECTU).

Case C-205/99, Judgement of 20 February 2001, Asociación Profesional de Empresas Navieras de Líneas Regulares (Analir) and Others *v.* Administración General del Estado.

Joined cases C-223/99 and C-260/99, Judgement of 10 May 2001, Agorà Srl and Excelsior Snc di Pedrotti Bruna & C. *v.* Ente Autonomo Fiera Internazionale di Milano and Ciftat Soc. coop. Arl.

Case C-309/99, Judgement of 19 February 2002, J. C. J. Wouters, J. W. Savelbergh and Price Waterhouse Belastingadviseurs BV. *v.* Algemene Raad van de Nederlandse Orde van Advocaten, intervener: Raad van de Balies van de Europese Gemeenschap.

Joined cases C-414/99 to C-416/99, Judgement of 20 November 2001, Zino Davidoff SA *v.* A & G Imports Ltd. and Levi Strauss & Co. and Others *v.* Tesco Stores Ltd. and Others.

Case C-443/99, Judgement of 23 April 2002, Merck, Sharp & Dohme GmbH *v.* Paranova Pharmazeutika Handels GmbH.

Case C-475/99, Judgement of 25 October 2001, Firma Ambulanz Glöckner *v.* Landkreis Südwestpfalz.

Case C-143/00, Judgement of 23 April 2002, Boehringer Ingelheim KG, Boehringer Ingelheim Pharma KG, Glaxo Group Ltd., The Wellcome Foundation Ltd., SmithKline Beecham plc, Beecham Group plc, SmithKline & French Laboratories Ltd. and Eli Lilly and Co. *v.* Swingward Ltd. and Dowelhurst Ltd.

Case C-218/00, Judgement of 22 January 2002, Cisal di Battistello Venanzio & C. Sas *v.* Istituto nazionale per l'assicurazione contro gli infortuni sul lavoro (INAIL).

Case C-433/00, Judgement of 19 September 2002, Aventis Pharma Deutschland GmbH *v.* Kohlpharma GmbH and MTK Pharma Vertriebs-GmbH.

Case C-106/01, Pending Case, Novartis Pharmaceuticals.

Court of First Instance

Case T-41/96, Judgement of 26 October 2000, Bayer *v.* Commission of the European Communities.

EFTA Court

Case E-6/98R, 11 December 1998, Norway *v.* EFTA Surveillance Authority.

About the Authors and Editors

Christa Altenstetter

Christa Altenstetter is Professor of Political Science at The City University of New York (CUNY, Graduate Center and Queens College). She has written extensively on health care reform and is currently working on a forthcoming book on Regulatory Regimes in Transition: The Case of Medical Devices and Patient Care, with a focus on France, Germany and the United Kingdom.

Rita Baeten

Rita Baeten is Researcher at the *Observatoire social européen*. She has worked for several years as a policy advisor on health care issues at the Cabinet of Belgian Ministers of Public Health and Social Affairs.

Leigh Hancher

Leigh Hancher is Professor of European Law at the Catholic University of Tilburg, the Netherlands, and a Partner in the law firm Allen & Overy. She specialises in European competition law, including state aids law, and free movement of goods law.

Vassilis G. Hatzopoulos

Vassilis G. Hatzopoulos is Lecturer in European Institutions and Policies at the Democritus University of Thrace and a lawyer at the Athens Court of Appeal, specialising in EC and procurement matters. He has also advised the Greek Government on issues of regulatory reform.

Tamara K. Hervey

Tamara K. Hervey is Professor of Law at the University of Nottingham, UK. She is the author of a number of texts and articles on European social law, and is currently working on a monograph on health law and the European Union.

Yves Jorens

Dr. Yves Jorens is Professor of social security law (national and international), at the Faculty of Law of the Ghent and Antwerp University in Belgium. Previously, he was head of an Independent Junior Research Group for European and International Social Security Law at the Max-Planck-Institute for Foreign and International Social Law, Munich, Germany.

Beatrix Karl

Beatrix Karl is Assistant Professor at the Institute for Labour Law and Social Law, Karl-Franzens-University Graz, Austria. She is currently engaged under a grant awarded by the Austrian Academy of Sciences at the Max Planck Institute for Foreign and International Social Law, Munich, Germany.

Martin McKee

Martin McKee is Research Director of the European Observatory on Health Care Systems and Professor of European Public Health at the London School of Hygiene and Tropical Medicine.

Elias Mossialos

Elias Mossialos is Research Director of the European Observatory on Health Care Systems and Brian Abel-Smith Reader in Health Policy, Department of Social Policy, London School of Economics and Political Science.

Jason Nickless

Jason Alan Nickless graduated from Grey College, University of Durham in Law and has a Master's Degree in European Community Law from the Catholic University of Leuven, Belgium. Since January 2000 he has been running his own business as a consultant and in October 2001 he was called to the British Bar.

Willy Palm

Willy Palm is a lawyer, specialising in social security law. He is the director of AIM, the International Association of Mutual Health Funds.

314

"Work & Society"

The series "Work & Society" analyses the development of employment and social policies, as well as the strategies of the different social actors, both at national and European levels. It puts forward a multi-disciplinary approach – political, sociological, economic, legal and historical – in a bid for dialogue and complementarity. The series is not confined to the social field *stricto sensu*, but also aims to illustrate the indirect social impacts of economic and monetary policies. It endeavours to clarify social developments, from a comparative and a historical perspective, thus portraying the process of convergence and divergence in the diverse national societal contexts. The manner in which European integration impacts on employment and social policies constitutes the backbone of the analyses.

Series Editor: Philippe POCHET, *Director of the* Observatoire social européen *(Brussels) and Digest Editor of the* Journal of European Social Policy.

Series Titles

N°40– *Protection sociale et fédéralisme. L'Europe dans le miroir de l'Amérique du Nord*, Bruno THÉRET, (2002), *ca.* 500 p., ISBN 90-5201-107-9

No. 39– *The Impact of EU Law on Health Care Systems*, Martin MCKEE, Elias MOSSIALOS & Rita BAETEN (eds.), (2002) 314 p., ISBN 90-5201-106-0.

No. 38– *EU Law and the Social Character of Health Care*, Elias MOSSIALOS & Martin MCKEE, (2002), 259 p., ISBN 90-5201-110-9.

No. 37– *Wage Policy in the Eurozone*, Philippe POCHET (ed.), Observatoire social européen (2002), 286 p., ISBN 90-5201-101-X.

N°36– *Politique salariale dans la zone euro*, Philippe POCHET (dir.), Observatoire social européen (2002), 309 p., ISBN 90-5201-100-1.

No. 35– *Regulating Health and Safety Management in the European Union. A Study of the Dynamics of Change*, David WALTERS (ed.), SALTSA (2002), 346 p., ISBN 90-5201-998-3.

No. 34– *Building Social Europe through the Open Method of Co-ordination*, Caroline DE LA PORTE & Philippe POCHET (eds.), SALTSA–Observatoire social européen (2002), 311 p., ISBN 90-5201-984-3.

N°33– *Des marchés du travail équitables ?,* Christian BESSY, François EYMARD-DUVERNAY, Guillemette DE LARQUIER & Emmanuelle MARCHAL (dir.), Centre d'Études de l'Emploi, (2001), 308 p., ISBN 90-5201-960-6.

No. 32– *Trade Unions in Europe: Meeting the Challenge* (provisional title), Deborah FOSTER & Peter SCOTT (eds.), forthcoming, *ca.* 250 p., ISBN 90-5201-959-2.

No. 31– *Health and Safety in Small Enterprises. European Strategies for Managing Improvement*, David WALTERS, SALTSA (2001), 404 p., ISBN 90-5201-952-5.

No. 30– *Europe – One Labour Market?*, Lars MAGNUSSON & Jan OTTOSSON (eds.), SALTSA (2002), 306 p., ISBN 90-5201-949-5.

No. 29– *From the Werner Plan to the EMU. In Search of a Political Economy for Europe*, Lars MAGNUSSON & Bo STRÅTH (eds.), SALTSA (2001), 526 p., ISBN 90-5201-948-7.

N°28– *Discriminations et marché du travail. Liberté et égalité dans les rapports d'emploi*, Olivier DE SCHUTTER (2001), 234 p., ISBN 90-5201-941-X.

No. 27– *At Your Service? Comparative Perspectives on Employment and Labour Relations in the European Private Sector Services*, Jon Erik DØLVIK (ed.), SALTSA (2001), 556 p., ISBN 90-5201-940-1.

N°26– *La nouvelle dynamique des pactes sociaux*, Giuseppe FAJERTAG & Philippe POCHET (dir.), Observatoire social européen–European Trade Union Institute (2001), 436 p., ISBN 90-5201-927-4.

No. 25– *After Full Employment. European Discourses on Work and Flexibility*, Bo STRÅTH (ed.) (2000), 302 p., ISBN 90-5201-925-8.

N°24– *L'Europe syndicale au quotidien. La représentation des salariés dans les entreprises en France, Allemagne, Grande-Bretagne et Italie*, Christian DUFOUR et Adelheid HEGE, IRES (2002), 256 p., ISBN 90-5201-918-5.

N°23– *Union monétaire et négociations collectives en Europe*, Philippe POCHET (ed.), SALTSA–Observatoire social européen (1999), 284 p., ISBN 90-5201-916-9.

No. 22– *Monetary Union and Collective Bargaining in Europe*, Philippe POCHET (ed.), SALTSA–Observatoire social européen (1999), 284 p., ISBN 90-5201-915-0.

No. 21– *The Regulation of Working Time in the European Union (Gender Approach) – La réglementation du temps de travail en Europe (Perspective selon le genre)*, Yota KRAVARITOU (ed.), European University Institute, (1999), 504 p., ISBN 90-5201-903-7.

EU Law and the Social Character of Health Care

Elias MOSSIALOS & Martin MCKEE

With Willy PALM, Beatrix KARL & Franz MARHOLD

European law is an increasingly important factor in the development and implementation of national and local health policy. Yet for many it remains shrouded in mystery. The situation with regard to laws impacting on health care is especially problematic as, typically, consequences arise from policies designed primarily to address problems in other sectors, which then establish general principles whose applicability to health care only becomes apparent once interpreted by rulings of the European Court of Justice. This book, written with the health and social policy community in mind, provides a comprehensive assessment of the main implications of EU law in certain key areas of health care.

The importance of this subject cannot be overestimated and the authors have approached the issues in a comprehensive and innovative way. Through this project, the Belgian EU Presidency has created the conditions for a focussed debate on future health care systems in Europe.

Michel ROCARD, Member of the European Parliament and former Prime
Minister of the French Republic

This book provides a comprehensive and in-depth picture of the legal foundations and political discussion taking place. The analysis provides a firm basis for further developments within the European Union.

Bernd VON MAYDELL, Professor of Social Security Law and Director of
the Max Planck Institute for Foreign and International Social Law, Munich

This is a timely book that brings together in both an accurate and critical way the various aspects in which health care and European legislation have become intertwined. The Belgian EU Presidency is to be praised for taking the initiative and revitalising the debate; the authors for providing a well documented basis for assessing that debate.

Jos BERGHMAN, Professor of Social Policy, Katholieke Universiteit Leuven,
President of the European Institute of Social Security

Elias MOSSIALOS is Research Director of the European Observatory on Health
Care Systems and Brian Abel-Smith Reader in Health Policy, Department
of Social Policy, London School of Economics and Political Science.

Martin MCKEE is Professor of European Public Health at the London School
of Hygiene and Tropical Medicine and Research Director of the European
Observatory on Health Care Systems.